Arnulfo L. Oliveira Memorial Library

HORACE GREELEY

ROBERT C. WILLIAMS

HORACE GREELEY

Champion of American Freedom

New York University Press • *New York and London*

NEW YORK UNIVERSITY PRESS
New York and London
www.nyupress.org

Library of Congress Cataloging-in-Publication Data
Williams, Robert Chadwell, 1938-
Horace Greeley : champion of American freedom / Robert C. Williams.
p. cm.
Includes bibliographical references and index.
ISBN-13: 978-0-8147-9402-9 (cloth : alk. paper)
ISBN-10: 0-8147-9402-5 (cloth : alk. paper)
1. Greeley, Horace, 1811-1872.   2. Presidential candidates—United States—Biography.
3. Newspaper editors—New York (State)—New York—Biography.   4. United States—
Politics and government—1849-1877.   I. Title.
E415.9.G8W55   2006
973.7'11092—dc22   2006000867

New York University Press books are printed on acid-free paper,
and their binding materials are chosen for strength and durability.

Manufactured in the United States of America

10 9 8 7 6 5 4 3 2

Contents

All illustrations appear as a group following p. 222.

Acknowledgments

I came to Horace Greeley from the outside, not the inside. I had no intention of writing his biography. Rather, I was engaged in a study of the shifting meanings of the words *liberty* and *freedom* in trans-Atlantic political discourse in the nineteenth century. This included a wide variety of research and reading into some major figures of the time—James Fenimore Cooper, Margaret Fuller, Henry David Thoreau, Ralph Waldo Emerson, William Lloyd Garrison, Theodore Parker, Karl Marx, Julia Ward Howe, Giuseppe Mazzini, Alexander Herzen, John Brown, William Linton, Adam Gurowski, Elizabeth Cady Stanton, Thomas Carlyle, Abraham Lincoln, and Francis Lieber. I soon began to realize that virtually all roads led through them to Greeley. He and his newspaper, the *New York Tribune*, were a kind of international switchboard for a trans-Atlantic conversation about liberty and freedom at a time when the main issue of the day was no longer British tyranny, but American slavery.

Doing history is always a collective effort. Like Horace Greeley, I had conversations with many friends and scholars before completing this book. Clearly the historian is ultimately responsible for the words on the printed page. But this book simply could not have existed without the kind assistance of many other people. Listing them below is a very small measure of gratitude for what they have given me over the past few years as I attempted to follow the trail of Horace Greeley, a prolific writer and correspondent who left his traces all across America. They listened patiently, they commented intelligently, they corresponded efficiently, they searched diligently, and they cooperated fully. None of them, of course, bears any responsibility for the shortcomings of a work to which they gave their attention in many ways, large and small. I am grateful to all of them:

Ben Alexander, New York Public Library; Polly Armstrong, Stanford University, Libraries, Palo Alto, CA; Gabor Boritt, Gettysburg College, Gettysburg, PA; Laura Grace Bruss, Bancroft Library, University of California, Berkeley; Melissa Bush, Hargett Rare Books and Manuscripts Library, University of Georgia, Athens; Philip L. Cantelon, History Associates Incorporated, Rockville, MD; Ruth Czar, East Poultney, VT; Christine Derby-Cuadrado, Barker Library, Fredonia, NY; Leslie Fields, Gilder Lehrman Collection, J. P. Morgan Library, New York City, NY; Peggy Ford, City of Greeley, CO, Museums; Edwin Geissler, New York City, NY; Melissa Haley, New-York Historical Society; Britta Karlberg, Peabody Essex Museum, Salem, MA; Erik Lunde, Michigan State University, Lansing; Harold Miller, State Historical Society of Wisconsin; Steve Nielsen, Minnesota State Historical Society; Kristin Nyitray, State University of New York, Stony Brook; Catherine Rod, Grinnell College Library, Grinnell, IA; Suzanne Schultze, Greeley, CO; Betsy Towl, New Castle Historical Society, Chappaqua, NY; Ann Williams, Center Lovell, ME.

I am grateful for the generous support of Davidson College, especially to the late James Vail and his wife Peggy, friends whose generosity provided the Vail Professorship I was privileged to hold. I am also in debt to my daughter Katharine for a superb editing job on the original manuscript, and to Deborah Gershenowitz and Despina Gimbel of NYU Press for their fine and final editing job. They all must be credited, but not blamed, for what follows.

Robert C. Williams

Center Lovell, Maine, August 2005

Abbreviations

APL	Amherst Public Library, Amherst, NH
BL	Barker Library, Fredonia, NY
BPL	Boston Public Library, Boston, MA
BrPL	Brattleboro Public Library, Brattleboro, VT
CPL	Concord Public Library, Concord, MA
CSL	California State Library, Sacramento, CA
DCL	Dartmouth College Libraries, Hanover, NH
DPL	Denver Public Library, Denver, CO
DUL	Duke University Library, Durham, NC
FHS	Fenton Historical Society, Jamestown, NY
GLC	Gilder Lehrman Collection, J. P. Morgan Library, New York, NY
HGP	Horace Greeley Papers
HL	Houghton Library, Harvard University, Cambridge, MA
LC	Library of Congress, Washington, DC
MHS	Massachusetts Historical Society, Boston, MA
MNHS	Minnesota Historical Society, St. Paul, MN
NCHS	New Castle Historical Society, Chappaqua, NY
NYHS	New-York Historical Society, New York, NY
NHSL	New Hampshire State Library, Concord, NH
NYPL	New York Public Library, New York, NY
NYSL	New York State Library, Albany, NY
PEM	Peabody Essex Museum, Salem, MA
RPL	Rochester Public Library, Rochester, NY
SUL	Stanford University Libraries, Palo Alto, CA
SUNY-SB	State University of New York, Stony Brook, NY
UCB	University of California–Berkeley, Berkeley, CA
UGL	University of Georgia Libraries, Athens, GA
UIL	University of Iowa Libraries, Iowa City, IA
UMO	University of Maine Libraries, Orono, ME
UNHL	University of New Hampshire Libraries, Dover, NH

URL   University of Rochester Libraries, Rochester, NY
USCL   University of South Carolina Libraries, Columbia, SC
UVL   University of Virginia Libraries, Charlottesville, VA
WCA   Westchester County Archives, Westchester, NY
WHS   Wisconsin Historical Society, Madison, WI

Preface

"Going West"

Let the old man sleep. His has been a long and unflagging life's work,
And he is tired and toil-worn. And just as the shades of his last, long night
Had begun to deepen the twilight of his life, disaster and sorrow had come
When he needed rather rest and joy to smooth his pathway down to the river.
And so he died just as the day yesterday was done and night hovered with the
Angels that waited for his life and soul to come out to them and fly away.

God bless the old man's memory.
— *Kansas City (Mo.) Times*, 1872

HORACE GREELEY was free at last. The "tribune of the people" had died, his voice now silenced by a higher power. Ordinary citizens grieved. The most widely known editor in America had gone, leaving an empty place at the table in millions of homes. Through his newspaper, "Uncle Horace" did many Americans' thinking for them for two dollars a year, as Ralph Waldo Emerson once wrote. He spoke their language and shared their joys and sorrows. His vivid and slang-ridden prose helped transform the liberty of some into freedom for all. Now, in the language of Elizabethan English and American frontier slang, Horace Greeley had finally "gone West."

Greeley had been a famous and visible figure in New York life, in large measure because of his recognizable, odd appearance. He stood nearly six feet tall, well above average, but was stooped from sitting at a desk and reading. His clothes were rustic and out of place in the city —an old white Irish linen coat (purchased from an Irish immigrant in New York for twenty dollars), large boots, baggy black pantaloons. He never did learn to tie a cravat. He wore thick wire-rimmed glasses and had a pink baby face, sometimes framed with a fringe beard or throat whiskers.

The editor of the *New York Tribune* died at 6:50 p.m. on Friday, November 29, 1872, at the home, and private asylum, of Dr. George S. Choate. Choate was a friend and neighbor who lived a few miles away from the Greeley farm in Chappaqua, north of New York City. For days the dying editor lay in a kind of "acute mania." He broke a watch at one point and threw a kerosene lamp on the floor. On occasion, he would blurt out utterances and prayers: "I know that my redeemer liveth," then later "I died before I was born," and finally, around 4:00 p.m. that afternoon, "It is done." At the end, only his daughter Ida was present. The doctors said he died of "brain fever."[1]

On Saturday, Greeley's body was brought down to New York City by train from Chappaqua to the home of Samuel Sinclair at 69 West 45th Street in the city, then displayed in a black walnut casket lined with white satin and covered with black cloth. In death as in life, his dress was formal but ordinary—black pantaloons, black dress coat, a velvet vest.

New York City in 1872 was a study in contrasts. Its population was approaching one million people. Greeley's new eleven-story Tribune Tower—the highest in New York City—was beginning to rise at the corner of Nassau and Spruce Streets, a massive brick-and-granite structure two years away from completion. Macy's, B. Altman's, Tiffany's, and F.A.O. Schwartz ran prosperous new retail businesses. New York City bonds were selling internationally on the markets of London, Paris, and Frankfurt. The Grand Central Depot, opened a year earlier, welcomed and dispatched over one hundred trains every day. Contractors were building new paved streets and avenues, new sewer, water, and gas pipelines, new buildings with newfangled elevators. The Third Avenue horse cars carried more than sixty commuters in each car at rush hour. Staten Island was becoming a new suburb, rather than a malaria-infested and inaccessible expanse. There were more than one thousand factories in Brooklyn alone. A new Brooklyn Bridge was under construction over the East River.[2]

In contrast, there were the rotting tenements and slums of the city, a warren of saloons and shanties from which many New Yorkers regularly averted their eyes, ears, and noses. Immigrants from Europe continued to pour into town, struggling to find a place to live and work. The New York Elevated Railroad, still an experiment, was both dirty and noisy. Some eighty "concert saloons" plied their trade—liquor and prostitution—especially in the new "Tenderloin District." When the poor and the homeless voted, they voted Democrat. The Republican Party fought a rearguard minority action against William "Boss" Tweed and Tammany Hall, who controlled City Hall, as well as the New York State Assembly and State Senate up the Hudson River in Albany. Corrupt politicians and contractors amassed fortunes, while raising the prices for land and rent. There were twice as many lawyers as two decades earlier.

On the day following Greeley's death, even the arch-rival *New York Times* paid grudging tribute to the editor. Without him, wrote the *Times*, his beloved *Tribune* was an "empty shell." Perhaps Greeley had died after an exhausting campaign for the presidency against U. S. Grant. Or perhaps the death of his wife, Molly, a few weeks earlier had simply overwhelmed him. Greeley was a man of odd styles with an "almost violent energy of mind" who was more of a champion than a leader. Yet millions knew his name and hundreds of thousands considered Uncle Horace another member of the family whose opinions they valued. He was the last of a breed of editors, great men who developed an enormous public following. But newspapers were now big business, not personal fiefdoms. His like would not be seen again.[3]

In Washington, the U.S. Senate opened its session on Monday, only to suspend deliberations until Thursday so that Senators who wished could attend the Greeley funeral. The House of Representatives paused for prayers and a moment of silence in Greeley's honor. Word was already out that the President and Vice President of the United States would be in New York City for the funeral.

On Tuesday, December 3, the citizens of New York City paid their respect as the body of Horace Greeley lay in state at City Hall. "All day and far into the night," wrote the *Tribune*, the rich and the poor, the old and the young, fathers with their little children, maimed soldiers on crutches, generals, merchants, lawyers, beggars, came to take a last look at his kind face." A double line stretched four blocks north from 10:00 in the morning to 10:00 at night. Democratic Party leader Samuel J. Tilden was there, along with Albany political boss Thurlow Weed, Greeley's former Whig mentor and ally, then his Republican enemy and rival, now simply another silent man in tears.[4]

The newly elected mayor of New York City, William Havemeyer, came by and paid his respects. Members of the city's Common Council

—Greeley called them the "Forty Thieves"—arrived. So did Republicans and Democrats of all shapes and sizes, and just plain citizens—businessmen, bankers, factory owners, Germans and Irish, white and black, and Civil War veterans of all conditions.

But the most moving sight came after 6:00 p.m. with the arrival of thousands of ordinary working men and women, including the "colored population" of the city, many of them former slaves. They included young newsboys who delivered the *Tribune* across Gotham. The newspapers estimated that three thousand people every hour, perhaps forty or fifty thousand in all, came by to pay their respect and say their farewells to Uncle Horace.

On Wednesday, Greeley's funeral suited a president more than a simple freeman.[5] The weather was cold and gray, homes and shops draped in mourning black, offices closed and shuttered. Flags flew at half-mast. Crowds lined the avenues as many people wept openly.

President Grant had only recently defeated Greeley in the election for the presidency of the United States, and came up from Washington by train to attend the services. He can hardly have been overjoyed at honoring the candidate who had so recently charged him and his administration with corruption, bribery, and general criminal activity. But Grant had won, and decisively so.

Republican politicians abounded. Vice President Schuyler Colfax, Greeley's old friend and editor from Indiana, later a U.S. Congressman and Speaker of the House of Representatives, was in attendance. Grant had just dumped Colfax from the ticket in favor of the Vice President elect, Senator Henry Wilson of Massachusetts, a former Natick shoemaker and radical republican friend of Greeley. The Chief Justice of the United States, Salmon P. Chase, was there. So were two cabinet members, Secretary of War William W. Belknap and former Secretary of State Elihu Washburne. Both New York Senators were there, along with the governors of New York, New Jersey, and Connecticut.

Whitelaw Reid, Greeley's editorial successor, and the entire *Tribune* staff attended the funeral as a group. R. M. Hoe, the inventor of the high-speed rotary press, was there. So was the rest of the New York newspaper world.

Funeral services were held at the Universalist Church of the Divine Paternity at Fifth Avenue and 45th Street. Here Greeley's own pew was strewn with camelias. The pew would remain vacant for the next thirty days out of respect for the deceased. Floral wreaths, like many banners across the city, carried his legendary last words—"I know that my Redeemer liveth" and "It is Done." "There could have been no political triumph for Horace Greeley living like this social triumph of Horace Greeley dead," wrote the *Tribune*. The *Times* agreed: "Seldom has an eminent man received greater proofs of the respect in which he was held by his fellow citizens." The packed church held only 1,500 people. Consequently, a huge crowd gathered in the streets outside the church, at times nearly overwhelming the police.

The service was brief and simple. The well-known minister Henry Ward Beecher, a close friend of Greeley, spoke of the dead man's lifelong crusade on behalf of the less fortunate. "He was feet for the lame," said Beecher, "he was tongue for the dumb; he was an eye for the blind; and had a heart for those who had none to sympathize with them." Greeley's own Universalist preacher, Edwin Chapin, noted that the "poor man's friend" spent his life showing that mercy could be greater than justice by his own example, "the magnetism of simple goodness." Beecher spoke to the heart, said one observer, and Chapin to the mind. Both were eloquent.

After the services, six men carried Greeley's coffin to a waiting hearse. At 1:15 p.m., the funeral procession—including 125 carriages, two abreast—wound its way by carriage and on foot to the Battery, then by ferry through the cold afternoon to Greenwood Cemetery on Gowanus Heights in Brooklyn. Greenwood was a sprawling sylvan meadow of curving paths, statues, iron railings, and picnic sites that for several decades served New York as a "romantic suburb for the deceased" and a Sunday afternoon escape from the cares of urban life. Greeley loved the place. Perhaps it reminded him of the farm life he had once escaped and later romanticized. Now it was his eternal home.

By the time the funeral cortege arrived at Greenwood, it was dusk. At the Greeley family vault on Locust Hill, his deceased wife and three children awaited his coming. Police had to clear a path through the crowd to get to the tomb. There were a few prayers. Then his daughters Ida and Gabrielle placed flowers on the coffin. That was the end.

Greeley's passing was an American, as much as a New York,

moment of grief. In 1869, *Harper's Weekly* called Greeley "the most perfect Yankee the country has ever produced." He "obeyed his impulses" and said what he thought. He could be crude, peevish, intellectual, childish, headstrong, moody, irascible, impractical, and absent-minded. But he was also humane, optimistic, principled, sincere, kind, generous, and physically fearless. He was a crusader for moral reform. At his *Tribune* office, Greeley was accessible to virtually anyone at any time, to the consternation of his staff. He worked endlessly and long hours. He rose early and slept little. He generally eschewed any stimulants, such as tea or coffee. He never drank alcoholic beverages (he was a lifelong temperance man). He could talk at length about virtually any subject. But he could also listen well.

Greeley was no orator. When he spoke—which was often—he had a high, somewhat squeaky voice. People loved to listen to him talk—a plain man reading and speaking plain sense to plain men, as his British biographer James Parton put it in 1855. But print was Greeley's true medium. When he wrote, he made the language sing for ordinary Americans, writing a colloquial prose they could easily understand. And the audience for his written words was enormous and attentive.[6]

But behind appearances lay a giant mind and heart. From his youth, Greeley was an omnivorous reader with a photographic memory. He read the poetry of Lord Byron and Robert Burns, the essays of Robert Browning and Thomas Carlyle, the Bible and Shakespeare, the novels of Nathaniel Hawthorne and the Universalist writings of Hosea Ballou. To his contemporaries, he seemed to read and retain everything, from poems to political speeches and voting statistics. He was also a polymath, who wanted to know and do everything. Some found him busy but not wise, humane but acerbic, sincere but stubborn, and a man of ideas but not thoughts. He had few friends and no cronies, and hated public dinners and parties. But he loved jokes and songs (he wanted to write a "Songbook for the People" but never did), told great stories, and held tenacious opinions on all subjects.

Greeley was a workaholic. He was always in a hurry and rarely seemed to have had any rest or sleep. He usually showed up at the *Tribune* offices between noon and 1:00 p.m., his pockets stuffed with the morning newspapers, many of which he had already read. He rarely greeted anyone, but went immediately to his roll-top desk. Here he opened and answered numerous letters. He then began reading drafts of the next day's articles before they went to press, a merciless editor, especially critical of typographical errors of any kind. His own prose was clear and crisp, usually sixteen words to a line as opposed to the usual twelve. Around 4 or 5:00 p.m., he went out to dinner at a nearby restaurant, usually returning to the office and staying well into the evening. "He worked," recalled one close friend, "because he could not help it."[7]

"Horace Greeley was a great man," wrote his friend James Gilmore, another editor, "—undisciplined, ill-regulated, but great, and measured by his influence upon his time, and on the upward progress of the American people, it may be questioned if this country has produced any greater, excepting Benjamin Franklin."[8]

His critics responded in kind. William Henry Seward, for example, considered Greeley's habits and eccentricities annoying: "What can you do with a man of sixty ideas, and every one of the sixty an impracticable crochet?" That legendary scribbler of New York happenings, diarist George Templeton Strong, wrote in his diary the day after Greeley died, "Had God granted him a little plain practical sense, Horace Greeley would have been a great man."[9]

But the traditional picture of Greeley the eccentric and impractical editor and talker needs revision. As at least a few contemporaries recognized, Greeley was a very consistent, if unsystematic, thinker with a lifelong and passionate commitment to the cause of freedom and reform. He readily imbibed new ideas. But he was not really inconsistent. In the words of a modern scholar, Greeley was a kind of "one-man switchboard for the international cause of 'Reform'" who tried to "accommodate intellectually the contradictions inherent in the many diverse reform movements of the time."[10]

Horace Greeley was a trans-Atlantic republican who inherited the Stoic, Christian, and Roman republican virtues of the western tradition. Like the Stoic philosophers of ancient Greece and Rome, Greeley believed in the power of reason, justice, hard work, kindness, generosity, temperance, self-control, and universal brotherhood. Like the early Christians, he believed in the importance of love, the Word, humility, conscience, liberty, moral reform, and universal salvation. And like the Roman republicans, he believed in civic virtue, citizenship, and political participation by the people.

In an age of liberal nationalism and national liberalism, Horace Greeley helped fuel the Second American Revolution, transforming the liberty of the first American Revolution into the freedom and equality forged in the fires of Civil War. He did this under the influence of the radical republicans of 1830 and 1848 in Europe who found their way to America, and often to the columns of the *Tribune*. American freedom was the moral and political heart of Horace Greeley's words and actions. So was his form of Christianity, Universalism. "He was for freedom in the broadest sense," recalled his friend Beman Brockway, "freedom from everything tending to fetter and debase."[11] He was the enemy of human slavery in the South and wage slavery in the North. "No man ever lived," read the Syracuse, New York, resolution in Greeley's honor after his death, "who had so large a share in securing the elevation of the thought of America to liberty and freedom as Horace Greeley."[12]

Greeley himself never wrote a great book on freedom or anything else. But his life and work epitomized the search for American freedom. In an unpublished note he wrote toward the end of his life, Greeley scribbled, "Political Freedom too, that priceless boon to those fitted to enjoy it, that rough but never stagnant school to those as yet unequal to its exalted requirements—we cannot be too thankful for its manifold blessings. Where each is a sharer in the National Sovereignty, there will be many monarchs without majesty, many rulers without capacity; but shall not Liberty teach even the lowest dignity and the most sordid magnanimity?" "Let us resolve," he added, "never to be unfaithful to Freedom and our Country."[13]

American freedom was, for Horace Greeley, a universal divine mission. "Either God rules the world," Greeley wrote a friend in 1872, "or he does not. I believe he does."[14]

Introduction

From *Liberty* to *Freedom*

Liberty and freedom, although often interchanged, are distinct in some of their applications. Liberty has reference to previous restraint, freedom to the simple, spontaneous exercise of our powers. A slave is at liberty. His master had always been in a state of freedom.

—Noah Webster, *American Dictionary of the English Language* (1828)

HORACE GREELEY (1811–1872) was a philological incendiary with a vision of universal freedom. As editor of the influential and widely read *New York Tribune* in the decades before the Civil War, Greeley's words helped to add fuel to the fires of slavery and sectionalism that divided North and South. His newspaper had a larger circulation than any other newspaper in the world by 1860. Indeed, the *"Trib"* both shaped and reflected political discourse and American slang. Now almost forgotten, Greeley was probably the best-known American public figure of his day. He contributed, or disseminated, words like *border ruffian, Copperhead,* and *slavocracy* to hundreds of thousands of readers across the country. He helped name and create the Republican Party. He fought slavery. He fanned the flames of sectionalism, North and South. And he helped transform the *liberty* of the American Revolution into the *freedom* of the American Civil War.

Greeley recognized that the words *liberty* and *freedom* were twins, but not identical twins.[1] Most people have always used the two words interchangeably. Many still do. But during the period 1830–1870, Greeley and other republican politicians and anti-slavery supporters gradually abandoned the idea and language of liberty under civil law for a broader and more radical idea of freedom under moral law, one

I

that would exclude slavery. Liberty for gentlemen of property became freedom for all—or at least for adult white (and later black) males. The image of "liberty leading the people" during the French Revolution of 1830 became the "battle cry of freedom" of the Union during the American Civil War.

Greeley inherited an idea of freedom that had its roots in the opposite condition of slavery. In the ancient world of Greece and Rome, a free man was a man who was not a slave but, rather, a citizen. But the *libertas* of the citizen was always distinct from the *licentia* of unbridled freedom, and from the servitude of the slave.[2]

In seventeenth-century England, radical proponents of equality claimed that true freedom required the elimination, not the possession, of property. Gerard Winstanley observed that "without exception, all sorts of people in the land are to have freedom" and that freedom meant "Christ in you and Christ among you."[3] Many of the outlaws of England—pirates, highwaymen, gypsies, diggers of the common land—took up the view that true freedom lay outside the law, not within or under the law.

Greeley also inherited the Enlightenment distinction between liberty as the right to do whatever the law allows (Montesquieu) and freedom as the emancipation of a human self that was "born free" but everywhere in chains (Rousseau). John Locke linked liberty with property under the law and warned against license. Mary Wollstonecraft called liberty the "mother of virtue" but hoped that some day women would breathe the "sharp invigorating air of freedom."[4]

Greeley also recognized that European immigrants to America brought with them their own views of liberty. These views varied from region to region. The ordered liberty of the Puritans from East Anglia found its way to New England and emphasized freedom of religious conscience and free town meetings. The hegemonic liberty of Virginia Anglicans from southwest England emphasized the right to rule others, including slaves, guaranteed by charter from the crown. Pennsylvania Quakers from the Midlands and Wales brought with them the inner light of conscience, the right to trial by jury, and a fierce opposition to slavery. And out in the backcountry, men escaping northern England and Ireland sought a new freedom in nature, the frontier, the wilderness, and free land.[5]

German immigrants likewise brought from Europe a dual concept of liberty, meaning freedom from constraint and a positive obligation to serve God. German Protestants stressed Christian liberty and inward piety over public life and worldly possessions.[6]

Before Greeley's time, the keyword of the American and French Revolutions was *liberty*. Everywhere men and women planted Liberty Trees, sang Liberty Songs, and joined the Sons and Daughters of Liberty. Liberty as order and the absence of restraint, defended by law and property, was matched by the freedom to pursue happiness and seek one's own welfare by taking advantage of opportunity.

For Greeley, any republic was a polity contingent in time, where only virtuous citizens could guarantee civil society against future corruption and degeneration. Liberty was a function of republican virtue. Thus the founding documents of the United States—which Greeley revered—sought to guarantee personal liberty, as well as national independence from Great Britain. But they too reflected the two strands of liberty and freedom. The Constitution of the United States defined a system of representative government with a Bill of Rights that defended personal liberty under the law, including the right to own property in slaves. But the Declaration of Independence stated that "all men are created equal" and suggested a future emancipation of slaves, if not their full citizenship.[7] This distinction between liberty with slavery and freedom without slavery would be vital to abolitionists, republicans, and Greeley himself.

"Liberty," said Reverend Jeremiah Atwater in a sermon to the Vermont legislature in 1801, "if considered as a blessing, must be taken in a qualified sense. The freedom which it implies, must be a limited, not absolute, freedom."[8]

But Greeley recognized that *liberty* dominated *freedom* in popular discourse. Only when the liberty of gentlemen gave way to the freedom of all equal citizens—as the American Revolution promised it would—would that revolution become complete. After 1800, *freedom* meant not simply the right to vote, but the right to rise, to buy and sell in a free market. The old paradox of slavery in a land of liberty became a new paradox of political democracy in a land of economic dependence and poverty.[9] Universal freedom required the elimination of slavery and poverty.

Greeley also knew that in Europe, too, the nineteenth century saw a growing divide between liberty and freedom. In Germany, Italy, Ireland, and Poland, liberty generally meant national liberation. Liberty depended on the law. Freedom meant individual and national autonomy. Negative liberty, added scholars in the twentieth century, meant individual rights guaranteed in law against government restraint. Positive liberty, or freedom, meant the freedom for individuals to develop themselves educationally, economically, and socially.[10]

Around 1830, as Greeley embarked on his journalistic career in New York City, the European words for *liberty* and *freedom* diverged in meaning. Liberty under the law often meant economic conditions close to poverty and slavery. Germans distinguished *Libertät* and *Freiheit* as very different conditions—personal and corporate rights, or personal, national, or social self-realization. The French only wrote and spoke of *liberté*, but they sought a republic with democratic representative government. Whatever the national and linguistic differences, there were two distinct clusters of meaning around *liberty* and *freedom*, rights and development.[11]

In Greeley's America, *liberty* and *freedom* also divided over slavery. In 1831, Garrison's *Liberator* and Nat Turner's rebellion put slavery on the front pages as a national issue. And then in 1863, President Abraham Lincoln spoke of a nation "conceived in liberty" that would produce a "new birth of freedom."[12] He knew perfectly well that his audience understood the distinction between *liberty* and *freedom* and that the distinction involved the difference between slavery and the Union.

Greeley also knew that men and women were increasingly talking of *freedom, liberation,* and *emancipation,* rather than *liberty.*[13] But in the South, the word *liberty* had different connotations. Slaves were not citizens, but property, and therefore crucial to the rights and liberties of their owners under the law. Slaves were like any other piece of real estate, houses, trees, or land. Many states had repressive slave codes that presumed slaves were simply property. Political discourse in the South continually used Locke and liberty to defend slavery.[14]

Horace Greeley thus lived in a world where *liberty* was restricted to the rights of adult white men of property, and *freedom* was a more universal concept requiring liberty for all men, women, and children. Freedom meant the political freedom to determine who should govern and how; the economic opportunities for individuals to consume, produce, or exchange value; the social opportunities to live better and healthier lives; an open society that guarantees transparency rather than secrecy and corruption; and protective security through a social safety net that protects individuals from poverty and unemployment.[15]

Horace Greeley was a republican. He believed that the transformation of liberty for some into freedom for all was essential if the American republic was to be saved. Republics existed historically in time, contingent on the continuing virtue and commerce of their citizens. They are not eternal, nor God-given. Without virtuous and active citizens, republics would become corrupt and might even perish. Only innovation and reform could prevent such corruption and an Aristotelian decline into tyranny, oligarchy, or anarchy. Moral reform of the republic was not simply desirable, but imperative. Only republicanism, grounded in universal Christian virtue, could transform liberty into freedom and thus save the republic of the founding fathers.

I

Yankee Apprentice

NEW HAMPSHIRE FREEMAN

Freedom was rooted in the soil of New Hampshire since it became a state in 1788. As a free state, New Hampshire had no slaves: only free labor—white men and women (and a few free blacks) free to fail as well as to succeed, free to fall as well as to rise. Entering the twenty-first century, New Hampshire had no state income tax, no state sales tax, only license plates reading "Live Free or Die!" Horace Greeley was a New Hampshire boy, and for the first eleven years of his life, his family would live free on the edge of economic ruin.

The terrain of southern New Hampshire has rolling and wooded hills, sandy flats, and bogs. Mount Monadnock to the west constitutes the only major peak, and stands in noble isolation below the rocky and rugged White Mountains far to the north. The inhospitable rocky soil was a constant challenge and frustration to early settlers, who nevertheless chopped down and cut up every tree in sight to obtain firewood and lumber. Subsistence farming was the rule inland; fishing predominated along the short coastline around Portsmouth and Rye. When Horace Greeley was born in 1811, New Hampshire had become a refuge for nonconformists, especially the Presbyterians, Baptists, and Methodists fleeing the cold Puritan rigidity of Congregational (and then Unitarian) Boston.

The Greeleys, like most Americans, were perpetually moving west in search of land and freedom. Greeley's ancestors came to America around 1640 from somewhere near the town of Nottingham, England. Andrew Greeley arrived in Salisbury in Essex County, Massachusetts, an area full of refugees from East Anglia as a consequence of religious persecution and the English Civil War, around 1640.

In 1643, Andrew Greeley married Mary Moyse and began to raise a family, while running a gristmill and sawmill. Their son Joseph, born in 1652, also married a local girl, Martha Corliss Wilford of nearby Haverhill, in 1694. Joseph then moved west to the frontier town of Hudson, New Hampshire (a British royal province), in the county of Hillsborough, where he built a mill. Joseph died there in 1745, leaving Martha to return to her family in Haverhill, where she died in 1757.

Joseph and Martha Greeley's son Benjamin was born in Haverhill, where he remained for the rest of his life. Benjamin (1699–1785) married Ruth Whittier (1701–1745) in 1722 and fathered Ezekiel Greeley— Horace's great-grandfather—in 1725 in Haverhill. Ezekiel later moved to Hudson to join his grandfather, Joseph. Around 1750, Ezekiel married Ester Lovewell, age twenty-two, of Dunstable, Massachusetts. Their son Zaccheus—Horace's grandfather—was born on November 27, 1753, in Hudson and named after Ester Lovewell's father.[1] Zaccheus Greeley was a tenacious and long-lived character of strong personality. He knew the Bible by heart and eked out a living as a farmer, first in Hudson and then in the nearby town of Amherst, New Hampshire. He had inherited some of his father's land, but hardly enough to divide up fruitfully among his own thirteen children. He died at the age of ninety-three in June 1846, five years after his famous grandson founded the *New York Tribune*.

Born in 1782, Horace's father, also named Zaccheus, inherited no land from his father. But somehow he earned enough money as a young man to buy a small farm in Amherst. In 1807, Zaccheus, at the age of twenty-five, married nineteen-year-old Mary Woodburn.

By 1809, at the age of twenty-seven, Zaccheus had made enough money to buy a farm five miles from the town of Amherst, New Hampshire, in the woods near Bedford. The one-and-a-half-story frame house still stands today about halfway down a gentle, rocky slope overlooking a flat and boggy area, and it was here that Zaccheus and Mary made a home for themselves and their family, which would soon include Horace. Mary Woodburn Greeley was a "republican mother" who set an example of piety and virtue for her small family. In addition to keeping house and raising seven children, she spun wool and linen, weaving them into cloth for the nearby mills of Manchester and Nashua. By 1800, steam-powered looms were greatly reducing the cost of turning cotton into yarn and weaving yarn into fabric in the mills of England and New England. When Eli Whitney invented the cotton gin in 1793, making it easier to separate seeds from fiber of short-staple cotton, annual cotton production in the United States rose. More than half of the cotton grown in America was shipped to England, and an increasing amount was shipped to New England.[2] By 1810, the steam-power loom was widely used in England, but in the United States the yarn produced by the mills was piling up at the feet of thousands of hand-loom weavers like Mary Greeley.

Gradually, the factory system of making cloth, begun at Lowell, Massachusetts, spread to the growing mill towns not far from Amherst. For a time, the mills disbursed cotton to neighboring towns after the cotton was whipped on a frame. Women like Mary Greeley then made yarn in their homes on hand looms.[3] As the supply of cotton increased, and the mills produced more cotton goods, the price of clothing dropped. Cottage weaving could not compete with steam power, and women like Mary Greeley became unemployed because the slave labor of the South was far cheaper. So were British cloth imports. As her son would later realize, she represented the free labor of an expanding and developing America that needed protection from free trade competition with cheaper foreign and slave labor.[4]

When Horace was born in 1811, the United States consisted of seventeen individual states with a combined population of more than seven million inhabitants. President James Madison was completing his first term in office and preparing to run for a second. James Monroe was Secretary of State. The National Road was under construction. The Lewis and Clark Expedition had opened up the recently acquired Louisiana Purchase (1803) for exploration and future settlement west of the Mississippi River. The Republican Party of Thomas Jefferson and Madison was dominating the Federalists of Alexander Hamilton and John Adams at the polls. And the great flood of settlers westward into Jefferson's "empire of liberty" was beginning.

Shortly after Horace Greeley's birth, the War of 1812 began, lasting from June 1812 through February 1815. British violation of American neutral maritime rights during the Napoleonic Wars in Europe and American land hunger for Canada and the expanding western frontier both helped cause the unpopular "Mr. Madison's War." Farmers south and west of Pennsylvania thought the war was a good thing, if it would recover markets for their grain, cotton, and tobacco. In New England, shipping merchants and Federalist politicians attacked the war, since they had profited from traffic on the high seas whether or not the British impressed American seamen or boarded American ships.

The nadir of the war came in August 1814, when British troops burned the U.S. capital of Washington and destroyed the White House. A month later, the spirited American defense of Fort McHenry near Baltimore, Maryland, led Francis Scott Key to write down the words to "The Star Spangled Banner." Future president Andrew Jackson became a national hero overnight for his victory over British troops at the Battle of New Orleans in January 1815. The United States gained little from the Treaty of Ghent except for a piece of western Spanish Florida. And the Hartford Convention of December 1814 showed that New England Federalist opposition to the war threatened even secession from the Union.

The results of the War of 1812 were more significant than the war itself, which one historian characterized as a "futile and costly struggle."[5] The war cost some twenty thousand American lives and $158 million. Was it worth it? The Republic had survived, but the Republican Party had failed to conquer Canada or reverse British domination on the high seas. Social and economic consequences were perhaps more significant than the political ones. An unprepared United States suddenly embarked on a massive program of "internal improvements"—building canals, roads, bridges, and federal coastal forts—that would deter future foreign enemies. A new factory system emerged to improve production and manufacturing. Economic independence and tariff protection became central goals of public policy. Banking recovered from the lost loans and uncollected taxes of the war effort.

New Hampshire shared the country's postwar modernization. The Middlesex and Amoskeag Canals dated from the 1790s. Coaches had been running overland regularly since 1807 from Boston to Concord, where a new state house was built in 1816. Now the first power loom went into operation at Amoskeag Falls in 1819. The old political fault lines of the war began to disappear. The Federalist Party nearly died out, and New Hampshire went Republican.

Horace Greeley, then, entered a Republican world where the young American Republic was fighting an unpopular war. He was born on February 3, 1811, in Amherst, the third of Zaccheus and Mary's seven children. Two had already died before he was born. One was a son, also named Horace. "Having suddenly lost her two former children, just before my birth," Horace later recalled, "my mother was led to regard me even more fondly and tenderly than she otherwise might have done."[6] Moreover, Horace himself very nearly died at birth. For the first twenty minutes of his life, the child did not breathe. "There were no signs of life," recalled a neighbor present at the delivery; "he uttered no cry; he made no motion; he did not breathe." Yet twenty minutes later he was a "red and smiling infant."[7]

Early oxygen deprivation can lead to Asperger's Syndrome, a neurological disorder among males that produces social isolation, eccentric behavior, a striking precocity with language, a huge vocabulary, a prodigious memory, intellectual brilliance, and an obsession with facts. Asperger's is a kind of mild autism—sufferers read the dictionary by age three, talk repeatedly about one subject, can't sit still, are easily frustrated, and do not fit in with others easily. Sometimes known as the "Little Professor Syndrome," Asperger's Syndrome is a lifelong developmental disorder which bears a striking resemblance to some aspects of the life of Horace Greeley.[8] But in the nineteenth century, the condition was unknown.

Far more than Zaccheus, who had all he could do to make ends meet by farming, Mary was a constant presence in the young life of "Hod" Greeley, as he became known among his friends. She taught him to read, showed him hay raking and hoeing, and told him stories at night. She sang ballads, related anecdotes, and shared family traditions. By the age of two, Hod was playing with newspapers and looking through the Bible. He learned to read "at her knee" before he learned to talk. He asked incessant questions. By the age of four, Hod could read virtually any book in any direction—left to right, right to left, and upside down. He was already an excellent speller, thanks to Noah Webster's *Spelling Book* and the *American Preceptor* of author Caleb Bingham, a collection of famous speeches with a strong antislavery tone. "I could read very fluently at 4 years of age," Greeley later recalled, and "spelling was my forte." He had a "tenacious memory" and arithmetic came easily, although grammar was difficult.[9] He was, and remained, a prodigy.

At some point, Horace's Uncle Perry gave him a copy of *The Columbian Orator* (also by Caleb Bingham) to read while he was sick in bed at his grandfather's home recovering from a case of the measles. This remained his "prized text book" for years, and he became "thoroughly familiar with its contents."[10]

The Columbian Orator was a collection of great speeches intended for children and public speakers. But it was also an anti-slavery tract. Frederick Douglass later discovered the same book in Baltimore when he was twelve, and considered it a "rich treasure." Greeley read and reread John Aikin's "Dialogue between a Master and a Slave," which argued that humans, not God, created slavery as an institution.[11] Another speech described slavery as an "odious traffic in human flesh." Still another praised Benjamin Franklin as a "genius of liberty" and a great man, the founder of "trans-Atlantic freedom."[12] *The Columbian Orator* provided Horace Greeley his first instruction in patriotism, Christianity, moral reform, and anti-slavery.

In 1817, Zaccheus Greeley moved his family to Bedford and a larger farm, leaving his own small farm to a needy brother. Young Horace attended school intermittently. Mostly, he helped with the farming. He killed the grubs in the ground ahead of where his father was hoeing corn. He learned to lead oxen and horses, to pick stones, and to burn charcoal.

In April 1819, the family moved back to Amherst. But farming was hard, and they remained destitute. The fifty acres Zaccheus had bought for $1,300 during the War of 1812 were now worth only $600. By now the family numbered six, Hod having acquired two sisters, Esther and Arminda, and a brother, Barnes. But times were hard and the debts mounted. Zaccheus had speculated in the lumber business and lost. In 1818, the local sheriff and his men had seized his home at Bedford for debts. He faced the ignominy of returning to his own house and cultivating the land "on shares," raising hops under an arrangement to satisfy his creditors. But the hop market was depressed, and he failed again. He ran up his account at the general store. He drank heavily and began to distribute too much rum to his neighbors. Zaccheus Greeley was going bankrupt.

Around 1820, a Bedford minister, Mr. McGregor, and one or two of his friends offered to pay Hod's way to exclusive Exeter Academy. But his parents were too proud to accept the offer, resisting charity from others. In January 1821, he watched as his father's house, land, and goods were sold at auction by the sheriff. Zaccheus decided to flee New Hampshire, fearing arrest, his debts unpaid. For several months, he took his family to Hampton, New York, where he helped Col. Parker French with his large farm and tavern. Then he decided to move on.

The answer to bankruptcy and the imminent arrival of the sheriff to imprison him for debt was to move west—to Vermont. "I have several times removed," Zaccheus later recalled from his home in western New York, "and always toward the West; I shall never remove again; but were I to do so, it would be toward the East."[13] As it was, Zaccheus in January 1821 piled his family into a rented two-horse sleigh and moved west to Westhaven, Vermont, crossing the Connecticut River on the ice. Here, where the Poultney River flows into Lake Champlain, he rented a small outbuilding at sixteen dollars a year from a Boston banker, Christopher Minot, on whose estate he lived. Zaccheus Greeley now made a living by chopping wood for fifty cents a day. He and his sons, Hod and Barnes, ages ten and eight, also cleared fifty acres of wild land of its yellow pine, white pine, black ash, beech, alder, and poplar trees. They were day laborers engaged in "mindless, monotonous drudgery" in the eyes of young Horace, who craved an "ennobling, liberalizing, intellectual pursuit."[14]

Life was difficult, and there were more mouths to feed. In 1823, another sister was born. The family subsisted on bean porridge. The men hoed, tended a sawmill, kept sheep and cattle fed and watered, drove oxen, and cut trees. They harvested and sold nuts and honey at the local store. Slowly the Greeleys began to save up some money for luxuries such as books or checkers. The children attended the District 1 School intermittently. And Hod continued to read every book he could lay hands on—the Bible, the *Arabian Nights, Robinson Crusoe,* Shakespeare, histories, tales, romances. Moreover, he could read these in the comfort of the Minot mansion's library.

Gradually, Hod got into his head the idea of becoming a printer. He not only wanted to read books and newspapers, but to make them. In 1822, at age eleven, he walked nine miles to Whitehall, Vermont, to see about becoming a printer's apprentice, but was told he was too young.

Horace Greeley's early New Hampshire years were critical to his personal and social development. He learned to help the family work hard in order to survive. He discovered that the world of books was more important than formal schooling. He learned that the capitalist free market could ruin a family overnight because of faraway economic trends and events. He learned that such families needed protection from the brutal effects of slave labor and free trade competition. Slavery was wrong, a moral evil that separated North and South. Freedom meant the opposite of slavery, and the right to rise in society by dint of hard work and free labor. But liberty under the law meant imprisonment for debt, foreclosure, and bankruptcy. In the free state of New Hampshire, only hard work and good luck promised freedom. And when economic ruin threatened, there was only one real escape —to the West.

VERMONT REPUBLICAN

In April 1826, Horace Greeley, age fifteen, answered an advertisement for an apprentice printer at the *Northern Spectator* newspaper in the little village of East Poultney, Vermont. Once again, he walked from Westhaven to a nearby Vermont town to seek employment. This time he was successful.

Poultney was a place of "considerable business."[15] In 1822, two young printers, Sanford Smith and John R. Shute, had started up a local newspaper in East Poultney, the *Poultney Gazette*, a four-page sheet some fifteen by twenty-two inches in size. After producing 114 issues, in January 1825, they changed the name to the *Northern Spectator*, then sold it a year later to Amos Bliss and left town. The paper emerged from a relatively new (1823) building near the town green that had a law office on the first floor and a harness shop attached to the building. The printing office was on the second floor.

The *Northern Spectator*, edited by E. G. Stone and Amos Bliss, from New York, was a relatively new country newspaper. Bliss was about thirty years old, and had come over from Greenwich, New York, to Poultney around 1817. Here he became a successful merchant and built a store next to the Eagle Tavern, a local watering place and hotel. In addition to editing the *Northern Spectator*, Bliss also became the town clerk, inspector of common schools, and the founder of the Poultney bank. Legend has it that Bliss was reluctant to accept young Greeley as an apprentice printer, but half an hour of conversation with the voluble and obviously intelligent towhead spelled promise, and Bliss and his foreman decided to take on the fifteen-year-old boy.[16] Bliss wanted Greeley bound over for five years in return for board and twenty-dollars-a-year salary. Zaccheus objected to this arrangement and demanded that Horace would serve until age twenty, getting his board for six months and then an additional forty-dollars-a-year salary for clothing and necessities. The compromise was that young Horace would not be bound over, would receive no money for the first six months, and then could choose to bind himself for five years at forty dollars a year plus board.

> Mr. Greeley says his boy may stay as an apprentice to Dewey and Bliss in the printing business till he is twenty years of age: That he may stay one year, and he will clothe him, and then determine whether he may stay another year. He means that the boy shall stay till twenty years old, and that he will not take him away for anything except ill usage. If the boy stays till he is twenty years old he is to have $40 a year in clothing after the first six months, and have his board. The boy is to be faithful and serve with the best of his ability in the office under the direction of the foreman. He is to be allowed reasonable time to go home to see his friends, occasionally and as other apprentices do. The boy's name is Horace Greeley. (A. Bliss, Poultney, April 18, 1826)

The actual contract was somewhat unusual, a signed statement by Amos Bliss that stated the terms of an oral agreement. Standard indentures were rarely used in Vermont at this time to define apprenticeships. The statement was unusual in that it failed to require any prior education or training at all. Thus began Horace Greeley's career as an apprentice printer in East Poultney, Vermont.[17] Like Ben Franklin, he found that his father had sold him into a kind of indentured servitude.

Not that he was unhappy. Vermont had a barter economy and little money in those days. Young men were plentiful and labor was cheap, averaging fifty cents a day in 1825. So young Horace was glad to get an apprenticeship at all.[18]

The apprenticeship began at a bittersweet moment. His father had now decided to move his family west once more. This time he proposed to give up New England farming and join his two brothers in Erie County, in far western New York, near the town of Clymer. Here he ultimately acquired some three hundred acres of forest land, heavily wooded and barely arable. As Horace recalled the scene twenty years later, his father "went West." "The parting was a sore trial to me," he wrote, "and I was almost persuaded to go off with them, my place being then hard and disagreeable, but I said goodbye and went back to my cold, strange home with a dry face but a sore heart."[19] Horace was on his own, bound over to a man he did not know and living in a room at the Eagle Tavern.

During the late 1820s, Horace Greeley learned the printer's trade —how to set type, ink typeface, and operate the hand-run Ramage press on the second floor of the *Northern Spectator* offices. Adam Ramage was a Scot who came to America in 1795 and soon began to make quality wooden presses. Using an enlarged screw and a reduced pitch, he could produce twice the pressure of conventional presses of the time. By 1820, Ramage presses used an iron, rather than wooden, press plate faced with brass bolts. As a result Ramage presses were lighter and easier to move than the all-iron presses commonly in use, and became popular on the frontier and in country towns because of their size, efficiency, and mobility.[20] Even so, the old hand-cranked presses produced fewer than two hundred sheets an hour and required nine separate operations. All type was set by hand.

From his office, Horace could look out the window to the river and the town cemetery as he rolled ink balls used to ink the typeface. During the 1820s, presswork was being changed by the introduction of an ink roller to replace leather balls for inking typeface, and by the new steam-powered press. Since very young boys could be trained to use the ink roller, older pressmen began to lose their jobs to "roller boys." Typesetters could survive more readily than pressmen.[21]

Outside the office, Horace became a recognized young man about town. Although he attended no local school while living in the area, his grammar was superior to that of most teachers. He devoured books in the East Poultney library. He also played chess, checkers, and cards, and went hunting for bees and honey. He joined the local debating society. He gained a reputation as the town encyclopedia, a fount of information on virtually every subject imaginable. He was good at math and quick to recite poetry. He neither danced nor drank nor gambled.

A fellow apprentice later recalled Greeley at this time: "He was then a remarkably plain-looking unsophisticated lad of fifteen, with a slouching, careless gait, leaning away forward as he walked, as if both his head and his heels were too heavy for his body." Other boys teased him at first, but then accepted him as an "unusually intelligent and honest" person. After boarding with several local families, in 1827 Greeley settled into a room at the Eagle Tavern, kept by Harlow

Hosford. Here he lived at the town social center and became a well-known figure, opposed to President Andrew Jackson, the Democratic Party, and their "Albany Regency" over in New York.[22] As a budding republican, Greeley opposed the forces of corruption—the British, the city, the politicians, alcohol, and secret societies like the Freemasons who sought to establish themselves as an aristocracy.[23]

On July 4, 1826, shortly after Greeley settled in East Poultney, both Thomas Jefferson and John Adams died. Patriotism, ignited by the Marquis de Lafayette's recent visit to the United States, was rekindled by the death of the last two major founding fathers of the republic. Aging Revolutionary War veterans still appeared on the Fourth to tell their war stories and legitimize their patriotism. In Vermont, patriotism translated into strong support for the National Republicans and protective tariffs, and hostility to Andrew Jackson and the Democrats with their free trade policies. In the presidential election of 1828, Poultney went for John Quincy Adams and Henry Clay of the National Republican Party over Jackson and John Calhoun, 334 to 4. The *Northern Spectator* was equally republican.

Vermont was a stronghold of republican protectionism—the doctrine that national tariffs should be used to protect local industry and manufacture against the competition of cheaper foreign (usually British) goods. The wool industry was central to the Vermont economy. In New Hampshire, Greeley learned that free trade easily led to local hardship, poverty, and unemployment. Vermont sheep owners and grain growers agreed. They strongly supported the protectionist tariffs of 1824 and 1828, which stimulated local industry in the face of British competition.

Greeley was still too young to vote. But he followed political developments with a passion, and had a practiced political eye and ear. He debated, read about, and followed politics. "He early learned," recalled one friend, "to observe and remember political statistics, and the leading men and measures of the political parties, the various and multitudinous candidates for governor and Congress, not only in a single State, but in many, and finally in all the states, together with the location and vote of this, that, and the other congressional district (whig, democrat, and what not) at all manner of elections."[24]

In Vermont, probably in reaction to his father's drinking, Greeley also became a temperance man. That is, he refused to drink alcoholic beverages (intoxicating liquors, as the phrase went) of any kind, a resolution he made in public at age twelve on January 1, 1824, while living in Westhaven. At the time, Greeley had heard of temperance people, but had never met one. Nor had the American Temperance Society yet been founded. In June 1824, when some other boys forced young Horace to drink an alcoholic beverage, he realized that temperance would be a lifelong passion. He would abstain not only from alcohol, but from coffee, tea, and other stimulants as well.[25]

Alcohol consumption was at an all-time high between 1790 and 1830—five gallons of drink per person per year, triple today's average. Consumption peaked in the 1820s, when the average male consumed a half pint of liquor every day. Whiskey, rum, gin, brandy, and tobacco were the poor man's luxuries. In New Hampshire, the common drinks were hard cider and malt beer, made from barley and brewed by virtually every farmer. Some preachers drank before preaching.[26] Alcoholic cider, at one dollar a barrel, could last a family of six to eight people for a week. Holidays and rituals like Election Day, the Fourth of July, and funerals were for getting drunk. For example, demon rum was freely ladled out on Election Day, so that the addled would vote for the right ticket.

Taverns and pubs had been nurseries of liberty during the revolutionary era, when liberty meant the right to drink. "To be drunk," wrote one historian, "was to be free."[27] But to temperance leaders of Greeley's generation, abstinence was the new freedom from King Alcohol, the descendant of King George III.

Moral reform lay at the heart of the temperance movement, and deeply affected the young Greeley. Like Universalism and Anti-Masonry, temperance helped define a new moral being trying to perpetuate the republic in a corrupt and sinful world. Alcohol was not only corrupt and evil, but economically wasteful. Thrift, frugality, and abstinence were virtues. Many future abolitionists had begun as temperance men. If slavery killed the body, did not liquor kill the soul as well? The chains of intoxication were everywhere in 1820s America, including East Poultney, Vermont, where Horace Greeley helped establish Poultney's first temperance club.

Temperance was a lasting legacy of Horace Greeley's stay in Vermont. The temperance pledge he took in 1824 was to become a lifelong moral gyroscope in his life. In 1849, he published a pamphlet on the adverse effects of alcohol for the Sons of Temperance. "Sensible, moral, intelligent men," he argued, acted irrationally under the effects of demon rum. Alcohol was a poison and a deadly enemy, especially dangerous for the young. In 1852, he supported the recent Maine law prohibiting the sale of alcoholic beverages and worked to establish prohibition in the State of New York. Selling alcohol—"for the privilege of poisoning their neighbors"—should be illegal. He urged New York voters to elect temperance men to the State Assembly.[28]

Horace Greeley's Vermont years also happened to coincide with a remarkable political movement that swept New England at this time, Anti-Masonry. An Anti-Masonic political party began to form in 1826 around the case of William Morgan, a New York Freemason (and by chance a stonemason as well) who threatened to reveal Masonic secrets. Morgan had published a book, *Illustrations of Masonry*, with national circulation. Now he threatened to expose the secret order in a series of articles in the Batavia, New York, *Republican Advocate*. A mob burned his printing office. Local Freemasons had Morgan arrested. He then vanished from jail on September 14, 1826, kidnapped by other Masons and taken to Fort Niagara, where he disappeared from sight.[29] "What became of Morgan?" became the watchword of a new Anti-Masonic political movement.

Freemasonry was a benevolent secret society that originated in Scotland and Germany in the eighteenth century. The first American lodge appeared in Boston in 1733. By the time of the American Revolution, the Masons were popular in both Britain and the emerging United States. Twenty-one Freemasons signed the Declaration of Independence. George Washington and thirty-two generals in the Continental Army belonged to the same fraternal order. The first Masonic lodge appeared in Vermont in 1781. By 1790, forty percent of all lodges were located in New England. By 1828, there were nearly four hundred lodges in New England, seventy-three in Vermont alone.[30] Many Masons were Revolutionary War veterans, businessmen, and professional people, with secret signs, symbols, handshakes, and oaths. Masons began to vote for other Masons for public office and in jury trials.

Anti-Masons contended that Freemasons were secretly controlling the Republic and plotting to restore British influence. The movement against Freemasonry was strongest in the countryside, especially the small towns and villages suspicious of cities, lawyers, and corrupt civilization in general. Anti-Masonry represented the rural poor against the new aristocracy of American leaders in the towns and cities. The

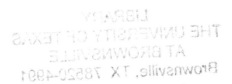

ideal of Anti-Masonry was the Christian Republic, a nation of patriotic white men devoted to the defense of republican liberty against the Masonic conspiracy.

Anti-Masonry was grounded in a belief that liberty and freedom were at risk in a modernizing and industrializing America. "The spirit of Anti-Masonry can never die," wrote one Anti-Mason in 1830; "'tis the spirit of liberty. . . . The coal that kindled the fire of anti-masonry, is the same that burned on the altar of freedom in '75."[31] An Anti-Masonic song of 1834 urged "Masonry no more shall reign / Freeman shall be free!"[32] For the Anti-Masons, Christian Republicans were the true guardians of American liberty, bequeathed to them by their fathers. But that liberty was in danger. Keepers of the flame needed to impose moral standards of civic virtue and piety on all American citizens before they succumbed to the Masonic plot.

Anti-Masonry burned even more fiercely in Vermont after the election of Andrew Jackson as president in 1828. People believed that Jackson was removing Anti-Masons from political office and replacing them with Masons. Vermonters voted for Adams over Jackson that year, while dozens of Anti-Masonic newspapers, reading rooms, lecturers, mobs, and riots brought the Anti-Masonic message of political paranoia home to Vermont citizens. By 1831, Anti-Masonry was the largest political party in Vermont, attracting two-thirds of adult males in 1832, and then dying out suddenly in 1836. For Anti-Masons, the transition from a self-sufficient farming economy to a market economy based in the cities was a threat to the Christian Republic. Statistics show that Anti-Masonry was strongest in towns undergoing a high rate of population change, and Vermont had been the fastest growing state in the Union from the 1790s.[33] Now thousands of young Vermont men began to "go West."

Horace Greeley became, while living in East Poultney, a fervent Anti-Mason and a lifelong opponent of secret societies. Rutland County, where East Poultney was located, was one of four centers of Anti-Masonry in Vermont at the time. Here Morgan's disappearance created a sensation, as it did throughout New England and the Northeast. "No man, in many of our towns, who was a Mason, could hold even the smallest office," recalled one of Greeley's friends; "many lodges surrendered their charters." Moreover Greeley himself now "entered zealously into the contest, and was a strong anti-Mason."[34]

In a letter to a friend in November 1829, Greeley tried to persuade him to join the "good cause" of Anti-Masonry, despite the presence of some "unprincipled demagogues" within the movement. The Anti-Masons needed "good fellows" like them to "keep them as they should be." "Do all you can against masonry," Greeley urged his friend, "whether in an editor's chair or in a bar-room debate." The *Northern Spectator,* he noted, was not sufficiently Anti-Masonic itself and would soon find "total extinction . . . some time in the year 1830." (It did.) He signed the letter, "Your devoted Anti-Mason."[35]

In June 1830, as revolutionary clouds stormed across Europe, the *Northern Spectator* closed its doors. Horace Greeley took his leave with twenty dollars in his pocket and walked across New York to join his family near Erie, Pennsylvania. He was nineteen.

Horace Greeley left Vermont a staunch republican, an Anti-Mason, and an enemy of Andrew Jackson and the Democrats. The Vermont years contributed to Horace Greeley's character and understanding of republican freedom's three essential elements: the importance of hard work, temperance, and a commitment to save the Republic from the secret aristocracy of Freemasons. Learning a craft and working long hours to rise within a profession characterized the hard and dirty years with other young apprentices at Amos Bliss's Ramage printing press. Temperance and moderation in all things, especially in refusing liquor and stimulants, freed one from the tyranny of King Alcohol. Working hard and maintaining a healthy body facilitated the lifelong goal of freedom and independence. And Anti-Masonry showed the contingency of the republic, a political experiment that could become temporary if corrupted. Without hard work and sobriety, freedom could turn into tyranny again. This was the mantra Greeley developed in Vermont, where by age nineteen he had become a workaholic, a tee-totaler, and an Anti-Mason: that is, a republican.

NEW YORK CITIZEN

When Horace Greeley left Vermont to join his family in western New York, he was a republican, but not yet a citizen of the republic. At nineteen, Greeley already had well-formed political ideas—he disliked Andrew Jackson and the Democrats, he abhorred Martin Van Buren and the Albany Regency, he favored protectionism, and he was a staunch temperance man and Anti-Mason who believed the American republic was in danger of corruption. He was also a minor, a young man of no income who could not vote until he reached the age of twenty-one, a ward of his father who still owed the old man whatever income he might come by. In addition, some of the newspaper editors with whom Greeley worked in the next two years were quite convinced that young Horace was a runaway apprentice who had broken his contract.

Zaccheus Greeley and his family had settled near other Greeley relatives in the woods of northern Pennsylvania up against the New York State line. In Wayne Township, Erie County, Zaccheus's brothers, Benjamin and Leonard, had arrived with their families in the late 1820s.[36] Here Zaccheus cleared the woods and built himself a log house. He also began rearing sheep. The nearest village was Clymer, New York. And the nearest large towns were Jamestown, New York, to the east and Erie, Pennsylvania, to the north.

Going West was time-consuming and difficult. To reach his family, Horace had to travel some four hundred miles on foot and by canal boat. He caught a wagon ride from East Poultney to the Champlain Canal, then a canal boat down to Troy, New York. Here he found a boat to take him to Buffalo on the Erie Canal, then a steamboat on Lake Erie to the town of Dunkirk. From here, he walked with an injured leg the last forty miles by himself, arriving at the family cabin in the dead of night. Elapsed time: twelve days. Total cost: seven dollars.

After his mother had ministered to his injured leg, Greeley then walked the twenty miles to Jamestown, New York, in search of another typesetting job. After a week of seeking work, he walked home again. A doctor treated his leg with electric current, aiding in his recovery, but leaving him with a reddish scar. He then walked the fifty miles to Lodi, New York, and worked briefly on a Democrat newspaper, "a Jackson paper, a forlorn affair," he wrote a friend in East Poultney, "else I would have sent you a few numbers."[37] Working for a Democratic newspaper was sheer desperation.

Western New York at the time was known as the "burned-over district" because of the variety of religious and political enthusiasms that prevailed. Evangelic Christianity took many forms. Revivalism was in the air. So was Anti-Masonry, imported by northern New Englanders who had traveled west to New York in search of cheap land and new lives. The Second Great Awakening led to thousands of conversions of mainstream Protestants and nonbelievers to a more robust Christianity. Joseph Smith founded the Mormon Church of Latter-Day Saints. By 1823, Greeley's religion—Universalism—had ninety congregations between Rochester and Buffalo.[38] And western New York was a hotbed of anti-Jackson sentiment where Anti-Masons and National Republicans waited for their chance to throw the Democrats out of office.

Greeley soon became a familiar figure around Clymer, New York. As a young printer in search of work, young Horace joined the cracker-barrel crowd at Steve Steward's general store in Clymer to talk politics, religion, and anything else. Years later, Clymer townsfolk remembered Greeley as polite, good natured, and kind hearted, a young man with "the face of an angel and the walk of a clodhopper."[39]

In the summer of 1830, Greeley walked to Erie, Pennsylvania, a bustling town of five thousand people, in search of a printing job. For six weeks, he had been essentially unemployed, cutting wood for his father and taking temporary jobs as a journeyman printer. In Erie, he visited the offices of Joseph M. Sterritt, editor of the *Erie Gazette* and a staunch Anti-Mason, who hired him as a typesetter and compositor at $12 a month plus board.[40]

Greeley quickly proved to be a reliable and accurate worker. Over the course of the next seven months, he spent a paltry $6 on himself, saved $15, and sent the rest—some $300—to his father, who was legally entitled to young Greeley's earnings until he reached age twenty-one.[41]

Greeley's closest friend at the *Erie Gazette* was another staunch Anti-Mason, Obadiah A. Bowe, who would remain a lifelong friend and correspondent. Both young men were bright and ambitious. They talked often of starting their own newspaper and printshop. Bowe had about $400, Greeley $20. Horace described himself as an "ill behaved, ill looking, and worse dressed chap." "I have nothing to risk but my carcass," he wrote Obadiah that winter, "which will not probably be placed in any imminent peril, by accepting your proposal."[42] A newspaper seemed like a grand adventure, if they could only find the start-up funds. If they succeeded, the paper would surely be Anti-Masonic. "No publication over which I have any control," Greeley wrote Bowe, "shall ever oppose and defame the cause of Anti-masonry." And Anti-Masonry was moving from a moral crusade to a national political party, nowhere more so than in western New York.

On April 31, 1831, Horace Greeley's five-year apprenticeship contract with Amos Bliss in East Poultney, Vermont, legally expired. He was now twenty, and nearly free to make his own way in the world. But his father still needed his support. The "old man," Greeley wrote his friend Bowe, needed his money. Should he break with his father or continue to support him and remain in a kind of bondage? Bowe and Greeley planned to go to Cortlandville, New York, start up an Anti-Masonic newspaper together, and make their own way in the world. Both were tired of Sterritt's orders and stern regimen at the paper.[43]

Greeley later recalled that his time with Sterritt at the *Erie Gazette* was "among the pleasantest of all the months I now recall." He admitted that as a young man, he was a "diligent, faithful, correct, though not very rapid typesetter" who "made many friends and no enemies."[44] But in the spring of 1831, he was restless, anxious about his continuing ties and obligations to his father. When the sick employee he was replacing at the *Gazette* returned to work, Greeley was let go. He had no funds to pursue his joint venture with Bowe. Failing to find work in Wilkes-Barre, he returned to his father's farm. He gave Zaccheus most of the earnings he had saved from the newspaper. In return, his father agreed that Horace had no more obligation to support him.[45] He was free to move on to adulthood and citizenship.

In addition to pursuing an independent living, Greeley also began to discover an independent faith. In New Hampshire, his parents had been inactive Congregationalists. In Vermont as a teenager, he was already "little better than a Universalist," according to his neighbors. He rejected the Calvinist world of sin and damnation prominent in New England Congregationalism in favor of a much less orthodox form of Christianity that emphasized free will, self-reliance, moral reform, and salvation through Christ for all people. But he did not hear a Universalist sermon until he passed through Buffalo, New York, in 1830. When he did, he became a convert.[46]

In 1831, Greeley began to reread the Bible, impressed by its "spirit and general scope." He believed that salvation was not restricted to an elect, but universal. Nothing was entirely predestined, and man was free to reform himself and his world.[47] Like Stonewall Jackson, the Confederate general, and many other Americans, Greeley believed— following the Dutch theologian, and critic of Calvin, Jacob Arminius (1560–1609)—that all people, not just an elect, could achieve salvation from a loving God. Original sin did not determine who would be saved and who would be damned after death. Man had never lost his ability to be good of his own free will. Arminianism was at the root of the Second Great Awakening, the belief, trumpeted by the evangelist Charles Grandison Finney and others, that anyone could be saved through Christ. Finney's revivalism swept across the burned-over district after 1830.

Universalism was much more popular among reformers and lower-class rural enthusiasts than the Unitarianism of educated Yankees.[48] Greeley's friend P. T. Barnum called it the religion of success. John Murray (1741–1815), a Scot from Hampshire, England, brought the movement to America after 1770. Like the Baptists, Universalists championed religious liberty. Universalists believed that God was benevolent, not wrathful, and would, in the end, save everyone. Individuals were free to interpret scripture for themselves. The emphasis was on conscience, benevolence, humanitarianism, and reform. Christ had died to atone for all men's sins, not just for a few. Reform could triumph over evil. In New York, as elsewhere, Universalists were at the forefront of reform—against slavery, against capital punishment, for labor reform, and for temperance.[49]

Greeley also understood that religious liberty was central to Universalism. The Winchester Profession included a "liberty clause" that permitted any Universalist society to adopt its own articles of faith. Elias Smith (1769–1846), the most popular Universalist preacher in New England, linked primitive Christianity with republican virtue. "Let us be republicans indeed," wrote Smith in 1809. "Many are republicans as to government, and yet are but half republicans, being in matters of religion still bound to a Catechism, creed, covenant, or a superstitious priest. Venture to be as independent in things of religion, as in that which respects the government in which you live."[50]

Universalism was popular in both New Hampshire and Vermont when Greeley was growing up. Congregationalism dominated the region (there were 138 Congregational churches in New Hampshire in 1800), but the new faiths—Baptist, Methodist, and Universalist—were making inroads in rural areas. By 1831, there were fifty-seven Universalist societies in Vermont, one for every four towns. Universalists were influential in the Vermont legislature, and tended to be Anti-Masonic, egalitarian, respectable defenders of the Christian republic against corruption, just like Horace Greeley.[51]

Universalism made Greeley rich in spirit, but not pocket. In mid-

August 1831, Horace moved to New York City to look for work. He came by the Albany boat, debarking at the Whitehall Street Pier in the early morning hours. He had paid off his debts to his father, but had only a few dollars in his pocket and a "scanty wardrobe." He carried all his worldly possessions on his back. In Gotham, Greeley was one of thousands of young printers in search of work. He knew no one. For a time, he boarded with Edward McGolrick, a pub owner, at 168 West Street for $2.50 a week, and walked the city streets in search of employment. Some young Irishmen referred him to John T. West's printing establishment over McElrath and Bang's bookstore at 85 Chatham Street. Here he laboriously composed a pocket New Testament in double columns with Greek references and superscripts in very small type—"the slowest, and by far the most difficult, work I had every undertaken," he later remembered. He tried some typesetting jobs, attended a Tariff Convention meeting as a spectator, and then composed the Book of Genesis, again in small pages and close type. "I obtained work pretty soon," he wrote, "but it was such as older hands would not do, and I had to work fourteen hours a day to make about $5.50 per week."[52]

New York City was overwhelming. The teeming metropolis of 1831 had some 242,000 people living in the greater metropolitan area, many of them in squalid conditions. The winter of 1831–2 was hard and cold. Greeley worked a variety of printing jobs—two months for John West; a week for the *Evening Post* newspaper; two or three weeks for a literary weekly, *The Amulet*, for which he received no wages; some weeks for the *Commercial Advertiser*; a few days for William T. Porter's *Sporting News*, a betting magazine; then for another sporting magazine, the *Spirit of the Times*. Here he became a close friend of the foreman, Francis V. Story, a young man of about Greeley's age. He also took up residence at a boarding house operated by Sylvester Graham, whose lectures that winter advocated a vegetarian diet and abstinence from all alcoholic beverage and coffee.[53]

Eventually Greeley went back to John West to set type for the Book of Genesis. "He hires me," Greeley wrote his friend Obadiah Bowe, "because he knows I can set any manuscript, however abominable, and make a cleaner proof than almost anybody else." Bowe should come to the city too, Greeley advised, leaving his current newspaper—"that infernal vehicle of masonic Jackson slander and nonsense." Greeley's old master, Amos Bliss, had come down from

Vermont, Greeley told Bowe, and "we held a regular antimasonic caucus. He's whole hog."[54]

In New York, Greeley quickly found a religious home in the Second Universalist Society on Orchard Street, headed by Thomas J. Sawyer, a twenty-seven-year-old minister from Vermont. At the time, Universalism was a minor faith in the polyglot city. The society had brought in Sawyer in 1830 as its first ordained preacher. Greeley also attended Sawyer's weekly Bible study class. "Horace Greeley was generally present," recalled Sawyer, "and entered with great interest into the discussions to which our lessons gave rise. He soon distinguished himself by the quickness of his apprehension, the pertinence of his observations and inquiries, and by the general grasp of his mind on every topic that came before us."[55]

Sawyer emphasized man's moral freedom to reform a fallen world. "Man is a free moral agent," he preached, "and of this necessary constituent of his moral nature God will never deprive him for the purpose of making him either holy and happy, or sinful and miserable."[56] "All human government," he wrote in 1853, "is predicated on the same conviction of human freedom."[57] Slavery was a moral evil, and anti-slavery was a moral imperative.

After he left his Grahamite boarding house and married Mary Cheney in 1836, Greeley and his bride were frequent guests at the Sawyer home. Caroline Sawyer may well have given the name *Tribune* to Greeley for his famous newspaper when he launched it in 1841, and she predicted that "it shall be a power in the land!"[58] But this is to get ahead of our story.

On February 3, 1832, Horace Greeley celebrated his twenty-first birthday. He was now economically free of his father and Amos Bliss, and politically free to be a citizen of the republic, eligible to vote in local and national elections. He continued to eke out a living setting type for a prominent publisher, J. S. Redfield, but the winter of 1831–2 was hard, and the cholera summer of 1832 nearly paralyzed the city, as it already had paralyzed Europe from Moscow to Paris. Tens of thousands died of disease amid the open sewers and filth of the crowded streets and tenements. In the autumn, Greeley went north to see his relatives in New Hampshire and Vermont—by ship from New York to Providence, Rhode Island ("an inferior ill-looking place"), by stagecoach from Providence to Boston ("it does not equal my expectations"). In Boston, he heard the famous Universalist preacher Hosea Ballou preach on Sunday ("too high toned, even for me") and visited several cousins and his aunt. He then walked to Lowell ("damn my poverty!") and on to Amherst, New Hampshire, some fifty miles away from Boston.[59]

Greeley returned to New York City in October, "just in time to vote against Andrew Jackson's reelection."[60] Although Greeley later became a staunch supporter of one candidate, Henry Clay, the National Republican, he probably voted for the Anti-Masonic candidate, William Wirt. A former Attorney General of the United States, Wirt believed that his God-given mission was to save the republic from corruption at the hands of Jackson and the Democrats. He modestly hoped that he could "become an instrument in the hands of Providence of rescuing the country from its present fallen condition," factionalism, corruption, and intrigue.[61]

During the winter of 1832–3, Greeley joined his friend Francis Story in setting up a new printshop to publish the weekly *Bank Note Reporter* and a penny daily newspaper. He rented two rooms at 54 Liberty Street and had less than two hundred dollars to his name. Somehow, in January 1833, Greeley and Story managed to come up with the funds from a physician, H. D. Shepherd, to edit a daily newspaper, the *Morning Post* (two cents). The goal was to sell fifteen thousand copies a day, but the paper quickly failed. Despite losing fifty dollars in the bargain, Greeley and Story persisted with a tri-weekly newspaper, the *Constitutionalist*, actually a lottery sheet based in Delaware. In July 1833, Story tragically drowned while swimming in the East River, and Jonas Winchester, Story's brother-in-law, replaced him as Greeley's partner in H. Greeley & Co., Printers. "I bitterly mourned the loss of my nearest and dearest friend," recalled Greeley. In the meantime, Benjamin Day had begun to publish the first penny daily in New York, the *New York Sun*, and was immediately successful, selling fifteen thousand copies a day by 1835.[62]

Greeley was beginning his publishing career at an auspicious moment. A growing and extensive American reading public was avid for the latest news, at home and abroad. American literacy rates were the highest in the world. New steam presses were printing two thousand sheets an hour, a vast improvement over the old hand presses. There had been two hundred newspapers in the country in 1800. There would be 2,500 by 1850. Newspapers were at the heart of the political process, informing their readers of the latest votes and election campaigns in every town, village, and state in the Union. No wonder that Europe saw republican America, as the London Working Man's Association put it in 1832, as the "beacon of freedom" for the world.[63]

2

Whig Politico

WHIG EDITOR

In 1834, Horace Greeley transformed himself from a printer into an editor, from an Anti-Mason into a Whig, and from a political novice into an anti-slavery man. Editing gave him a chance to speak his mind on the great issues of the day without having to bend to any other man's will. The newly formed Whig Party was a party of freedom opposed to the Democrats of Andy Jackson and Martin Van Buren. Jackson and the Democrats ruled the nation from Washington. They espoused a doctrine of equal rights for all, no privileges for individuals or corporations, low tariffs and minimum government protection (the 1828 "tariff of abominations" was too high, they said), and no national bank. The North, charged some Democrats, was exploiting the South through high tariffs on manufactured goods. Only a gradual reduction in such tariffs, warned Henry Clay, could avert secession and civil war.

Protection was not a new issue. Since 1789, the nation and the individual states had launched a barrage of tariffs on imported and exported goods. Goods imported from Europe, especially cottons and woolens, at first carried a tariff of five percent. Then came the inflated land prices of 1815–8 and the crash of 1819. After the War of 1812 a flood of cheap British imports threatened American farmers and start-up companies. By the 1820s, American protective tariffs averaged twenty percent or more. As the new American mills and factories began to produce their own cloth and fabric, a strong protectionist movement arose to maintain high tariffs at twenty-five percent. The 1828 Tariff of Abominations raised some tariffs to fifty percent of the price of European goods.[1] The purpose was to protect farmers and emerging American industries from foreign competition and to reduce the prices of protected goods. The movement for protection was strongest in the North, from Ohio and Kentucky through New York and Pennsylvania to New England. The South, in contrast, supported slavery, free trade, and lower tariffs. High tariffs thus helped widen the sectional gap between North and South.

The leader of the protection movement was Henry Clay, a Kentucky U.S. Senator since 1806. Clay was a Jeffersonian republican and economic nationalist who believed that the federal government should encourage economic growth in agriculture, commerce, and manufacturing to stimulate the home market and avoid dependence on foreign imports. The government should also fund "internal improvements" such as canals, harbors, roads, and railroads. Government thus should play a role in modernization and development, supporting the economy and providing harmony, mutual advantage, and higher wages for labor. Clay also supported the Second Bank of the United States, chartered in 1816, whose re-chartering Jackson vetoed. In 1824, Clay became Secretary of State after the "corrupt bargain" where Clay helped engineer the vote for John Quincy Adams for president in the House of Representatives.

In 1830, as Horace Greeley trudged across upstate New York, the U.S. Senate considered a bill to restrict land sales that were leading so many New England men to "go West" with their families. Senator Thomas Hart Benton of Missouri attacked the bill, and was supported by Senator Robert Y. Hayne of South Carolina. Hayne argued that the Union was simply a compact of individual states that had the right to secede from that Union. Senator Daniel Webster of Massachusetts responded to Hayne with his famous words, familiar to every American school child for generations: "Liberty and Union, now and forever, one and inseparable." Senator John Calhoun of South Carolina responded with the admonition, "The Union. Next to our liberties, the most dear." Mayor Harrison Gray Otis of Boston, Massachusetts, spoke of the unfinished business of the American Union, namely, the equality of freedom for all, rather than liberty for some. "We are now before the altar," he said, "whence the coals were taken which have kindled the flame of liberty in two hemispheres . . . [and will lead us] on the railroad which leads to universal freedom."[2]

In 1832, Jackson proposed to lower tariffs. Calhoun raised the possibility that a state unhappy with tariffs might "nullify" federal laws. South Carolina promptly declared the federal tariffs of 1828 and 1832 to be null and void, refusing to collect any federal duties after February 1, 1833. The state legislature even voted funds to raise an army. In response, President Jackson declared nullification illegal and the Union indissoluble. He asked, and received, from Congress a Force Bill enabling him to send federal troops into any state to execute federal laws. We are a single nation, Jackson said in effect, and no state has the right to secede. Civil war seemed imminent.

The man who saved the day was Henry Clay. His compromise proposed a gradual reduction in tariffs acceptable to the majority of both Whigs and Democrats, northern businessmen and southern planters. By 1842, no tariff would exceed twenty percent. Although the South remained unhappy, the compromise tariff rates of 1833 prevented a national breakdown.

The consequence of the nullification crisis for Horace Greeley was that he became absolutely devoted to his new hero, Henry Clay, but retained his Yankee protectionist enthusiasm. He also became an enthusiastic Whig.

The Whig Party developed out of divisions within Thomas Jefferson's National Republican Party. By 1832, an anti-Jackson coalition began to form of National Republicans, Anti-Masons, and states' rights southerners. But Whigs were more than an ill-defined anti-Jackson coalition. They had an ideology grounded in political principles. Specifically, they supported the defense of liberty against power and tyranny. They synthesized virtue and commerce in defining active citizenship in the republic. And they contrasted the "liberty of the freemen" with the "slavery of party" offered by the Democrats. In an age of Democratic Party dominance, the Whigs emerged as crusaders for political freedom.[3] They became the party of small business and finance in the cities, linked to trans-Atlantic trade networks. They favored protective tariffs, the power of markets, and internal improvements subsidized by the federal government. They believed in the virtues of industry, thrift, and sobriety.

The Whigs sought greater liberty through the economic transformations of capitalism. This meant recognizing the profit motive, the need for money as a medium of exchange, active markets, and government support and protection. In a world of burgeoning cities, eager consumers, and a literate reading public, the Whigs welcomed liberal capitalism as the successor to Jeffersonian agrarianism.[4] In the Whig view, Jeffersonian republicanism had now given way to a Jacksonian democracy that threatened to corrupt the republic.[5] The liberty of the founding fathers differed from the more universal freedom associated with economic development, territorial expansion, and anti-slavery. "In Greece, in Rome, in Venice, in France," said a conservative Whig attorney, Rufus Choate, in 1834, "men have called on the Goddess of Liberty, but they were not wise enough, they were not virtuous enough, for diffused, steady, lasting freedom."[6]

In 1834, the Whig Party began to organize in New York State. In local city elections in April, Horace Greeley joined a group of anti-Jackson politicians that adopted the Whig name in their modest, and sometimes violent, campaign. Greeley printed their short-lived campaign newspaper, *The Constitution*. The Whigs lost badly, Greeley and his partner Jonas Winchester lost money, and New York City elected a Jackson man as mayor. Yet the Whigs did succeed in electing a majority of the city's governing body, the Common Council, thus gaining some control over patronage in city appointments to public office. The Whigs had entered the New York political arena, and Greeley had become a Whig.[7]

Greeley's professional life was moving in a more auspicious direction than the Whigs. In the spring of 1834, at the tender age of twenty-three, Horace Greeley began to edit his first journal, a weekly magazine called the *New Yorker*. Jonas Winchester was the business manager, since Greeley himself was hopeless with both money and figures. The first issue appeared in March and sold only one hundred copies. Yet it met a public need. By September, the magazine sold 2,500 copies, then the following spring 7,000, until it reached a sales peak of 9,500 in the spring of 1837. Although the journal continued to lose money, which Greeley begged and borrowed from friends around the city, it had an established readership and became widely popular.[8]

A weekly of sixteen pages that cost three dollars a year for subscribers, the *New Yorker* featured literary, political, and social articles, as well as book reviews. Editorials held forth against liquor, slavery, exploitation of Indians, and imprisonment for debt, praising the common man, education, and useful knowledge. Greeley admired the July 1830 revolution in France and the movement for Irish reform, that is, for independence from England. He was an American liberal nationalist, a conservative, a promoter of national welfare and Clay's American System. He was a patriot and a moral man. He believed that a woman's place was in the home, and he distrusted the masses. He believed in distributing public income from the sale of public lands. And he wanted a national bank to control currency and credit.

In October 1834, Beman Brockway was looking for work as a compositor when he met Horace Greeley for the first time. He was stunned by the appearance of the young editor. "He was sitting at a small table at one side of the little composing room, writing furiously, of course, and had barely time to look up when I was introduced to him. He was not yet twenty-five years old, and the greenest specimen of an editor I had ever seen. His hair was flaxen and long, he had handsome blue eyes and a complexion white and delicate as that of a woman. My interview with him was of the briefest character. He was busy, and I did not wish to bore him."[9]

In 1835, New York City had a population of 270,000 and offered fifteen daily newspapers on the streets to an eager reading public. The first newsboys were starting to hawk daily papers on street corners, rather than selling them over the counter or providing home delivery. There were twice as many newspapers in America as there had been in 1810, with a combined annual circulation of around one hundred million copies. In addition, there were some eleven semi-weeklies and thirty-one weeklies in New York City alone, for a combined circulation of around thirteen million.

Into this competitive marketplace of news came James Gordon Bennett, a Scot who had immigrated to America in 1820. Now, at the age of forty, Bennett, who had been a journalist in Charleston and Washington, proposed to start a new daily newspaper, the *New York Herald*. He was a Tammany Hall Democrat who attacked the Anti-Masons in his writings. Expelled from the *New York Courier and Enquirer* by its volatile editor, James W. Webb, Bennett decided to go it on his own. In 1834, Bennett approached Greeley about joining him in publishing a new daily newspaper. But Bennett had only five hundred dollars in cash, and Greeley declined to be simply a printer. Bennett, following a recommendation of Greeley and Winchester, then turned to some other printers on Ann Street and in May 1835 brought out the first edition of his *Herald*. He would become one of Horace Greeley's greatest rivals as a newspaper editor in New York.[10]

Bennett's offer had been tempting, but the *Yorker*, as Greeley called it, required all his time and energy for the moment. After a year, subscriptions had risen, but the journal was still losing money. Winchester said he wanted to quit. Greeley wrote his friend B. F. (Fitch) Ransom in East Poultney, Vermont, about his troubles. "I paid off everyone tonight," he wrote in July 1835, "Have $10 left and have to raise $350 on Monday. Borrowing places all sucked dry. I shall raise it, however."[11] Somehow he did.

On December 17, 1835, a fire started on Merchant Street near Greeley's offices. Freezing temperatures turned water in hydrants and hoses into ice. High winds took the fire down Wall Street to the East River, then westward to Exchange and Post, becoming the worst conflagration in America before the Chicago Fire. Many newspaper offices, including Greeley's, were burned out, together with their records and supplies of paper. Seven hundred shops with merchandise valued at forty million dollars were destroyed. People in Philadelphia and New Haven could see the flames of New York.[12]

Undaunted, Greeley persisted. By early 1836, after two years of "humble but assiduous labors," he told his readers that the *Yorker* now had over seven thousand subscribers. But paper was expensive, he added, and he could no longer give credit or tolerate subscribers who did not pay.[13] The new double-quarto edition provided an enticing mix of news and literature, essays and poems, music and financial reports. Greeley in his editorials (he pioneered in setting his own opinions apart from the news) supported a national paper currency. He urged harmony between labor and capital, the two great mutually dependent sources of national wealth. He followed the doings of Congress in Washington. He railed against prostitution, liquor, and the spoils system. And he welcomed the independence of Texas from Mexico, "free flourishing and independent—but not a portion of the United States."[14]

Finances remained a problem. In May 1836, Greeley again wrote to his friend B. F. Ransom offering him a partnership in the journal, in the event that Jonas Winchester should decide to leave (Winchester ultimately went west to California, where he became the first state printer in 1850). Ransom would run the publications office and Greeley would handle the printing.[15] As usual, Greeley needed a businessman to make his enterprises actually work.

Greeley also began to take up the cause of social reform. He argued against capital punishment, which often killed innocent people and did not deter crime. Likewise, the laboring man needed help. The worker was not a serf or a slave, but a free man. War between labor and capital was only "injurious to the interests of both." Strikes for higher wages were not the answer. Society needed reform to help the poor and needy get on with their lives. And the greatest cause of social reform was the elimination of slavery.[16]

Horace Greeley was not an abolitionist. But he did have a deep aversion to the institution of slavery that threatened free labor. The managing editor of the *Tribune*, John R. Young, later recalled that "the anti-slavery atmosphere surrounding the *Tribune* was not inspired by Greeley," but enjoyed only his "reluctant grumbling acquiescence."[17] Yet even in the pages of the *Yorker* in the 1830s, Greeley took on the peculiar institution with his tongue and his pen.

To the Whigs before 1850, slavery meant any relationship of economic restraint that fixed labor for life without compensation. Only a market economy offered liberation from the slavery associated with agriculture and the plantation. Slavery robbed workers of their labor value. Wage slavery was the enemy of white, as well as black, workers. Henry Clay himself admitted that slavery was a "manifest violation of the rights of man."[18] The federal government could not emancipate the slaves. That must be left to the states. But slavery was wrong —and inefficient.

Abolitionism was in the air. Greeley's distant cousin, the poet John Greenleaf Whittier, noted that "the pure republican principles of Anti-Slavery are rapidly gaining ground in Essex County [Massachusetts]."[19] But for Horace Greeley, anti-slavery was simply one part of a developing universal struggle for freedom. In July 1834, New York endured a series of violent race riots. On August 1, there was a celebration at Philomathian Hall of the British emancipation of slaves in the West Indies. The British Unitarian abolitionist Harriet Martineau arrived in New York from Boston in September. Then came George Thompson, another British abolitionist. Greeley in the *New Yorker* duly noted that slavery was an evil institution in the American South that the founding fathers had cleverly avoided in drafting the Constitution, leaving it as a matter for individual states to resolve. "The Union was formed," he wrote, "with a perfect knowledge, on the one hand, that slavery existed in the South, and, on the other, it was utterly disproved and discountenanced at the North." "We entertain no doubt," he concluded, "that the system of slavery is at the bottom of most of the evils which afflict the communities of the south." Slavery had retarded economic growth in Missouri and Indiana. But abolition was not the answer yet. Clay's American Colonization Society, with its plans to send slaves back to Africa, was a step in the right direction. More likely, once southerners recognized the disadvantages of slavery, they too would welcome the "ultimate extinction of the evil."[20]

Anti-slavery continued to gather steam in 1835. Thompson and Anglo-American abolitionist Charles Stuart both came to New York in May to address the second congress of the Antislavery Society. Liberty, republicanism, and Christianity were rhetorically set against the "legalized tyranny" of slavery. Cousin Whittier, now editor of the *Essex Gazette*, recognized the "glorious liberty" of the founding fathers and the "freedom which they toiled to win." Increasingly Whittier wrote not of liberty, but of "freedom's cause" and "freedom's light." "Be ours to strike in Freedom's cause, As Christians may,—as Freemen can!"[21] But abolitionism was a risky business. George Thompson was mobbed twenty times on his two-hundred-lecture tour, and his landlord evicted him from his New York City apartment. Attacked by the mainstream press and assaulted by mobs, he bemoaned his cause of abolition at the end of the year: "How long shall the deeds of America clog the wheels of the car of Universal Freedom?"[22]

Yet the abolitionists persisted. William Lloyd Garrison's anti-slavery newspaper, *The Liberator,* however small its readership, hammered away at the slavery issue—the moral law was superior to the civil law, civil disobedience was justified against slavery, slavery was a form of war, disunion was preferable to union with slaveholders, and so forth. Abolishing slavery was every Christian's moral obligation. The overarching goal was "universal emancipation," a world of freedom for all, not liberty for some. Only then could man perfect himself and attain the Kingdom of God.[23] Likewise, the Grimke sisters of South Carolina, Sarah and Angelina, published their own *Appeal to Christian Women of the South* in 1836 in New York, pitting freedom against slavery and noting that "slavery is contrary to the declaration of our independence."[24] And in Congress, former president John Quincy Adams proclaimed that the "holy cause of human freedom" raged against the "slavocracy" of the South, and called for the "total abolition of slavery on earth."[25] Slavery was a sin, one that must be redeemed by emancipation.

Greeley, as a Whig, was not yet ready to argue that both economic progress and the moral law argued for the abolition of slavery. But as a newspaper man, he was well aware of the abolitionist current, and the backwash of pro-slavery sentiment in the North. In the spring of 1836, Greeley wrote of the anti-slavery convention held in Granville, Ohio, that "abolitionist declaimers" were "exciting the public mind." Whigs were divided, often within themselves, about slavery, not only the "conscience Whigs" of the North who questioned the institution and the "cotton Whigs" of both North and South who sought to preserve their business and property. The *Cincinnati Whig* charged in 1836 that British abolitionists were behind the American agitation (in fact, one-third of American abolitionists were born abroad, most of them in Great Britain).[26]

But slavery was becoming a major issue in 1836. Within a few months, Wendell Phillips told the Massachusetts Anti-Slavery Society that "disunion is coming unless we discuss this subject; for the spirit of freedom and the spirit of slavery are contending here for the mastery. They cannot live together."[27] Greeley was not yet a disunionist, although in 1860 he came close to arguing that North and South should separate. He recognized that slavery and freedom, not tyranny and liberty, were becoming words in the vocabulary of a new struggle. He would later play a major role in that struggle. But at the moment he was more concerned about getting married.

In a republic, Greeley believed, virtuous citizens were crucial in order to avoid corruption of the body politic. He had already taken one step toward virtue with his temperance pledge a decade earlier. Another form of virtue was good bodily health and hygiene. Virtuous citizens must take care of their own body by proper exercise and diet. In his youth, Greeley had been—and continued to be—a great walker, hiker, and outdoor enthusiast. Now he turned to diet and the new health cult of Sylvester Graham, a recent arrival in New York. In the process, Greeley met his future wife and lifelong companion, Mary Youngs Cheney.

Mary—or Molly, as Greeley called her—Cheney was a Connecticut Yankee and a schoolteacher. Her father, Silas, was born in 1776, the year of independence, near Hartford and had died in 1821. Her mother, Polly Youngs, of Waterbury, now lived in Litchfield. In 1836, Molly was a vivacious five-foot-four-inch brunette of twenty-five, the same age as Greeley. Like her future husband, she had an active mind, a retentive memory, and strong opinions. She was a well-educated schoolteacher who seemed "crazy for learning," as her friend Margaret Fuller put it.[28]

Horace met Mary around 1834 when both were living at a New York City boarding house run on Sylvester Graham's principles of diet. Graham began as a temperance speaker in Philadelphia and a Presbyterian minister in New Jersey. He was fluent, forceful, and clever. He read widely and could converse on matters of physics, metaphysics, and theology. In 1831, he moved to New York and began to give lectures on the "science" of human health, life, and longevity. He recommended lots of baths, fresh air, regular exercise, a vegetarian diet, lots of sunlight, and sexual hygiene—all of which were novelties or nonexistent in the smoggy industrial world of the burgeoning city. Alcohol, tobacco, coffee, tea, opium, spices, condiments, and meat were all off limits. Instead, Graham recommended that people eat coarse-grained wheat or rye bread more than twelve hours old, along with fruits and vegetables. He also recommended sleeping on hard mattresses, opening the bedroom windows at night, chastity, cold showers, loose clothing, pure water, and vigorous exercise.[29]

Graham was at war against alcohol and atheism. Emerson ridiculed him as a "poet of bran and pumpkins." But he attracted a great following in New York and Boston in the 1830s, among them Horace Greeley and Mary Cheney. For a couple about to be married, Grahamism was hardly romantic. Continence and vegetarianism appealed more to the Puritan and the frugal than the passionate in them. But Graham recognized that at the time rural communities were being transformed by urban and industrial capitalism. The filth and disruption of this transformation required a new commitment to a conscious regimen of health in daily routine. The first Graham boarding houses opened in Boston and New York in 1833.[30] At first, the one in New York was a temperance hotel for men only. William Lloyd Garrison stayed there when he came down from Boston to lecture fellow abolitionists. There were two vegetarian meals daily, cold water to drink, and no keys for the residents, who had to be up at five o'clock in the morning (six o'clock in the winter) to exercise, and in bed by ten o'clock at night.

Greeley later recalled that he was a "Grahamite" in those days, and continued to eat meat "sparingly" even afterwards. He exercised by walking, cutting wood, clearing brush, and felling trees. He also got into the habit of lifting weights at a New York City health club called "The Lifting Cure."[31]

In 1835, Mary Cheney left the boarding house and moved south to

Warrenton, North Carolina, to teach at a private school for young gentlemen and ladies, run by Harriet Allen. Warrenton was the wealthiest town east of the Mississippi River at the time, with a thriving economy based on cotton and tobacco. Here Mary boarded with the family of William Bragg, a wealthy builder whose son Braxton—the future Confederate general—was off studying at West Point. In Warrenton, both Mary Cheney and her courting visitor, Horace Greeley, got the reputation—probably in retrospect—of being abolitionists. "He came down here and got Miss Cheney," one Warrenton resident later recalled, "after the Warrenton people found out what she was up to and withdrew their children from her instruction."[32]

More likely Greeley came down to Warrenton simply to marry Molly on July 5, 1836. They apparently told very few people. Greeley got round to telling his co-worker Jonas Winchester about the wedding only a day before. "I mean to be in New York Saturday evening," he wrote in a jocular vein, "but this will depend on my getting married tomorrow morning and on the road July 7, and in Petersburg [VA, 105 miles from Warrenton] the same evening."[33] Greeley promptly wrote his friend O. A. Bowe informing him of his marriage. He also signed the customary North Carolina marriage bond, stating that there was neither legal nor moral reason why they should not marry, and that he could support them both. He agreed to pay a five-hundred-dollar fine if the bond was violated.[34] If there was no "lawful cause or Impediment to obstruct the said Marriage, then the above obligation to be void."[35]

On July 16, the *Yorker* duly announced the occasion in a matter-of-fact way: "Married. In Immanuel Church, Warrenton, North Carolina, on Tuesday morning 5th inst., by Rev. William Norwood, Mr. Horace Greeley, editor of the New Yorker, and Miss Mary Y. Cheney of Warrenton, formerly of this city."[36] The wedding breakfast and reception was given by William and Margaret Bragg at their home a few blocks from the church.

Despite his change in marital status, Greeley remained wedded to his first love, politics. On his way down from New York to Warrenton, he took a detour at Washington, DC. Here he visited Congress and witnessed his hero, Henry Clay, in action. "The most striking person on the floor [of the U.S. Senate] is Mr. Clay, who is incessantly in motion, and whose spare, erect form betrays an easy dignity approaching to majesty, and a perfect gracefulness, such as I have never seen equalled." Clay was surely "no common man," but "one of the driest, hardest speakers I ever listened to."[37]

Instead of a honeymoon, Horace and Molly headed home to New York to begin life as man and wife by going back to work. Horace edited the *Yorker*. Molly went back to schoolteaching. They took up keeping house at 35 East 19th Street, where they also kept three goats in the back yard. Yet all was not harmony in Gotham: to Greeley's dismay, he returned to a city on the brink of a financial crisis that would lead him to urge his fellow citizens to "go West," rather than face a life of poverty in the East, in order to find freedom.

Horace Greeley probably did not coin the phrase that made him famous. But he essentially espoused its message from 1837 until the end of his life. For Greeley, as for most Americans, the West meant freedom, the chance to begin life anew. Santa Fe trader Josiah Gregg spoke of the "perfect freedom" of the prairies and the unknown lands of the American West. Henry David Thoreau told the Concord Lyceum in 1851 that he wanted to "speak a word for Nature, for absolute freedom and wildness."[38] Greeley's own ancestors and relatives had been part of the great westward migration to the New World, the Greeleys from Nottingham, England, to Massachusetts, the Woodburns from Scotland to Ireland to New Hampshire. His father had gone west from New Hampshire to Vermont, then to the burned-over district of western New York. Greeley himself would travel westward for the rest of his life, first to Pennsylvania, Ohio, Michigan, and Minnesota, later to Kansas, Nebraska, Colorado, Wyoming, and California. Like most Americans, Greeley dreamed of the West as a state of mind and a new opportunity for freedom.

One story has it that in 1851, John Babson Lane Soule, the editor of the Terre Haute, Indiana, *Express*, bet his friend and future Secretary of the Navy Richard Thompson that he could write an article that would be attributed to Greeley. Sure enough, Soule dashed off a newspaper column that used the phrase "Go West, Young Man!" and the *New York Tribune* reprinted it. Despite the *Tribune*'s disclaimer that the words were "attached to the editor erroneously," people from that moment on did indeed attach them famously to Horace Greeley.[39]

Another story attributes the phrase to Greeley via the famous *Tribune* correspondent and abolitionist minister Josiah Bushnell Grinnell (1821–1891), who went west to found Grinnell College in Iowa. Grinnell was born in New Haven, Vermont, and in 1851 became pastor of the First Congregational Church in Washington, DC, at a time when that town was a muddy backwater of forty thousand people, many of them slaves on their way to and from the pens of the slave market. In 1852, he moved again to New York City, where he got to know Greeley through the temperance speaking circuit. Greeley would often take over for Grinnell when he lost his voice.

In September 1853, Grinnell claimed that he lost his speaking voice and headed for the *Tribune* offices to find Greeley. Greeley reportedly said, "Don't get ready for a fashionable European health trip, or to lounge in the city, which is no place to stay except with occupation and good health. Go West, young man, go West. There is health in the country, and room away from our crowds of idlers and imbeciles." According to Grinnell, "in regard to the more than legendary counsel, 'Go West, young man, go West,'—a shot at thousands of dullards since my day; I was the young man whom Mr. Greeley told to go, and I went. I have never found occasion to regret the fact that I was a protégé of his—a life-long correspondent and friend."[40] Grinnell accordingly went west to Iowa to found a temperance town of teetotaling abolitionists, and then Grinnell College. He covered the Iowa State Fair for the *Tribune* to cover his initial expenses. In 1859, Grinnell hid John Brown and other abolitionists and slaves in his home, a stop on the Underground Railroad. And he maintained to the end that he was the young man whom Horace Greeley advised to go West.

In fact, Greeley had urged young unemployed men of eastern cities to go West ever since the financial panic and national crisis of 1837.[41] In that year, a depression in England had led to a sharp drop in the price of American cotton. British banks and investors stopped investing in American companies and refused to extend loans, driving up interest rates. The result was a wave of foreclosures and rising inflation. States stopped building roads and canals, throwing thousands of young men out of work. Dozens of banks failed. The government lost some nine million dollars in the depression. By the autumn of 1837, nearly one-third of all adult males in eastern cities were unemployed. Wages of those fortunate enough to work dropped by one-third to one-half over the next two years. Consumer prices rose sharply. In New York City alone, there were some two hundred thousand homeless people roaming the streets in search of food and shelter.

Even before the crisis, Greeley was urging young working men to leave the cities and go West if they could not find a job. In June 1836, he urged newly arrived European immigrants to buy guide books on the American West. "If there are not more adventurers exploring the far West, there will at least be fewer unfortunate ones." In September, he urged Congress to begin making public lands available to future settlers at $1.25 an acre, to "convert a tract of wild land into a productive farm." The government was selling more and more western public land, but mainly to speculators wanting to hold the land and then sell to settlers at a profit. Land speculators were the real evil and should be taxed, argued Greeley. Congress should pass laws prohibiting usury and protecting the poor from the "devouring fangs of heartless and calculating avarice" by regulating interest rates.[42]

The hard winter of 1836–7 moved Greeley in the direction of social reform. He was in charge of poor relief for the Sixth Ward that winter, and he watched as hundreds starved or froze to death and the unemployed went door to door begging for money and food. He continued to publish the *Yorker*, but also continued to lose money. Loans were hard to come by. The five thousand dollars Mary had brought to their marriage was evaporating. But Greeley remained optimistic, undoubtedly pleased when his "Ode to Printing" was sung at the annual meeting of the Southern Typographical Association in Mobile, Alabama, lauding journalists and the press as "Freedom's vanguard adoring."[43] But there was not much adoration or happiness in the streets of New York that spring, and Greeley began to look for other solutions to the devastating problems of economic and social conditions in the cities.

In April 1837, Greeley began his campaign to move the unemployed out of the cities and westward. "We advise every laborer, of whatever trade, to take up his march for the new country whenever he shall find himself unable to get employment at a fair price, unless his circumstances forbid the attempt." By now, twenty thousand mechanics and thirty thousand seamstresses were unemployed in New York City alone. "Fly, scatter through the country, go to the Great West," he advised his readers, "anything rather than remain here. . . . Away, then, hardy adventurers, to Ohio, Michigan, Illinois, Indiana, and Wisconsin. . . . The West is the true destination."[44]

Then, on May 10, New York City banks suspended all specie payments. Other banks followed. Credit was unavailable, loans were called in, and a national panic started. Prices dropped, and a cycle of recession, recovery, and depression began. The Whigs blamed the Democrats and President Martin Van Buren for the catastrophe, calling for economic growth and recovery. "The country is in a wretched condition," wrote Greeley in June, "and there are no signs of speedy improvement." Immigrants were pouring into New York at a rate of a thousand a day, finding instant poverty and unemployment. Greeley wanted to support the "virtuous and industrious immigrant" and convert him into an American citizen, but only after a naturalization period greater than five years.[45]

Greeley was also concerned about the extension of slavery to the West. He did not want to see the newly independent republic of Texas become a slave state, and opposed its annexation for that reason. The murder of an abolitionist newspaper editor, Elijah Lovejoy, in Alton, Illinois, further aroused his indignation. The mob that killed Lovejoy had denied an editor's rights to the "lawful expression of a freeman's sentiments" and was an "outrage." A few years later Greeley argued that Oregon too should remain independent, as opposed to a new state. Emigration to Oregon was a dangerous step verging on madness, a "cherished delusion" of life in freedom beyond the bounds of civilization. Only in 1845 did Greeley finally recognize the feasibility of overland travel to the Pacific, by which time tens of thousand of young men and women were following his advice to go West.[46]

"If any young man is about to commence the world," Greeley wrote in 1838, "we say to him, publicly and privately, Go to the West; there your capacities are sure to be appreciated, and your energy and industry rewarded."[47] Greeley's campaign for western migration thus began as early as 1837, not 1853, as Grinnell claimed. Land and freedom lay to the west. For the next twenty-five years, Greeley would campaign for free homesteads and land in the West for anyone willing to settle and improve that land. Western land reform and eastern unemployment were inextricably linked.[48] The Republican Homestead Act of 1862 was in part a monument to Greeley's long drive for land in the West as a crucial foundation of American social reform and moral improvement. Going West marked a step toward freedom, at least for white men.

WHIG POLITICIAN: THE *JEFFERSONIAN*

In 1837, Horace Greeley cemented his position as an up-and-coming Whig politician. In addition to continuing to edit the *Yorker,* Greeley became the hired gun of the new Whig Party and its New York political boss, Thurlow Weed, editor of the *Albany Evening Journal*. Weed needed someone to edit a Whig campaign journal for the elections of 1838, and the young and energetic Greeley caught his eye. Thus began a sixteen-year political firm of Greeley, Weed, and New York governor William Henry Seward that dominated Whig politics in New York and ultimately helped form the Republican Party.

After his term expired in 1836, President Andrew Jackson left Washington in the care of his hand-picked successor, Martin Van Buren, the "Little Magician" or "Red Fox" of Kinderhook, New York. At fifty-five, Van Buren had served as an attorney, U.S. ambassador to London, and then vice president under Jackson. In the 1836 presidential election, Van Buren won forty-two of fifty-six counties in his home state of New York. Van Buren stood for Albany Regency machine politics, and for Jacksonian Democracy. The Democrats retained power in Washington and Albany, but the national financial panic of 1837 gave the Whigs a new opportunity.

Greeley believed that "the only security for public liberty is found in the absolute and unqualified freedom of thought and expression."[49] He also felt that the Whig Party was committed to such freedom. Lovejoy's murder in Alton might have been at the hands of the "soldiers of Louis Philippe" in Paris or the "sterner despotism of Russia" under Tsar Nicholas I.[50] Greeley was ever attuned to public opinion on the issue of freedom, and in 1838, the Whigs won a startling series of election victories in New York—the governorship (Seward), sixty-eight percent of the seats in the lower house in Albany (up from thirty-six percent in 1836), and fifty-eight thousand more votes than two years earlier.[51]

In the late autumn of 1837, Thurlow Weed arrived in New York City unannounced to ask Greeley to edit a Whig journal for the forthcoming election campaign. Weed exuded power. He was a large man, with a florid face and a genial, robust, and shrewd personality. He was manipulative, but also resolute. His goal was to elect William Henry Seward—a red-haired lawyer with a large nose, great oratorical ability, and a commitment to destroy slavery—to the governorship of New York State. Weed invited the young editor to dinner at the City Hotel, and promptly offered him the editorship of a cheap weekly journal for the 1838 campaign to be known as the *Jeffersonian*.

Greeley would receive a salary of one thousand dollars for one year, and would publish the journal in Albany.

Weed recalled the occasion well. "In casting about for an editor," he wrote later, "it occurred to me that there was some person connected with the *New Yorker*, a literary journal published in that city, possessing the qualities needed for our new enterprise . . . a strong tariff man, and probably an equally strong Whig." He found Greeley at work in the composing room to be a "young man with light hair and blond complexion, with coat off and sleeves rolled up, standing at the 'case' 'stick' in hand." When Weed offered Greeley the job, the young editor was surprised but gratified.[52]

But then Greeley heard nothing from Weed. He continued with the *Yorker*, publishing a prophetic article in late December warning of the danger of dissolution of the Union over the issue of slavery.[53] At about the same time, Greeley wrote Weed and asked whether Weed had abandoned the idea of a Whig weekly. The *Yorker* was in its usual financial straits. Subscribers owed Greeley $8,000. He could not pay his bills. The income from the Whig project would be desperately appreciated. He signed his letter "Yours perplexed."[54]

But Weed was as good as his word. In February 1838 Greeley produced the first issue of the *Jeffersonian*. The weekly, subsidized by Weed and the Whigs, claimed to have fifteen thousand subscribers (at fifty cents for the year) when Seward won the election by some hundred thousand votes. The first issue described itself as a cheap weekly journal of political intelligence that was devoted solely to the "temperate discussion of public measures and the elucidation of the true principles of republican liberty."[55] The journal was eight pages long and included congressional speeches, legislative reports, facts and figures, news, and a brief editorial, in Whig language, "reliable information upon political subjects."[56]

Greeley was elated to be politically active. "So," he kidded his friend O. A. Bowe in a letter, "you don't like my *Jeffersonian*, ha? That shows you've no taste. But I rather guess that your old Federalism revolts at the name, isn't that it?" Greeley told Bowe that he went to the Albany Assembly every day at ten in the morning to try to pick up political news items and help write speeches. He would then return to his boarding house in Albany to work on the *Jeffersonian* and write letters. He considered Seward "the finest fellow I ever knew." He was delighted that there were thirty-three subscribers to the *Jeffersonian* in his old hometown of East Poultney alone.[57] He wrote Fitch Ransom there that he hoped to get to Vermont at some point, but that "I am at any rate a prisoner for the year 1838."[58]

Shuttling back and forth between New York City and Albany every week was no mean feat. Mostly Greeley went by boat up the Hudson River. In the winter he might face a three-day trip by horse-drawn sleigh. But he was young, bubbling over with energy, and up to the task. Seward was impressed by the "slender, light-haired young man, stooping and near-sighted, rather unmindful of social usages, yet singularly clear, original, and decided in his political views and theories."[59]

Greeley's new enterprise enabled him to get a much clearer picture of the emerging Whig Party. The Whigs, he noted, were a coalition of former National Republicans (Jefferson's party), followers of Henry Clay's American System, states' rights southerners, Nullifiers, Anti-Masons, dissident Democrats unhappy with Jackson, and new voters—"numbers who had not before taken any part in politics, but who were awakened from their apathy by the palpable usurpations of the Executive" by the Democrats.[60]

Greeley now helped shape Whig ideology himself. He lamented the "doom of the Indian" and the "utter destruction of the Red Man" by Jackson's Indian removal policy, which created the Trail of Tears from Florida to Oklahoma. Smallpox was tragically wiping out the Mandan tribe. Annihilating Indians was inconsistent with national honor. Young unemployed men should go not to the eastern seaboard cities, but to the "inviting prairies and forests of the Great West."[61]

Heartened by the success of his short-lived *Jeffersonian*, Greeley continued to hope for greater success at the *Yorker* as well. "I am getting along by hook or by crook, in New York," he wrote Fitch Ransom, and "I mean to make the *New Yorker* the best weekly going, if that is in me."[62] To help handle both enterprises, Horace took on Molly's brother, Silas Cheney, but learned only that Silas lacked the "close application required by the printing business."[63]

In the late autumn 1838, family tragedy struck. Mary Greeley had given birth to her first child, a son, that summer, but the infant died at the age of three months. Five months later she had a miscarriage and was cruelly injured by the medical practices of the day, including bleeding, purging, and giving morphine. Virtually abandoned by her workaholic husband, who traveled back and forth to Albany every week, she felt isolated, lonely, and trapped in a marriage where her "fire would not burn." She became distracted and apathetic. She loathed the sexual routine of her marriage, and she was depressed and irritable. In March 1839, Greeley wrote a friend about Mary's troubles: "Broken in health and come down with dyspepsia for years, she sustained a serious injury before the birth of her child, and was nearly killed while that birth took place." Now she lay in bed helpless from the "cruel surgical operating" that ravaged her body.[64] Mary Greeley's health would remain poor for the rest of her life.

Personally distraught about Molly's illness, Greeley turned to political journalism with renewed energy. Seward and the Whigs had won by a landslide the previous November, after all, and he was optimistic. "I do not intend to back out of the *New Yorker* this year," he wrote Fitch Ransom, "though I may. There is some prospect that it will begin to support itself." But, in addition, Greeley felt that he needed "something to live by." The Whig Party offered to extend his contract, but he declined.[65]

By March 1839, Greeley was already thinking ahead to the presidential election of 1840. Anyone except his hero Henry Clay was out of the question, he felt, and yet Clay would suffer from his Kentucky slaveholding past and his equivocating on slavery. "I wish," wrote Greeley, "Vermont could find it in her heart to vote for Clay."[66] But that seemed unlikely. The Whigs were after Greeley again that spring to repeat his successful performance as editor of a party campaign weekly, based in Albany. He initially demurred, complaining about his "slender means" financially. He would need ten thousand subscribers and two thousand dollars if he were to make a go of it again. He saw Weed, who agreed that the *Jeffersonian* had done its work "middling well." They agreed that a big battle for votes lay ahead for the presidential election of November 1840. Soon Greeley was "enlisted for the campaign, at least" and planning another "internal improvement paper." He wrote for several other Whig newspapers, and got an additional twelve dollars a week for editing their *Daily Mix* in the city.[67]

In the summer of 1839, Greeley took a small break from editing and traveled west, to Clymer, New York, to see his father and mother, then on to Buffalo and, by steamboat, to Cleveland, Sandusky, Toledo, and Detroit. This trip marked one of his very first railroad train rides across New York State—five days of travel from Saratoga to Lake Erie, by both rail and stage coach. By mid-July, he had reached Detroit, the furthest west he had ever traveled.[68]

That autumn, he was back in New York City complaining about his family life. Molly had spent the summer with her mother in Litchfield, Connecticut, before returning to the city. They were now fixing up a three-room apartment on three different floors at 93 Barclay Street, near the East River. Money remained a problem. "I am hard up, as usual," he wrote Bowe, and "must have money or break, but of course I shall fish it up somehow." He continued to work for several Whig journals in anticipation of the presidential campaign. "We shall probably try Clay," he anticipated, "and get licked."[69]

Greeley's pessimism at this time was personal, financial, and political. In the winter of 1839–40, the *Southern Literary Messenger* published one of his poems entitled "The Faded Stars." Heaven's grace and nature's marvels have faded, he mused, but he would continue to "war on Fraud, entrenched with Power— / On smooth Pretence and specious Wrong—."[70] He would try to reform a fallen world. Then in his short story entitled "Adolph Bruner" for *The Lady's Book* in Philadelphia, Greeley considered the consequences of a failed love.[71] Adolph Bruner is a young German student who rescues a young lady, Bertha Lindhoff, from malicious ruffians who have assaulted her, marries her, but then believes that she is unfaithful to him. Disgraced, she drowns herself. He lives on in torment, an eminent scholar widely recognized for his achievements. When he dies, "a people's tears and a stately monument proclaimed the usefulness and proud renown of a life embittered by one fatal error."

Was Greeley's marriage a fatal error? Would the Whig party become his stately monument? Greeley's literary musings suggest that he may have seen his life in terms of personal tragedy and public achievement through moral reform of society. His major achievements still lay ahead. But even in 1839, he sensed that his public campaign as New York editor and Whig journalist on behalf of freedom might help him escape his domestic tragedy, which was just beginning. The Whig Party had recognized and rewarded Greeley's editorial and political talent. But at home, Molly Greeley was becoming a lifelong emotional and physical burden to herself and others, isolated and lonely with a husband whose political and journalistic career she did not fully appreciate. Horace Greeley's public ideal of universal freedom would never completely reflect his private family life, but it would get him out of the house. Monuments to him would be built.

"TIPPECANOE AND TYLER TOO!"

In 1840, Horace Greeley and the Whig Party virtually invented the modern political party campaign. Until then, party organization and activity before an election was minimal. But with the rise of the Whig Party and the departure of Andrew Jackson from office, the stage was set for real competition to obtain votes. Expecting an easy Van Buren reelection, the Democrats were shocked by the victory of a political unknown, William Henry Harrison, a retired general. Greeley, who never met Harrison, played a central role in that victory.

A major reason for Greeley's success in 1840 was his command of popular language and slang. Greeley was a philological incendiary who used words to incite his readers. "I can write better slang than any editor in America," Greeley once boasted. Both major political parties began to use slang in their campaign literature to appeal to the often uneducated but highly literate American reader. Reaching the people, at a time when nearly eighty percent of adult males voted, was politically essential. Although later critics would assault Greeley for his "stupid rusticity of diction" and "school-boy use of expletives" that were "offensive to good taste," his readers understood his language and came back for more.[72]

In 1840, Greeley himself understood this all too well. "Writing for the common people, I have aimed to be lucid and simple. I write for the great mass of intelligent, observant, reflecting farmers and mechanics, and if I succeed in making my positions clearly understood I do not fear that they will be rejected."[73]

Greeley's fascination with words included Noah Webster's *An American Dictionary of the English Dictionary*, published in 1828 and running through many subsequent editions. In particular, Webster distinguished *freedom* from *liberty*. Freedom meant a "state of exemption from the power of control of another." But he went further to add "an exemption from slavery, servitude, or confinement." Freedom was broader than liberty, implying privileges, immunities, ease of doing anything, frankness, boldness, license, and improper familiarity. In addition, the word *slavery* meant the absence of freedom, "bondage: the state of entire subjection of one person to the will of another."[74]

By distinguishing the words *liberty* and *freedom*, Webster helped define a crucial distinction between liberty under the law, where slaves were property, and freedom under the moral law, where slavery was abolished. In the 1870 edition of his dictionary, he made the distinction even more clear: "*Liberty* has reference to previous restraint, *freedom* to the simple, spontaneous exercise of his powers. A slave is set at *liberty*; his master had always been in a state of *freedom*."[75] Soon enough the abolitionists would shift their rhetoric from the classical *liberty* guaranteed under the Constitution to the *freedom* and equal rights expressed in the Declaration of Independence.

In December 1837, Greeley wrote Webster offering him free advice on his dictionary and suggesting that Webster issue different editions of the publication, serialized—"at a moderate price and at intervals—bimonthly, for example." Webster responded point by point to Greeley's spelling suggestions, and admitted he could only come close to the idiosyncratic nature of American English. "An approximation to uniformity is all that can be expected in a language so abominably irregular as ours," he wrote.[76]

Reviewing the latest edition of the dictionary in 1841 in the *New Yorker*, Greeley praised Webster's book as useful, instructional, and generally accurate, the best dictionary around. After several examples of etymology, the editor concluded "we recommend it again, as we have before, to all the youth of our country in pursuit of science—to everyone who would obtain a correct knowledge of the English language."[77]

In 1843, shortly before Webster died, Greeley wrote the old man with some friendly advice on the etymology and origins of modish terms of the day—*Fourierism* and *Phalansterian* among them.[78] The two men probably never met. But they shared a common love of the language and a desire to get it right in terms of usage, as well as syntax and grammar.

Greeley's own language ultimately became precise, earthy, and even belligerent at times. When he called the rival *New York Times* a "mealy-mouthed" newspaper, the *Times* fired back in response: "As a matter of personal taste, we do not believe Mr. Greeley enjoys hearing men calling others liars, or d——d liars, or any other epithets, more or less ornamented with theological adjectives. . . . Why, then, does he put them into his newspaper? . . . We see no reason why the language of a newspaper should be very different from the language of a decent society, from the language used by gentlemen in their daily intercourse."[79]

But by 1840, Greeley was not interested in gentlemen. He wanted to reach the common man. The *Times* complained that Greeley's language was "such as to unfit him for the society of gentlemen, inasmuch as it is the sort commonly confined to blackguards."[80] That was the point, of course. *Liberty* was for gentlemen. *Freedom* was for the people.

The Whigs began to prepare for the presidential election by holding their first national convention in Harrisburg, Pennsylvania, in December 1839. The mood was clearly anti–Van Buren. But it was also Anti-Masonic. From the outset the Whigs were therefore divided on candidates. Henry Clay was the favorite, but he was both a former slaveholder and Free Mason. Conscience Whigs dedicated to abolition and Anti-Masons would find him unacceptable. Thaddeus Stevens, an anti-slavery attorney from Gettysburg, was the leader of the Whig Anti-Masons in Pennsylvania. Indeed, he had chaired the national meeting of what was left of the Anti-Masonic Party that May, also held in Harrisburg. When Pennsylvania Whigs supported Henry Clay at their state convention in June, Stevens and the Anti-Masonic wing of the Whigs pulled out and endorsed William Henry Harrison, whose one claim to fame was a victory over Tecumseh and his Indian confederacy at the Tippecanoe River in Indiana in 1811. Stevens thus came to the national Whig convention in December as the leader, together with Weed and Seward, of the "stop Clay" movement within the Whig Party.[81]

Greeley abhorred the division within the Whig Party. "The die is cast," he wrote Weed after the state convention in May, "and it is resolved that the Whig party shall be ruined." He was sick at heart about the feuding within the party. Something needed to be done, he told Weed, and fast. ("Burn this," he added.) But Weed saw that Clay was not the man to do it. He resolved to try to persuade him to step aside in favor of Harrison. Despite Molly's perpetual poor health, Greeley resolved to attend the Harrisburg convention himself.[82]

On December 5, Greeley arrived in Harrisburg with the deeply divided New York delegation, headed by Weed. Twenty delegates favored General Winfield Scott, a hero of the War of 1812, ten favored

Henry Clay, and two favored Harrison. Thaddeus Stevens was there with his Pennsylvania Anti-Masons to fight for Harrison. Greeley attended the meetings in Stevens's hotel room as the delegates tried to come to an agreement on a candidate. Greeley reported in the *Yorker* on December 7 that "Henry Clay will be nominated for President."[83] He was quite wrong. After several ballots, the Whigs nominated William Henry Harrison for President and John Tyler of Virginia for Vice President. Despite the defeat of his hero, Henry Clay, Horace Greeley agreed to work for their campaign.

Greeley immediately began negotiating with Thaddeus Stevens to edit a Whig campaign newspaper along the lines of the *Jeffersonian* in Pennsylvania. He wrote Stevens that he was determined to move to Harrisburg himself and produce a newspaper without advertisements but affordable to "everybody who can be induced to take it at fifty cents per annum."[84] A few days later he wrote his friend O. A. Bowe that "we had a great time in Harrisburg. I talk of going there to edit three or four papers. I can't get rid of the 'Yorker,' but must work for that also." Molly, he added, was very ill and "down-hearted" because of another miscarriage. She was showing signs of blindness and could not bear to be in the light. "I think," he added, "that she will ultimately recover."[85]

Greeley did not move to Harrisburg, however, and remained in New York laying plans for his new Whig paper. "It will be an advocate of Freedom, Improvement, and National Reform," he promised, complete with songs and cartoons, as well as facts and figures. Discovering Harrison's humble origins in Indiana, Greeley entitled his paper the *Log Cabin*. He would publish fifteen issues over the next six months (May 1 through November 1) and try to collect five dollars for each subscription. Having neither steam presses nor mailing facilities in Albany or New York City, he outsourced them and printed eighty thousand copies, a massive effort. The first issue promised to disseminate the truth to readers, to refute Democratic "slander and calumny," and to provide the full story of General Harrison, one of America's "noblest and most illustrious patriots." "Freemen!" he exclaimed, "Americans! The hour of deliverance has come. . . . Press on to the polls."[86]

In the spring of 1840, Greeley helped invent modern political campaigning. Every issue of the *Log Cabin* carried an image of a log cabin and (ironically for teetotaler Greeley) a jug of hard cider, symbols of Harrison's folksy origins on the Indiana frontier. The newspaper printed campaign songs on the back page. Greeley also helped organize mass meetings, torchlight parades, log cabin raisings on public squares, Harrison clubs, and choruses to sing Whig songs. He wrote epigrams and jokes, penned the Whig lyrics to popular songs, passed out Tippecanoe Songbooks free around New York. Then came the Tippecanoe medals, badges, flags, handkerchiefs, almanacs, and shaving soap. Every town in America seemed to have a log cabin, a Harrison club, and a chorus singing Whig songs that summer.

Weed was skeptical, but Greeley delivered. "Our songs are doing more good than anything else," Greeley wrote Weed, "really, I think every song is good for five hundred new subscribers." The hit song was "Tippecanoe and Tyler Too!" with endless variations. A favorite slogan was "Van, Van is a Used Up Man!" in reference to the Democratic candidate, Martin Van Buren. Greeley even collected Whig songs together in the *Log Cabin Song Book*.[87] By late July, Greeley could report to Weed that he was now printing sixty-two thousand copies of the *Log Cabin,* and prophesied victory in November at the polls, as long as the Whigs remained united behind Harrison. "Our dirty, disgraceful, miserable exhibitions of selfishness and faction alone," he added, "prevent our sweeping all before us. This is too deplorable to think about."[88]

Greeley's political slang included the "sick Vanocrats" and "foul party" of the Democrats. He would raise "freedom's voice" against corruption in high places. *Freedom* was the new watchword of the day. The "friends of reform" would defeat "fair freedom's foes" and fight off the corruption of "freedom's high and holy land." America was a land where "freedom's banner high / gleams as it fills." Citizens were merely slaves to the arrogance of power of "freedom's foes." Greeley's lyrics swept the country and roused Whig voters to action.[89]

Greeley not only wrote song lyrics, he led crowds in singing them during stops along the campaign trail in New York, especially at the new railroad stations. "His dress, his figure, with the white hat set several degrees farther upon his head than usual, and the old white overcoat hanging free and clear from his shoulders, gave him an appearance that was grotesque."[90] There he would stand, waving his arms frantically in the air in an effort to conduct, flailing about with great enthusiasm as the crowd roared out the tune and the words.

Greeley's political language helped turn Harrison into a republican hero, and a man of the people, while the Democrats charged that he simply drank himself into oblivion on his front porch in Ohio and would prefer retirement to election. Greeley responded in kind: "Wherever you find a bitter, blasphemous Atheist and an enemy of Marriage, Morality, and Social order, there you may be certain of one vote for Van Buren."[91] Greeley promised that his journal of "national reform" would continue publication after the election, and would support a one-term president, reduction of federal expenses, elimination of executive patronage, and punishment of "speculators and defaulters." He would continue to publish only "political truth."[92]

In the end, the Whigs' and Greeley's freedom campaign resulted in Harrison's stunning victory over Van Buren and the Democrats. The largest number of voters in American history turned out for the election. Harrison carried nineteen of twenty-six states, and won in the Electoral College 234–60, getting fifty-three percent of the popular vote (1,275,000 to 1,128,000). The Whigs won control of both the presidency and Congress. How much money Weed had raised and spent on the campaign remained a mystery. But he was a persuasive fundraiser, emptying the pockets of land speculators, businessmen, and Erie Canal workers to help pay for the *Log Cabin*. Whatever the cost, the Whigs had come to power in the name of freedom against corruption in the republic.[93]

In Greeley's mind, 1840 was a free election whose result promised greater freedom for all Americans. The Democrats had tried to violate the "vital principles of Freedom" during the election campaign itself. Democratic officials at the New York Customs House recruited immigrant voters off the boat, telling them that the Whigs were "Aristocrats, Monarchists, Enemies of the Poor, especially hostile to Foreigners, and desirous of excluding them from all rights and privileges, if not the country itself." In fact, the Whigs too had paid particular attention to attracting German, Irish, and English voters. They published two biographies of Harrison in the German language, and proclaimed "liberty is equally dear to all of us."[94]

Greeley himself might have been expected to share in the spoils of victory after the election. But he denied any interest. "I s'pose I might have got some wretched claw at 'the spoils' by hard elbowing," he wrote his friend Bowe, "but I have told all the magnates that I won't have the smell of anything."[95] His old Anti-Masonic editor friend Joseph Sterritt nominated him for State Printer of Pennsylvania. Some newspapers mentioned Greeley's name as a possibility for Postmaster General. But Greeley claimed to have no desire for any position in Washington. Within a few months, Harrison died and John Tyler was the new president of the United States.

The campaign of 1840 was significant in refining Greeley's philosophy as a Whig as well as testing his use of political language. In a campaign pamphlet entitled *Why I Am a Whig*, Greeley noted that the two ideas of Liberty and Order divided the world. Both were needed under the rule of law. The freedom to speculate in land at the expense of the poor was unacceptable. The protection of home industry was a necessity. Democracy was vital to the survival of the Republic. In addition, the "abject and powerless Negro" and the "plundered, homeless, and desolate Indian" also needed government protection from rapacious whites. "If without Liberty," he concluded, "human existence is bitter and irksome, without Order it is precarious and beset with constant perils."[96]

Greeley's charged political language had helped win an American presidential election for the Whigs. Flush with the election victory, but unwilling to share in the spoils, he made the difficult and dramatic decision to leave the *Yorker* and embark on another adventure by editing his own daily newspaper, beholden to no one but himself. He would make himself the Tribune of the People. His newspaper would be called the *New York Tribune*. Its friends would call it simply, "the Trib." It would be his monument.

3

Tribune of the People

THE PAPER

In the spring of 1841, Horace Greeley launched the newspaper that would make him the most famous editor in America before the Civil War. At thirty, he was still young and energetic, fresh from the Whig triumph in the election of 1840. On April 4, President Harrison died, one month after his inauguration, and John Tyler became president. "His Accidency," as Greeley called Tyler, was a Virginia states'-rights man opposed to the Missouri Compromise of 1820 on slavery. (The Whigs would later expel Tyler from their party for vetoing bills on a national bank and protective tariffs; they even tried to impeach him.) Greeley had little desire now to go to Washington. Instead he decided to abandon his beloved *New Yorker* and enter the competitive market place of New York daily newspapers.

New York was the literary and cultural center of a growing and expanding new nation. Yet it was hardly a modern city, but more of a sprawling medieval village of about 315,000 people.[1] Stagecoaches rumbled over the cobblestones. There was no indoor plumbing or sewers, no garbage collection. Residents emptied chamber pots from upstairs windows onto muddy and unpaved streets and alleys. They drew their drinking water from wooden pumps and cisterns. Refuse littered the streets, where pigs rooted about for sustenance. The stench from noxious gases was often overwhelming. Cholera and yellow fever were frequent and deadly visitors to the metropolis, which extended north to only about fiftieth street. In Greeley's words, for New York "the Past is torture, the present misery, and the Future despair."[2]

To enter the world of daily newspaper publishing in 1841 was exciting and difficult. Competition for readers and subscribers was fierce. Nationally, American newspaper circulation had tripled since 1830. Most daily papers were dull, inaccurate, and biased. They generally reflected the low taste and poor education of the editor. Fisticuffs between rival editors and newsmen were common. New York had dozens of newspapers, most of which filled their pages with news of murder, boxing matches, prostitution, and society dinners. James Gordon Bennett's *New York Herald* dominated the market with daily, weekly, and extra editions, and boasted a circulation of some 55,000 readers. All of his competitors combined had a circulation of only 36,550.[3]

The race for news from Europe led many editors to send fast packet ships out to meet the incoming steamers to get the latest information. Bennett used Sandy Hook pilot boats to pick up the news, then the newfangled Long Island Railroad to get it back to the city for printing and distribution. The *Herald* had its own fleet of three fast sailboats. In 1841, Bennett also sent the first regular reporters to Washington, DC, to cover Congress and national events.[4]

Greeley had been looking for a way to rescue or abandon the *New Yorker* for some time. "The poor old Yorker," he wrote O. A. Bowe in December 1840, "I am afraid the hand of death is upon it, though I am doing everything I can to keep the breath in its body."[5] Whig campaign journals provided vital supplemental income. He therefore told Thurlow Weed that he was getting along all right financially, but was seeking other options. He had declined Sterritt's offer of the State Printer job in Pennsylvania, or at least of its prospect, because the politicians in Harrisburg were "rapacious" and "unprincipled."[6]

In Greeley's mind, the sad state of the daily newspapers in New York required reform. The "revolution" in printing technologies since 1830 meant that the dailies were gradually replacing the weeklies to supply faster and more complete news to an ever growing audience. This revolution must continue until the "character" of the press generally was "purified and elevated, its independence asserted, and its influence extended."[7] He would be no man's man, not even the Whig Party's. He would be independent. He would reform the press. And he would speak for the people who had no voice.

But how? In 1841, Greeley had "no partner, little credit, and no powerful backing." He had no money to buy a new steam-power press, or even new hand presses. Yet somehow he scraped some funds together from Whig friends, presumably including Weed, who wanted a cheap daily newspaper that could reach the working-class men and women of New York City. The only major contributor was his friend

James Coggeshall, who loaned him a thousand dollars to help him get started. On April 10, 1841, a "leaden, funereal morning" of cold temperatures, sleet, and snow, Horace Greeley produced the first issue of the paper that would be his monument, the *New York Tribune*. He promised that the newspaper would be a "new morning Journal of Politics, Literature, and General Intelligence." Following the "political revolution" brought on by Harrison's election, the new paper would epitomize a "triumph of right Reason and Public Good over Error and sinister Ambition."[8] On the same gray day, New York held a sad funeral parade and pageant for the late president of the United States, William Henry Harrison.

The *Trib* was edited and printed in a crowded and badly lighted attic in a decaying two-story building at 30 Ann Street, near City Hall. After one week, receipts totaled $92 and expenses $525. It was not an auspicious beginning. Greeley's main assistant was a young twenty-one-year-old from Vermont, Henry J. Raymond, who would later (1851) found and edit the rival *New York Times*. Raymond had helped Greeley with the *Yorker* for the past year doing reporting, rewriting, and reviews. Now he worked for the *Tribune* at twenty dollars a week.[9]

The *Tribune* was an immediate publishing success (fifteen thousand copies published each day), but not a financial one. Subscribers outnumbered advertisers. So Greeley wisely hired a New York attorney friend, Thomas McElrath, as publisher and partner in the enterprise. McElrath was wealthy and respected and knew how to run a business. He promptly purchased a half interest in the new paper for two thousand dollars.[10] Greeley and McElrath became a highly respected publishing partnership that lasted through most of the 1840s and 1850s.

Politically, Greeley stated that he was devoted to the Whig program of Henry Clay: incorporation of a national bank, new and higher tariffs to increase government revenue and protect home industry, distribution of the proceeds of public-land sales to the people, and so on. He also announced that the *Tribune* expected Congress to "work rather than talk" in Washington, and to demonstrate the "fruits of Statesmanship, not the flowers of declamation." But Greeley did not ignore Washington. He visited every session of Congress between 1840 and 1860. He sent a full-time correspondent (code-named "Argus") to Washington to cover congressional debate and politics. Within a short time, other newspapers followed suit.[11]

Clearly Greeley was taking a risk. "I am poor as a church mouse," he wrote his friend Rufus Griswold in July 1841, "and not half so saucy." He was nostalgic about the old *Yorker,* which he continued to edit that summer and fall. It had reputation, character, talent, and energy, and he hated to see it go under. He was getting on well with the *Tribune,* he wrote Weed, "but not as well as I expected." "Well, the Tribune is going to live," he wrote O. A. Bowe. In September he did, as promised, cease to publish the *New Yorker* and combined it with the new weekly edition of the *Tribune.*[12]

As usual, Greeley succeeded because he was a workaholic. His hours were becoming more irregular and unreasonable. He had so many visitors he had to limit them to two hours during the day. Most evenings he did not get home until well after midnight. In addition, some Whigs were trying to persuade him to move to Washington and edit their national journal, the *Madisonian.* Greeley promised to come down and look the situation over. Weed fretted that Greeley was needed more in New York, although he wrote Daniel Webster and told him that Greeley was "all honest and true" and could "reflect whatever is useful and salutary from the President, the Cabinet, and the Congress, to the People"—dramatically underestimating Greeley's independence of mind.[13]

In December, Greeley went to Washington. In part, he wanted to explore the *Madisonian* opportunity. He also wished to investigate the widening gap between Tyler and the Clay Whigs, claiming that Tyler and his entire cabinet "do not want to harmonize with the Whig party." He had not removed enough Democrats from office. The "restoration of concord" between Tyler and the Whigs over a national bank seemed unlikely. Greeley also visited the Whigs who edited the *Madisonian* and wanted him to take over as editor. He asked for "chief control of the paper," but did not get it. Greeley returned to New York a committed Clay Whig.[14]

When the Whigs lost the congressional elections of November 1842, Greeley retreated from politics for a time. The election news was "wretched stuff." The Democrats had won back the Congress. But Greeley was convinced that Henry Clay was the man for the 1844 presidential election, when the "uprising of the people" would support Clay Whigs everywhere. "We shall make a glorious fight in Clay," he wrote, "and, if beaten, why we shall have as good a Government as those who make it."[15]

As the Whigs licked their electoral wounds, Greeley met, for the first time, a man who would become one of his closest lifelong friends. Phineas Taylor Barnum was a year older than Greeley, a Universalist, and a recent immigrant to New York from Connecticut. Barnum had started his own newspaper, the *Herald of Freedom,* in Bethel, Connecticut, in 1831. In it he trumpeted the virtues of religious liberty and Universalism in the face of Congregationalist conformity and Calvinism. His bare-knuckled prose soon resulted in three libel suits. He abandoned the paper in 1834 and moved with his wife and infant daughter to New York, where he sold hats and tended bar. Now he had just opened his new American Museum across from the Astor House near the photographic studio of a young Irishman, Matthew Brady. Barnum found Greeley to be a "gangling, wispy-haired, pasty-cheeked man, high-domed and myopic, with the face of somebody's favorite grandmother." Soon Barnum and Greeley began to eat dinners together and to attend the Orchard Street Universalist church of Thomas Sawyer.[16]

The *Tribune* now replaced the Whig Party as the center of Greeley's life. Within a few years, the telegraph was transmitting news with the speed of lightning from Washington to New York, from the Mexican War to the small towns of America, replacing older forms of news transmission—the courier, the carrier pigeon, pilot boats, and the railroad. The first telegraph office in New York City opened in January 1846, at 16 Wall Street. By 1850, continental Morse code was adopted across the country, and telegraph messages were used to dispatch railroad trains and carry news bulletins.

In February 1845, the four-story *Tribune* offices on the corner of Chatham and Spruce Streets burned to the ground. The fire started at 4:30 a.m. in the publications office from sparks off a match used by a boy to light a stove. High winds fanned the flames into an inferno. A snowstorm kept horse-drawn fire engines away. Some workers barely escaped with their lives from the burning building. Paper supplies and all of Greeley's papers and manuscripts vanished in the fire. Only a few books were saved. Yet Greeley was able to rent another office and somehow get his edition of the newspaper out as usual the following morning.[17]

After the fire, the paper recovered and flourished. Greeley maintained a correspondent in Washington, William E. Robinson, to keep up with Congress. He sent foreign correspondents to Europe. He hired

Bayard Taylor to write for the Literature and Music Department of the newspaper at twelve dollars a week. He employed George Ripley, after the collapse of his Brook Farm utopia, to replace Margaret Fuller, another Brook Farm alumna, as book review editor. He hired Charles A. Dana, also of Brook Farm fame, as his first managing editor. He helped form the Associated Press in 1848, to share resources in the competitive race for news, with James Gordon Bennett and eight other editors. He was the first to adopt the new four-cylinder rotary press of Richard M. Hoe, the Lightning, which could produce twenty thousand sheets an hour. And he established the *Tribune* as a joint-stock association, selling shares to his employees (he sold off most of his own shares to friends at sub-par values).[18]

By the end of the 1840s, Greeley and his paper were New York fixtures. The city's population had increased to over half a million, half of those of Irish or German descent. More than three hundred horse-drawn omnibuses carried more than seventy thousand passengers a day. Fresh water was flowing into the city from the new Croton Reservoir. New York was replacing Boston and Philadelphia as a publishing center, with new names like Harper, Van Nostrand, Scribner, Wiley, Putnam, Dodd and Mead. The writers Herman Melville, Edgar Allan Poe, and Walt Whitman all lived in the city.[19]

While New York City was the epicenter of the *Trib*, the paper's real audience lived in the small towns and rural areas of America. The journalist Bayard Taylor called the weekly edition second only to the Bible "all through the West." Editor E. L. Godkin said the paper was "an institution more like the *Comedie Francaise* than anything I have known in the journalistic world." The *Trib* was not a newspaper, but an article of faith, faith in Uncle Horace, the philosopher of the paper. "My father," wrote attorney Clarence Darrow much later, "like many others, had early come under the spell of Horace Greeley, and as far back as I can remember, the *New York Tribune* was the political and social Bible of our home."[20]

The *Tribune* ultimately gained such a sizeable readership that its editor would mold public opinion even more effectively than the U.S. president, especially in rural areas, where the weekly edition became a Bible. Although he never wrote them down, Greeley developed the principles of editorial writing to a fine art, using rhetorical strategies and persuasive techniques worthy of the Roman writer Cicero. Despite his own personal quirks, Greeley's newspaper followed a consistent editorial policy over the years flexible enough to respond to changing public sentiment. Lincoln's secretary, John Hay, called the editorials the "Gospel according to St. Horace." The schoolmaster and autocrat of the *Tribune* would, despite his "loose habits of reasoning" and "snap judgments," issue clear pronouncements on all subjects that would both influence and reflect his readers' tastes and sentiments. "He dipped his pen of infallibility," wrote Hay, "into his ink of omniscience with as little self-distrust as a child plays with matches."[21]

McElrath put the newspaper on a firm financial footing. Over the next twenty-four years, the *Tribune* would earn its owners and shareholders more than one million dollars a year, investing a surplus of over three hundred thousand dollars. The one hundred shares of the Tribune Corporation paid annual dividends of more than five hundred dollars. Greeley himself would make an annual salary in excess of thirty-five thousand dollars. But he frittered away much of that money in bad loans to friends, and sold all but six of his thirty-one shares before he died. The *Tribune* brought Greeley personal fame, but not fortune.[22]

The *Tribune* also made Greeley a lifelong defender of freedom of the press. In 1841, the patrician writer James Fenimore Cooper, a Democrat, sued Greeley, McElrath, and the *Tribune* for libel in a story regarding swimming rights on Cooper's family property near Lake Otsego. Greeley argued his own case that libel involved malicious intent, and that "in this Free Land I had a right to cherish an opinion and to express it."[23]

The judge, unimpressed, found Greeley guilty of libel and assessed him two hundred dollars in damages and six cents in court costs. Greeley's account of the trial appeared in an eleven-column story in the *Tribune*, entitled "The Cooperage of the Tribune." Freedom of the press, Greeley wrote, requires an editor "to rebuke wrong and to exert a salutary influence upon the Public Morals." All newspapers would face the threat of libel suits if Cooper's case was upheld. "But the Liberty of the Press has often been compelled to appeal from the bench to the People. It will do so now."[24] If opinion by itself were libel, "the press becomes the crouching slave of every vice, a spaniel at the feet of inhumanity and villainy."[25]

Horace Greeley in 1841 might have become the U.S. Postmaster General, the State Printer of Pennsylvania, or the editor of the Whig

Madisonian in Washington, DC. He did none of these things. Instead, he became his own man, free of party political entanglements but still a dedicated Henry Clay Whig, defender of a free press, editor of the *New York Tribune,* a tribune of the people, in whose name he would speak for a generation and more. He created the paper and was identified with it until the day he died. But the *Tribune* was not simply the product of one man, but an association. And in 1842, association became Greeley's new enthusiasm.

FREE ASSOCIATION

The *Tribune* was Greeley's first major experiment with an association of like-minded individuals to achieve a common goal. True, Greeley himself was already a married man, a temperance man, an Anti-Mason, a Whig, a Universalist, and an active member of his Sixth Ward in New York City. But by 1842, Greeley was also a moral and social reformer open to new ideas who realized that men and women had to live in social communities. Freedom meant free association with others, as well as individual liberty. Individuals needed to cooperate with one another and to share their labor efficiently in order to be more productive. America in the 1840s was becoming a nation of joiners—citizens of the republic, members of a political party, Masons and Anti-Masons, members of benevolent societies, trade unions, companies, corporations, and so on.

Like many Americans, Greeley was also drawn to a variety of "isms" and reform movements in the 1840s. At the center of his interest was the movement to build small communities, or associations, dedicated to human happiness and productivity. The father of these communities was the French socialist dreamer Charles Fourier (1772–1837). Through Fourier and his American disciple, Albert Brisbane, Greeley came to believe in associationism—"the combination of many hands and heads to achieve a beneficent result, which is beyond the means of one or a few of them." Associationism meant economy and efficiency more than socialism, a universal instinct that "impels each worker to produce and save for himself and his own."[26] Greeley's own variant of Fourierism was a kind of utopian middle-class capitalism, where laborers could become property owners, and where hard work would lead to individual rewards and civic virtue.

The word *association* in French commonly meant the association and cooperation of individuals, guilds, and workers in their own interest. Association could also mean socialism, as reflected in the urban workshops of the 1830 and 1848 revolutions in Paris. But in America, association had a broader meaning in the 1830s, as Tocqueville observed on his travels. Associations were not only working-class organizations, but religious, economic, Masonic, Anti-Masonic, benevolent, social, and educational. Hundreds of newspapers, social clubs, tract societies, and other voluntary organizations were constantly springing up across the country in the name of reform. Women too joined such organizations, but were often kept in roles subordinate to men—cooking, housework, child care, and so on.

Greeley had turned to Fourier's social experiments after the terrible winter of 1837–8. He had gone door to door in his neighborhood of the Sixth Ward and encountered only "filth, squalor, rags, dissipation, want, and misery." Poor himself, he tried to help others with charity work. He wrote an article for the *Yorker* entitled "What Shall Be Done for the Worker?" about the great need for social reform to solve the urban problems of hunger, unemployment, begging, prostitution, and crime. One of Fourier's students, Albert Brisbane, read Greeley's article and helped stimulate the editor's interest in the French social thinker.[27]

Charles Fourier, in the 1820s, had developed an elaborate theory of association based on the "natural" or "attractive" qualities of individuals. Association would gratify individual desires, serve the general good, make labor attractive, and harmonize social conflicts among individuals. Fourier called groups with common property "passionate series" that would associate producers, credit unions, collective kitchens, and laborers. The ideal association would be a Phalanx of exactly 1,620 people, double the complete "scale" of 810 "passional types" of individuals, where everyone worked for the good of the association.

Fourier, like Greeley, recognized that liberty was impossible without economic prosperity. "In civilized societies," Fourier wrote, "liberty is illusory if the common people lack wealth."[28] Through association, men and women would be able to liberate their repressed passions (there were twelve main ones). The ideal community would be one of complete harmony among diverse individuals. People preferred labor to idleness, Fourier believed, so that work was not necessarily painful drudgery, but could be pleasurable. Unlike Marx, Fourier and Greeley believed in class harmony, not class struggle, grounded in small communities of hard-working individuals.

Brisbane proselytized for Fourier in America. By the time Greeley met him, Brisbane was an avowed socialist returned from Europe, patient, abstract, absorbed in his mental world, gentle, kind, and original. Born in Batavia, New York, in 1809, Brisbane was the child of an English father and a Scottish mother. He went to Paris in 1828 to study at the Sorbonne. The European revolutions of 1830–1 helped transform him from a republican to a socialist. He imagined a socialist federation of European nations linked together by railroads. In the spring of 1832, Brisbane met Fourier, who tutored him for twelve sessions on his teachings, and in the spring of 1834, Brisbane returned to his home in Batavia and began teaching associationism to anyone who would hear him.[29]

In 1840, Brisbane published a massive summary of Fourier's ideas entitled *The Social Destiny of Man; or, Association and Reorganization of Industry*. He organized a Fourier Society in New York City and, with the help of Horace Greeley, set up a journal called *The Future*. Brisbane edited the journal, but Greeley let him work out of his own office. Brisbane also began writing articles for the *Tribune*.

Even before Greeley founded the *Tribune*, however, Brisbane had drawn Greeley's attention to the importance of Fourier and association. In an article on social reform in the *New Yorker* in January 1841, Greeley again described the widespread social unhappiness in America—poverty, unemployment, prostitution, and foreign immigration. The answer, he felt, lay in association. One hundred families working together could do better than if they worked in isolation. Living in common and "sharing the products of their industry" was better than living in poverty and separation. Associational communities along the lines suggested by Brisbane and Fourier could be a "mine of wealth for the poor, the unthrifty, and the destitute."[30]

Some laughed at Greeley's new enthusiasm. Henry Raymond wrote that the editor had "got himself into a scrape" by associating with Brisbane and his Fourierist ideas. Weed was very skeptical of a Whig flirting with socialism, despite Greeley's promise that associationism was supported by "some of the strongest and most practical minds of this city and elsewhere." "Finding Greeley imbued with that heresy," Weed wrote later, "I remonstrated early against his determination to espouse it in the *Tribune*." But Greeley was quite "inflexible" on the subject.[31]

Greeley wrote Weed that he thought Weed was taking "the wrong view of the political bearing of this matter." The Whig Party had ignored social discontent in the country, and the discontented chose to vote Democrat. "This forms a heavy dead-weight against us," he added. The Whigs would never profit by being considered the "enemies of improvement" or the "bulwark of an outgrown aristocracy in this country." He only wanted the chance, he told Weed, "to think for myself."[32]

A few months later, Greeley wrote Weed again that he was unwilling to sacrifice his freedom of thought and expression for the Whig Party. "We differ radically," he told Weed, on the need for a national bank and other matters. "You take me to task" for my Fourierism, he continued. Yet Greeley had given Weed good service as a paid journalist for the Whig Party. "Do not assume to dictate or lecture me," he warned Weed, "I can surrender to no man" and would "do no man's bidding but speak my own thoughts."[33]

In 1842, Greeley allowed Brisbane to run a series of almost daily front-page columns in the *Tribune* on Fourierism. Brisbane consequently paid the editor for the privilege of the column, and signed each column "B." In them, Brisbane argued that Fourier was a genius, and that the future lay with associationism, which offered the only way to improve the workingman's condition under capitalism. Throughout 1842 and 1843, Brisbane reported regularly in the *Tribune* on the poverty and miserable conditions created by capitalism, and the benefits offered by Fourier's system. The free market had terrible consequences for the poor and the unemployed. A commercial oligarchy produced degradation for all workingmen. Greeley distanced himself from Brisbane's columns by noting that their authorship was "entirely distinct from that of the *Tribune*."[34]

But Greeley was clearly drawn to associationism. "The system of Association, or sharehold property," he wrote in May 1842, "blended with Attractive industry, promulgated by Fourier, does away with the last objection, that a Social Order adverse to the present must generate improvidence and idleness, and so perish through human infirmity. Its vast economics will bring wealth within the reach of all." Association in the interest of brotherhood and humanity reflected the "visible Harmony of God's universe" and would help bring an end to tyranny and slavery. Many Universalists, in fact, were turning to Fourier at this time. They created six Phalanxes in the Rochester, New York, area alone, and their own utopian community of Hopedale in Mendon, Massachusetts. Hopedale consisted of thirty people living on five hundred acres of land. They cooperated and agreed to give up swearing, drinking, unchaste behavior, slave-holding, war, capital punishment, and violence. Greeley certainly shared these sentiments.[35]

Charles A. Dana remembered that Greeley "embraced the associative doctrine very early and with great enthusiasm and zeal."[36] Yet Greeley was not about to become a card-carrying Fourier disciple. Instead, he accepted the principles of associationism generally and reworked them as his own: the elimination of private property, unemployment, and waste in food consumption; increased productivity; technical education for young men; support for farmers; and the sharing of common land, livestock, and machines. He also asserted his own independence. "I accept unreservedly the view of no man, dead or alive."[37] Fourier had taught Greeley a good deal about life in community, and about the need to work out his own views on associationism. "We are furnishing a theme," he wrote his friend Bowe, that later generations would "contemplate with some respect."[38]

In the spring of 1842, Greeley encountered the world of Boston transcendentalism and Brook Farm. Transcendentalism appeared in New York in the person of Ralph Waldo Emerson, who ate dinner with Greeley and Brisbane at a Grahamite boarding house in the city. Emerson was exploring the New York literary marketplace. He was little known outside New England at the time, although Greeley had already reviewed Emerson's early essays enthusiastically in the *Tribune*. Brisbane held forth on the views of Fourier, as usual, and promised a "full exposition" as soon as Emerson settled in at his hotel. Emerson was delighted to meet "two new friends" who were "bent on popular action." He found Greeley to be a "young man with white, soft hair from New Hampshire, mother of men, no scholar but such a one as journals and newspapers make, who listens after all new thoughts and things but with the indispensable New York condition that they can be made available; likes the thought but must keep the power; what can I do with such an abetter? He declares himself: Transcendentalist, is a vegetarian, a defender of miracles, etc. I saw my fate in a moment & that I should never content him."[39]

Greeley immediately approached Emerson about helping publish

Emerson's work in New York. If he wished, Greeley would plump for a volume of Emerson's poems in the pages of the *Tribune*. He would also help place favorable reviews in the papers of Albany and Philadelphia. Greeley also reprinted, without permission, Emerson's lectures (and promised not to do so again). By the way, he asked Emerson, what of the prosperity of "Mr. Ripley's community at Roxbury," otherwise known as Brook Farm?[40]

Brook Farm was the utopian community set up in 1841 by George Ripley (1802–1880), Emerson's cousin, in Roxbury, outside Boston. At Brook Farm, the residents ate together, shared the farm chores, and gave papers and lectures on a wide variety of topics. Ripley and Theodore Parker were Unitarian ministers. Writers like Henry David Thoreau, Nathaniel Hawthorne, and Margaret Fuller were often visitors. Some were vegetarians and Grahamites. Most opposed slavery. They talked frequently about associationism. Everyone paid for room and board, and private property was encouraged. All received wages for the work they performed. "Mr. Greeley," wrote Emerson, "is greatly interested in Ripley's community. His wife an amiable pleasing woman wishes to board there. I told her what I knew of it. He said he should write to G. R. very soon."[41] So Molly, having lost another infant in childbirth recently, wanted to escape to Boston, and did so in the summer of 1842, boarding with a Mrs. Hunt near Watertown and frequenting Brook Farm.

Greeley himself visited Brook Farm in July 1842. He arrived in Watertown to see Molly, and found her "quite solitary here—in fact, lonesome." He managed to visit the Roxbury farm, where he gave a paper on associationism. Amelia Russell, a Brook Farm resident, recalled him wandering about with his white hair, white hat, and off-white Irish linen coat, a "singular apparition" resembling a ghost.[42]

Greeley's response to Brook Farm was mixed. "My fear for your system," he wrote Charles A. Dana, Ripley's assistant, "is that it is adopted only to angelic natures and that the entrance of one serpent would be as fatal as in the Eden of all." One selfish individual could ruin the associationist garden and spoil the apples, saying, "Why should I labor, when another in wanton idleness consumes the product?" Utopias would have a hard time overcoming Original Sin and the Old Adam in its members. Fourier's system, he felt, would avoid this problem by having a "rampart of equal people in every Phalanstery," presumably chosen for their harmonious passions and interests. But he generally approved of the Brook Farm experiment. "Don't let anything daunt you," he wrote Dana, "much less destroy you."[43]

A week later Greeley wrote Dana again, indicating that Molly was still in Watertown, "very eligibly situated in most respects, but almost isolated from society, which in her state of virtual blindness, so far as reading and study are concerned, is a great privation indeed." He hoped that a stay at Brook Farm would help her "find all she needs" and that her "recovery to health and vision" would be "sure and rapid."[44]

Greeley then went to see family and relatives in New Hampshire and Vermont, as well as his parents in Clymer, New York. He also visited Washington, DC, which he found to be a city of "ceaseless intrigues, the petty strifes, the ant-hill battle." The Whig Party seemed unbroken by recent "disasters and treachery" under President Tyler. And he denied a rumor that he had actually eaten breakfast with two African-Americans.[45]

Greeley's encounter with the idealism and transcendentalism of Boston Unitarians, Concord writers, and Brook Farm residents helped him continue to rethink the meaning of freedom and the place of associationism in that freedom. By the autumn of 1842, and into the winter of 1842–3, Greeley was thoroughly immersed in Fourierism and the politics of associationism. "I think Associationism the most natural thing in the world for a properly civilized and Christianized society," he wrote Ralph Waldo Emerson.[46] By 1843, Fourier's association communities were proliferating across the nation. Greeley thought the movement could save the world. "Not through hatred, collision, and depressing competition; not through War, whether of Nation against nation, Class against Class or Capital against Labor; but through Union, Harmony, and the reconciling of all Interests, the giving scope of all noble Sentiments, and Aspirations," he wrote, "is the Renovation of the World, the Elevation of the degraded and suffering Masses of Mankind, to be sought and effected."[47] The solution to the ills of capitalism was not revolution born of class struggle, but reform born of class harmony.

Noah Webster's son wrote Greeley asking for his definition of Fourierism for another edition of the dictionary. Greeley replied that Fourier was the "founder of a school of philosophy—which now has many ardent apostles in this country and in Europe." Fourierism was an attempt to reform society by reorganizing it "upon principles analogous to those of a joint stock company." He was busy trying to help organize a Phalanx in New York now. He thought that even out in Ohio many people were now "ripe for a Social Reformation." "Only study Fourier's system," he wrote a friend there, "and the dumb can speak its praises."[48]

In addition to Fourierism in New York, Greeley was also involved in similar projects with the Unitarian Bostonians. William Henry Channing was just forming a Christian Union society in New York that spring that included transcendentalist writer (and Molly's friend) Margaret Fuller. A Unitarian minister and graduate of Harvard College and Harvard Divinity School, Channing's unorthodox views ended his ministry in Ohio and brought him back to New York. Here he joined the Fourierist network and organized his society, seekers after truth who believed in God as a universal father of all. He also believed in reforming society in the interest of future harmony and happiness. Channing also helped form the Society for Universal Inquiry and Reform, following the meeting of the American Anti-Slavery Society. This society favored community property and socialist reform, which Greeley and the *Tribune* criticized as a "destructive conception" and not an "organic Social principle." Channing's own society broke up in 1845, when he returned to Boston and joined Brook Farm, then helped organize the Religious Union of Associationists with George Ripley.[49]

The Union began in January 1846, at the Boston home of James Fisher, a wholesaler in salt. About thirty men and women interested in Fourier's ideas met to form a study club. George Ripley, Channing, Greeley, and Marcus Spring were all involved, linking the Union with the North American Phalanx in New Jersey. By 1848, they called themselves the Church of Humanity and met every Wednesday evening to espouse ideas of reform and universal love and harmony. Greeley served on the executive committee, along with Charles Dana, J. S. Dwight, Fisher, Ripley, and Channing.[50] Greeley also began to act as Emerson's agent in the New York literary marketplace, arranging to place advertisements and favorable reviews for his books in order to improve their chances.[51]

Greeley did more than serve on committees. He was active in the spring of 1843 helping organize the Sylvania Association along Fourierist lines. The Association consisted mainly of young New York mechanics, men who recognized labor as the "true and noble destiny of Man on earth." Sylvania claimed to be the first attempt in North America to organize along Fourierist lines (Brook Farm was not yet a Fourierist community). This meant organizing a Phalanx divided into twelve "tribes" as a kind of corporation, or joint-stock company, rather than a socialist community. The purpose was to establish a "new, more trustful, more benignant relationship between Capital and Labor," reflecting the philosophy of the Whigs, based on class harmony, not class conflict. Greeley was treasurer of the corporation, which purchased some three thousand acres of land in Pennsylvania along the Delaware River in wilderness Pike County for seven thousand dollars, much of it Greeley's own money. The land was poor and dotted with scrub pine and oak. "I hold myself but the steward of a kind Providence," he claimed, but the steward in the end lost twelve thousand dollars on the project. "I might have lost more," he recalled, "had I bought many of the stocks and bonds urged on me by securities salesmen."[52]

The Sylvania Phalanx consisted of a gristmill, sawmill, store, barns, and three two-story houses. Stockholders purchased shares for twenty-five dollars each. They agreed to invest their labor, capital, and talent in the project. By autumn 1843, there were twenty-eight married couples there. Ultimately, there were three hundred residents, and a governing board of twelve men. Women could vote at age eighteen on Phalanx issues, men only at age twenty. Female wages were set at five-eighths the rate for males. Social life consisted mainly of lectures and dances. Greeley made frequent visits to the community, helped with the farming, and wrote editorials on the Phalanx for the *Tribune*. Unfortunately, the experiment did not survive for long, as the harsh winter of 1844–5 killed off most of the crops. Many members proved too incompetent or lazy at farming to succeed. In 1849, the community sold its property to the Reverend Thomas Taylor, who promptly renamed it Taylortown. (The town was renamed Greeley in July 1892.)[53]

Sylvania was not Greeley's only association. The second was the North American Phalanx located five miles from the town of Red Bank on Colt's Neck, New Jersey. The project began in Albany in August 1843. Greeley subscribed to help a capital fund of one hundred thousand dollars. Again, the project was not socialist but capitalist; the right to earnings was not equal, and laziness was not rewarded. But this time the founders were some sixty doctors, grocers, shoemakers, druggists, lawyers, painters, carpenters, and blacksmiths from the Albany area, together with their families. All of them had suffered financially from the panic of 1837. Somehow they scraped together fourteen thousand dollars to buy a 673-acre farm on Colt's Neck. Again, they were inspired by the vision of Fourier and his American apostle, Brisbane. The *Tribune* supported the project and recruited members, promising that Red Bank was a great place to settle because of the "mildness and salubrity of the climate" and the "invigorating atmosphere" of the nearby (nine miles) Atlantic Ocean, "excellent meadows," and "good water power."[54]

The key organizers of the North American Phalanx were two Albany businessmen, Allen Warden (president) and Nathan R. French (treasurer). Greeley was vice president and owned the largest number of shares. By 1844, the Phalanx had ninety residents, forty of them children. The farm soon began to produce wheat, rye, buckwheat flour, mustard, corn meal, and hominy. It sold the first boxed cereal in the United States, and marketed dried fruits and tomatoes. The North American Phalanx trademark was well known in the vast emporium across the bay, New York City, where products were shipped from Red Bank or Keysport. Workers received a monthly salary, divided profits annually, paid rent for their lodging, and ate together in a common dining room. Earnings were low, but so were costs. Each type of work was organized in a "series." The "chiefs" of the "series" formed an "industrial council." Each normally worked at the job he or she preferred to perform. In 1847, a Phalanstery building was erected which contained a salon, with a piano, designed for dancing, singing, and dining. Values were nonsectarian but religious. In 1848, the Phalanx incorporated itself in New Jersey with a capital stock of some two hundred and fifty thousand dollars. The corporation then purchased the property from Warden in 1850. By then, Red Bank was a friendly community of plain living and hard work, a kind of middle-class capitalist utopia.[55]

By 1844, associations had established a national network. In August 1843, a convention met at Rochester, New York, to organize more Phalanxes. Brisbane lectured across the state and helped found Fourier associations, five in the Rochester area alone. The Friends of Association met in Boston the following winter representing associations at Brook Farm, Hopedale, Northampton, and Skaneateles. Brisbane repeated his sermons on Fourier. Charles A. Dana urged that Brook Farm become a Fourier association. Greeley, George Ripley, and William Henry Channing all gave lectures. The meetings lasted into the new year. Although all wished reform, they ranged from socialists to capitalists, farmers to ministers, and evangelicals to Unitarians. A few months later, on April 4, 1844, they reconvened at Clinton Hall in New York City, where Ripley presided over another Fourier convention. Dana described Brook Farm as the "oldest Association in the United States." They had "abolished domestic servitude," and "no man is master." Labor was for the "mutual benefit of the laborer and the capitalist." Indeed, at Brook Farm one could find Dana pitching manure, Hawthorne feeding the pigs (unreliably), and Margaret Fuller cooking (badly).[56] Brisbane ended the meetings by toasting Horace Greeley for the "manly, independent, and generous support" and added that "he has done the work of a century."[57]

Unlike most Phalanxes, Red Bank lasted for more than a decade. The Boston abolitionist Lydia Child heard from Greeley and his friend Marcus Spring that the North American Phalanx was "on a much more safe business foundation than any association that has ever been formed in this country." By 1849, the land and buildings of the community were valued at more than fifty thousand dollars. Greeley served as a trustee, and meetings were often held at his office in New York.[58] Several years later he wrote an open letter highly critical of Red Bank because some of its members "fail to work steadily and efficiently." Phalanx members held a public meeting and rejected Greeley's findings.[59] But Greeley was a prescient critic. In April 1854, a fire destroyed many of the main buildings at Red Bank, including the mills, their main revenue source. Still, when it disbanded, the community showed a balance sheet of nearly one hundred thousand dollars.[60]

For Greeley, associationism was part of his moral and religious search for universal freedom. He saw associationism as a Christian doctrine consistent with his Universalist religious beliefs. When Universalist leader Hosea Ballou criticized Fourier and associationists for their utopian dreaming, Greeley responded with a ringing defense. Associationists, he said, wanted not "universal perfection," but simply to improve the lot of the less fortunate. The Shakers too were good examples of moral reform, because they had abolished slavery in all its forms in their communities. So were the Moravians, the Rappites, the Brook Farm crowd, and other intentional communities seeking a better way of life. Social reform was a vital mission in a fallen world. Slavery was an evil, and "the abolition of Servitude except for Crime and of Pauperism" would be a good thing. Free labor was far more economically effective than slave labor. Socialism was but a "rude and imperfect" solution to the world's ills, but it was at least trying to do something. Associationism, Greeley concluded, was nothing less than "the application of Christianity to the Social Relations of mankind."[61]

By 1846, Brook Farm was disbanding in the wake of economic failure and a March 3 fire that destroyed the main building, still under construction. Greeley, like the rest of the New York stockholders in Brook Farm, gave up his stock in the corporation.[62] But he did not abandon his enthusiasm for the associationism movement. Throughout the year, Greeley conducted a long *Tribune* campaign in defense of associationism against the rival *Courier and Enquirer* and his former employee Henry J. Raymond. Between November 1846 and May 1847, the two newspapers ran six articles for and against associationism. Greeley continued to fend off charges that he was a socialist by arguing that associations should have private property belonging to those who contributed capital and purchased shares of stock. Raymond charged that Fourier's passions were self-indulgence, and his socialism irreligious. Greeley responded that associationism was really Christian social reform. Emerson concluded that Greeley "has a conscience."[63]

Greeley concluded his campaign with breathless enthusiasm: associationism sought the "truth of the Universal Human Brotherhood." Christian love in a world of poverty, hunger, and war required that reformers "redress the palpable wrongs before us by prompt action." Fourier's vision was a "grand and inspiring one—it may possess great practical value when we come fully to understand and apply it."[64] Greeley remained an active supporter of associationism throughout the 1840s.

Yet by 1848, associationism had pretty much run its course in America. Most of the Phalanxes had disappeared. Three survived: Greeley's North American Phalanx at Red Bank, the Trumbull Phalanx in Ohio, and the Wisconsin Phalanx at Ceresco. Each owned a good deal of land, was improving the soil and exporting agricultural produce, and was doing some manufacturing. But Greeley continued to believe in the efficacy of association grounded in harmonious relations with others, the right to labor, and joint stockholding. The well-organized Phalanx was a cooperative "republican organization." Labor, not capital, would benefit from this arrangement by making work more attractive, providing education for all children, and increasing productivity and efficiency. He favored radical reform to obtain "universal justice." But he also favored private property rights and opposed socialism and communism as "utterly subversive of justice not merely, but of individual freedom."[65]

Greeley was in 1850 President of the American Union of Associationists, the most public national figure in a declining utopian movement. In his presidential address that year, he noted that America's problems were social more than political or economic. Individual selfishness and "incoherent" commerce were corrupting society. Only harmony and unity could produce order and freedom in the "wild, weltering chaos of the social world," he wrote. Private property was essential to freedom. The ideal community would be a joint-stock company, a "true fraternal, Christian association" where men and women were free from "industrial slavery." Freedom meant the freedom to work, to enjoy the arts and sciences, and to improve oneself in mind and body. Abolitionism, pacifism, temperance, and women's rights were merely attempts at partial reform. Real social reform meant "social reorganization" based on the "Christian spirit of this American nation." Association was the duty of "every branch of the Universal Church" to produce the union of free men in a free America.[66]

Greeley retained his ties to the North American Phalanx until it collapsed in 1854. By then he was nationally well known, a trustee of another association, the Grand Prairie Harmonial Institute in Indiana, and involved with the utopian community of Etienne Cabet in Nauvoo, Illinois.[67] His instincts remained reformist, on the side of justice for all in community. He retained a strong commitment to associationism until he died, toward the end of his life helping to establish the western joint-stock community of Greeley, Colorado.

Horace Greeley's involvement with associationism in the 1840s was not simply another "ism" but a stage in his lifelong search for freedom, linked to his anti-slavery and his Universalism. Association with others made people stronger, more productive, more efficient, and more free. Strength lay in unity. Men and women could achieve more together than they could accomplish in isolation. The most effective associations were those in which men and women contributed freely of their own talents, time, energy, and labor to a community that could benefit all its members. Association strengthened freedom.

But Horace Greeley was no socialist. His enthusiasm for Fourier's teaching was limited. He was not interested in abolishing, but in encouraging, private property. His central concern was not the equal distribution of the fruits of production to all, no matter how hard they worked. Real freedom depended instead on the combined efforts of all to produce more according to their different abilities, to invest in a joint venture, and to benefit in unequal measure from the unequal efforts to improve productivity. For Greeley, as a Whig politician and journalist, the ideal association was not a utopian, proletarian, socialist commune, but a middle-class joint-stock company whose investors reaped what they had sown. Such companies might well become communities that escaped the evils of the city and achieved social reform and harmony as small towns leading a happy and productive life off the land. Greeley's ideal association was a capitalist utopia somewhere to the west, where freedom beckoned and followed the setting sun.

THOREAU, FULLER, AND THE LITERARY FREE MARKET

Through Brook Farm and the Boston transcendentalists, Horace Greeley became a major link between emerging literary talent in Boston and New York. For writers, freedom meant the freedom to publish their work and succeed in a highly competitive capitalist literary marketplace. In the cities, "sublime thoughts" could become "penny wisdom," with profitable employment for the unknown writer seeking to establish a reputation. Horace Greeley enabled the Boston transcendentalists—Margaret Fuller, Ralph Waldo Emerson, and Henry Thoreau—to succeed in New York.

Margaret Fuller (1810–1850) was a remarkable woman, a schoolteacher, a pioneer in the campaign for women's rights, a New England transcendentalist, and a frequent visitor to Brook Farm. She was a close friend of Emerson and others in the Concord literary community. Margaret Fuller was probably the most important woman in Greeley's life, aside from his mother and his wife. Although the editor found her a bit of a fanatic on the subject of equal rights for women, rights he considered a "logically defensive abstraction," he admired her greatly as "the best instructed woman in America." Editor of the transcendentalist journal *The Dial*, Fuller also wrote *Woman in the Nineteenth Century* (1845), a call for women's liberties, which Greeley considered the "ablest, bravest, broadest assertion yet made of what are termed woman's inherent rights." In his introduction to her book, Greeley described Fuller as "one of the earliest, as well as ablest among American women, to demand for her sex equality before the law with her titular lord and master."[68]

Greeley greatly admired Fuller's generosity, her commitment to seeking the truth in all things, and her belief in immortality. He hired her as the first literary editor of the *Tribune* and helped establish her reputation as one of America's finest woman writers. He welcomed her as a boarder into his own house outside New York for nearly two years. But he always claimed she was really Molly's friend, not his. There was ongoing "sharpish sparring between us" on the question of equal rights for women, he remembered. "Margaret was only known to me," he wrote after her tragic death in a shipwreck in 1850, "through the two years previous to her departure for Europe, and by some letters afterward, and though she lived in my house a year and a half, I never was really intimate with her. I only met her at breakfast, leaving soon after for the office and not returning until long after the whole family had gone to rest." And his public memory of Margaret was decidedly mixed. "Noble and great as she was," he wrote in his memoirs, "a good husband and two or three bouncing babies would have emancipated her from a good deal of cant."[69]

Public condescension hid Greeley's private affection and admiration for a remarkable woman. Her father, Timothy, was a leading New England Anti-Mason, who, like Greeley, wanted to eliminate corruption and restore the virtuous republic. A graduate of Harvard College, he became an attorney, a U.S. Congressman from Massachusetts for several terms, and a close friend of John Quincy Adams. As a good father, he inculcated his precocious daughter with the virtues and values of the Roman Republic. Margaret grew up well-educated and widely read. By the late 1830s, she was a schoolteacher prominent in Boston and Concord literary circles, where her judgments and her mind were highly regarded.

Fuller had her own views on the spiritual nature of freedom. Political freedom, she believed, "does not necessarily produce liberality of mind." There was outer freedom and inner freedom. Outer freedom meant "independence from the encroachments of other men," in essence, civil liberty. But inner freedom was deeper, more significant, transcendental, and of the soul. Freedom for women meant not simply the equal rights of citizenship, but freedom "as a nature to grow, as an intellect to discern, as a soul to live freely and unimpeded." Freedom meant self-development, intellectual rigor in the search for truth, and freedom of the spirit. God was spirit, felt Fuller, and our true selves are divine. "By becoming more ourselves, i.e. more divine—destroying sin in its principle, we attain to absolute freedom, we return to God, conscious like himself, and, as his friends, giving, as well as receiving, felicity forevermore."[70]

Horace Greeley met Margaret Fuller through his wife. Molly probably encountered Margaret for the first time in 1842 during her visits to Boston and Brook Farm. They became friends and shared a correspondence. But Molly was slipping slowly into despair with her poor health, her workaholic husband, and the deaths of her babies. She lived in a cheerless house devoid of furniture, curtains, rugs, and pictures, subsisting increasingly on a Grahamite diet of bread, vegetables, and water. "It takes both of my hands," Greeley wrote his friend Bowe in spring 1843, "to wait on one woman and then it is hard work."[71] In the summer of 1843, Greeley discovered Margaret Fuller for himself when he read her article in *The Dial* entitled "The Great Lawsuit— Man versus Men, Woman versus Women." Her talent impressed him deeply. The usually hypercritical editor considered Fuller's article the product of an original mind.

In early 1844, Greeley purchased a wooden farm house on ten acres of land at Turtle Bay on the East River in New York City across from Blackwell's Island (where 34th through 50th Streets are now). Greeley could get to his office and City Hall by stage—a trip of two hours in good weather. In March, he installed Molly and their new infant son, Pickie, there. Here, in what Margaret Fuller would call "Castle Doleful," Molly turned increasingly agitated, anxious, irritable, isolated, and depressed. She sought solace in spiritualism, but lived in a world without music, good food, or company. That spring, after a visit from Margaret, the editor took time out from his trips to the Sylvania Association to offer Fuller advice on her publishing contract with Little Brown in Boston. She should publish her book, Greeley recommended, in a limited first edition, then in a cheap edition in order to gain a broader "hearing before the country."[72]

That summer, Margaret Fuller was basking in the warm reception accorded her new book, *Summer on the Lakes*. She wrote her publisher,

Little Brown, asking them to send Greeley a copy for review in the *Tribune*. Greeley was impressed yet again. He offered Margaret a job as book review editor of the newspaper, at an annual salary of five hundred dollars. Margaret accepted. She wrote a friend in September that she planned to move to New York before Christmas to "try that city for the winter, with a view to living there, if my position suits me."[73] It did.

Not only did Greeley hire Margaret Fuller for the *Tribune*, he offered to put her up indefinitely at his own home on Turtle Bay. "Mr. Greeley has taken a beautiful place near New York," she wrote her brother in October. "If this home should be as pleasant within as without I should much enjoy living there."[74] Turtle Bay was indeed a spacious and secluded place, with trees, a pond, and a lovely garden. But Margaret was not sure about living with Molly. She arrived in December 1844 to find a "happy family of eccentrics" in residence, complete with a bouncing baby (Pickie was eight months old).[75]

Fuller admired the editor greatly. "Mr. Greeley," she wrote, "is a man of genuine excellence, honorable, benevolent, of an uncorrupted disposition, and of great abilities. In modes of life and manners, he is the man of the people, and of the *American* people." But Molly was another matter. The two women had enjoyed and admired each other when they met a year or two earlier in Boston at some "conversations" among the literati. But now Margaret had literary ambitions of fame, if not fortune, and Molly was becoming a tiresome and irritable recluse. One story had them meeting in the streets of New York shortly after Margaret's arrival there. Molly despised wearing fur from animals. She met Margaret attired in kid gloves. They shook hands. "Skin of a beast! Skin of a beast!" shrieked Molly. "Why, what do you wear?" asked Margaret. "Silk," Molly replied. "Entrails of a worm!" shouted Margaret.[76]

On December 7, 1844, Margaret published her first review in the *Tribune*, of Emerson's essays. For the next two years she wrote on average three articles a week for the newspaper. "A home in my family was included in the stipulation," Greeley later recalled; "I was myself barely acquainted with her when she came to reside with us, and I did not appreciate her nobler qualities for some months afterward."[77] Fuller was equally pleased with the arrangement. "I like Mr. Greeley very much. He is a man of the people, and outwardly unrefined, but he has the refinement of true goodness, and a noble disposition. He has, in his own range, great abilities. We have an excellent mutual understanding."[78]

Fuller's articles covered a wide variety of subjects—the difference between wealth and poverty in New York City, the nobility of the working poor, the need to reform prisons and asylums, equality for women and African-Americans, anti-slavery, and opposition to capital punishment. Many of these were Greeley's reform causes as well. He admired her writing; she tolerated his editing. During the two years she wrote for the newspaper, she published over two hundred articles and two books, all with Greeley's assistance. They worked well together.[79] "Mr. Greeley I like, nay more, love," Fuller wrote. "He is, in his habits, a slattern and plebian, and in his heart, a nobleman. His abilities, in his own way, are great. He believes in mine to a surprising extent. We are true friends."[80] And their friendship was mutually profitable.

But by 1845, life with Greeley was getting less profitable. Fuller had taken a lover, James Nathan, a German businessman from Hamburg. The "intense" Molly Greeley was getting on her nerves. "Our friend Mrs. Greeley," she wrote Nathan, "is more dejected than ever, indeed she has much cause, but I cannot now speak of this." Fuller was distracted from her work. She told Nathan that she was trying to "revive my energies about the paper." Greeley depended on her now for the literary column and book reviews. But she could not focus. He needed to travel, but was afraid to leave her unsupervised at the office. "Unless I took more interest," wrote Fuller, "he should not feel that he could go away."[81] And Fuller herself was waiting for a "better state in life."[82] Was the well-known Margaret shopping for a new position? We don't know. But the affair with Nathan seemed to open up avenues for a new life.

"Mr. Greeley is all you say," Fuller wrote a friend in August 1845, "he teaches me many things, which my own influence on those who have hitherto approached me, as also that we attract in mutual relations those congenial with ourselves, has prevented my leaving. He and I are in business and friendly relations. There is a solid good will and natural respect without intimacy. I think him the most disinterestedly generous person, except my own Mother, that I have ever known."[83] But apparent contentment masked growing resentment. At the end of the year, Fuller wrote James Nathan that she would be leaving Greeley's home. There was some question as to whether or not her contract would be renewed. She planned to stay at least through the following September so that Greeley could travel during the summer. She found Molly to be in a "sad state of mind and body." Pickie Greeley, now almost two years old, was a beautiful "picture of health and gaiety."[84] Nevertheless, life at Castle Doleful was increasingly tense and uncomfortable for Margaret.

Nor was life at the *Tribune* much better. "These clouds between me and the *Tribune*," she wrote, were becoming more ominous. Her growing reputation made her think that she might do better with another employer. "If I leave the *Tribune* by and by I think I can do well," she believed.[85]

In March 1846, Margaret Fuller moved out of the Greeley home and to an apartment in Brooklyn. She planned to take the steamer that summer from Boston to England, where her wealthy friends Marcus and Rebecca Spring had invited her to tutor their children. She still expressed "unbounded confidence and respect for Greeley himself."[86] Greeley too remained active on Margaret's behalf, urging his friend Rufus Griswold at *Graham's Magazine* to read her book and give it a favorable review.[87] In August 1846, Margaret Fuller left for Europe, apparently still on good terms with Greeley. He appointed her a foreign correspondent for the *Tribune*. She arrived in England, where she met the Italian revolutionary Giuseppe Mazzini, a friend of the Thomas Carlyles.

The Greeleys, meanwhile, were relaxing at the recently opened Brattleboro Hydropathic Establishment in Vermont. Here they engaged in a daily routine of temperance, abstinence from smoking, regular exercise, baths, showers, and wet-packs, and a diet of homemade bread, crackers, and cereal from wheat, hominy, and oatmeal.[88] While in Brattleboro, Greeley gave lectures to attentive audiences and made contacts with a number of influential visitors to the spa, most of them well-to-do women. He also plumped for the spa in the pages of the *Tribune*, proclaiming that Brattleboro had fresh springs, pure water, and proprietors of "perfect honor and candor."[89]

Greeley also maintained contact with Margaret Fuller, who had taken up with an impoverished Italian nobleman, Giovani Ossoli, in Rome. In May 1847, Greeley wrote Margaret that he and Molly had lost yet another child, a daughter named Mary Inez, who died in infancy. Pickie asked after Margaret frequently. "His mother whips him but never rules him." In fact, Pickie was apparently an unruly, undisciplined, and unloved brat. "He is unvaccinated, his hair uncut, and in his baby attire, and will long remain so," even though he was nearly three years old. "I have no voice in his management," added Greeley.[90] Pickie was a healthy bouncing boy now, but a bit wild. He broke dishes. He smashed watch crystals. Greeley hired a governess to take care of him, but she lasted only a month.[91]

In addition to getting Margaret Fuller started on her New York literary career, Greeley made Ralph Waldo Emerson into an American literary genius by praising his work in the *Tribune* and helping him make contacts in the New York publishing world. According to one historian, Greeley was "the single most important source of popular knowledge of Emerson's name and ideas."[92] When he learned from Margaret Fuller that Emerson had received the sheets of Thomas Carlyle's biography of Cromwell, Greeley asked if he could publish a cheap edition. But the Wiley and Putnam publishing houses got there first, and promised to sell more copies than any Boston publisher. "I can do nothing in the matter of Cromwell," Greeley wrote Emerson in March 1846. Greeley wanted to put out a complete edition of Carlyle's works, but he had, again, given up the U.S. rights to Wiley and Putnam. Carlyle himself was to blame for his failure to take advantage of the American marketplace.[93]

Greeley was also the man who made Henry David Thoreau famous in the literary free market. The two men first met on December 19, 1842, when Thoreau invited Greeley to speak in Concord, Massachusetts, at a conference on "Protection and Free Trade."[94] Thoreau was twenty-five, a recent graduate of Harvard College (1837) who had published some articles in *The Dial* and little else, and a budding surveyor who worked in his father's pencil factory. Within the next few months, Greeley became Thoreau's literary agent in New York, a position he would retain for more than a decade. As with Emerson and Fuller, Greeley would puff Thoreau's work in the pages of the *Tribune*, place his articles in the best new literary magazines, collect his fees, and pay him.

Thoreau also added another dimension to Greeley's evolving concept of freedom, the freedom of the wilderness frontier of the expanding United States. Nature, for Thoreau, was the citadel of freedom, indeed of "absolute freedom and wildness." Natural freedom was superior to civil freedom and civilization. "Eastward I go only by force," Thoreau wrote, "but westward I go free." Freedom was greatest to the west, along the wild frontier zones beyond the Mississippi River. "I must walk toward Oregon, and not toward Europe," added Thoreau. "The West of which I speak is but another name for the Wild; and what I have been preparing to say is, that in Wilderness is the preservation of the World."[95] Freedom under the higher moral law, in Thoreau's view, trumped civil law, as in his opposition to slavery and the Mexican War.

In May 1843, Thoreau arrived on Staten Island to tutor the children of Emerson's brother, William, a county judge. The experiment failed, however. Thoreau was in poor health. He was unhappy with the city, and no journal would publish his work. He soon came to dislike the Emerson family and its rambunctious brood of three boys under the age of seven. On December 17, 1843, he left New York for Concord. "Even the little I write," he complained, "is more than will sell."[96]

While in New York, Thoreau renewed his acquaintance with Greeley. "Cheerfully in earnest," Thoreau wrote his sister, "at his office of all work—a hearty New Hampshire boy as one would wish to meet. And says 'now be neighborly'—and believes only or mainly, first, in the Sylvania Association somewhere in Pennsylvania—and secondly and most of all, in a new association to go into operation soon in New Jersey [Red Bank], with which he is connected."[97] Thoreau also met William Ellery Channing, now assisting Greeley at the *Tribune*.[98] Despite Greeley's associationist enthusiasms, Thoreau found him much more impressive than the dreamy Albert Brisbane or the retiring Channing.

The *Tribune* connection with the Bostonians continued throughout 1844. Greeley utilized Channing as an "experiment" in literary work. But Channing was "shy and retreating to an extreme," in Emerson's words, and the experiment was not a great success. Channing referred to Greeley behind his back as "Mumbo Jumbo." He ridiculed him for his dress ("canvas trousers, scarlet jacket, and cocked hat") and for his attempts to criticize and demolish ideas he did not like.

In addition to developing professional contacts in the publishing world of New York for the unknown Thoreau and continuing to publish regular articles by Margaret Fuller, including the book review of Emerson's essays,[99] Greeley supported other writers as well. In November 1845, he loaned Edgar Allan Poe fifty dollars when Poe was desperately seeking money to finance his *Broadway Journal.* (Poe never paid him back.) Greeley also continued to try to place articles in the New York magazines for Thoreau. And he was generous with his time and his money, frequently loaned and rarely repaid. "Greeley surprises by playing all the parts," wrote Emerson in his journal, "only possible in America."[100]

One example of Greeley's efforts on Thoreau's behalf was his work placing Thoreau's essay on Thomas Carlyle in New York magazines. In the summer of 1846, Greeley wrote George R. Graham, the editor and publisher of *Graham's Lady's and Gentleman's Magazine,* to introduce him to Thoreau: "Thoreau is a young man, a scholar, poor of course, and sends this to me to get utterance and bread." Greeley described Thoreau's piece as "a brilliant as well as a vigorous essay," a regular "Daguerrotype of Carlyle." If Graham would publish the essay, Greeley would advertise it in the *Tribune.* If Graham did not want the essay, Greeley would offer it to *Godey's Lady's Book* or another magazine.[101] In September 1846, Graham still had not accepted, although his associate editor, Rufus Wilmot Griswold (Poe's successor in that position), was a close friend of Greeley. Griswold, thirty-one, had worked for Greeley at the *Tribune* and was a fellow literary promoter, Whig, and Vermonter.[102]

Privately, Greeley judged Thoreau's Carlyle essay "solidly good," but too long. He should shorten it to appeal to a wide audience. He should enter the New York marketplace if he wanted any attention paid to his work. "In my poor judgment, if any thing is calculated to make a scoundrel of an honest man, writing to sell is that very particular thing," wrote Greeley. Yet "writing to sell" was exactly what the self-styled hermit and anti-materialist Thoreau was about. He became impatient. He asked Greeley to send the essay back. Greeley wrote Griswold that he was disappointed in the magazine's delay, asking "Why don't Graham publish my friend Thoreau's article on Carlisle [*sic*]?"[103]

Thanks to Greeley's pressure on Graham, Thoreau's essay "Thomas Carlyle and His Works" appeared in *Graham's Magazine* in spring 1847. Greeley offered Thoreau twenty-five dollars if he would produce another essay on Emerson or Hawthorne.[104] Greeley also wrote Griswold that he might get Thoreau to produce a first-rate essay on Emerson if he, Griswold, wrote Thoreau in confidence: "He has leisure and talent," promised Greeley.[105]

Greeley continued to flatter and promote both Emerson and Thoreau. "Your poems have rejoiced everybody," he wrote Emerson, "but the most stubbornly bull-headed." He asked Emerson to send him an essay when Emerson was abroad. He got Thoreau published and handled his payments from publishers. When Graham was late with a payment, Greeley promised that Thoreau would be paid and soon. "I have made Graham pay you $75.00," Greeley wrote Thoreau in March 1848, "but I only send you $50 for, having got so much for Carlyle, I am ashamed to take your 'Maine Woods' for $25." Thoreau was grateful for Greeley's efforts, having lived on twenty-seven cents a week for two years at Walden Pond. "You have been so active on my behalf," he wrote Greeley, "you have done well for me." Except for manual labor, this was the first money Thoreau had earned from his writing in five years. "I know not how to thank you for your kindness," he wrote the editor.[106]

In 1848–9, Greeley praised Thoreau's lectures on self-reliance and called him a "thorough classical scholar" and a "true poet" who "never sought to make a livelihood by his writings, though there are not six men in America who can surpass them. We feel honored indeed by his friendship." He ran selections from Thoreau's long essay on Katahdin and the Maine woods, praising the "freshness and odor of the pine-forests" and "unrhymed poetry" that pervaded the work. He also sent Thoreau fifty dollars after placing the essay in John Sartain's *Union Magazine of Literature and Art* for seventy-five dollars. "One day Horace Greeley came to me with a thick roll of manuscripts," recalled *Tribune* staffer Bayard Taylor, "saying 'Now you must do something for this young man. His name is Thoreau; he lives in a shanty at Walden Pond near Concord, on $37.21 a year, and he must be encouraged.'"[107]

Indeed, Greeley continued to encourage and support Thoreau for the rest of Thoreau's life. He helped place his works in magazines throughout the 1850s. He encouraged Thoreau to give public lectures. He asked him for articles on Emerson and on Canada. He loaned Thoreau money. He published the first draft of *Walden* in the *Tribune* in 1849 under the title "Life in the Woods." There was "not a young man in the land," Greeley puffed, who would not profit by reading Thoreau, who believed that "a man's soul is better worth living for than his body." His observations of nature were superb. His prose was better than his poetry, even if Thoreau launched a "misplaced Pantheistic attack on the Christian faith." Greeley advised Thoreau to send review copies of *Walden* to England. He assured Thoreau that publishing excerpts in a magazine was "the best kind of advertisement whether for a publisher or readers."[108]

On July 16, 1850, Margaret Fuller drowned tragically with her husband and infant son when the ship *Elizabeth* broke up in a storm off Fire Island, fifty miles from New York City. They had been returning from Europe together with future Senator Charles Sumner's brother Horace. "The Ossolis had, as it seems to me, little to hope in our country," wrote Sumner. "I fear their future would have been bitter." Greeley actively sought to promote her memory. "We must have a proper edition of Margaret's works," he wrote Emerson, asking whether he would be willing to write an introduction. It was essential to publish her work "very fast" before public interest in her subsided. "Her friends will buy it anyhow; but I wish it to reach a larger circle." What would a Boston publisher offer for her writings? Two volumes should suffice. Would Emerson be her literary executor? In the end, Greeley gave up the project for a few years, then took it up again in 1854. Thoreau too helped round up friends in the Boston and Concord area who could contribute their memories of the departed Margaret.[109]

By 1856, Greeley and Thoreau were such good friends that Greeley asked him to tutor his children at Castle Doleful. "Our home is two hours (36 miles) from New York," the editor wrote Thoreau, "in a quiet Quaker neighborhood. You would be out of doors nearly all pleasant days, under a pleasant shade, with a pleasant little landscape in view from the open hill just back of our house." With such a Waldenesque description, and money no issue between them, Greeley hoped Thoreau would join his household in early summer, while Molly was still away in Europe. Molly "is heartily gratified with the prospect that you will come to us and teach our children," he wrote Thoreau. Thoreau accepted, then changed his mind and stayed in Concord. But he visited the Greeleys with Bronson Alcott in November and engaged in a prolonged discussion with the editor as to whether forest trees sprang up only by seed dispersal (Thoreau) or by spontaneous generation (Greeley, following the naturalist Louis Agassiz). In 1860, Greeley published Thoreau's essay "The Succession of Forest Trees" in the *Tribune*. They still disagreed. "Yours is pure theory," Thoreau wrote Greeley, while mine is "observation."[110]

Horace Greeley helped establish the Boston transcendentalists in the New York and American literary marketplaces. His generous support improved their opportunities to publish. In addition, Fuller, Emerson, and Thoreau all shared with Greeley a passion for ideas and a belief that freedom was something beyond personal liberty. Freedom for Fuller implied freedom for women as well as men. Emerson's freedom was something spiritual, moral, transcendent. Thoreau thought freedom meant resisting war, attacking slavery, opening up the West. But if Thoreau sought to preserve wilderness, Greeley sought to develop it. Thoreau was a pantheist, Greeley a Universalist. Thoreau sought a natural existence in the woods of Concord. Greeley sought to be the people's voice in the bustling streets of New York. Greeley's notion of freedom involved farming and railroads more than sauntering through the woods or living alone by a pond. Freedom in the white man's republic required an opportunity to settle and improve the land.

4

Freedom Fighter

FREE LAND

Thoreau helped convince Greeley that free land was central to the idea of freedom. Freedom, without private property in land, was an illusion. A man could not truly be free without the economic power that underlay and supported freedom. America was vast. Land was cheap. The solution to the problems of immigration, poverty, and unemployment among the young men of eastern cities lay in the West. The West meant open land, and the development of open land meant freedom for citizens of the republic. True republican government meant giving fifty acres of land to "every person of full age" who was landless, thereby enhancing their "liberty."[1]

This idea was not new. The Roman Republic featured numerous land-reform plans, including state retrieval of illegally held public lands from private owners. The philosopher John Locke believed that God gave humans the earth in trust. Every individual, therefore, had a natural right to own some land. "As much land as a man tills, plants, improves, cultivates, and can use the product of," wrote Locke, "so much is his *property*." Land in itself was not of value, except insofar as human labor "puts the greatest part of value upon the land."[2] Land and labor were inseparable as a social good, known as "improvement."

From the beginnings of American independence, the U.S. Congress viewed public land as a source of government revenue. Land sales meant income without taxation. And land was cheap. A 1796 law enabled the federal government to sell public lands at auction for two dollars an acre. In 1800, a buyer who paid down five percent of the purchase price in cash had four years to finish paying for his land. In 1804, Congress reduced the minimum acreage to be acquired through purchase of public land from 640 acres to 160 acres, then to 80 acres.

Cashless squatters often acquired public land simply by occupying it. Sometimes troops drove them off. Congress responded by granting the right of "preemption," whereby longtime squatters who had worked to improve their land could acquire the right of ownership by paying the minimum price established by Congress, rather than lose their land. Squatters would thus acquire indisputable title to their land specified in clean surveys. In 1841, Greeley's hero, Henry Clay, pushed the Preemption Act through Congress, allowing any single male adult or head of household to preempt 160 acres of public land and pay the minimum government price of $1.25 an acre to purchase it. The profits of any land sales would be distributed among the states by the federal government. Greeley, in the end, supported distribution over preemption as a principle for opening up western lands.[3]

Speculation was the enemy of land reform. What was to prevent a speculator from buying huge amounts of cheap land, holding it, and then selling it on the open market for an inflated price? Every dollar made by a speculator was a dollar less for the U.S. Treasury. Andrew Jackson tried to limit public-land sales to settlers, not speculators.[4] Many blamed the financial panic and depression of 1837 on speculation. But Greeley argued that credit, not speculation, was to blame. As unemployment rose, land sales declined. Why not solve the problems of immigration and urbanization in eastern cities by giving free public land to settlers who moved west? How else could the workingman find economic independence?

Speculation and land reform were volatile issues in New York. New England settlers who moved across the Hudson River to New York as tenant farmers perceived land as the basis for their freedom. The desire for independent proprietorship produced a hunger for property in land. Many tenants were at the mercy of their landlords, producing a culture of hierarchy and deference. In 1836, the Holland Land Company purchased lands west of the Genesee River. The company sold much of this land to absentee rich landlords, who leased it to poor farmers. The company's attempt to collect rent and evict those who would not, or could not, pay rent soon led to mob violence, especially in Chautauqua County, where Greeley's family still lived.[5] The panic of 1837 made rent payments even more difficult. By 1840, the Whigs and Greeley had taken up the cause of tenant farmers, and a powerful anti-rent movement had emerged, especially in the back-country of the frontier.[6]

As land became an important regional and national issue, Horace Greeley continued to edit the *Tribune* and urge young men to go West. What catalyzed his views on land reform was a little book by Thomas Carlyle (1795–1881) called *Past and Present*. Carlyle was a British friend of Emerson, a dour and gloomy Scot drawn to Goethe and German romanticism, and an opponent of industrial capitalism. Carlyle preferred a kind of feudal society that promoted individual rights, but not socialism. Greeley encountered Carlyle's *Past and Present* because Emerson gave him a copy in May 1843. At first he was not impressed. But a second reading convinced him that this was a great book. In it, Carlyle attacked liberal democracy and free trade as the "law of the stronger," which defined freedom as "the liberty to die by starvation." Free trade meant unemployment and famine. Liberty, he wrote, "requires new definitions." Liberty did not mean simply the absence of oppression, but the means to labor on the "right path." Unemployed men should be put to work. "Men cannot live isolated," wrote Carlyle, "we are all bound together, for mutual good or else for mutual misery, as living nerves in the same body." Free men should have access to "new western lands" by emigration. They would become a "land aristocracy" essential to the nation. "Freedom, not nomad's or ape's Freedom, but man's Freedom. This is indispensable. We must have it, and will have it!" Liberty under the law meant only the right to starve; freedom under God's moral law offered hope. "The Laws of God," concluded Carlyle, "all men obey these, and have no 'Freedom' at all but in obeying them."[7]

For Carlyle, as for Greeley, freedom was an essential and divine part of the human condition. Just as men dressed themselves to clothe their nakedness, so wisdom meant that one had to get beyond clothing, the visible outer self, to understand the divine self within, the human being. The naked center of human existence, believed Carlyle, was freedom.[8]

Carlyle thought going West meant trans-Atlantic migration from Great Britain to America. Greeley was thinking of western expansion across America. Both agreed that emigration and free land could solve problems of poverty and unemployment. They also agreed that liberty under the laws of men should give way to freedom under the moral, higher, or divine law. But who would define that law?

In the *Tribune*, Greeley praised Carlyle's book as a "fearless and thorough exhibition of the abyss of social evils and miseries." It required a "new soul in man" that would create a "truer and more genial relation between Rich and Poor, High and Low, Laborer and Employer." This book, Greeley told his readers, "will do great good." It was a "great book—a noble book." Its ideas could work in America as well as in Great Britain. Workers everywhere had a right to the land and to the fruits of their labor. Working men should not be oppressed by an "idle aristocracy."[9]

"Do you want to know something?" Greeley wrote his friend O. A. Bowe. "If you do, just beg or borrow Carlyle's *Past and Present.* There's been no work containing so much gospel since the days of John the Beloved. I have read it all once, a good deal of it twice or more, and will go without sleep but I'll have one or two more readings of it. It does tell folks more truth than they have ever yet known, depend on't, get the book."[10]

In addition to Carlyle, Greeley's ideas about free land were influenced by George Henry Evans (1805–1856), a British-born printer and editor of the *Radical* and the *Working Man's Advocate.* Evans maintained that every freeman had a right to enough land to sustain his family. Free homesteads should be available to all men willing to work the land. Northern workers were as much slaves as those who worked the plantations of the South. "White slavery" was a disgrace, "even more destructive of life, health, and happiness than chattel slavery." "The white laborers are beginning to understand that *liberty* means something more than the privilege of exchanging taskmasters," Evans wrote in 1841.[11]

In March 1844, Evans organized his National Reform Association to push for free land. Its first meeting produced a collection of workers, intellectuals, and radical Democrats. They believed that the "land question" involved three distinct elements: (1) federal homestead legislation by Congress that would permit landless men to settle public land virtually free of charge; (2) the states should exempt any family lands from sale or seizure for nonpayment of debt (as had happened to Greeley's father, Zaccheus); (3) there should be a ceiling on land allotments and acres owned to prevent speculation and resale.[12] In time, free land in the West became a rallying cry for the Whig party, then the Republicans. And one of Evans's most important converts to the cause of land reform would be Horace Greeley.

Greeley watched Evans's movement closely from the beginning. He published articles by and about Evans in the *Tribune*. Greeley himself argued that society must "secure future generations against the fateful evils of monopoly of land by the few." For a time, Greeley was lukewarm about Evans's land-reform program, although he read Evans's pamphlets and attended his weekly meetings in New York. Evans himself drifted toward the Democrats and the emerging Young American movement, insinuating that Greeley was a "popularity hunter" suspicious of Evans and his "workingmen's party." But ultimately Greeley converted to Evans's plans and saw "freedom of the public lands to actual settlers" as "vitally necessary" to the health of the republic. He attended a convention of land reformers in New York in October 1845. A few months later, he wrote that the public-land distribution plan of the National Reform movement was "the best that can be devised."[13] Free citizens in a free republic deserved free land.

Greeley remained ambivalent, however, about the growing anti-rent movement in New York. He defended the right of tenant farmers to organize, but advised the anti-rent leaders that "the law is against you" and opposed mob violence (with anti-renters dressed up as Indians) that could ruin the anti-rent cause. He recognized that the tenant movement could not be suppressed by force, but would simply elect more and more legislators in Albany. He was alarmed by anti-rent radicalism, but appreciated the quasi-slavery of tenant farming. Rising rents defrauded tenants of their right to a fair share of the fruits of their own labor. "The fact is," he wrote, "abstract notions of natural right and justice cannot override and nullify sovereign grants and title-deeds."[14] A negotiated compromise between landlords and tenants was the best solution.

Both Greeley and Whig boss Thurlow Weed hoped to get more Whig support among the anti-rent farmers in counties east of the Hudson River. Whigs were prominent at the Anti-Rent State Convention in Albany and the May 5 national meeting of the National Reform Association in New York City in 1845. The convention demanded abolition of distress (the auctioning off of personal property of tenant farmers who could no longer pay their rent), taxation of rental income to the landlords, and abrogation of the laws that kept tenant farmers from challenging in court any landlord's title to the land.[15]

Greeley was heartsick at the rising immigration, poverty, and unemployment that plagued New York City in the winter of 1845–6, and saw free land as a solution. He estimated that there were thirty thousand unemployed in the city. He advised them to leave the city for rural areas, but few were willing or able to do so. He proposed rural workshop-farm complexes along Fourierist lines, landed estates with cotton and woolen factories to employ workers. He asked for private donations to help fund public-works projects. And he noted that many new settlers on public lands in western states were still in debt and paying high interest rates. "The freedom of the public lands to actual settlers, and the limitation of future acquisitions of land to some reasonable amount," he wrote in May 1846, "are also measures which seem to us vitally necessary to the ultimate emancipation of labor from thralldom and misery."[16]

In the summer of 1846, the National Reformers again called for a state convention on land reform in New York. Ira Harris, a liberal Whig, was the main anti-rent candidate. Some Whigs wanted him to run for governor. Both Whig and Democrat anti-rent leaders were calling for free public land for settlers, who had a natural right to that land. A consensus was building that cut across class and political lines to open the West to free white settlers. Most of the anti-renters, in fact, would soon join the ranks of anti-slavery men. Many would join the Free Soil Party in 1848. Greeley, Seward, and Harris all saw the political possibilities of such an alliance. Harris, predicted Greeley, "could be elected out of sight if the Whigs would vote for him, but they won't: He would lose thousands all about, on account of the terrors of anti-rent."[17]

By 1847, Greeley saw National Reform as the best possible land policy for the moment. His *Weekly Tribune* spread land reform through the tiny towns and villages of the expanding Northwest, from Ohio to Minnesota. The "Vote yourself a Farm!" movement in New York (1845) now became a national cause. Greeley claimed that by 1847, some fifty papers across the nation endorsed land reform. Both Carlyle and Fourier had inspired him to new ideas of land reform and association that required individual enterprise as much as socialist redistribution of wealth. He certainly defended the natural right of working men to public lands that they would improve. He continued to fight for social justice, intellectual and moral progress, and universal well-being. But critics said he was denying the equal right to private property in land.[18]

The foundation of "True Democracy" in America for the next

twenty years, Greeley wrote a friend in 1847, would be "land reform, not alone as applied to the public lands, but to all lands." He supported various national homestead proposals until the Homestead Act passed Congress in 1862. He continued to urge young men to "go West" and become settlers on the frontier. Any republic where citizens all held rights in land would be the "strongest on earth." Inviolable homesteads were the basis of "Republican Freedom."[19] In short, Greeley believed that freedom and land were inseparable.

For Greeley land remained the solution to the labor problems of the big cities. Free land granted to settlers would transform "orphans and mendicants" into farmers and homesteaders. There would be no need for strikes and labor unrest when every citizen could work for himself rather than for others. Unemployed workers leaving the urban labor market would reduce the pressure on employers for jobs. By the late 1850s, the new Republican Party supported the homestead bill, opposed by the Democrats. In early 1859 the bill again passed the House but was tabled in the Senate. Finally, it passed the Senate in June 1860, but President Buchanan vetoed the bill. Greeley scorned the bill as "half a loaf," but remained hopeful. "Does anyone suppose," he mused, "that Abraham Lincoln would ever veto such a bill?" He reminded his readers that only the Republicans were committed to free public land for settlers on the "virgin soil of the great West."[20]

Free land was crucial to Horace Greeley's evolving concept of freedom. Fourier's ideas on free association and Carlyle's book on land for the landless provided important stimuli along the road. But this was no socialist project. Free land was only for those willing to labor. Without labor to improve the land, it could become wasteland, as John Locke had noted two centuries before. A man willing and able to work the land was truly free. Labor, as much as land, was the key to republican freedom.

FREE LABOR

Free land would not produce free men without free labor. In a republic, a free man who owned land that he himself did not work was either a speculator or a non-producer. His land would contribute nothing to the greater good of society without being worked and improved. Land was a necessary, but not sufficient, condition for prosperity in the republic. Only labor would make the land sufficient.

In the 1830s, a movement to protect American labor from cheap foreign competition, especially in textiles, became the "protectionist" alternative to Free Trade liberalism. The main proponent of protectionism was the young economist Henry Charles Carey, son of an Irish immigrant to Philadelphia who had become a prominent Pennsylvania industrialist. Carey retired from his family's firm in 1835 at the ripe old age of forty-two and became an active Whig and proponent of protectionist trade and tariff policies. Carey was irascible, dogmatic, one-sided, and disagreeable, and he became a prominent American economic nationalist.

In 1835, Carey published an essay on wages and labor in which he argued that "whatever has a tendency to prevent the growth of capital is injurious, while everything that promotes its growth is advantageous." New factory machinery could help the laborer become more productive and thus raise his wages. Employment itself was no virtue unless it increased the amount of goods produced. Taxation was equally unproductive except as a short-term source of revenue because taxation did not increase productivity. The key to a successful American economy was what Carey called "freedom of action"—no internal passports, easy mobility, no apprentice laws, the ability of men to change jobs as often as they wanted. The absence of government interference was the key. "The best system of government," Carey concluded, "is that which gives security of person and property at the lowest cost, either of money or of freedom of action, and its most important maxim is embraced in the words "LET US ALONE!""[21]

Carey was the favorite economist of both Horace Greeley and Abraham Lincoln. He argued that the key to a healthy national economy was cooperation, not conflict, between labor and capital, workers and capitalists. He accepted the labor theory of value. He favored high protective tariffs. He believed that association and cooperation could increase productivity. Agriculture and industry could complement each other to their mutual advantage. Government non-interference (except for protectionist tariffs) was crucial. It all came down to freedom—freedom of action, freedom of thought, freedom of discussion. Freedom bred innovation and increased productivity. "The man who is conscious of the right to think and act freely," wrote

Carey, "is a superior being to him who feels that he is liable to punishment for entertaining or expressing opinions different from those of his fellow man."[22]

Greeley shared Carey's enthusiasm for free labor in a free society as the key to republican prosperity. Manual labor, Greeley wrote, was a "blessing and a dignity." Hard work was a virtue. Labor was the rational and natural way for society to improve itself. Labor was part of God's design for man on earth. Common sense, reason, and Christianity all placed a high value on human labor. The "right to labor" was a precious right. There was nothing more pathetic than the sight of unemployed men wandering the streets of cities in search of work. Americans lived in a land of "Political and Intellectual Freedom," Greeley noted, "a land boastful of its Liberty, its Happiness, and its general superiority to other Nations," but America was a land of the poor, the homeless, and the unemployed. Full employment was a good thing. Capitalism alone could solve the problems of poverty and disease. "Organized and attractive industry is the magic which is to transform the hovels of penury and pestilence into the abodes of health, intelligence, and comfort."[23] But how?

In 1842–3, Greeley edited a little monthly magazine entitled *The American Laborer, Devoted to the Cause of Protection in Home Industry.* In it, he argued that the doctrine of Free Trade only reinforced Great Britain's monopoly on global industries. That monopoly meant "depressing and disastrous foreign competition" for American businessmen and workers. Only high tariffs could protect American companies and laborers from foreign competition and produce national prosperity and independence. The whole purpose of government was to protect its citizens. Free-trade talk of "unrestricted freedom" was an illusion that merely disguised British dominance in the world market. Real freedom meant American national independence, stability, and prosperity. Only a strong national economy protected by high tariffs could produce such an outcome.[24]

Greeley's protectionism landed him somewhere between socialism and capitalism, between the laboring classes and their employers, in the emerging middle, or middling, classes in American society. For Greeley labor was not a separate class at all. There was no working class. There were simply workers who were nascent capitalists. Economic failure was not due to exploitation, but to extravagance and ostentation, or perhaps to laziness. All men had to do was to follow the Protestant ethic of frugality, hard work, and sobriety. Then they could take advantage of their "right to rise" and become successful at anything they wished. Labor and capital had a harmony of interests that overrode the divisive forces of class conflict, strikes, and industrial warfare. The answer to low wages was to change jobs or move west to a new homestead. Greeley's world was a fluid structure of individuals capable of moving across class boundaries whenever they wished to apply themselves.

The "miserly" approach of Free Trade—"buy where you can cheapest"—did not satisfy Greeley. Americans should buy their products at home, not abroad. Free Trade ignored the needs of government and society as a whole in order to favor a few individuals. But the "common interests of the People" were more important. Free Trade was morally wrong, throwing workers out of their jobs by allowing the cheapest products to flood the market. Free Trade favored the capitalist countries. Protection favored labor by supporting "free institutions" at home.[25] Greeley also believed—following a New York businessman friend, Edward Kellogg—that the government should help labor share in the fruits of production by circulating interest-bearing currency and creating a National Safety Fund to back it up.[26] The government could use banking, as well as tariffs, to protect labor and home industry.

As a printer and an editor, Greeley espoused the cause of the workingman since the 1830s. Human labor was the efficient and productive engine of society. Those who monopolized and speculated on land, those who were homeless, hungry, and landless, were on the edge of that society. "Labor must be organized," he wrote, in order to promote the cause of social reform.[27] Progress meant converting poverty into wealth, barbarism into refinement. Industrial associations, joint-stock companies, and labor unions were all worthy organizations.

In January 1850, Greeley helped organize the printers of New York City into the New York Typographical Union. Printers associations had existed since the eighteenth century. The Franklin Typographical Association emerged in New York in 1844. But this was something new. The union promptly adopted a fair-wage scale of thirty-two cents for every thousand ems (units) of type set. In addressing the printers of New York on Benjamin Franklin's birthday (January 17), Greeley noted that labor was becoming ever more efficient, thanks to technology. But workers were not getting their "just reward." Unemployment was still a massive social problem in the grimy, noisy, overpopulated cities of the eastern seaboard. Greeley proposed a Laborers' Exchange as a joint-stock company, or Fourierist association. There were toasts to truth, enlightenment, and a free press. Three thousand workers roared their approval, listened to band music, and ate an alcohol-free temperance supper.[28]

Greeley was the workingman's workingman. The printers elected him the first president of their union, and Greeley promptly issued the very first union card to a printer and received one himself. He helped establish unions in most of the printing establishments of New York City, and became the first union negotiator on behalf of collective bargaining.

The key to free labor for Greeley was free association. Workers had the right to organize themselves. Throughout the 1840s, the editor espoused various forms of emancipation for laborers, whom he considered less of a class and more of an upwardly mobile set of future capitalists. Slavery was an unjust impediment to free labor, and free labor for Greeley lay between slavery and speculation. Slavery was an unjust and inefficient system of labor. Speculation was profit by the idle rich who did not have to labor. "No man," he argued, "can really enjoy more than his own moderate daily labor would produce, and none can truly enjoy this without doing the work."[29] Poverty below and idleness above were the enemies of free labor. Industry, thrift, moderation, and harmony were the virtues of free labor. Work was noble. Workers should be neither wage slaves nor speculators, but honest and frugal men working for an honest wage at a job they enjoyed. Capitalism as an economic system was best suited to a republic of free men. But capitalism worked only if social justice and harmony overcame exploitation and class conflict. "The wage system is totally vicious," he wrote a friend in England in 1868. "I am for cooperatives to the fullest extent practicable. Never till the workman is paid from the proceeds of his work and according to its tested excellence, will our laboring class be other than servants and prodigals."[30]

Free labor in the end depended on the right of association, the right to free speech and assembly, the right to own and improve land, and the right to compete in the marketplace. Only free citizens could be free workingmen. For Greeley and many other Americans in the 1840s, the enemy of free labor was increasingly clear. It was slavery.

ANTI-SLAVERY

Anti-slavery was at the heart of Horace Greeley's concept of freedom, and southerners before the Civil War thought that Greeley was an abolitionist or an African-American or both. He was neither. He was by 1850 becoming an anti-slavery man. But his road from Whig journalist to anti-slavery man was neither rapid nor direct.

How and when Greeley moved into the anti-slavery camp is difficult to ascertain. By 1850, Greeley was no abolitionist, but he was certainly a Henry Clay Whig who opposed slavery as economically inefficient and morally unjust. Reluctant to accept the single-issue third-party anti-slavery efforts of either the Liberty or Free Soil parties, Greeley sought to bring anti-slavery into the Whig Party as a single party of freedom.

Indeed, anti-slavery was a consistent part of Greeley's evolving Whig ideology. In the 1830s, Henry Clay could still argue that the "liberty of the descendants of Africa in the United States" was quite "incompatible" with the "safety and liberty of the European descendants." But by the 1840s, the Whigs had adopted anti-slavery—but not abolition—as a political form of moral redemption. Abolition meant immediate emancipation of the slaves. Anti-slavery opposed slavery as an institution, but hoped that in a free labor market slavery would ultimately disappear. Anti-slavery also implied that freedom was not to be limited to white men. "Free institutions," wrote the *American Review* in 1848, "are not proper to the *white* man, but to the courageous, upright, and moral man."[31] Under a system of ordered liberty, all men (but not women) should have the right to vote.

The abolitionists were also developing into a vociferous and well-connected movement. By 1840, British and American abolitionists conducted a trans-Atlantic conversation on the need to abolish slavery worldwide. In England, Lord Brougham demanded liberty for slaves "in the name of justice and of law—in the name of reason—in the name of God, who has given you no right to work injustice." In William Lloyd Garrison's *Liberator*, Boston abolitionist Wendell Phillips called for America to "finish what our fathers left unfinished when they declared all men free and equal." The equality mentioned in the Declaration of Independence should apply to all men, white and colored, even if the Union were to dissolve over the slavery issue. "'Freedom' and 'Slavery' will soon be the rallying forces," wrote abolitionist

Maria Chapman, "not 'Clay' and 'Van Buren.'"[32] Former slave owner Henry Clay, trying to appease southern Whig voters, was more cautious. "I am no friend of slavery," he told the U.S. Senate in 1839, "but I prefer the liberty of my own country to that of any other people, and the liberty of my own race to that of any other race."[33]

In 1840, the London Convention of the British and Foreign Anti-Slavery Society (BFASS) brought American and English abolitionists together for the first time as organized groups. Emerson became more vocal in his anti-slavery views. Unitarian minister Theodore Parker thundered against slavery from his Boston pulpit. So did William Ellery Channing. Garrison boycotted the conference because it would not seat female delegates from America. He hammered away at the issue in the *Liberator* and met with Frederick Douglass, an escaped slave, at an anti-slavery meeting on Nantucket Island. And Gerrit Smith in New York helped organize the first anti-slavery political party, the Liberty Party, which ran James Birney for president in the elections that fall. Birney garnered only 7,059 votes, but slavery was now on the national political agenda. In 1844, the Liberty Party would run again, this time getting sixty-two thousand votes nationwide.[34] Anti-slavery was becoming a trans-Atlantic moral crusade. The Liberty Party was fighting "freedom's battle."

Greeley was cautious where abolitionists were concerned. He had denounced the murder of abolitionist publisher Elijah Lovejoy in 1837 more as a violation of freedom of the press than as the mob murder of a righteous abolitionist. In 1841, he responded with equal caution to the "Virginia Controversy," when some Virginia slaves escaped from their ship to New York and Governor Seward refused to return them to Virginia. "Whoever offends against a local institution, like Slavery," Greeley wrote, "must take his chances of escaping from its dominion or incurring its penalties; but when a surrender from one State to another is demanded, we insist that there must be an offense against general or moral laws, else compliance is out of the question."[35] Unless the slaves had broken the law in Virginia or elsewhere, New York was justified in its refusal to return them.

When the House of Representatives finally rescinded the "gag rule" that prohibited discussion of slavery, Greeley wrote that "we rejoice" that an "arbitrary and extraordinary" provision of the law was reversed. The gag rule was, in his view, "eminently calculated to foster and inflame the spirit which threatens the dissolution of the

Union."[36] And to dissolve the republic over the issue of slavery was unthinkable.

In 1842, in *Prigg v. Pennsylvania,* the U.S. Supreme Court held that the 1793 Fugitive Slave Act was constitutional. Owners had a legal right to recapture their runaway slaves as lost or stolen property in any state of the Union. "The effect of this decision," wrote Greeley, "will be to deepen the impression on the public mind that the existence of slavery for some is inconsistent with, and fatal to, the preservation of perfect freedom for any."[37]

According to his biographer, James Parton, Greeley began to adopt a more radical anti-slavery stance in 1843 after he saw two black men denied a cabin on a Boston–New York steamboat. The incident, however, is uncorroborated by any other testimony. He did publish a pamphlet by Henry Clay's cousin, Cassius M. Clay of Kentucky, entitled *Slavery: The Evil—The Remedy.* But Greeley at this point repudiated higher-law doctrine (slavery was immoral in the eyes of God) in favor of gradual legal emancipation of the slaves through reform. And he distrusted the abolitionists. Garrison was "a clever fellow, but not a great man." The abolitionists seemed to him long on free advice and short on practical measures. They should help elect Henry Clay president and then ask him to help abolish slavery once in office. They should recognize that the "white niggers" of New York City, urban blue-collar workers, were as bad off as southern slaves. "I do not think the mass of the Whig party prepared for any other than defensive action against Slavery," he concluded, "and I cannot see the wisdom of any other."[38] Abolitionist agitation only prolonged slavery. The answer lay in the associationist movement to emancipate all the poor, not just slaves.

By 1844, anti-slavery was an established, if small, movement on the national level. Many of its supporters were churchgoers—Quakers, Methodists, Universalists, Unitarians—who considered slavery a moral evil as well as an economic brake on industrialization. Anti-slavery poets wrote of the "heralds of freedom," of liberty against tyranny, of "freedom's gathering" through universal rights for all. The Liberty Party in its songs for the 1844 election told of how slaves were "praying for freedom," for liberty or death, for "independence from slavery." "We're for Freedom throughout the Land," and "Freedom's battle is begun!" But even as the Liberty Party in its noisy political lyrics trumpeted the call for "freedom's car, emancipation," Greeley remained wedded to the Whigs.[39] An anti-slavery single-issue party could not succeed without broader political and philosophical goals. There were but two major political parties, and anti-slavery would rise or fall with the Whigs.

Throughout the 1840s, therefore, Greeley remained a Henry Clay Whig regarding anti-slavery matters. "I have admired and trusted many statesmen," he wrote later in his recollections, "I profoundly loved Henry Clay."[40] Clay was generous, gallant, and eloquent, thought Greeley. He had been a conservative slaveholder, then an advocate of returning slaves to Africa, then a national protectionist and patriot. Beaten five times for president, Clay made his most notable attempt against James Polk in 1844 and lost again. Greeley worked frantically for Clay's election from May through November, staying up until two or three in the morning writing speeches and articles, traveling across the country to Whig rallies on Clay's behalf, and accumulating fifty or sixty boils on his body as a result.

Clay reciprocated Greeley's respect and admiration. He found the *Tribune* to be a "very great" newspaper, even though he regretted its "eccentricities." "I regard Mr. Greeley," he wrote in a private letter to a Whig friend, "as surpassed by no other editor in the Union."[41]

Greeley had worked hard for Clay's nomination since 1842. He urged Schuyler Colfax to bring the Indiana Whigs "heartily" in line behind Clay. He continued to speak out for "wise, just, necessary, and Republican" measures. He worked for free land and a protectionist tariff. He assured fellow Whigs that Clay would make a "glorious fight" in 1844. "Our Harry Clay," he wrote one of his *Tribune* staffers, "if alive and well, will then be elected President."[42]

In 1844, Greeley and Thomas McElrath published a *Clay Tribune* as a separate political newspaper for Whigs, featuring excerpts from the daily and weekly *Tribune* and "thoroughly dedicated to the advancement of the Whig cause and the election of Henry Clay." Greeley sent Molly off to rest on a farm in rural Massachusetts. He went without sleep, lived in the office, and gave up to six speeches a week on Clay's behalf. The result was mental anguish and declining health—headaches, irritability, nervousness, insomnia, and flashes of hot temper. Clay's loss to Polk in November 1844 was a crushing blow to the famous editor. "I was the worst beaten man on the continent," he later declared.[43]

Greeley continued to develop his ideas on the moral reform of society. Free Trade crushed the working class beneath the burden of high prices. "Moneyed capitalists" raised interest rates and made high profits while prices rose. Only protection could equalize prices and protect home industry.[44] Only a campaign of "Christian reform" would "fearlessly grapple with War and Slavery." Virtue was more important than any financial reward. Man was engaged throughout history in a "struggle with darkness and evil." But continued human progress required a "perilous and doubtful struggle for Freedom."[45] In February 1844, Greeley had announced the formation of the American Society for the Collection and Diffusion of Information in relation to the Punishment of Death, and argued against capital punishment in the pages of both the *New Yorker* and the *Tribune*.[46] For Greeley, capital punishment remained both morally wrong and politically inept. He advised Weed that a stronger stand on that issue would bring "thousands of conscientious, reflecting, serious men to the polls who will not otherwise come, and would have helped our vote." Hanging sometimes killed innocent people, and certainly did not deter crime.[47]

Clay's loss to Polk in the 1844 election marked a watershed in the history of the Whig Party. Greeley was crushed, and quickly blamed a number of factors: the "two hundred thousand foreign votes" of immigrant Irish voters; the Democratic Party "concealed or mystified" the issues for the electorate; the "third-party wire-workers" of the anti-slavery Liberty Party of James G. Birney had siphoned off some fifteen thousand Whig votes. While Greeley cursed the "infamy" of the Liberty Party, he felt that the real enemy was not anti-slavery or abolitionism, but emerging nativist "Know-Nothings," the self-appointed patriots who espoused a virulent form of anti-Catholic and anti-immigrant nationalism.[48]

Clay's defeat, coupled with Polk's annexation of Texas (March 1, 1845) and the implied war with Mexico, helped turn Greeley and the *Tribune* more strongly towards the anti-slavery cause. Slavery had always seemed immoral and unnecessary. Now anti-slavery seemed imperative to prevent the spread of slavery. Adding new states and territories to the Union raised the question of whether their representatives in Washington would be from slave or free states. And this was a national, not sectional, issue.

Texas declared its independence from Mexico in 1836. When Sam Houston's army defeated the forces of General Santa Anna, Houston helped create a "free, sovereign and independent republic." Greeley favored such independence. He wished the newly independent Texans "victory, glory, independence—anything but an amalgamation with the Federal Union. To this we stand unalterably opposed."[49] The admission of Texas to the Union, Greeley correctly predicted, would revive the slavery controversy and undo the Missouri Compromise of 1820. The issue of Texas and the issue of slavery were inseparable.

Thus, the election of 1844 placed the issue of Texas annexation—and therefore the issue of slavery—in sharper relief. Joshua Giddings pointed out that Texas presented a special problem for the Whig Party. It raised the "great question of slavery or liberty. Will we extend slavery or will we promote Liberty and Freedom? To give the South the preponderance of political power would be itself a surrender of our Tariff, our internal improvements, our distribution of the proceeds of the public lands." Greeley and the *Tribune* continued to oppose annexation of Texas "so long as a vestige of slavery shall remain within her borders." The House of Representatives, he charged, wanted annexation merely as a tool for extending slavery. "This project was conceived in Slavery and must be carried on as a Slavery-extending measure, or it cannot be carried on at all." In February 1845, Greeley visited Washington, DC, and wrote Molly that "Texas is the only matter thought of."[50]

Yet Greeley's caution on anti-slavery continued to infuriate the abolitionists. In June 1845, he refused an invitation to attend an anti-slavery convention in Cincinnati, arguing again that wage slavery for both white and black workers in the North was as bad as real slavery in the South. Free blacks in the North needed new schools, churches, and towns as much as slaves in the South. Improving their condition would do more to "pave the way for Universal Freedom" than "reams of angry vituperation against slaveholders." "How can I devote myself to a crusade against distant servitude when I discern its essence pervading my immediate community?" he asked. He was less troubled by slavery in Charleston or New Orleans than in New York City.[51]

Throughout 1846, Greeley remained with the Whig line. The Whigs were the champions of "general CONCORD or united interests," and the Democrats, the "the party of DISCORD, divided, repugnant, hostile." The Whigs wanted a strong commonwealth, a government through which "vast and beneficent ends may be accomplished." The Democrats looked upon federal government with distrust as an agency of "corruption, oppression, and robbery." Greeley thought he might run for lieutenant governor of New York if Weed thought him a likely candidate.[52]

In the meantime, the war with Mexico over the annexation of Texas dragged on. Couriers traveling by ship and horse brought battle reports and mounting casualty lists to the newspapers of eastern cities. Greeley denounced the war as "a fathomless abyss of crime and calamity," calling Polk the "Father of Lies." One denunciation was particularly stunning: "The laws of Heaven are suspended and those of Hell established in their stead. It means that the Commandments are to be read and obeyed by our People thus—Thou *shalt* kill Mexicans; Thou *shalt* steal from Them, hate them, burn their houses, ravage their fields, and fire red-hot cannon balls into towns swarming with their wives and children." He saw the war as simply an adventure of the southern "slavocracy." He called for peace at any price: "Sign anything, ratify anything to end the guilt, the bloodshed, the shame."[53] But the war went on.

U.S. Senator Charles Sumner of Massachusetts called the war "an enormity born of slavery." Garrison too railed against the war. On August 8, 1846, congressman David Wilmot of Pennsylvania, a Democrat, introduced an amendment to a House of Representatives bill that would grant President James Polk authority (and two million dollars) to negotiate an end to the Mexican War. The so-called Wilmot Proviso prohibited slavery in any part of territory acquired from Mexico after the Mexican War ended. The proviso passed the House, then failed in the Senate. Both Greeley and Lincoln voted for it later in the thirtieth Congress. The Wilmot Proviso also fueled the mounting campaign to limit or abolish slavery. "The last foot of slave territory has been conquered," wrote Thurlow Weed, "and if the issue is to be more Slave territory or no Union, the sooner the issue is tried the better. We have no fears of the result. Freedom will triumph and the glory of our beloved country will be maintained."[54] The Wilmot Proviso had opened up the main question for the ensuing decade—the future of slavery in the western territories. Either freedom or slavery must triumph. There was no middle ground.

In the autumn of 1846, Greeley began to hammer away against slavery and for the Wilmot Proviso in the pages of the *Tribune*. He promised that the "great mass" of New York Whigs would support another Clay run for the presidency, even though Clay had not yet announced his candidacy.[55] But he was also feeling the pressure from abolitionists and anti-slavery forces to abandon Clay and the conservative Whigs, and to take a stand on slavery in the pages of the *Tribune*. If Clay ran again, Greeley wrote Seward, "it will be impossible to make our Northern Anti-Slavery people follow and confide in him." Charles Sumner called for a new "Northern Party of Freedom" to bring together the anti-slavery voters of every stripe, a "new crystallization of parties." (He was nearly a decade ahead of his time, and of the future Republican Party.) Abolitionist Joshua Giddings wrote Greeley from Ohio denouncing the Mexican War as a "war of conquest" to extend slavery and asked the editor for support in the *Tribune*. From Boston, Sumner wrote Giddings that public opinion was now "moving on" with regard to the question of "freedom on the Atlantic Ocean." It was time to stand on principle. "We are all disappointed by the silence of Greeley in the *Tribune*," wrote Sumner. "Why does he not speak out?"[56]

Perhaps Greeley was preoccupied that winter with other matters —financial, personal, and political—and did not want to jeopardize his newspaper by taking an unpopular stand on a divisive issue. "I need money," he wrote a friend in Buffalo, and would be glad to "get anything for my Buffalo land." He was selling off some of his stock in the *Tribune*. "Money! Money! Money!" he complained. "I always want money." His son Pickie was now a noisy toddler fighting with his mother and stealing doorstops. Horace and Pickie were sleeping in the same bed, while Molly and their daughter Mary Inez slept in another bed in another room. Whig politics also concerned him. He wrote Weed in Albany urging him to run Seward as a candidate for vice president with Clay ("our best if not our only hope for success next time"). Seward might help regain the anti-rent vote in upstate New York. Combined with "anybody but Webster or a slaveholder" for president, the ticket could well carry the state of New York in 1848.[57] But Whig success at the polls required caution.

In January 1847, the Greeleys' infant daughter Mary Inez died, adding yet another family tragedy to the growing list of despair. Greeley lost himself in his work. He finally ran a series of anti-slavery columns and messages on the front page of the *Tribune*. In February, he came out solidly for the House passage of the Wilmot Proviso under the headline "Freedom Triumphant!" He compared it with the battles of Saratoga, Yorktown, and Marathon. He was consequently disappointed when the Senate voted down the same amendment, calling those who voted against it "betrayers of freedom." But Greeley had emerged as an anti-slavery man in public. "I am glad," wrote Charles Sumner to Joshua Giddings, "the *Tribune* has spoken at last."[58]

Seward, in the meantime, expressed his delight that the anti-slavery case of *Prigg v. Pennsylvania* (on the matter of fugitive slaves) was now before the Supreme Court. He promptly sent Greeley a copy of his argument. "Publish or not as you think best," Seward advised the editor. "Slavery and freedom are antagonisms," Joshua Giddings told the House of Representatives in Washington. "They must necessarily be at war with each other." Greeley was reluctant to run the popular general Zachary Taylor, rather than Henry Clay, for president in the next election. Taylor was a hero of the hated Mexican War, and not known as an anti-slavery man. Greeley and Charles Sumner had a long conversation in May, in which Greeley "avowed warm opposition to Taylor," despite the "war spirit" in New York City, and seemed solidly in the anti-slavery camp. Sumner was delighted.[59]

Throughout the summer of 1847, Whigs across the nation began to see Zachary Taylor as their next presidential candidate. Perhaps a general could win, where a politician might lose. Yet Greeley continued to support Henry Clay, not Taylor, as one of the "master minds" of the age. "What man lives except Henry Clay," he asked rhetorically, "whom any great proportion of the People really desire to see President?" Only Clay, in Greeley's view, could stop Taylor, win the election, and hold the Whigs together as a political party.[60]

Economic development continued to inform Greeley's anti-slavery stance. That summer Greeley went west to visit his investments in a new mining operation on the shores of Lake Superior, where Greeley held some stock in a copper mine. He also saw the need for lighthouses along the Great Lakes, a project that he helped push through Congress.[61] He made a second trip to Lake Superior in the late summer of 1848, writing Weed that he could not attend the Buffalo State Fair and enclosing the draft of an anti-slavery speech for Weed to consider.[62] He also led the New York delegation to the Northwest River and Harbor Convention in Chicago (July 5–7), organized to discuss federal "internal improvements," including the dredging of harbors and damming of rivers for navigation and commerce. Here he first met Abraham Lincoln, a "tall specimen of an Illinoisan," according to Greeley, who "spoke briefly and happily" to the gathering. Greeley addressed the meeting and was—according to Weed—"listened to with great attention, and warmly cheered in concluding. Every word that he uttered was full of truth and wisdom."[63] Greeley also wrote up the convention for *DeBow's Commercial Review*.[64]

In late October, the New York City Whigs met in Lafayette Hall to nominate candidates for statewide office in the coming elections. Rival editors Greeley and James Webb "as usual disturbed the meetings with personal squabbles in which the friends of each participant took part," noted diarist Philip Hone. Webb supported the Mexican War, while Greeley was sharply opposed to it. But in the end Webb's resolutions passed. "Webb should not have thrown in a firebrand to such combustible materials," concluded Hone, "and Greeley would do better to confine his crudities to the columns of the *Daily Tribune*."[65]

But the Mexican War had radicalized Greeley on the slavery issue. The U.S. Army was "tearing down the houses of trembling cities with bombs and cannon shot, until the streets [of Mexico] run red with the blood of massacred women and children." Henry Clay wrote Greeley that he was still not decided about his candidacy and would wait until the spring of 1848 before making a decision.[66] And before he decided to run, the war was over, and public opinion focused on the revolutionary events unfolding in Europe.

Horace Greeley was still a Clay Whig. He wrote Weed that he would be interested in running for Senator from New York. He assured Weed that Henry Clay was in favor of "Free Territory" and not slave states, and was willing to push the Wilmot Proviso again at the next session of Congress. In February, Greeley helped the city Whig committee host a massive rally for Clay at Castle Garden that attracted some ten or twelve thousand people. But Seward and Weed thought General Zachary Taylor had a better chance to win the election than did Clay. And the Whigs would ultimately win the presidential elections of both 1840 and 1848 not by their principles, but by running popular generals who could claim military success.[67]

On February 2, 1848, the Treaty of Guadalupe-Hidalgo pronounced an end to the bloody war with Mexico. Under its terms, Mexico gave up its claims to the territory that would become California, Nevada, Arizona, New Mexico, and Utah. Mexico recognized Texas as U.S. territory as far south as the Rio Grande River. In return, the United States withdrew all its forces from Mexican territory and paid an indemnity of fifteen million dollars to compensate Mexico for its loss of territory.

The "Mexican cession" brought an end to the war, but marked only the beginning of the battle over slavery in the new territories. Although the war had drawn Horace Greeley deeper into the anti-slavery cause, he still refused to abandon the Whigs, whose philosophy he articulated in the pages of the *Tribune*. Although he shared its anti-slavery principles, he refused to join the Liberty Party in 1840 or 1844. Now in 1848 he faced a new choice: whether or not to join the new anti-slavery Free Soil Party.

FREE SOIL

Horace Greeley was never a member of the Free Soil Party, formed in the summer of 1848 to run another anti-slavery candidate for president of the United States. Free Soil meant that no slavery would be permitted in the new territories in the West acquired from Mexico. Greeley shared Free Soil ideology, but he continued to believe that a single-issue third party was not the way to eliminate slavery. He remained a staunch Whig, despite the fact that the Whigs were badly divided on the slavery issue.

"Cotton Whigs" tolerated slavery as a central institution in the production of that plant in the South. "Conscience Whigs" moved steadily toward eliminating slavery as a moral evil. Most Whigs were typically racist toward African-Americans, even when they opposed slavery. They understood freedom as freedom for white men only. Abolitionists saw this as pure hypocrisy. The black abolitionist William Wells Brown, back from England, noted that even American sympathizers with the republican revolutions of 1848 in Europe often supported slavery. They "pretended sympathy for people in foreign countries, while they chain, whip, and sell their own countrymen."[68]

Greeley was a Conscience Whig. In the *Tribune*, he spoke out against slavery with increasing belligerence. "Human slavery," he wrote in January 1848, "is at deadly feud with the common law, the common sense, and the conscience of mankind; nobody pretends to justify it but those who share in its gains and its guilt. God, Man, Nature, Religion, Law, Reason, are all against it. . . . If the slavery propagandists are ready for the inevitable struggle, let no retreat be beaten by the champions of universal Freedom. The people are looking on."[69] He continued to support Clay for president and was lukewarm about General Taylor, but the Taylor candidacy marched on.

The death of John Quincy Adams on February 28 seemed to galvanize the anti-slavery forces into action once more. In his eulogy on Adams, Theodore Parker claimed Adams stood for the greatness of politics in a country that favored "the government of all, for all, and by all." Parker praised Adams's love of "human freedom in its widest sense." Liberty was embodied less in the laws of the Constitution than in the divine law of the Declaration of Independence that found all men created equal and endowed by God with inalienable rights.[70]

By May, Greeley began to realize that Taylor would win the nomination over Clay. He wrote Indiana congressman Schuyler Colfax that "if we nominate Taylor, we may elect him, but we destroy the Whig party. The offset to Abolition will ruin us. I wash my hands of the business."[71] Greeley wrote Henry Clay that the cause was now lost. "I believe we are doomed to be beaten," he mused, because of "the men who control the counsel of the Whig Party through the machinery existing at Washington." Clay was a proven loser and a former slave owner. In June, the Whig national convention meeting in Philadelphia nominated Zachary Taylor for president of the United States. Greeley stomped out of the building with a scowl on his face, saying only that he was going home to New York. Hearing that no trains would run that night, he growled, "I don't want any train. I'm going across New Jersey afoot."[72] And so he did.

Greeley remained a Whig, but he would not support Taylor. Martin Van Buren, a Democrat, the "old fox of Kinderhook," was talking about running on a third-party anti-slavery ticket. At first Greeley urged his readers to support Van Buren. He flirted with Gerrit Smith and the old Liberty Party. He thought that most Free States could be carried by the Free Soilers against both Whigs and Democrats. Then he had second thoughts. A Whig alliance with the emerging Free Soil Party would simply help elect another Democrat to the White House, undercut anti-slavery congressmen in Washington, and "enable the Extensionists [of slavery] to carry Slavery to the Pacific without a struggle in Congress."[73]

On August 9, 1848, a mixed bag of anti-slavery Democrats and Whigs, plus Liberty Party men, gathered in Buffalo, New York, to form the Free Soil Party. Abolitionists of all shades united for a moment to nominate Van Buren for president. Their platform resolved to support "free soil, free speech, free labor, and free men." This meant a national battle against any extension of slavery into the newly acquired territories in the West. Freedom meant free land for free white men. "The cry of Free Men," wrote Frederick Douglass, "was raised, not for the extension of liberty to the black man, but for the protection of the Liberty of the white."[74]

But neither Lincoln nor Greeley wished to break Whig ranks and join the new party. "I am going to vote for Taylor," Greeley admitted to a friend in mid-September, "—at least I think I am—and I am not clear that this is right. If I could make Van Buren President tomorrow I would. I don't like the man, but I do like the principle he now embodies—Free Soil and Land Reform. And, very properly, the Free Soil Party is the only live party around us. It ought to triumph, but God works out his ends by other instruments than majorities; wherefore it will fall, but fall gloriously. You needn't ask me to do any more than I am doing for Taylor. I do all I have stomach for. Let him whose digestion is ranker do more." Greeley went on to say he "could have been the oracle of the Free Soil Party . . . had I chosen." But he remained loyal to the Whigs, "a party which never loved me."[75]

Greeley promised Weed that he would continue to support Taylor reluctantly for president, now that the Clay candidacy had ended. But he remained unenthusiastic. Weed talked of running Greeley for Congress, hoping to keep the erratic editor in Whig harness. Greeley was flattered. But he continued to argue the Free Soil case against extending slavery in the territories as a matter of "national concern, for which the People are morally and every way responsible." "The Clay Whigs," wrote diarist Philip Hone, "are falling into the Taylor ranks, reluctantly in some instances and with a bad grace." Greeley —the "oracle of the party"—was hoisting the Taylor flag in the *Tribune* but "thinks proper to make an apology for his course." Greeley damned Taylor with "faint praise." "This is in abominably bad taste," wrote Hone, "as well as impolitic in the last degree."[76]

Ideologically, Greeley remained wedded to the cause of freedom against slavery. Americans needed to "establish firmly the righteous principle that Slavery can never more be planted on our National Soil." The Whig Party should stand against any extension of slavery to the territories, and staunchly for "the cause of Humanity and

Freedom." William Seward echoed Greeley's thoughts. "Slavery must be abolished," he wrote. "Freedom insists on the emancipation and development of labor; Slavery demands a soil moistened with tears and blood—Freedom a soil that exults under the elastic tread of man in his native majesty." The Whigs must become the "party of freedom" and seek "complete and universal emancipation."[77]

And the Whigs did win. In November, Taylor received 1,360,967 votes to 1,222,342 for the Democratic candidate, Lewis Cass. Even more significant was the astounding gain of the anti-slavery third party. Some 291,804 men voted Free Soil for Van Buren, an increase of 244,000 over the Liberty Party's tally in 1844. Taylor beat Cass handily in the electoral college, 163–127. The Whigs had captured the White House, but Greeley was unlikely to be invited to General Taylor's party. "Old Zack," he wrote bitterly a year later, "is a good old soul, but don't know himself from a side of sole-leather in the way of statesmanship." His cabinet too was a "horrid mixture" of incompetent men. "We have done the best we could do," he lamented, "for Freedom and Free Soil."[78]

Although he never joined the Free Soil Party, Greeley learned much from its success in 1848. Its campaign virtually made slavery extension impossible without a national struggle. He praised the "self-forgetting, single-minded champions of Free Soil" for helping stop that extension. He knew he was now an outsider in Whig Washington. He would get no public office (he always coveted Postmaster General), but he joked to Colfax that he would love to be minister or chargé to a Free Republic of Ireland. "Till then," he concluded, "I have office enough."[79]

The Free Soil Party continued to flourish for a time. Greeley spoke at several rallies in Vermont, where the number of party members had doubled between November 1848 and November 1849. But by then, he was feeling some contempt for the party, even accusing them of having allied with pro-slavery Whigs to win elections. Northern Whigs and Free Soilers began to go their separate ways, until the formation of a new Republican Party reunited them. But ideologically, Greeley had become a Free Soil man without joining the party. There should be "no compromise which will admit slavery into the territories," he wrote in early 1850. "Prudence as well as principle abide in the camp of Free Soil." He sought to include a "free soil" plank in Whig platforms in New York. And he concluded with a ringing endorsement: "Let the Union be a thousand times shivered," he wrote, "rather than we should aid you to plant Slavery on Free Soil."[80]

Free Soil was yet another step in Horace Greeley's long journey to define and propagate the ideals of American freedom. Free Soil meant freedom in the West, freedom grounded in land ownership, freedom to labor and improve that land as private property, and freedom for white settlers without competition from black slaves. Free Soil was another variant of Greeley's emerging capitalist utopia of free men in a free society.

Horace Greeley embraced Free Soil ideology, but not its politics. Why? Single-issue third-party politics seemed to him a recipe for political failure at the national level. Anti-slavery needed to be a plank in the platform of a national party—the Whigs, and later the Republicans—and not the entire platform of a minor party. The Free Soil Party in 1848 certainly outpolled the old Liberty Party. It made freedom and free land for white men the centerpiece of anti-slavery. But the 1848 elections were only one moment in the evolving two-party political system and the drive to eliminate slavery in the United States.

Free Soil was utopian politics, a swirling eddy in the moving waters of anti-slavery. Horace Greeley wanted to bring it into the mainstream. He understood its significance, shared its ideology, and supported its actions. But Free Soil was only a brief stop on the long road to freedom, and Greeley knew it.

FREE ELECTIONS: CONGRESSMAN GREELEY

The Free Soil movement of 1848 illustrated that Horace Greeley was first and foremost an editor and a journalist, not a politician. Yet he longed to roam the corridors of power in Albany or Washington, and was perpetually disappointed. While he publicly disavowed any interest in holding office, he lusted privately for just that. In the winter of 1848–9, Greeley was finally appointed to serve out an incomplete term of a New York congressman in Washington. "I was once sent to Congress for ninety days," he later growled to Thurlow Weed, "merely to enable Jim Brooks to secure a seat therein for four years."[81]

Greeley's appointment was a reward for coming out belatedly and unenthusiastically for Whig candidate Zachary Taylor in November 1848. "Our success in 1848," he wrote later, "was the triumph of

General Taylor, if not of our principles." Taylor led the Whigs to victory but knew little about Whig ideology. By winning the election, the Whigs were "at once triumphant and undone," but Greeley's support was lukewarm: "While I frankly avow that I would do little . . . to make General Taylor President," he wrote in the *Tribune* shortly before the election, "I cannot forget that others stand or fall with him . . . to whom I cannot now be unfaithful."[82] If the Whigs could win with Taylor, so be it.

In November 1848, the Democratic incumbent in the mainly Irish Sixth Ward of New York City, David Jackson, was unseated from the U.S. House of Representatives on charges of election fraud. Under the political rules of the day, Whig district electors chose Greeley, a well-known Whig, to fill out Jackson's unexpired term of three months. They also chose James Brooks, another Whig, to run for Jackson's next full term. The ebullient Greeley assured the members of his district that he would continue "the efforts made last summer to aid the people of Ireland in their anticipated struggle for liberty and independence."[83] Ireland, like the rest of Europe, witnessed violent national, liberal, and socialist unrest in 1848. But when Greeley departed for his three months in Washington, he ended up not as an agitator for Irish independence, but as a loose cannon shooting at every target he could identify in Congress.

Washington, DC, in December 1848 was a disorderly and dirty town of some thirty-five thousand inhabitants, many of them black, some slaves. The Washington slave market was a flourishing contradiction of ideals of liberty and freedom for all. Muddy streets often went nowhere except to a dead end. The Potomac Flats incubated malaria and other contagious diseases. The U.S. Capitol was in a constant state of construction with the help of slave labor. Gas lamps had just appeared in the streets to provide nightly illumination. And among the newly arrived congressional representatives were Horace Greeley and Abraham Lincoln.

Despite the fact that he owed his appointment to a few Whig cronies, rather than being elected by the people of his district, Greeley was optimistic and enthusiastic. He predicted to a friend that the issue of slavery in the territories would be "satisfactorily adjusted" at this session of Congress. Congress would admit both California and New Mexico as free states, since "neither of them, if organized now, will tolerate slavery, however friendly to it we may be." By mid-December,

Greeley had filed his own land-reform bill. Any citizen could file for 160 acres of public land. If he settled on it and improved it, he could purchase the land for $1.25 an acre. Local land offices would issue a "warrant of preemption" that guaranteed the claim for seven years. If speculators bought land, it would cost them $5.00 an acre. False affidavits would lead to five years of hard labor in a state prison and loss of land held.[84]

Greeley became notorious quickly because he launched a series of assaults upon Congress itself. He kept track of congressmen absent from votes. He opposed the job of House chaplain and declared it worthless. And he launched a campaign against abuse of mileage reimbursement for travel to and from Washington. As usual, Greeley was ready to save the republic from corruption.

According to the rules of the day, congressmen traveling to and from Washington received eight dollars a day, or forty cents a mile for twenty miles, for coming by the "usually traveled route." On December 22, Greeley published in the *Tribune* a list of every congressman, the number of miles by the shortest route, the number of miles actually charged, and the excess of charged mileage over the mileage by the usual (postal) route. For example, he showed that Congressman Lincoln had traveled 780 miles from Springfield, Illinois, but had charged the public weal for $1,300.80 when the actual charge should have been $676.80. He calculated that overall Congress had charged the public an excess of $62,105.20 for that session, a considerable sum of money.[85]

Congress was outraged, but Greeley persisted. In January, he gave several speeches in favor of a new mileage bill that would have corrected the excesses, but the House roundly defeated it. "There is no disposition in a majority of Congress," announced the much maligned Greeley, "to make its own crooked paths straight." A few days later he wrote Rufus Griswold that he had "divided the House into two parties—one that would like to see me extinguished and the other that wouldn't be satisfied without a hand in doing it."[86]

On January 25, Greeley tried again, attaching an amendment to a bill on funding for the U.S. Army. Under the amendment, military officers "or any other person whatsoever" would be reimbursed according to "the shortest mail route between the points traveled from and to respectively." The government would reimburse travelers only for the "shortest route," not the "usual route."[87] The House promptly ruled Greeley out of order for introducing a general amendment to a bill devoted to army matters.

Mileage was not the only issue for Greeley. He promised a friend in New Hampshire that he would restore his mail route. He worked hard on behalf of a new railroad across the Isthmus of Panama, and spoke out frequently against slavery in the newly acquired territories. He opposed the emerging anti-Catholic, anti-foreign, anti-black "Know-Nothings" and introduced another land-reform bill in committee that would allow any citizen to claim and settle a quarter section (forty acres) with a "right of preemption" that would allow him, within seven years, to purchase the land for $1.25 an acre. (The bill was tabled.)[88]

Greeley also proposed a new boundary between Texas and New Mexico. Another congressman promptly accused him of wanting to "steal from Texas enough land for his Fourierite bill to operate upon." Greeley responded that "land stealing" was what Texas was trying to do to New Mexico. "This question of boundary," he argued, "was more than a mere question of law; it was a question of liberty and right." The people of New Mexico should not have to submit to the people of Texas on the question of slavery. The people of New Mexico should be able to decide a matter of "republican principle."[89]

As his term came to an end, Greeley recognized that he had achieved very little political success. Even the New York delegation of Whigs did not support him on mileage or preemption. Only in 1862 would his far-sighted homestead proposals become law. "I am not very high in the confidence of the Taylor leaders," he wrote a friend. "I don't belong to their particular squad, but to the old Whig phalanx." He could seek no favors from the "new dynasty" until he saw how it "means to behave." "I am about dead with hard work," he wrote his old friend O. A. Bowe. "We can do little good, and may as well go home."[90]

So home he went to New York on March 4 when his term ended. He had failed to achieve much except notoriety. Who could miss the thirty-eight-year-old agitator with his white hair and squeaky voice lamenting the sins of Congress? The *Congressional Globe* mentioned Abraham Lincoln eleven times during this session; it mentioned Greeley seventy-one times. But Greeley and Lincoln had become friends and allies for the first, but not last, time. They voted the same way on bills ninety-five times, and voted differently forty-nine times. On the

December 13 bill to repeal slavery and the slave trade in the District of Columbia, Greeley voted in favor and Lincoln against.[91]

Freedom depends on free elections and representative government. Even during his short term in public office, Congressman Greeley had made his mark by assailing corruption in the republic. Moral reform, not political business as usual, was to be his order of the day. Abuses of mileage reimbursement were but one example of the way corruption threatened virtue in a free republic. Politics was a dirty business in the rude republic of 1849. But citizens had a right to expect their representatives to play by the rules, to be fair and honest, and to represent their interests. Greeley did his best to do that, but showed that he would remain a far better journalist than a politician. Defending freedom could be more easily done in the pages of the *Tribune* than in the halls of a corrupt and immobile Congress.

FREE SPIRITS

Upon his return from Congress, Greeley went back to his office at the *Tribune.* His rambunctious seven-year-old son, Pickie, was "very hearty," although his mother would not let him attend school yet because of its "evil associations."[92] In April 1849, Greeley made a hurried trip of twelve days to Maine, speaking to Whig audiences in several cities. That summer, a cholera epidemic ravaged New York again. One of its victims was Pickie, who died on July 12. The next day one of Greeley's friends at the North American Phalanx, Edmund Tweedy, wrote a friend in Boston that the editor had "lost his darling boy, Arthur Young Greeley, by the cholera. This will be a great blow to his father, for he doted upon the child." Pickie, thought Tweedy, was "almost the only attraction of his home and hearth," given the poor health and mental instability of Molly Greeley. Pickie's death was devastating to both parents. "We had previously lost three children," Greeley wrote to O. A. Bowe, "but all was nothing to this." And to Schuyler Colfax out in Indiana: "We have now lost four children . . . yet we were never utterly desolate till now." Greeley thought for a time that Molly's "health and reason" would not survive the shock of Pickie's death. "I knew," he wrote later in his memoirs, "that the Summer of my life was over, that the chill breath of its Autumn was at hand, and that my future course must be along the downhill of life."[93]

The death of infants and very young children was all too common in Victorian America before the Civil War. Every family, from the White House to the local farm house, had its tragic experiences and stories to tell. Many grieving parents in response to the missing place at the table turned to the belief that they could still communicate with the spirits of their dead children on the "other side." "I cannot help feeling that I have more in the unseen world than in this," the distraught Greeley wrote, "and that all future exertion and achievement must be comparatively lifeless and joyless."[94]

Greeley was one of many deeply religious people who turned to spiritualism in the 1840s. The Universalists were particularly drawn to the unseen world, as they were drawn to temperance and opposition to capital punishment. They began with a belief in immortality, a reasonable and rational God, and the power of all individuals to find their own way to salvation. Every human being was sacred and could be saved. Many Universalists, like Greeley's minister, Thomas J. Sawyer, were receptive to phrenology, the pseudoscience of plotting character and intelligence by measuring bumps on the head. (Sawyer believed that only Jesus was phrenologically perfect.) Others took up listening to spirits rap on tables, undergoing hypnosis, levitating bodies, or having séances. Universalist preachers like Andrew Jackson Davis and Thomas Lake Harris became spiritualists and attracted large followings across the "burned-over district" of upstate New York. They became mediums to the spirit world, holding séances with the dead.[95]

Universalists and spiritualists shared the belief that all die and are saved in heaven, where they become spirits. There is no real barrier between the living and the dead, and no elect that can claim salvation for itself alone. Divine power is visible in the material world. Spiritual science can map that power. Man is morally free to make his own choices, but would in the end be saved. God is benevolent, not malicious or vengeful. The dead are with God in heaven and are in communication with the living.

Greeley had been an active Universalist since before he arrived in New York City in 1831. God ordered all things wisely, he believed, and only Christianity could eliminate that evil and emancipate people from the "ills of our earthly condition."[96] Throughout the 1840s, Greeley wrote articles for Universalist journals. In them, he noted that a true life must be "genial and joyous," grounded in faith in God and

Jesus Christ. "Is not the world yet prepared," he asked, "to realize that, in the fullness of the Christian dispensation is contained the remedy for all evil, for all that is incident to our mortality, even here?" Christians should feed the hungry and house the poor. The goal should be wealth and full employment for all. Universalists should oppose slavery, felt Greeley. He and Thomas Sawyer introduced anti-slavery resolutions at the Universalist Convention in 1843 and got them passed with only one dissenting vote. He was proud of the fact that the Universalists were the "first Christian sect which has declared against Slavery."[97]

Universalism underlay many of Greeley's theories of reform and progress. Man, he believed, conquered nature by his energy, intellect, and civilization. His efforts were heroic and divine. Greeley believed that whites should work for the "elevation of the African race." Men should seek truth, become truly human, and find freedom. Fourier's associationism was still the best solution. Fourier wanted social improvement, without the delusion of "universal perfection." Men could often be lazy and selfish, fallen and divided. But through Christianity, they could be "raised and reunited." War and slavery were evils. Industry should replace war. All men had a right to happiness and freedom.[98] Christian reform could save the world. "To me," Greeley once wrote, "Christ, the Son of Mary and the Son of God, is the actual and veritable Saviour of every child of Adam."[99]

Greeley was affected deeply by two new ministers who arrived to take over the Fourth Universalist Society in New York from Thomas Sawyer. Thomas Lake Harris (1823–1906), a twenty-two-year-old Christian mystic, arrived in December 1845 and stayed for only seventeen months. Born in England, he came to upstate New York as a child and grew up amid the swirling currents of spiritualism, universalism, and socialism that surrounded him. While in New York, he read poems inspired by trances, performed séances as a medium, and organized his own First Independent Christian Society, which Greeley joined. In 1847, Harris met another mystic and seer, Andrew Jackson Davis, and turned for a time to his esoteric brand of Swedenborgianism. Harris then moved on with his followers to western New York and then California.[100]

Greeley was interested in spiritualism, attended spiritualist performances and séances, and watched his brother Barnes become a spiritualist out in western New York. The Kiantone movement, a mix of spiritualism and communism, had its base at Spiritual Springs (Harmonia), a few miles from Greeley's parents' home near Jamestown. Thomas Lake Harris set up his own commune at neighboring Brocton on Lake Erie. The medium Lucinda Colton lived on Spirit Hill a few miles from the Greeley farm. But Greeley remained skeptical. "Don't take this Spiritualism too seriously," he wrote his friend Margaret Allen in Jamestown, "I have known many to turn to it but none to whom it brought comfort or anything but heart-break. I am convinced that Spiritualism has nothing to offer and that there is nothing in the claims of its mediums and prophets."[101]

Not long after Harris left the Fourth Universalist Society, in February 1848, a new minister, Edwin Hubbell Chapin, age thirty-four, came down to New York from Boston as pastor. An accomplished orator, poet, and punster, Chapin quickly gained a reputation as an outstanding preacher. He spoke spontaneously from notes with exuberant wit and charm. Like Harris, Chapin had lived for a time in Utica, New York, and converted to the Universalist faith. He believed in universal restoration and salvation, the continuing progress of humanity, and moral reform of society. He was open and undogmatic in his views. He was also a staunch temperance man who believed in total abstinence from stimulants and alcoholic beverages. And he believed in human Free Will, and the great possibility of universal freedom under the moral direction of a benevolent God.[102]

Chapin took over a church in transition. Housed since 1838 in the rented New Jerusalem Church on Pearl Street, the Society purchased a new church on Murray Street to serve a growing congregation of merchants, many of whom did business in the South as well as the North. The mood of the church under Chapin was unionist, moderately antislavery, reform oriented, temperance minded, and open to all views, including spiritualism. Harris had left his mark on the community. But Chapin would give it leadership and direction for another thirty-two years. His vision was of universal freedom for all as a blessing.[103] Both Harris and Chapin inspired Horace Greeley to deepen his commitment to Universalism, but also to appreciate things of the spirit.

Spiritualism burst out into the open suddenly in 1848 with the appearance in Hydesville, New York, of two remarkable sisters, Maggie and Kate Fox. The daughters of John D. Fox claimed to have heard mysterious rappings in their home that could only have come from invisible spirits. Fox was a Methodist, a blacksmith, and a reformed alcoholic. Hydesville was a small town (forty inhabitants) some thirty miles east of Rochester, and the "Rochester Rappings" made sensational news. According to the girls, during March they heard mysterious noises and vibrations throughout their house over the course of a week. On March 31, the girls imitated the noises and were astounded to receive answering raps. Various witnesses confirmed the existence of spirit communications from the dead. Tourists arrived to see the remarkable house. They rapped out questions and received answering raps in return.[104]

Emmanuel Swedenborg, the Swedish mystic, had long taught that the living could communicate with the dead and the spirit world. (He himself claimed to have had conversations with Plato and Aristotle.) In his arcane and complex writings, Swedenborg claimed that there was a correspondence between the natural and spirit worlds. "Man is so created," he wrote, "as to live simultaneously in the natural world and in the spiritual world."[105] Heaven was an enormous community of deceased friends and relatives with whom communication was possible. Angels had wives and husbands. Many Universalists and Brook Farm intellectuals were drawn to Swedenborg's teachings. Greeley too had his enthusiasms for the Swedish seer.

Pickie's tragic death came at a time when the Greeleys and other New York Universalists were deeply attracted to spiritualism. The idea that Pickie had simply gone to another, better world but could still communicate with his family had enormous appeal for Molly, and even for Horace. In August 1849, Greeley went to Hydesville to see what the mysterious rappings were all about. He wanted, mainly on Molly's behalf, to see if eleven-year-old Kate Fox could contact Pickie, but remained skeptical.

In February 1850, another Fox sister, Leah, escorted her younger sisters Kate and Maggie to Albany for three weeks, and then toNew York City, to demonstrate their powers of communication with the spirit world. In New York, they stayed at Barnum's Hotel and gave séances to paying customers. They gave a demonstration at Rufus Griswold's home, attended by Greeley, George Ripley, James Fenimore Cooper, and other notables, which Ripley wrote up in the *Tribune*. Greeley brought the sisters to his farm at Turtle Bay to hold séances and console Molly. He began to run columns in the *Tribune* sympathetic to the claims of the spiritualists. He became convinced that the entire Fox family had integrity and good taste. Kate conducted a séance at the house, attended by the Swedish singer Jenny Lind, P. T. Barnum's touring "Swedish Nightingale." Greeley's Universalist friend Barnum soon had the Fox sisters on display at his American Museum in New York, where he increased ticket prices from twenty-five cents to a dollar. The Greeleys convinced themselves that Kate Fox was in contact with their beloved Pickie on a daily basis for several months. Whatever the success of her séances, Kate Fox was lonesome and upset with Molly's oppressive behavior, bad food, and isolated and unhappy home. On August 1, 1850, the Fox sisters left New York via the Greeley home and headed back to Hydesville. They had grossed about one hundred dollars a day on their tour.[106]

In his grief, Greeley could not dismiss out of hand the possibility of communicating with Pickie. Spiritualism might be subject to "frauds and impostures," he wrote in the *Tribune*, but there had also been "real and momentous communications from the unseen world." Spiritualist claims should be judged rationally on the basis of available evidence, not dismissed out of hand. Miracles were possible. After all, a convinced spiritualist should also believe that God "did raise Lazarus and Jesus, as recorded in the Gospels."[107] Another *Tribune* staffer, Bayard Taylor, was a somewhat skeptical believer. "Greeley's boy has twice sent a message to me from the spirit-world," he wrote a friend, "at least, a request to speak to me. He lately rapped on the floor a number of lines of poetry, which are said to be quite good. In spite of all, I will not believe that intelligent souls pass their future lives in such trifling employment."[108]

Greeley remained intrigued by spiritualism for the rest of his days, although his enthusiasm in the wake of Pickie's death diminished. "What have you seen or heard about 'Spirit Rappings'?" he asked his old friend O. A. Bowe in August 1851. "Now don't stiffen your (unshort) ears, for *there's something in them!* What it is, I am not yet sure; but it isn't knee-joints or toe-snaps—notwithstanding the wise pill-peddlars of Buffalo." The Greeleys had another baby boy, he told Bowe, "but the loss of the last still weighs." A few months later Greeley wrote his friend Emma Newhall, "About the Rappings. I have seen nothing lately, having no time; yet I have heard a good deal; and I am quite inclined to the belief that *some* super-terrestrial agency is involved in them. They are still growing and spreading." A year later, Greeley wrote in the *Rose of Sharon* that he was "utterly unable to decide" whether spiritualism was serious or not. Despite Christ, we are not even sure about our own resurrection. Living in an age of materialism tried one's faith. But man still lived an "essential and immortal existence."[109]

While Molly continued to assuage her grief with rappings and spiritualism, Greeley remained undecided. "I am sure it cannot be accounted for by merely human agency," he wrote a friend, "it is a puzzle which you will some day be interested to investigate—don't look on it till then." The editor believed that one could not simply reject the existence of spiritual reality. Even "rational beings" could not ignore spiritualism or reject it as a "mere human juggle or imposture." Mediums were not all swindlers. We all need to "open our eyes" and avoid "preconceptions" about the spirit world. Rappings and knockings in the end would be shown to be consistent with nature, reason, and "God the Father of us all."[110]

Pickie's death reminded Greeley of the inevitability of his own death, that "dim pathway to that 'Father's House' whence is no returning." He was certainly saddened and devastated by his son's demise. But his faith in a benevolent God was unshaken. "God is above all, and gracious alike in what He conceals and what He discloses—benignant and bounteous, as well when he reclaims as when He bestows. In a few years, at farthest, our loved and lost ones will welcome us to their home."[111]

When writing down his recollections in his later years, Greeley tended to make light of the story of the Rochester Rappings and to appear more skeptical than he was at the time. The failures of the mediums, he wrote, were "more convincing to me than their successes." "To sit for two dreary hours in a darkened room, in a mixed company, waiting for some one's disembodied grandfather or aunt to tip a table or rap on a door, is dull music at best; but so to sit in vain is disgusting."[112] Such acerbic dismissal was understandable. But death was an all too familiar visitor in the Greeley home, and the hope of communicating with Pickie was more significant in the wake of his departure than the grief-stricken editor would later remember.

Death is an ultimate limit on human freedom. But belief in a victory over death, spiritualist or Christian, promises eternal freedom from the cares of this world. Horace Greeley was a deeply believing Christian Universalist who rarely doubted that his benevolent God would guide his reformist mission, and ultimately grant him a freedom beyond this world. Pickie's death in 1848 tested his deepest beliefs, hardened his faith, and opened the way for him to embrace the hopeful republican revolutions breaking out all across Europe.

5

Trans-Atlantic Republican

1848: FRENCH *LIBERTÉ*

The wave of republican revolutions that swept across Europe in 1848 further helped shape Greeley's idea of freedom. Since 1775, Europeans had looked to the young American republic for inspiration in their struggle for freedom against tyranny, despotism, and aristocracy. Now Europe again, as in 1789 and 1830, witnessed a massive struggle of people and nations against monarchs and empires. In the end, the republics of 1848 and the springtime of nations proved short-lived. Germany, Italy, Poland, and Hungary would have to wait decades for their national unification and liberation. But in the meantime, Greeley and the *Tribune* became a significant lens through which Americans saw the radical republicans of Europe.

The French republican image of liberty leading the people inspired many European immigrants to the United States. The revolutions of 1848 fueled radical trans-Atlantic republicanism and the more violent and prolonged struggle of the American Civil War. In the 1850s, some German liberal exiles in America saw the developing battle between free-labor republicanism and slavery as the "American 1848." Thousands of Germans and Irishmen participated in both struggles. After 1848, as one historian put it, "Central European radicalism found its most direct continuation in the United States, in the struggle against slavery, from the founding of the Republican Party to the outbreak of the Civil War."[1]

More than two million European immigrants arrived in America between 1845 and 1855, half of them Irish, most of the rest German. By 1854, the annual immigration rate was over four hundred thousand. Overall, some five million Europeans arrived in the United States between 1820 and 1860. As a result, the percentage of foreign-born Americans in the general population jumped from 9.7 percent in 1850 to 13.2 percent in 1860. The American population increased during that period by 8.2 million individuals, of whom 2.7 million were foreign-born and brought with them their own concepts of freedom.[2]

In 1848, Greeley and his *Tribune* became a critical switching station in the international network of freedom. Both American and European journalists played a crucial role in Europe that year in articulating the mood of the middle-class public and working classes who dreamed of a better world, national unity, political and social reform, and economic improvement. Greeley too used his newspaper to bring the political rhetoric of Europe into the lives of his American readers. He hired European revolutionaries to write columns for the *Tribune*. He sent his own foreign correspondents to Europe to report on events there. And he helped people understand that the words *liberty* and *freedom* had considerably different meanings in different nations.

Paris ignited the revolutions of 1848, as it had those of 1830 and 1789. On February 24, 1848, hostile crowds gathered in the streets around the Tuileries Palace and forced the abdication of King Louis Philippe, bringing the so-called July Monarchy of 1830 to an end. Barricades of paving stones, furniture, and firewood sprang up across the city. Liberty trees and statues of the goddess Liberty appeared in public spaces. The king fled to England. The National Assembly elected a new provisional government and formed a Second Republic. The new minister of labor, Louis Blanc, organized a series of national workshops to hire the unemployed. New elections were held in April, and radical socialists and workers took to the streets again in May.

Then, in June 1848, the revolution turned violent. Workers went on the rampage across Paris, battling with police and the national guard. The "red peril" was followed by the "white terror." The minister of war, Eugene Cavignac, ordered out the army to suppress the uprising. More than ten thousand people died in the fighting. After restoring order, the National Assembly produced a constitution in November (modeled on the U.S. Constitution) that guaranteed civil liberty, universal manhood suffrage, the separation of powers, and a parliamentary form of government. The Assembly then presided over the election of the forty-year-old Louis Napoleon Bonaparte, a nephew of Napoleon, as president in December. The Second Republic soon became the Second Empire.

Greeley understood that the French have only one word for liberty and freedom: *liberté.*[3] *Liberté* had broader connotations than the

English word *liberty*. *Liberté* remained linked in the popular mind with both *égalité* and *fraternité*. All adult males over twenty-one, not simply men of property, had an equal right to liberty and the vote in the elections of April 1848. And *liberté* was a matter not simply of individual rights, but of popular and national republican sovereignty. When the National Assembly in April 1848 emancipated slaves throughout the French colonies, it illustrated that *liberté* in France meant anti-slavery as well as liberal nationalism. The French also linked *liberté* and republicanism with the United States, the young republic they had helped achieve independence from Great Britain. But within French republicanism, 1848 brought a new division over classes. Bourgeois liberalism faced proletarian socialism across the barricades, creating new tensions in the meaning of *liberté*.[4]

Greeley, like Americans generally, applauded the republican revolutions of 1848 in Europe. "Liberty and order," promised Secretary of State James Buchanan, "will make France happy and prosperous." The U.S. minister in Paris, Richard Rush, promptly recognized the French provisional government. Congress passed resolutions on behalf of republican France. Thousands of citizens celebrated the revolution in City Hall Park in New York City with brass bands, roman candles, rockets, and patriotic songs. William Lloyd Garrison praised the French movement to abolish slavery in its colonies.[5]

The *Tribune* shared American enthusiasm for *liberté* and the new republic in France. Greeley's newspaper provided a long account of the events of February and editorialized that the French people were "worthy of the freedom they have won." They deserved a "new prosperity under a free and enlightened Republicanism." France was America's new sister republic. "The Emancipation of Europe," he prophesied, "has begun in earnest." The year 1848 would mark a "new era of Freedom for Europe," including Poland, Ireland, and other aspiring republics and nations.[6]

To find out what was happening in Europe, Greeley promptly dispatched his colleague, native Vermonter, Brook Farm resident, Fourierist, and Harvard graduate Charles A. Dana, to join his reporter Margaret Fuller in Europe.[7] In February 1847, Dana came to work for Greeley and the *Tribune* as city editor. Greeley paid him fourteen dollars a week at a time when the editor himself made only fifteen dollars. Dana had always wanted to study in Germany, and 1848 gave him his opportunity. Greeley told him that he, Dana, knew nothing about European affairs, but nevertheless offered him ten dollars a week for a letter to the *Tribune* on events there. Dana promptly made similar arrangements with the *Philadelphia American*, the *New York Commercial Advertiser*, the Brook Farm *Harbinger*, and the *Chronotype*.[8] Combined, the work could produce forty dollars a week.

Young Dana was more of a socialist than a liberal republican. "As the revolution of 1830 was the work of the bourgeoisie," he wrote, "so is the Revolution of 1848 the act and deed of the working class, who have sealed the inauguration of their power with their own blood." France was leading the way in establishing human rights and abolishing slavery. "Is the new French Revolution the product of Fourierism or Socialism?" asked editor Greeley in April, answering that "this is the problem of the day, and a great deal is to be said on either side." France, he proclaimed, "has already far outstripped us in the race for Universal Freedom."[9]

The bloody June Days in France gave Greeley pause. The street battles were the most violent conflicts in Europe since the Battle of Waterloo (1815). They were crimes against civilization, tragic events that illustrated the need for order to stem the forces of anarchy. Land reform was important, but only if it helped "sustain republican institutions" and was "conservative of law, order, property, and liberty." Dana, who arrived in Paris on June 23 in the middle of the riots, was also appalled by the violence. He estimated the dead at some twelve thousand people. In his first letter from Paris (June 26), Dana wrote that the "emancipation of labor is the present especial duty and destiny of this nation." The revolution of 1848 was a workers' revolution. Its aspirations went far beyond the limits of liberty and parliamentary democracy to include economic justice and reform. Freedom for workers meant something quite different than bourgeois liberty. "It is vain," Dana warned his readers, "for barbarism and tyranny to attempt to regain the conquests of liberty."[10]

Dana was in his element in Paris during the summer of 1848. He climbed over the barricades, sat in on the proceedings of the National Assembly, and wrote enthusiastic letters home. He visited workers' cooperatives and national workshops. He listened to the speeches of the anarchist Pierre Proudhon. He hoped that the revolution would be non-violent. He expected no new Robespierre and no terror. France had no duty to propagate the revolution elsewhere or to assist "every nation that in the name of *Liberty* invokes her aid." But France was fighting for liberty, Russia for despotism. It was "providential" that France was again leading the "final struggle between Despotism and Liberty." But the revolution would be socialist as well as liberal. "From political to social and industrial *freedom*," Dana prophesied, "the distance at times seems long, but it is not too long for humanity." "It is no longer Fourierism or Communism, nor this nor that particular system which occupies the public mind of France," he wrote, "but it is the general idea of social rights and social reorganization. Everyone is now more or less a socialist." The French Revolution of 1789 had created "political liberty." The revolution of 1848 promised "social liberty."[11]

By October, Dana was convinced that only socialism would produce true freedom for the workers of France. The Assembly represented only the propertied and privileged classes. Universal suffrage would not alleviate economic misery and starvation. France needed a "complete system of Association" along Fourierist lines. The way to spread republican principles was through ideas, not violence. France herself had achieved "popular Liberty." Now, wrote Dana in his last letter from France on October 4, she should "proclaim the era of Universal Emancipation."[12]

Charles Dana correctly perceived that 1848 marked a crisis in European civilization. Socialism had emerged to join liberalism and nationalism as the ideology of the hour. The working classes toiled under a system of wage slavery not that different from slavery itself. Labor reform was a necessity. Cooperation was more important than competition. By the time Dana returned to the United States in March 1849, he was a confirmed socialist. He urged Americans not to fear socialism. He praised Proudhon's ideas on association and a national banking system. France had emerged to defend the "liberties of the world" as their "sheet anchor." He wrote that in Europe the cause was no longer "political oppression or aristocratic privilege," but the "social structure."[13]

On returning to his old office at the *Tribune,* Dana became a shareholder in the newspaper. Greeley promptly made him managing editor and increased his salary to fifty dollars a week. Dana began to live comfortably for the first time. "The struggle for freedom may be terrible," he had learned in France, "but the stagnation of oppression is more so." As managing editor of the *Tribune,* Dana would soon become the major focus for radical republicanism at the newspaper.

Greeley was often out of the office, and Dana was able to translate his French experience of 1848 into a new campaign for freedom in New York. "The republicanism of the Continent," wrote Greeley's early biographer, James Parton, "[came] to a focus at the corner of Nassau and Spruce streets."[14]

With the election of Louis Napoleon, France moved ineluctably from revolution to reaction. The Second Republic gave way to the empire of Napoleon III. French republicanism went underground. The police removed the liberty trees from the streets. Republicanism meant radical opposition to the tyranny of Napoleon *le petit*. Ten thousand republicans and socialists, including Victor Hugo, fled the country. But the dream of *liberté* and universal freedom lived on, especially in America. Dana and Greeley would articulate the republican and socialist elements of that dream through the pages of the *Tribune*, especially in the articles of a young German journalist in London, Karl Marx, who expressed in social-class terms the dream of *Freiheit*.

GERMAN *FREIHEIT*

Horace Greeley recognized that, unlike France, there was no Germany in 1848, merely a complex collection of principalities and states left over from the Napoleonic Wars. But the dream of a free and united Germany as a republic was alive and well in *Libertät*, a medieval concept of liberty associated with guilds and corporate rights, and *Freiheit*, a modern concept of freedom associated with personal and national self-development and emancipation through history, the state, and nationhood.[15] In Germany, liberty and freedom carried quite distinct meanings.

Germany took its cue from revolutionary Paris that year. In March, republican revolutions broke out in Baden, Saxony, Silesia, and Austria. Barricades went up in Vienna, and prime minister Clemens von Metternich fled to England. In Berlin, the Prussian King Frederick William IV recalled his troops and promised a parliament. In Munich, King Ludwig I of Bavaria abdicated his throne in favor of his son, Maximillian II. In Frankfurt, a so-called National Assembly of middle-class representatives met in May to establish a constitution for a new liberal Germany. That summer, liberal intellectuals, lawyers, and journalists incessantly debated the merits of a large Germany under

Catholic Austria versus a small Germany under Protestant Prussia. But the talks ultimately came to nothing. The Austrian army put down an uprising in Vienna in October, and the young Franz Joseph came to the throne. In March 1849, the Frankfurt Parliament offered the throne of a united Germany (without Austria) to Frederick William IV of Prussia, but he turned it down.

Germans who fled to America after 1848 were predominantly anti-slavery republicans. They fanned out across the Midwest, especially to cities like Louisville, Milwaukee, Cincinnati, and St. Louis. Most came for economic rather than political reasons. But they shared the philosopher G. W. F. Hegel's dream of America as a place where freedom as an idea could be realized in history. Gustav Koerner, who had emigrated in 1833, told his fellow Illinois Germans in January 1849 that their "actual liberty" was being sacrificed to the idea of unity in Germany. "The whole nature of man is freedom," claimed the Cincinnati Hegelian Johann B. Stallo. "It is superfluous to mention that lawlessness, the indulgence of momentary caprice, is not freedom but slavery —because it is the subservience of the real nature of man, his reason, to his self-estrangement, his particularities and passions."[16]

German ideas of freedom found their way into the *Tribune* with the eager sponsorship of Dana and Greeley, as the newspaper's German readership expanded. During the 1850s, some 120,000 Germans settled in New York City, making up fifteen percent of the entire city population, the largest collection of Germans outside Berlin and Vienna. Cincinnati, St. Louis, and Milwaukee had even larger percentages of Germans, although fewer in number. Most New York Germans came from southwest Germany and Bavaria. Many were single men or young couples in their twenties and thirties eager to start a new life together. They concentrated in East Side neighborhoods from the Bowery to the East River, where the population quadrupled between 1845 and 1855. Here, in the crowded and dirty tenements and boarding houses flourished a community of enterprising German tailors, shoemakers, cabinetmakers, upholsterers, bakers, brewers, and carpenters. By 1850, more than twenty German-language newspapers appeared in New York City alone.[17]

In January 1850, a German-language New York newspaper, the *New York Staats-zeitung,* announced that it was now the New York agent for a German newspaper, the *Neue Rheinische Zeitung,* edited by one "Carl Marx." Charles Dana had met the thirty-year-old Karl Marx in Frankfort in October 1848 while covering the European revolutions for the *Tribune* and other American papers. In 1850, Marx was a well-known communist on the run from the French and German police. He had fled into political exile and settled with his family in London. Although the two men never actually met, Marx wrote for Greeley's newspaper for more than a decade. Greeley and Marx shared a broader radical republican vision of freedom that went beyond older notions of liberty under the law.

Marx was a harsh critic of the classical liberal ideas of freedom, bourgeois liberty, and legal contracts between workers and capitalists. He saw all values as class-bound ideologies grounded in economic and material forces. The only true freedom would come through communism and the abolition of private property. Marx acknowledged in his early writings that traditional liberty meant "the right to do everything which does not harm others." But in practice, liberty meant the right to own private property, defined the rights of the bourgeoisie, and would never liberate workers from their alienation and oppression by those who owned the means of production, capitalists. In the *Communist Manifesto,* published in 1848, Marx and his co-author, Friedrich Engels, predicted a communist revolution where "association" would produce a society in which "the free development of each is the condition for the free development of all."[18] Freedom for some was class oppression. Freedom for all required economic justice. Bourgeois ideas of freedom, argued Marx, were only the product of a social condition based upon Free Competition.[19]

Greeley himself was drawn toward the labor movement at this time. The condition of the "laboring class," he noted in his presidential address to the New York Typographical Union in January 1850, had hardly improved since he came to New York in 1831. The workers of Paris were far ahead of their American counterparts in their devotion to the "rights of labor." Greeley called for the "union and organization of all workers for their mutual improvement and benefit," through labor exchanges, cooperatives, joint-stock companies, and reading rooms. He encouraged a printers' union to negotiate with employers on wages. Since the 1830s, Greeley had gained a reputation for paying fair wages to his printers and for being a friend of labor.[20] By 1850, that reputation made him about the only newspaper editor in New York trusted by the nascent labor movement.

In 1850, freedom for workers meant the freedom to organize

themselves in trade unions, and even the freedom to go on strike. Greeley favored unions, but not strikes. In late May, he spoke to some six hundred New York printers, many of them Germans, who cheered him on as he proclaimed "good wages are of the first importance for all trades." He called for a twenty-five percent increase in wages for printers, and hoped that a strike would not be necessary. In June, Greeley told a gathering of New York printers that "nothing practical" had been done since January to improve their wages. Yet he did not advocate a strike. Rather, he called for employers to engage in collective bargaining to improve wages ("the adjustment of a scale"). He also encouraged a joint-stock organization of printers to look out for their own interests as a craft. In his 1850 collected lectures and essays over the previous decade, entitled *Hints toward Reforms*, Greeley called for reform, not revolution: meaning land reform, the emancipation of labor, and the gradual elimination of slavery—but not strikes.[21]

But there were strikes in New York in the summer of 1850. Mainly Irish day laborers and German tailors and other tradesmen took to the streets. Police arrested some forty German tailors and locked them up in twelve small cells in a city jail. Among city newspapers, only Greeley and the *Tribune* expressed any sympathy for the strikers, although Greeley continued to favor class cooperation, rather than strikes. By 1851, the wages of New York printers had, in fact, begun to increase and achieve some uniformity, largely because of Greeley's efforts on behalf of organized labor.[22]

In 1851, in the midst of this labor unrest, Charles Dana wrote to his 1848 acquaintance Karl Marx in London to see if Marx would forward a letter addressed to the German exile poet Ferdinand Freiligrath (1810–1876), a member of Marx's Communist League and the former editor of the *Neue Rheinische Zeitung*. Dana also hoped that Marx might write as a foreign correspondent for the *Tribune* to strengthen its appeal to German readers. (There were now eighteen such correspondents.) Marx himself needed a regular income to support his family in London. "Since we met in Cologne," wrote Dana, "the world has made many gyrations and not a few of our friends have been flung quite off its surface by the process. The play is not over, thank God! And they who wait today may have hot work to do tomorrow." Dana suggested that Marx might consider writing some articles about the German revolutions of 1848–9. Marx, busy doing research in the British Museum, was destitute. He agreed to write for the *Tribune* at a rate of one pound for each article. "When you reach New York," he wrote his friend Joseph Weydemeyer in Zurich, "go and see A. Dana of the New York Tribune and give him my and Freiligrath's regards. He may be of use to you. As soon as you arrive, write to me at once, but still care of [Friedrich] Engels, who is better able to afford the postage than any of us."[23]

In August 1851, Marx told his friend Friedrich Engels, then running a factory in Manchester, that Dana had invited them to write for the *Tribune* as "paid collaborators." "It is the most widely disseminated journal in North America," he noted. But Marx's English was much less developed than Engels's. Could Engels possibly send an article in English on conditions in Germany within a few days so Marx could send it on to Dana? "That would make a splendid beginning," concluded Marx. Engels wrote back that he could hardly produce an article on such short notice, and asked more questions about the *Tribune*. "I know nothing about the politics of the New York Tribune beyond the fact that they are American Whigs," he observed, asking Marx for "any other available information that may help me find my bearings."[24]

But Marx was persistent. He claimed he was too busy with his own research on political economy to write a series of articles on Germany in 1848. Engels obliged with his first article based on his memory of events, rather than on the newspapers. Marx found the article "splendid" and sent it on to Dana. "You hit just the right note for the Tribune," Marx assured Engels, "as soon as we get the first number of it, I'll send it to you, and continue to do so regularly from then on."[25]

Engels's letters, which later appeared as a book entitled *Revolution and Counter-Revolution in Germany*, finally came out in October in the *Tribune* under Marx's byline. In them, Engels described historical events driven by a combination of accident and necessity, individual will and social forces. "The sudden movements of February and March 1848," he wrote, "were not the work of single individuals, but spontaneous, irresistible, manifestations of national wants and necessities." The revolutions were born of "class antagonisms," and the alliance of different classes to achieve their freedom was only temporary. In the end, the middle classes proved cowardly and vacillating, throwing their support to monarchs and liberal politicians, fearful of the class violence that raged around them.[26]

But by December 1851, Engels had no idea whether or not his articles had even been published. He urged Marx to write to Dana or
Greeley in English asking them what had happened. They should also
send on copies of the *Tribune* in which the articles had appeared. Marx
should make the same request of Weydemeyer in New York, Engels
suggested. Otherwise Engels could hardly continue the series. Marx
wrote Weydemeyer that he needed to see copies of the newspaper "in
order to write the sequel, which I must do, if only for pecuniary reasons." In January 1852, Weydemeyer obligingly visited Dana at his
office to arrange for the articles to be sent to London—and to be published as a book.[27]

Thus began Marx and Engels's collaboration with the *Tribune,*
which would last until 1862. In all, the two communist journalists produced nearly five hundred articles. Dana was so pleased with the letters on Germany, which concluded in October 1852, that he appointed
Marx foreign correspondent in London and invited him to write on
Great Britain. Marx urged Engels to write somewhat longer articles for
Dana ("If we send him short articles, he will think he is being fleeced
and will cast me out of the temple"). Both Marx and Engels continued
to produce articles, often in German, which Engels translated into
English and which were further edited in New York, where they ran
either unsigned or under Marx's name.[28]

The relationship between the Whig protectionist newspaper and
the London German communist exile was not always smooth. "Mr.
Marx," Greeley editorialized, "has very decided opinions of his own,
with some of which we are far from agreeing, but those who do not
read his letters are neglecting one of the most instructive sources of
information on the great questions of current European politics."
Marx on his part claimed that the *Tribune* represented the "protectionist, i.e. industrial, bourgeois of America."[29] Marx complained that
the newspaper often signed his name to inferior articles and ran the
best ones without a byline. He criticized it for not attacking Russia
and Pan-Slavism more during the Crimean War (1853–6). He asked
for more money for his articles, and got Dana to raise the rate from
five to ten dollars an article in 1855. He threatened to leave if Dana
did not publish all of his submissions. He ridiculed Greeley as a
white-haired armchair philosopher. In 1861, Greeley became tired of
the whole business and asked Dana to fire Marx. After Dana simply

suspended publication of Marx's articles for eight months, Greeley fired Dana.

German *Freiheit* entered American political discourse mainly through the German émigrés who arrived before and after the revolutions of 1848. *Freiheit* was broader than liberty, a radical republicanism that shaded over into socialism and anti-slavery. Many Germans were staunch supporters of free labor and would support the Republican Party in the 1850s. Others were more radical. A speaker at a congress of Germans meeting in Wheeling, West Virginia (still Virginia at the time), in September 1852 argued that "We demand the extension of American freedom! An Empire, not of conquest and of subjugation, not of inheritance, not of international frictions and hatreds, but of fraternity, of equality, and of freedom." Friedrich Engels also appreciated the "thirst for freedom" expressed in the 1848 revolutions in Europe.[30] Liberty had come to mean bourgeois privilege in a capitalist society. Freedom implied worker emancipation.

Horace Greeley recognized the need to improve the lot of workers, but through class harmony rather than class conflict. In 1853, he supported New York journeyman printers in their demand for a wage increase from their employer, the *Tribune*'s rival *Journal of Commerce*. Greeley wrote that the latter journal "talks loudly of 'liberty' but acts autocratically and treats journeymen like slaves." The relations between workers and employers, he argued, should be established on the basis of "Order, Harmony, System, instead of Anarchy, Antagonism, and Chaos."[31] But what did this mean? How could workers obtain their objectives through reform rather than revolution? And what did words like *liberty* and *freedom* mean for people who wondered from where the next meal or the next job would come?

Greeley and Dana brought the European revolutionary and radical republican experiences of 1848 into the pages of the *Tribune* in many ways, none more curious than the articles of Marx and Engels. Throughout the 1850s, the two German communist exiles would remind American readers that economic freedom required more than bourgeois liberty. Their theory of class conflict leading inevitably to revolution hardly suited Greeley's republican ideas of association and class harmony. But the newspaper needed to reach its German readers across the country, and Marx needed money. And Greeley's concept of freedom always included the freedom to publish many writers, ideas, and opinions with which he disagreed.

THE ROMAN REPUBLIC

Horace Greeley recognized that freedom in Italy was no more a reality in 1848 than it was in Germany. In February, Rome proclaimed itself a republic, and Pope Pius IX fled the city, appealing to Austria, France, and Naples for help. That July, French troops entered Rome, and a month later Venice surrendered as well. As in the rest of Europe, republican revolutions gave way to armed intervention and the suppression of rebellion. Giuseppe Mazzini's Young Italy and Giuseppe Garibaldi's Red Shirts vanished before the forces of restoration and reaction.

Liberty in Italy was grounded in a vision of a national civic culture, of social life and political talk on the piazza, a kind of national family or brotherhood of liberal republicans. The word *liberty* to Italians meant equality before the law, male suffrage, freedom of the press, the right of association, and other classical liberal virtues. But it also conveyed an almost religious sense of national unification. Liberty must be "for all and in the sight of all," wrote Giuseppe Mazzini, Italy's leading radical.[32] Liberty was only a means, like duty and faith, to national unification as a republic. Mazzini called for a liberal nationalist revolution made "for the people and by the people"—a commonplace republican phrase of the day made famous later by Abraham Lincoln. True liberty required national unity, and resided in the nation, not the individual. Liberty, equality, humanity, and national unity were all intertwined.[33]

Beside Young Italy stood loosely organized Young Europe and its national clubs—Young England, Young Ireland, Young Germany, Young Hungary, Young Poland, and so on. Radical republicanism became an international and trans-Atlantic movement against the monarchies and aristocracies of Europe. Despite the blight of slavery, Mazzini recognized the United States as the first place where republican principles triumphed over limited monarchy. In Italy, liberty meant the crusade to unify a nation. "Inscribe on one side of your flag EQUALITY and LIBERTY," he told his followers, "and on the other GOD IS WITH YOU."[34]

The Swiss expelled hundreds of radicals in 1836, including Mazzini, who took up lodgings in London and proclaimed himself "head of the republican party of Europe." He opened a free school for Italian immigrant children in Hatton Garden, London, which Margaret Fuller visited. He organized a Young Italy chapter in New York under Felice Foresti, a Columbia University professor deported from Austria a few years earlier. Other Young Italy organizations soon sprang up in Boston, Philadelphia, and New Orleans.

Together with William J. Linton (1812–1897), his English follower and secretary, Mazzini organized the People's International League to spread the ideas of "national freedom and progress."[35] By 1848, Mazzini was the leading republican in Europe, head of a network of young radicals who hoped to overturn the monarchist establishments of the great empires. His moment seemed to have arrived.

Greeley was aware of Mazzini's movement primarily through his correspondence with Margaret Fuller, who was living in Rome in the late 1840s. In her letters to the *Tribune*, Fuller attacked American slavery and war with Mexico. She proclaimed war on tyranny wherever it raised its head, including the United States. Greeley asked Margaret to come home. "Why should you stay?"[36] He continued to send money to Fuller in Rome for her *Tribune* articles, and as loans. He paid her more than the agreed upon ten dollars per letter—"just twice what we pay for any other European Correspondence," presumably including Marx and Engels.[37]

But in July 1849, French and Austrian troops arrived, and the Roman republic came to a bloody end. Greeley railed against armed intervention that summer in the pages of the *Tribune*. Fuller worked in hospitals aiding the wounded. Then she learned from Greeley that the death of the Roman republic coincided with the death of his own son, Pickie, for whom Fuller had served as a surrogate mother when boarding with the Greeleys in 1843. "Ah, Margaret!" Greeley wrote Fuller on July 23, "the world grows dark with us. You grieve, for Rome has fallen; I mourn, for Pickie is dead."[38]

Fuller's life also ended tragically in July 1850 when she died with her husband and infant son in a ship accident off Fire Island, New York. She was returning from Italy, supposedly with a manuscript about the Roman republic and its historical antecedents in her luggage. Her friends mourned her death, and the death of the republican cause to which she had attached herself in Rome. "The best thing we can think to do in these worst news of last night concerning MF," Emerson wrote Greeley, "is to charge Mr. Thoreau to go, on all our parts, and obtain on the wrecking ground all the intelligence and, if possible, any fragments of manuscript or other property [looters were a common danger following shipwrecks]."[39] But the search for the lost manuscript failed to turn up anything.

Two years later, Horace Greeley wrote again about Italy's struggle for "liberty and progress" and bemoaned the loss of Fuller's manuscript. "Knowing intimately and sympathizing thoroughly with Mazzini and other republican leaders in the great movement of 1848," he observed, "her work would have presented that band of heroes more justly and worthily than anything that has been printed."[40] But such was not to be.

The republican ideals of freedom and democracy remained alive when Mazzini and other Italian republicans fled into exile in England, France, Switzerland, and the United States. They emphasized "Union" over individual competition and rejected all proposals for central control of the economy. They also rejected traditional "British liberty" as a cloak for upper-class interests. True republicanism should be based on universal suffrage, equality, anti-slavery, and educated citizens. Republicanism meant freedom, not liberty. "Freedom," wrote Mazzini's follower William Linton, "is the capability of healthily developing one's nature—the opportunity of self-regulation—of self-control. Freedom is the condition of excellence."[41]

Horace Greeley's subsequent visits to Italy only reinforced his enthusiasm for the Italian republican tradition that so enraptured Margaret Fuller. "I saw enough in Tuscany, Papal, Austrian Italy," he wrote, "to make me loathe forever the name of monarchy, and prize more dearly the liberty of our own happy land." Roman republican liberty should be spread throughout the world to help achieve universal freedom. Americans should glory not only in the past traditions of Roman liberty, but in the future promise of "Republican faith, in Republican freedom."[42]

YOUNG IRELAND

Greeley was equally enthusiastic about Irish freedom in 1848. Freedom for Ireland meant freedom from English rule, the right of Irish Catholics to sit in Parliament, and freedom from famine. Parliament should repeal the Union of January 1, 1801, which created the United Kingdom out of England, Scotland, Ireland, and Wales. Repeal men called for a united and independent Irish republic. Dublin mayor

Daniel O'Connell, "the Liberator," led the movement for Catholic Emancipation that would eliminate laws prohibiting Catholics from running for office in Protestant England. Irish republican rebels often found themselves exiled to Australia or other distant parts of the globe. And hundreds of thousands of Irish families sought relief from famine by setting sail for other shores, including America. For Irish republicans, liberty was only another word for English oppression. What they wanted was freedom in an Irish republic they could call home.

Greeley also sympathized with the more than eight hundred thousand Irish who came to the New World between 1825 and 1845, well before the potato blight and the Great Hunger. Two-thirds of them went to Canada, mainly to Nova Scotia, Newfoundland, and New Brunswick. Many were Ulster Protestant tenant farmers, not Catholics. But after 1835, some sixty percent of all Irish emigrants settled in the United States. Most were Catholic, and they believed O'Connell's promise that one day the "full moon of freedom shall beam around your native land."[43]

Horace Greeley, an Irish Scot on his mother's side of the family, was a lifelong supporter of Irish freedom. He wore proudly his Irish linen coat, "the best coat I ever wore. They do good work in the Old Country."[44] He was a public supporter of Irish Repeal. He produced an "Ode for the Meetings of the Friends of Ireland." "Oh, glad was the morning when FREEDOM awoke," he began, "From her slumber of ages in darkness and chains." Ireland, for Greeley, symbolized not only his own family heritage, but the worldwide struggle for freedom and the "Rights of Man." Some day the cause of Irish independence would be "nobly triumphant."[45]

By 1848, Greeley was well connected with the Irish independence movement in New York. He hired William Robinson, editor of the *Irish World*, to write for the *Tribune*. He led the crusade for money and food to assist victims of the potato famine in Ireland in 1847, joined the Tammany Hall Democrats and the Irish Relief Committee, and wrote that the Irish should enjoy "the right of the human race to live." Irish immigrants were welcome in America because they would help "create wealth" by settling on the "untilled lands of the great West."[46]

Most Irish, in fact, did go west to Pennsylvania, Indiana, and beyond. Some 850,000 of them entered New York between 1847 and 1851. Few stayed. There were 133,000 Irish living in the city by 1850, most of them concentrated in lower Manhattan east of Broadway and north of City Hall. Many of these were ditch diggers and day laborers living in squalor. Former smallholders, tenant farmers, and laborers in Ireland, they found themselves among the poor and destitute of American cities. Many of the women entered dressmaking or domestic service in wealthy homes.[47] They seemed no better off than slaves.

In 1848, Greeley became involved with the Young Ireland movement, in opposition to the Old Ireland movement of Daniel O'Connell. Young Ireland urged more radical action toward an Irish republic, reacted favorably to events in Europe that year, and organized its own Irish Republican Union to promote an Irish republic. There were plans to organize an Irish Brigade of volunteers for future use in Ireland. There were fife-and-drum parades, St. Patrick's Day celebrations, and a new Friends of Ireland organization. The Irish Republican Union formed the 9th Regiment of the New York State Militia.[48] Man is naturally free, wrote Irish exile John Campbell, a *Tribune* reporter, and the people must be sovereign. Freedom and equality without slavery should be the goal of all Irishmen everywhere.[49]

In July 1848, Greeley published letters in the *Tribune* that described a great Irish victory over British troops that never occurred. The letters, based on Dublin rumors, were never checked at the *Tribune*. Greeley was off looking at copper mines near Lake Superior, and did not see the letters until they appeared in his newspaper.[50] There were accusations that the whole affair was a deliberate hoax to sell newspapers. Greeley denied it. He was, he claimed, "doing no more for the Irish than we are ready to do for the Poles, the Italians, or the English should they ever convince us they were about to strike for liberty and justice against long endured and galling oppression." Irish patriots were "all for Freedom," and should be liberated.[51]

In September, Greeley wrote Weed recommending two Irish "friends" who "had to leave Ireland, you know why," for aid in "going West" to St. Louis to practice law. He asked Weed to recommend them to Edward Bates, a Whig politician and attorney there. When Irish republicans were tried and sentenced to exile in Van Diemen's Land in October, Greeley protested on their behalf. One was a "martyr to Freedom." His cause would continue. "The march of Freedom is onward," Greeley added, and "all Europe (Russia excepted) will ere long be republican." The whole trial was simply a case of "judicial murder." But Irish martyrdom would "teach us how to live."[52]

Greeley continued to support the Irish republican cause as refugees poured into the United States from Ireland. "The best of Ireland's population," he wrote, was in flight to America. They asked no favors, but fled oppression at home "because they loved liberty." "They are here," he promised, "because they would live only in the Land of Freedom." They needed jobs, money, shelter, and food. Greeley asked Governor Hamilton Fish to oppose extradition of Irishmen accused of political crimes in Ireland. He attended protest meetings and spoke for repeal of the Union with England. He praised Irishmen ready to "fight the battle of freedom." And he helped welcome Irish republican hero Thomas Meagher when he arrived in New York from exile in May 1852.[53]

Greeley may also have been involved in 1853 with Irish republicans in New York City who founded the Irish Republican Brotherhood (Fenians), an armed, secret organization that emerged out of the failures of 1848. The Fenians solicited members and funds from Irish communities and ghettoes in cities across the United States. By 1864, they claimed eighty thousand members inside Ireland. But the degree of Greeley's involvement with, and sympathy for, the Fenians remains unclear. He did help celebrate the arrival of the Fenian leader James Mitchell in December 1853. "The Monarchical East casts me out," proclaimed Mitchell, "the Republican West welcomes and embraces me. One slave the less in Europe—one free man more, America, to thee!"[54]

Many Irish republicans voted Democrat in the 1850s after they became naturalized American citizens. Meagher became an active supporter of Stephen Douglas and a pro-southern Democrat until the Civil War, when he organized the famous Irish Brigade for the Union Army. But for a moment, during and after the upheavals of 1848, Irish republicans found an enthusiastic reception in America that crossed party lines. Greeley and the *Tribune* continued to support the cause of Irish independence. And Irish dreams of freedom became part of the American dream.

EAST EUROPEAN INDEPENDENCE

Greeley also supported Hungarian dreams of independence. In April 1849, Hungary declared its independence from Habsburg rule and chose an attorney, Lajos (Louis) Kossuth (1802–1894), as governor of a new republic. Hungarian freedom fighters drove out the remaining Austrian troops. Kossuth was a romantic rebel and an effective political leader, whom abolitionist Frederick Douglass praised as a "liberator" who "commands the cooperation of the Sons of Freedom everywhere to emancipate the serf and the slave."[55] Kossuth was the leader of the radical party on the Hungarian Diet, a liberal nationalist, and an advocate of constitutional and democratic government for Hungary. He called for freedom of the press, of religion, of education, and of speech, as well as peasant land reform. In April 1849, Kossuth wrote a Hungarian Declaration of Independence that proclaimed Hungarian independence from the Habsburg Empire, now ruled by the young Habsburg emperor Franz Joseph.

The United States welcomed the Hungarian republic at first. Huge rallies were held on behalf of Hungarian independence and the "Freedom of the World." But by August, the Russian Emperor Nicholas I had sent Russian troops to intervene in Hungary. Kossuth resigned as governor, and hundreds of his followers fled with him to Turkey, and then London. Turkey (the Ottoman Empire) interned Kossuth and his followers for a year at Austrian request.[56] The bloody defeat of the Hungarians by the Russians brought to an end the abortive republican revolutions of 1848 in Europe. But the ideals of international freedom and republican revolution remained alive and well in exile. Kossuth became a political hero in America, eager to recruit followers, raise money, and purchase weapons in order to pursue republican schemes. For a time, Kossuth languished in a Turkish jail, until the U.S. Congress voted to send a warship, the *USS Mississippi,* to pick up Kossuth and some of his followers and bring them to safer shores, England and then America. Freed in September, Kossuth was in London by October 1851.[57]

Horace Greeley was much involved in the Hungarian cause of Louis Kossuth. In August 1849, he wrote that "the Hungarians are contending not merely for Liberty but for National existence, and they will hold out to the very last. . . . There is no choice between success and slavery." A few weeks later, he noted in the *Tribune* that all "servants of freedom" should rally in defense of "Hungarian Liberty" and "strike for Justice and Freedom." In March 1850, Greeley addressed a mass meeting in New York in support of Hungarian independence. He declared Austria's crushing of Hungarian independence a "crime." But freedom would ultimately triumph, he promised, because the worldwide commitment to freedom was not affected by the "accidents of Fortune," such as Kossuth's failure and exile. In May, he wrote Thurlow Weed urging him to push the new president, Taylor, to support "the Republicans of Europe." Taylor, said Greeley, should dismiss Lewis Cass, the U.S. representative in Rome, who was continuing to spread "the most atrocious libels on Kossuth, Mazzini, Ledru-Rollin, and every Republican leader in Europe."[58]

Greeley caught the "Kossuth fever" that swept England and the United States in the winter of 1851–2 as the famous Hungarian republican exile launched a triumphant fund-raising tour. Thousands greeted the *Mississippi* when it brought Kossuth and his followers to Southampton on October 23. Nearly half a million people later heard him speak in Birmingham, but many were confused. Was Kossuth a Free Trade liberal or a radical republican? Where did he stand on working-class goals? On slavery? No one really knew. He seemed to emphasize national independence and Free Trade, more than political and social reform. He was neither a socialist nor a classical liberal. He did not define words like *liberty* and *freedom*.[59]

Austria was furious. The Austrian representative in Washington did not relish the idea of a Hungarian rebel on the loose in America, especially with American government sponsorship. He wrote Secretary of State Daniel Webster that the United States wanted to "interfere" in European politics. If Kossuth came to America, he wrote, "the socialist wing of the Whigs, led on by Mr. Greeley, will do their best to keep Kossuth on their side; but the large conservative division of the Whigs will be inevitably thrown into opposition to him."[60]

On December 5, 1851, Kossuth arrived on Staten Island to a tumultuous welcome. "The spirit of liberty," he proclaimed, "has not only spiritually, but materially, to go forth from your glorious country, in order that it may achieve the freedom of the world." American liberty would give birth to universal freedom. During his speaking tour of the United States, there would be Kossuth marches, hats, buttons, flags, dances, restaurants, and even oysters. "Kossuth fever" infected virtually all Americans as the man Emerson called the "angel of freedom" brought his case before the jury of American public opinion.[61]

"I am a republican," promised Kossuth in a December 6 speech to the New York City common council, a "plain, straightforward man, a faithful friend of freedom—a good patriot."[62] Senator William Henry Seward welcomed Kossuth to his home in Auburn, New York, and then to Washington, DC, where he sponsored a congressional resolution favoring Hungarian independence. Seward wrote a friend that the ecstatic reception for Kossuth was ironic, given American slavery. "How strange that people will go mad for the freedom of *white* men, and mad *against* the freedom of black men." But Kossuth's call for American intervention in Europe, his Free Trade liberalism, and his refusal to condemn slavery soon cooled American opinion. Antislavery Senator Charles Sumner feared that "Kossuth has made a great mistake. By asking too much, he has missed a great opportunity of impressing the country."[63] But Greeley still praised Kossuth as a hero of "Hungarian Independence and General Freedom." He promised to give one thousand dollars to the cause. "I am the enemy of the Kingcraft and Priestcraft under which Europe is now crushed," he wrote a friend in Massachusetts, "and am determined to fight it to the death."[64]

Kossuth found a warmer reception when he went west on a speaking tour in early 1852 to Pennsylvania, Ohio, and Illinois. In Springfield, Illinois, Congressman Abraham Lincoln—who publicly supported the Hungarians in 1849 in their "glorious struggle for liberty"—attended Kossuth sympathy meetings, supported an invitation for the Hungarian to visit Springfield, and drafted a "Resolution on Behalf of Hungarian Freedom." In it, Lincoln supported the right of any people to "revolutionize their existing form of government." Kossuth was "the most worthy and distinguished representative of the cause of civil and religious liberty on the continent of Europe." He deserved the support of the "friends of freedom everywhere."[65]

Kossuth also found support among Democrats drawn to the expansionist and nationalist Young America movement. George N. Sanders of Kentucky, the newly named editor of the *Democratic Review,* had witnessed Kossuth's triumphal entry into New York and promised to help him with money and weapons. He also warned Kossuth not to speak out against slavery, or use "theoretic liberty" or other abstractions, because he would alienate southern slaveholders. In January 1852, Kossuth reminded Sanders of his promise to help Hungary with money and weapons. "The struggle in Europe can no longer be delayed," he warned.[66]

In February 1852, Horace Greeley caught Kossuth fever and wrote an introduction to an instantly popular biography by P. C. Headley entitled *The Life of Louis Kossuth.* In it, Greeley praised Kossuth as one

of the many popular leaders who were "upheaved by the great con-
vulsions of 1848" into the "full sunlight of European celebrity and
American popular regard." "Our fathers," he wrote, "declared all men
rightfully born free and equal, but left one million of their own countrymen in slavery." Kossuth was a living embodiment of the American
Declaration of Independence. He had helped emancipate the serfs in
Hungary in 1849, an example that showed only the "hollowness of
our boasted love of liberty." Other books praised "Hungary's freedom," her independence, her "struggle for freedom," and Kossuth as
an "eloquent champion of freedom for an entire continent."[67]

On February 6, Kossuth himself made an even more indelible
impression when he told the Ohio state legislature that "the spirit of
our age is Democracy. All for the people and all by the people. Nothing about the people without the people. That is democracy."[68] Like
Mazzini's government "of, by, and for the people," Kossuth's language would enter American republican political rhetoric.

By the time he left America, in July 1852, Kossuth's popularity had
waned. Plots with southern adventurers helped link Kossuth with the
states'-rights liberties of the South, rather than the anti-slavery republicanism and freedom of the North.[69] Despite an outpouring of sympathy for his cause, he had raised less than one hundred thousand
dollars and spent most of it on his fellow exiles before he disem-
barked. When he tried to borrow ten thousand dollars from George
Sanders to purchase more rifles, Sanders stalled him off. He also asked
Sanders to pay for printing counterfeit Hungarian banknotes and buying a steamship, but without success. Kossuth left America penniless,
in debt, and without the weapons and munitions.[70]

Even in London exile, Kossuth and Sanders continued their
scheming after the election of Democrat Franklin Pierce as U.S. president in November 1852. Pierce appointed a number of Young America
enthusiasts to diplomatic positions in Europe. He named Sanders to
the London consulate, only to have the U.S. Senate fail to confirm
him in 1854. Kossuth asked Sanders relentlessly for money and weapons for the cause of freedom in Europe. So did Mazzini and Garibaldi. But Sanders remained a shadowy link to European revolutionaries who would reenter Greeley's life later under much different
circumstances.[71]

Kossuth's legacy to Horace Greeley and American freedom was
largely rhetorical. Both men shared the dream of universal freedom

grounded in American liberty. Yet they were deeply divided over the question of slavery, which Kossuth chose to avoid and Greeley to confront. "Poor Kossuth!" wrote abolitionist Maria Weston Chapman, "The anti-slavery cause is dearer to me than other things, because its principles include all other things. If it were *only* the freedom of the Negroes, or *only* the freedom of Hungary, I could not honor it so much."[72] In America, the freedom of Hungary meant little without the emancipation of slaves.

Horace Greeley was as uninformed about the Poles as he was about the Hungarians in 1848. Polish *liberty* had a long tradition grounded in the legal rights of the nobility, famously symbolized by the *liberum veto*, or free veto, which allowed any single noble representative to the Polish parliament, or *sejm*, to veto any piece of legislation. The romantic Polish cult of *freedom*, on the other hand, was a product of modern national consciousness and republicanism. Although Poles tended to use the same word for liberty and freedom, *volnosc*, they recognized that "*freedom* [meant] the amassing of *liberties* rather than Liberty."[73] The Polish people dreamed of a new freedom from oppression by imperial Russians, Prussians, Austrians, and by their own nobility.

In 1830–1, the Poles made a noble attempt to emancipate themselves from the Russian imperial rule imposed by the Congress of Vienna in 1815. Thousands of Polish volunteers fell in battle to Russian troops sent in to quell the uprising. Five thousand veterans fled to Paris. The Poles wanted not liberty, but freedom. One slogan of the uprising read "For Our Freedom and Yours!" Samuel Gridley Howe of Boston, at the age of twenty-nine already a veteran of the Greek War of Independence, raised money for the Polish rebels through his friend Lafayette in Paris that year. And James Fenimore Cooper continued to exert himself on behalf of Polish republicans during and after the revolution.[74]

Greeley came into firsthand contact with Polish republicanism through the person of Adam Gurowski (1805–1866), who worked for the *Tribune* in the 1850s as an editor and columnist. Gurowski was one of the most colorful and remarkable men of his day. His friends called him simply "the Count," whatever the nobility of his lineage. Greeley loaned him three hundred dollars upon his arrival in New York, but the Count, a notorious borrower, never repaid the editor. Gurowski was an irascible character, a gossip, and would-be philosopher. He believed in a great future for the Slavs, and could "express his wrath in a great many languages," as one *Tribune* staff member put it.[75]

Gurowski, at age twenty-five, was active in the Polish rebellion of 1830–1, fought against the Russian army, and fled to Paris, where he hobnobbed with Lafayette before he became another isolated and frustrated Polish exile. "I tried to establish the republican government, and whose disastrous end threw me upon the world as a condemned exile," he recalled. "A homeless wanderer over the world, I reached America."[76]

After 1831, Gurowski became a journalist and an admirer of the Slavs. Amnestied, he worked in St. Petersburg, probably for the Russian political police, the Third Section. In December 1834, Gurowski published a pamphlet entitled *The Truth about Russia and the Revolt of the Polish Provinces*. In it, he argued that Russia was superior to Poland and had a God-given mission to save Poland from another revolutionary catastrophe such as 1830.[77]

Throughout the 1840s, Gurowski wandered about Europe, publishing his thoughts and impressions on Poland and the Slavs. He conspired with radical republicans. He reiterated Hegel's view of the historical mission of the Slavs and called upon Nicholas I to emancipate the serfs (something his son Alexander II would do only in 1861). Finally, shattered by the failures of 1848, Gurowski fled to the United States.[78]

When Gurowski arrived in the United States, he renewed his old acquaintanceship with Cooper, Howe, and Howe's wife, Julia Ward Howe, who introduced him to friends in Cambridge and Boston. He tried teaching law at Harvard for a time, established contacts in the Boston area with a number of leading intellectuals, and took on odd jobs at Harvard (he was a gardener for a time) and the Boston Museum of Fine Arts. He wrote articles on European affairs. By 1852, Gurowski had moved to New York City, where he went to work as a Russian expert for the *Tribune*.[79]

Throughout the 1850s, Gurowski added a Polish and Russian perspective to Greeley's newspaper, with articles on Russian and European affairs. (He wrote them illegibly in French, so that they required both translation and interpretation before appearing in English.) He wrote pro-Russian articles during the Crimean War (1853–6), for which he received some money from the Russian ambassador in Washington, Baron Stoekl. His book *Russia as It Is* appeared serially in the *Tribune* before publication in April 1854. In it, Gurowski criticized Russian autocracy as "bloody, pitiless tyranny" but glorified "ancient Slavic freedom" and "Polish democracy." A year later he wrote *A Year of the War* on the Crimean War, pleasing ambassador Stoekl enough that he sent a copy on to St. Petersburg. Gurowski also rewrote and edited some of the articles contributed to the *Tribune* by Marx and Engels, sometimes adding his own views to make them more favorable to the Russians. He also suppressed at least seven letters of which he did not approve. Marx and Engels simply assumed that Gurowski was a Russian spy. "We thus have also the honor," Marx wrote Engels in 1856, "that our articles are, or rather were, directly watched over and censored by the Russian embassy."[80]

Gurowski thoroughly enjoyed his job as editor, critic, and nuisance. "I can abuse everybody in the world," he wrote, "except Greeley, Ripley, and Dana." In addition to his *Tribune* job, Gurowski also contributed to the *New American Cyclopedia*, edited by Dana and Ripley. Marx and Engels were annoyed to learn that Gurowski was editing and altering their submissions. They assumed correctly that the eccentric Pole was in the pay of the Russians, either through the police or the embassy in Washington. "The devil take the *Tribune!*" wrote Marx in 1855, "certainly it is now absolutely essential that it should adopt an anti-pan-Slav line. If it doesn't, one might be compelled to break with the rag, which would be disastrous."[81]

In the 1850s, Gurowski became a well-known and colorful radical republican in both Boston and New York. Boston Unitarian minister Theodore Parker considered Gurowski a man of "famous family, ancient and patrician," who became a "fugitive from Russian despotism."[82] By 1861, Gurowski had moved to Washington, DC, where Charles Sumner got him a job translating German newspapers at the State Department. Gurowski quickly became a thorn in Lincoln's side as an abolitionist, radical-republican critic of administration policy. Gurowski crossed the path of Horace Greeley many times between 1850 and Gurowski's death in 1866. He ultimately became a fervent anti-slavery man, but retained his opportunist charm and ability to get money out of a wide variety of people.

Greeley's other expert on Russian and Polish affairs was Ivan Golovin (1816–1890), a liberal Russian army officer and diplomat who lived and studied in England, France, and Germany in the 1840s. In 1846, he produced *Russia under the Autocrat*, published in Paris in both

French and English translations in two volumes. In the book, Golovin described Russia as the most "wretched of countries" and added that "slavery has never been the education for freedom."[83] Liberty was unknown in Russia, where millions of oppressed serfs—"white Negroes"—needed their freedom. Golovin also published *A Russian Sketchbook* in 1847 and *Catechism of the Russian People* in 1849.

Golovin did not enjoy a good reputation among his fellow Russian exiles. He played the stock market in Paris and joined the elite Jockey Club; he was described as an "insolvent and quarrelsome man"—tactless, outspoken, illogical, and at times incoherent. In July 1849, the French police expelled Golovin from the country for publishing an article critical of the future Napoleon III. He moved on to Geneva, Nice, Belgium, and finally London, where he became a naturalized British citizen. He arrived in the United States in February 1855 and promptly began writing for Greeley and his *Tribune*.[84]

Meanwhile, Adam Gurowski continued his assault on Russian despotism in his *Russia as It Is* (1854). The "bloody, pitiless tyranny" of Nicholas I in Russia suppressed freedom, and serfdom in Russia was no better than slavery in the United States. America's "manifest destiny" was to extend freedom, democracy, and self-government worldwide.[85] A year later, Gurowski published a much more favorable book about Russia entitled *A Year of the War*, probably subsidized by the Russian representative in Washington. In it, he noted that, while Russia had never been an "apostle of constitutional liberty," neither had she suppressed it in other countries (ignoring Hungary in 1849). Russia was the lesser of two despotisms, the other being the Ottoman Empire. Russia and America both had a great future and mutual interests, independent of old Europe.[86]

When Ivan Golovin arrived in New York in early 1855, he established himself at the St. Nicholas Hotel and met some of Kossuth's followers, along with the editor of the *Democratic Review*, George Sanders. He soon began to write for the *Tribune*. Sanders and his wife, Anna, considered Golovin a Russian agent or spy who "pretends to be a Republican," but was in reality "a Russian agent and a slanderer of the European republicans."[87]

Despite such charges, Golovin continued to write for the *Tribune*. In 1856, he published his impressions of America as a book entitled *Stars and Stripes*. He praised the "republican freedom" of the United States, tarnished only by the "disastrous" institution of slavery. The "manifest destiny" of the country, if it did not emancipate the slaves, would be disunion. "The abcess must burst," he predicted. The great struggle between freedom and slavery was "at the bottom of all American complications."[88]

Tribune columnists Gurowski and Golovin—like Marx and Kossuth—showed American readers a Poland and Russia with republican hopes and dreams, even in the aftermath of the failed revolutions of 1848. These two "advocates of Freedom in America," as Greeley pointed out, recognized that "the preservation of the Ark of Liberty rests with us alone."[89] Indeed, the republican refugees of 1848 in Europe were crucial in cementing Greeley's view—informed already by Whig politics, Universalism, Pickie's death, and spiritualism—that American liberty would someday become universal freedom. But American freedom was still a fragile reed in a republic of virtue. Unless something was done about slavery soon, the United States might well face her own 1848, and suffer the same defeats and disappointments.

6

American Republican

HIGHER LAW POLITICS: THE COMPROMISE OF 1850

America might well have succumbed to her own revolution after 1848 but for the Compromise of 1850. The discovery of gold in California had produced a gold rush into the territory and higher prices in the East. Immigration of Germans and Irish to eastern cities was increasing, leading to over-population, hunger, and poverty. Labor unrest and strikes plagued urban factories. The addition of new territories after the Mexican War raised the question of whether new states added to the Union would be slave or free—the so-called Free Soil issue. Slavery, sectionalism, and industrialization all threatened social and political dislocation and disunity. Failure to compromise might well mean the secession of the South or North from the Union, or even civil war.

The compromise, passed by Congress and signed into law by the president, was complex. In return for admitting California to the Union as a free state, other Southwest territories acquired from Mexico after the Mexican War would be added without restriction regarding their free or slave status. The United States would assume Texas's debt and define its boundary along the Rio Grande River. In return for abolishing the slave trade in the District of Columbia, slavery would still be permitted there. In addition, southern slave owners could recapture their fugitive slaves in the North with the help of federal warrants and commissioners—a diabolical and immoral scheme in the eyes of northern abolitionists. Finally, Congress would have no legal right to interfere in inter-state slave trade.

The dying Henry Clay and Senator Daniel Webster both helped push the compromise through the halls of Congress. Clay appealed to his listeners to save "the Union." The ill John Calhoun, wrapped in flannels, watched the proceedings. Failure to pass the legislation, they

warned, would result in an American 1848, a bloody civil war between North and South. Boston abolitionist Theodore Parker warned
of a giant struggle between freedom and slavery, the two principles
now contending for power. In the end, the winner must be "the idea
of freedom," that is, "a government of all the people, by all the people,
for all the people."[1]

Greeley initially opposed the Compromise, despite Clay's role in
it, as a victory for the southern "slavocracy," as he called it, that dominated Congress. "Slavery," he wrote, "is not a mere industrial institution in this country, and does not depend for its existence on profits
alone. It is a great political machine, whereby the minority in the
Republic has long ruled the majority." Texas was trying to steal New
Mexico and make it a slave state. The Compromise of 1850 violated
the Missouri Compromise of 1820 that allowed states to be admitted
only in pairs, one slave and one free. The "cause of Freedom," he
wrote Thaddeus Stevens, required Americans to add no more slave
states to the Union. The Compromise was either "gross incompetency" or "flagrant treachery." The great issue facing the country, he
wrote Thurlow Weed, was "slavery extension." The territories acquired from Mexico should only be added to the Union as free states.
In February, he addressed the South in the *Tribune*: "Let the Union be a
thousand times shivered rather than we should aid you to plant slavery on Free Soil."[2] Disunion was better than continued slavery.

The Compromise of 1850 only helped fuel the fires of the slavery
question. Which was higher: human laws or the moral law? Congress
or God? For years, British and American abolitionists had argued that
Christianity and the moral law trumped any laws enacted by Parliament or Congress. But what if human laws violated divine law?
Was civil disobedience justified? Thoreau thought so. So did Theodore
Parker, who considered slavery a mortal sin, as well as Salmon P.
Chase, an Ohio attorney who considered slavery against natural rights
and argued in court that God gave every human being an equal right
to freedom. In England, member of Parliament Henry Brougham told
Parliament that "by a law above and prior to all the laws of human
law givers, for it is the law of God—there are some things which cannot be holden in property, and above everything else, that man can
have no property in his fellow-creature."[3]

Among the supporters of Higher Law theory in the United States
was William Henry Seward, former governor of New York, a political

mentor and ally of Greeley, and now a U.S. Senator. Seward's March 1850 attack on slavery in the name of a Higher Law shocked the nation and introduced the language of Higher Law doctrine into the national political discourse. But his interest in the doctrine was long-standing.

Higher Law doctrine was a "settled principle" of Seward's life by 1840. Seward believed that all men, including slaves, were "entitled of right, by the Constitution and the laws, and by the higher laws of God himself, to equal rights, equal privileges, and equal political favor, as citizens of the State, with myself." Seward's father had owned slaves, and Seward taught school in Georgia when he and his abolitionist wife, Frances, traveled in the South in 1835. (The British abolitionist Harriet Martineau helped convert Frances to the abolitionist cause.) Throughout the 1840s, Seward the Whig politician spoke of "moral sense" and the "universal laws of civilized countries" with regard to slavery. Gradually, his wife's opinions and the changing political times drew him into the anti-slavery camp. He railed against the Fugitive Slave Acts of 1793 and 1850. He spoke of "divine laws, paramount to all human understanding" that were higher than the U.S. Constitution. And in 1850, Seward propelled Higher Law concepts of freedom into national political discourse.[4]

In mid-February 1850, Seward wrote Greeley and asked him to review a speech he was about to give in the Senate on slavery. Greeley agreed, and made a number of suggestions that Seward found helpful.[5] On March 11, speaking to the Senate in a husky voice to a rapt and divided audience, Seward attacked Henry Clay and the entire Compromise of 1850. The battle was now between slavery and freedom, he thundered. The Constitution, devoted to principles of union and liberty, was not the final arbiter of the matter. There was a "higher law than the Constitution, which regulates our authority over the domain, and devotes it to the same noble purpose"—God's higher law.

Greeley, who sat through some of the Senate proceedings on the Compromise with Charles Dana, applauded his fellow Whig New Yorker. Seward's speech was "what it should be," he wrote in the *Tribune*. "It uttered the voice of the great State of New York and of Freedom." New York, of course, was as divided as the rest of the country on the matter of slavery. But Seward's speech, averred Greeley, would "live longer, be read with a more hearty admiration, and exert a more potential and pervading influence on the national mind and character than any other speech of the session." Greeley reprinted Seward's speech in entirety in the *Tribune* and published another fifty thousand copies for distribution across the country. Perhaps Seward could be the next Whig candidate for president in 1852. "You have read Seward's speech," Greeley wrote his friend Schuyler Colfax in Indiana, "Isn't it sane? If he can only maintain that position, he is our hope for 1852."[6]

In April, Greeley published his collected essays from the 1840s as *Hints toward Reforms.* He stood forth passionately for reform in the name of noble ideals—temperance, justice, peace, and truth, the virtues of the American farmer. He called slavery a "rebellion against God."[7]

In July 1850, President Zachary Taylor died of gastroenteritis and was succeeded by Millard Fillmore. Fillmore was an old political rival of Seward in New York who supported both the Compromise of 1850 and the Fugitive Slave Law. With Fillmore in office, Greeley moderated his attack on the Compromise. "The passage of the bill," he wrote on July 23, "would be more auspicious to the cause of Freedom than its defeat." A few days later he called the Compromise a "fair and equal compromise of the questions on which the North and the South are at issue."[8] Greeley was, in fact, already thinking ahead to the next presidential election (1852) and who should succeed Fillmore as the Whig candidate. "We shall probably run General [Winfield] Scott for next President," he wrote Colfax, "and probably get flogged at that."[9] He urged compromise to avoid civil war.

Higher Law doctrine continued to enflame the debate over slavery over the next several decades. "Wicked laws," wrote one critic, "not only may be broken, but must be broken."[10] Moreover, Seward's injection of Higher Law doctrine into the national political debate over slavery provided a critical new element in the quest for American freedom. Greeley himself rarely articulated the doctrine, knowing that it would have linked him too closely with the abolitionists. But he praised Seward for introducing Higher Law into American politics. As a Universalist and a Christian, Greeley recognized the ultimate significance of divine moral law in the struggle for universal freedom. As the U.S. Constitution and the recent debate in Congress indicated, liberty under the law condoned slavery, whereas freedom under the moral law required emancipation.

THE CRYSTAL PALACE

In 1851, following the Compromise, Horace Greeley made his first trip to Europe. In fact, his fellow editors at the *Tribune* urged him to do so, both to attend the famous "crystal palace" exhibition in London and, perhaps, to get him out of the office for a while. (The formal title of the world's fair was the Great Exhibition of All Nations' Industry.) In December 1850, the editor was still lukewarm about going, even though he admitted that he might learn something from the visit. Greeley remained an Anglophobe, remembering the War of 1812, the continuing flight of the impoverished and brutalized Irish from Britain to America, and the unfair competition of English goods with American manufacturers under the doctrine of Free Trade. The London exhibition celebrated Free Trade, but Greeley was a protectionist. It celebrated British progress, but Greeley was an American. England was a monarchy, but Greeley was a republican. English liberty seemed but a cloak for power and privilege, whereas American freedom was open to all who worked on its behalf.

Despite his Anglophobia, Greeley was excited by the opportunity to test American manufactured goods against competition from Europe in the world's great emporium, London. The latest developments in industry, agriculture, and technology would be on display. Moreover, he could see firsthand the Europe to which he had sent Charles Dana and Margaret Fuller in 1848. "I am going to the World's Fair," he wrote Schuyler Colfax in February, "poor business, but our concern wants me to go."[11] Indeed, Greeley's trip to Europe reminded him that freedom depended not only on legal rights and justice, but also on technology and economic productivity.

Greeley traveled on the latest technology at a time when steam travel was replacing sail and carriage. He planned to be in Europe without Molly until the end of the summer. Perhaps the trip would give him some rest and a chance to cool his "fevered brain." On April 16, 1851, Greeley set sail for England on the *Baltic*. Twelve days later, after a storm-tossed voyage and considerable seasickness, he arrived in Liverpool and rode the Trent Valley Railway to London. He then took a carriage to the home of a fellow publisher, John Chapman, with whom he stayed.[12]

The exhibition opened on May 1. The Crystal Palace was a gigantic building of glass and steel constructed on a twenty-acre plot of land near Hyde Park, London, by Joseph Paxton. Two hundred miles of wooden sash bars held together a million square feet of the glass. In five months, some six million visitors would attend the exhibit, the first "world's fair" of its type. Critics naturally pointed out that behind the façade of progress and prosperity lay the poverty, disease, smog, and filth of British working-class slums. Yet the Crystal Palace was a thing of beauty, a giant greenhouse celebrating human achievement with endless exhibits. "The Crystal Palace," wrote Greeley, "which covers and protects all, is better than any one thing in it."[13]

In May, American organizers designated Greeley to serve as a jury chair for a technology exhibit that included metals, gas generators, heat diffusers, and agricultural machinery, including the first McCormick reaper. In addition to his time at the exhibit, Greeley toured London, observing Queen Victoria at a parade and visiting model homes for workers, a public bathhouse, and a school for working-class children. He met Charles Dickens at a play and attended socialist Robert Owens's eightieth birthday party at the Colbourne Hotel. Greeley also attended the annual meeting of the British and Foreign Anti-Slavery Society, where he gave an impromptu fifteen-minute speech. In it, he praised free labor and attacked slavery, noting that the British could improve their own labor conditions, for which he received only polite applause. "Political freedom," he promised, "such as white men enjoy in the United States, and the mass do not enjoy in Europe, not even in Britain, is a basis for confident and well grounded hope."[14]

In June, Greeley crossed the English Channel from Dover and spent a week in Paris admiring the sights. He marveled at the Cathedral of Notre Dame, and visited the Hotel de Ville, where revolution had broken out in 1830. He spent two days wandering the corridors of the Louvre Museum, but found the building too low. Paris was a city of enjoyment, not happiness. French railroad porters were incompetent. And he predicted that the new Emperor, Napoleon III, would not last long in power. He then took a smoke-filled train to Lyons, then another train across the Alps to Turin, Italy.[15]

In Italy, Greeley spent a week in Rome before conducting a whirlwind tour of Pisa, Florence, Padua, Bologna, Venice, and Milan. By July 21, he was back in London after traveling quickly through Switzerland, Germany, Belgium, and France.

Again in London, Greeley visited the fourth (and final) annual international peace conference, along with Charles Sumner, Richard

Cobden, Alexis de Tocqueville, and the leader of the U.S. delegation, Elihu Burritt.[16] Sumner was on the steering committee of the congress, while Burritt headed the American Peace Society. Some three thousand people attended. The congress—the last in a series that began in 1848—featured lots of talk about the evils of war and the need for disarmament and a congress of nations. But Greeley was disappointed, finding talk of peace unreal and unacceptable as long as Europe's tyrannies and aristocracies survived. Without republican revolutions in Europe, war was unavoidable. Greeley also visited the Crystal Palace again, where the McCormick reaper was attracting admiration after an initial period of skepticism. The editor spent his final week touring Edinburgh and Glasgow, then Galway in Ireland. He returned home on the *Baltic* on August 6.

Overall, Greeley's European tour was a grand success. He played a central role in the greatest exhibition of modern technology ever assembled, and hobnobbed with famous people, including the Baltimore investment banker George Peabody. Throughout the trip, he sent back articles on his travels and experiences to the *Tribune*. The *Cleveland Plain Dealer* reprinted the articles with the comment, "Whatever opinion we may entertain of the justness of Mr. Greeley's inferences, we do not for a moment doubt his ability or zeal in the discovery of facts." (Greeley's rival *New York Herald,* to the contrary, wrote that "Horace Greeley's letters are about as silly as anything of the kind can be.") The Crystal Palace, Greeley believed, showed the great promise of universal peace and freedom through the cooperation and industrial progress of all nations. The "liberties of nations" were on display through their technical and cultural accomplishments. But Scots drank too much whiskey and British trains were slower than American trains. Greeley relentlessly defended American interests against the carping criticism of the British press. After 1848, Europe was involved in the "last decisive struggle" for "Justice, Opportunity, and Freedom."[17] The future of freedom depended on the industry of man, as well as on virtuous republics.

American manufactured goods had also done well in London, winning more awards than the vaunted British. The yacht *America* beat the British *Titania* in the first "America's Cup" race (not yet called by that name). Samuel Colt's revolvers, Cyrus McCormick's reapers, and American sewing machines were all new technologies to European visitors. A free republic had competed very well with the power and prosperity of European monarchies. Economic and technological efficiency went hand in hand with individual freedom.[18]

After returning to New York, Greeley began to plan an American exhibition of arts and industry. Construction of a glass and iron "crystal palace" in New York City (on Sixth Avenue between 40th and 42nd Streets) began in October 1852. Its purpose was to celebrate American "progress, power, and possibilities." Greeley's friend P. T. Barnum purchased one hundred shares of stock and agreed to serve as a director. The exhibition opened in July 1853 and attracted thousands of paying visitors. Hundreds of exhibits of art, agricultural and industrial machinery, guns, clothing, shoes, soap, and paper products testified to American achievement. Greeley produced a lavish book on the exhibition, praised by *Godey's Lady's Book* as a testimony to "progress of the arts" and the "dissemination of useful knowledge." The Crystal Palace in New York, Greeley wrote his friend Rebecca Whipple in Vermont, was a "beauty and a wonder."[19]

For Greeley, the Crystal Palace exhibitions—both in London and New York—were not simply signs of industrial progress, but of the universal aspiration to freedom. Technology and art knew no national boundaries. Neither did freedom. "Freedom," Greeley reminded his readers, "is the right of white men in this country; for our fathers, with French help, flogged the British, and made them acknowledge our Independence; but Freedom has no business in Poland, Hungary, Lombardy."[20] English liberty reflected the monarchy and aristocracy that spawned it. Freedom in America, the white man's republic, Greeley believed, also reflected the blight of slavery. American freedom could only be complete when extended to Europe, the world, and all men and women everywhere.

"FREEDOM NATIONAL!"

Greeley returned to the United States in the late summer of 1851 to find America convulsed by the growing controversy over slavery. The most controversial aspect of the Compromise of 1850, the Fugitive Slave Act, was anathema in the North. The South feared losing control of the national government as more free states joined the Union. The Free Soil movement continued its drumbeat against admitting any more slave states. More Whigs were drifting into the anti-slavery camp. Southern slave owners continued to dominate the U.S. Congress. "We are on the eve of great events," predicted James Fenimore Cooper in 1850, "a principle must prevail, and that principle will be freedom."[21]

In the autumn of 1851, Greeley was living on his own in New York while Molly and their two children, Ida, now three, and Raphael, eight months, stayed at a cottage fifty miles up the Harlem railroad line. "I keep bachelor's hall at our house," wrote Greeley, "making my own bed, etc. and eating here and there." Whig prospects looked quite dismal. Greeley thought that the Whigs could only win in 1852 with another military man like Harrison or Taylor. The likely candidate was General Winfield Scott, an old veteran of the War of 1812. Yet in Greeley's opinion, Scott (like many others) was a pompous fool. But Scott might very well win the election. He should therefore be tolerated. He could certainly carry New York State, thought Greeley. "We must run Scott for President," he complained, "and I hate it." He preferred John McLean of Ohio, an unelectable anti-slavery candidate, later a Supreme Court Justice.[22]

To add insult to injury, Greeley's former *Tribune* employee Henry Raymond founded the *New York Times*, in September. Raymond's newspaper immediately occupied an impressive six-story building on Nassau Street, fitted out with the latest model of a Hoe steam cylinder press. Raymond also hired away a number of the *Tribune* staff. Some thought that Thurlow Weed, tiring of Greeley's passions and moods, was setting up a rival Whig newspaper. Greeley fumed, threatening to take away routes from any carriers who deserted to the rival newspaper.[23]

Yet Greeley also found that the Fugitive Slave Act had deepened anti-slavery sentiment in the North, and that anti-slavery could sell newspapers. Harriet Beecher Stowe's novel, *Uncle Tom's Cabin*, was a runaway best seller about a slave who escaped across the Ohio River to the North. In February 1851, Boston police arrested a fugitive slave known as Shadrach (William Wilkins). Abolitionists quickly helped him break out of jail and spirited him off to Canada. Eight men were indicted, three tried, but none convicted in the plot. Theodore Parker called it "the noblest deed done in Boston since the destruction of tea in 1773." In April, federal agents arrested Thomas Sims, another fugitive slave, and had three hundred armed men escort him through the pre-dawn streets of Boston to a ship waiting to return him to his owner in Georgia. Again, Parker attacked federal law in the name of the Higher Law. The poet Longfellow called Boston a "city without a soul." "From the depths of our soul," thundered the *Tribune*, on November 6, "we hate and abhor human slavery" in general and "inhuman slave-hunts" in particular.[24]

Greeley attacked the Fugitive Slave Act throughout the 1850s. He favored emancipation of the slaves and even black suffrage. He contributed eight dollars a year to the Underground Railroad, which helped slaves escape to the North and to Canada. (Seward contributed fifteen dollars and Weed one hundred dollars annually, by comparison.) But he also continued to follow the more cautious line of his mentor, Henry Clay, supporting colonization of slaves in Africa, criticizing blacks for their conduct and lack of self-improvement, and refusing to go over to the abolitionist camp. Greeley's anti-slavery deepened, but he was still not an abolitionist.[25]

Greeley did agree with Massachusetts Senator Charles Sumner, however, that freedom was a national, not local, issue. Sumner's friend and mentor, Professor Francis Lieber, a German immigrant, argued in his legal textbooks that freedom and liberty meant different things."[26] Lieber supported *Freiheit* more than *Libertät*, freedom rather than privileges or rights. His book *On Civil Liberty and Self-Government* observed that "British liberty differs and must forever differ from ours, and both will differ from French liberty, whenever firmly established; as modern liberty differs, and cannot otherwise but differ, from the liberty of the Middle Ages and ancient freedom."[27] Liberty was "determined and limited by the acknowledgement of obligation." Freedom of action without limits was simply licentiousness.[28]

"As to the synonyms freedom and liberty," Lieber wrote, "the former is personal, individual, and relates to the whole being; the latter is granted, guaranteed, and, therefore, generally of a public character. The slave receives freedom, the captive liberty." "We say: the slave was restored to freedom; and we speak of the liberty of the press, of civil liberty." American freedom derived from English liberty. French *liberté* contained further notions of equality and democracy.[29] Lieber, Sumner, and Greeley all agreed that freedom was more extensive and broad than liberty.

Greeley was not sanguine about Whig possibilities in the election of 1852. President Millard Fillmore and Senator Daniel Webster were desperately trying to hold the Compromise together, even if it meant supporting the recapture of fugitive slaves. The Whig Party was deeply divided over slavery. Opponents of slavery had moved beyond the tiny Liberty Party of the 1840s and the Free Soil movement of 1848 in search of a new anti-slavery party. "If Fillmore and Webster will only use each other up," Greeley wrote Weed in December 1851 from Washington, DC, "we may possibly recover. But our chance is slim." Slavery, he wrote a friend in Rochester a month later, was now dividing the nation into "two great antagonist parties."[30]

Greeley expanded upon this point in a brief pamphlet entitled *Why I Am a Whig.* In it, he wrote "two grand and fruitful ideas attract and divide the political world. On the one hand Liberty, on the other, Order, but neither suffices without the other."[31] The Whigs were the party of peace and protection. The Democrats supported Free Trade, the Mexican War, then the acquisition of Cuba and Texas as slave states. To complicate matters, the Whigs were facing life without Henry Clay, who lay dying in Lexington, Kentucky. Greeley had agreed to write a life of Clay, but wished that "Uncle Harry" would live at least another year. He wrote Seward and Weed in April that Free State Whigs would go for Scott in the presidential election.[32]

Despite his antipathy for another politically untutored general as the Whig candidate, Greeley reluctantly supported Scott. He chided one of his Washington correspondents, James Pike, for damaging Scott by attacking Fillmore in his columns and undermining the Whigs at a time when they needed support. Greeley edited the rough draft of Scott's speech accepting the nomination. "You shall show this to General Scott," he commanded Pike, "and tell him I say we can stand it at the North." If the Whigs would only put a Free Land plank in their party platform, it would be worth thousands of votes in New York and in the West.[33]

On June 29, Greeley learned of the death of his longstanding hero, Whig Party Senator Henry Clay of Kentucky. He was devastated. Greeley promptly printed a new edition of Epes Sargent's 1842 biography of Clay. "We Americans of 1852," Greeley wrote in his introduction, "are the heated partisans or embittered opponents of Mr. Clay." Clay was an "ardent Patriot," a "chivalrous adversary," and an "unfailing friend." Greeley claimed that Clay regretted the Fugitive Slave Law.[34]

Clay's passing may have helped move the *Tribune* further into the anti-slavery camp. Charles Dana predicted that "the United States will extinguish slavery before slavery can begin to extinguish the United States." On July 5, Frederick Douglass, speaking in Rochester, New York, compared the U.S. Constitution, a "glorious LIBERTY document" that supported slavery, with true freedom. "We mean to stay in the Whig party," promised the *Tribune* after the Whig defeat at the polls that November, "and not to keep silence about slavery nor 'acquiesce' in fugitive-slave hunting."[35]

On August 26, Senator Charles Sumner delivered his famous speech "Freedom National, Slavery Sectional" to a crowded Senate chamber in Washington, DC. In it, he called for the repeal of the Fugitive Slave Law. "According to the true spirit of the Constitution, and the sentiments of the Fathers," he thundered, "Slavery and not Freedom is sectional, while Freedom and not slavery is national." Sumner's slogan quickly became a republican rallying cry of the 1850s against slavery across the country. Freedom under the moral law was now a national imperative. Liberty under the Constitution could no longer justify slavery in the South. Salmon P. Chase of Ohio, another Free Soil man, also told the Senate on another occasion that "Freedom is national; slavery only is local and sectional."[36]

Sumner's speech helped widen the great divide between the liberty of the founding fathers and the freedom promised by the Declaration of Independence with its promise of equality for all men. Sumner helped create a Manichean world of light and darkness, righteousness and sin, in American politics. "Are you for Freedom, or are you for Slavery?" he asked his audiences. Sumner the lawyer hoped to amend the Constitution so that "all persons are equal before the law" and "no person can hold another as a slave." Such a phrase, he believed, might give precision to "that idea of human rights which is enunciated in our Declaration of Independence."[37]

In the meantime, the Young America movement within the Democratic Party was eagerly trumpeting the virtues of "manifest destiny" as the American empire expanded its territories. George Sanders and the Young Americans—including writers like Walt Whitman, Herman Melville, and Nathaniel Hawthorne—identified with the failed European revolutionaries of 1848. They too extolled the virtues of American freedom against the tyrannies and empires of England and Old World Europe. They contrasted themselves with the "Old Fogies" of politics—Clay, Calhoun, and Webster—and dreamed of an expansionistic America. They supported O'Connell, Kossuth, Mazzini, and

Garibaldi in their attempts to create their own republics. They supported states' rights for the South and hoped to annex Cuba. Sanders supported Stephen A. Douglas for president. But in November 1852, the Young Americans voted for Franklin Pierce and the Democrats to lead America's "youngest and greatest generation to the battle for the world's liberty, and to the fulfillment of its magnificent destiny."[38]

In the end, the Whigs went down to a resounding defeat in November 1852, their last serious appearance as a political party. Voter turnout was low. Democrat Franklin Pierce, the New Hampshire supporter of slavery in the South, easily beat Scott in the electoral college, 254–42. New York Whigs took only 11 of 33 House seats, as opposed to 32 of 34 in 1848 and 17 of 34 in 1850. The party endorsed the Fugitive Slave Law, much to Greeley's disgust. He promptly changed the name of his annual *Whig Almanac* to the *Tribune Almanac*. He drafted his own program for the party—tariff protection, river and harbor improvement, a railroad to the Pacific, foreign policy in support of American interests abroad, no slavery in the new territories (but no interference with slavery in slave states), a single term for presidents, reform of Congress, and so on. Slavery, he wrote, was "morally wrong" and "ought to be terminated." He referred to "the late Whig Party."[39]

Greeley recognized that the Whig Party was as dead as Henry Clay. He talked openly of simply disbanding the party, which was "not merely discomfited, but annihilated," in Greeley's words. In part, Greeley blamed Joshua Giddings and other abolitionists for lumping Scott with Pierce in the pro-slavery camp. But Sumner wrote Giddings sympathizing with his position, criticizing Greeley for his attack on Giddings, and promising that "out of this chaos, the party of Freedom must rise."[40]

Thus was born the idea of a new political party grounded in opposition to slavery. Greeley could no longer be a Whig. "We cannot stifle our convictions respecting Slavery," he charged, "we choose to go out of the Whig party, if we must, rather than to remain in it subjects, servants, or prisoners."[41]

The cry of "Freedom National!" and the political collapse of the Whigs presaged a reformation of political parties that would pit freedom, not liberty, against slavery, and North against South. Lieber and Sumner made it clear that liberty and freedom were no longer the same. Greeley too realized that a new "party of freedom" was in the making. William Ellery Channing might have written of Greeley, as he did of abolitionist Charles Follen in 1840, that "the love of freedom glowed as a central, inextinguishable fire in his soul; not the schoolboy's passion for liberty, caught from the blood-stained pages of Greece and Rome, but a love of freedom based on knowledge of the inalienable rights of man."[42] That love of freedom would propel Horace Greeley into the forefront of American politics in the 1850s and make him a true anti-slavery man.

THE TRIBUNE ASSOCIATION

Horace Greeley became a popular writer and journalist in America in the 1850s, and his *New York Tribune* the most widely read newspaper. The paper was now a corporation, a business bigger than its editor, an association of garrulous and radical journalists and correspondents that aimed to make the world a better place. Inspired by the ideas of Fourier, Greeley transformed his newspaper into a joint-stock company in which many of his editorial staff could become part-owners. The company was a microcosm of Greeley's imagined capitalist utopia, an association in support of freedom.

Now in his forties, Greeley was a fixture in New York City, with its new mansions, bustling shoppers, and street railways, drifting uncertainly down the street in his old Irish linen coat, his pockets stuffed with newspapers, his wisps of white hair blowing in the wind. The New Hampshire philosopher was now famous, his columns read by an increasingly literate national public, his eccentricities, enthusiasms, and causes well chronicled. *Tribune* readers everywhere felt like he was one of them, a plain man speaking plain sense to plain folk.

In 1849, Greeley and McElrath renamed their newspaper company the Tribune Association. They issued one hundred shares of stock at one thousand dollars a share and made it available in principle to interested staff members, including twenty editors, foremen, and assistants. McElrath hung on to his fifty shares. Greeley sold ten to Charles Dana, and more to other employees, until he had only twenty-five shares himself. (By 1872, Greeley owned only six shares.) The newspaper had been steadily prosperous for years, Greeley felt, and paper was still cheap enough. But postage was increasingly expensive. He helped his printers organize their own union, and became the first president of the New York Typographic Union himself.[43]

In 1849, the *Tribune* was still a relatively small operation. Daily circulation stood at about 13,330, compared with 45,000 by 1860, then 90,000 by 1865. The weekly edition probably reached 217,000 subscribers by the Civil War. Annual profits were around $40,000 in 1849, but would reach $86,000 by 1859. On average, stockholders in the 1850s annually divided some $50,000 in dividends. These numbers sound small by today's standards, but were indeed quite substantial. In addition, many readers of the *Tribune* passed their newspaper along to friends and neighbors, so that the actual number of readers was significantly larger than the circulation figures might suggest. By all accounts, the *Tribune* was by 1860 the most widely read newspaper in the world.[44]

Greeley prided himself on staying ahead of his competitors for news. In 1850, the *Tribune* purchased a new four-cylinder "Lightning" press from the R. Hoe Company for $12,500. The press could produce eight thousand sheets an hour, after which the process was repeated on the other side of the sheets. Greeley increased the size of his daily sheets to the same size of his larger weekly newspaper and began producing fifteen thousand copies a day. He also expanded the paper from four to eight pages, and from twenty-eight to fifty-eight columns. In 1852, Greeley purchased the six-cylinder Hoe press, then an eight-cylinder one, and in 1855 a ten-cylinder giant, two stories high, the largest printing press made at the time, costing $25,000. By the late 1850s, the newspaper was running three Hoe presses simultaneously. The result was deafening noise, constant vibration, and dirty surroundings, all in the name of increased efficiency.[45]

People remained as important to Greeley as technology. He was constantly on the lookout for better editors, printers, and correspondents. He wanted good writing and instant news, aided now by the telegraph. Managing editor Charles Dana remained his right-hand man, and handled most of the daily operations of the *Tribune* throughout the 1850s. Dana thus had a relatively free hand in hiring radical republican journalists to help with the paper, which he did, including Brook Farmer George Ripley, who reviewed literature, and agronomist Solon Robinson, who wrote columns on agriculture. Greeley's old friend Obadiah Bowe served as a proofreader until his eyes failed him in 1851. Other writers included a family friend from Clymer, New York, Beman Brockway, and Samuel Sinclair, later the company cashier and publisher. Jane Swisshelm, an abolitionist editor from Pittsburgh, became the first female political reporter in Washington. Swisshelm promptly got attention by attacking Daniel Webster, an architect of the Compromise of 1850, as a drunkard and father of illegitimate mulatto children—Greeley promptly fired her and hired James S. Pike from Calais, Maine. At first, Greeley edited some of Pike's letters. Then, recognizing Pike's talent, Greeley wrote Pike, "I don't think I shall ever take liberties with your letters, except that it may be the liberty of dissenting from some of their positions."[46]

A letter from Greeley to William Davis Gallagher, editor of the *Cincinnati Gazette,* gives us an intriguing glimpse into Greeley's thinking regarding newspapers of the time. Make sure to have a telegraphic reporter in Baltimore, Greeley advised, who could send on dispatches even before they appeared elsewhere in print. Have a confidential man in Washington who could send on one or two hundred words a day on political goings on, "ahead of the usual dispatch." Have separate telegraph offices in New Orleans and San Francisco. Get the European news by translation from the *Zeitung.* Be a good Whig! Run a daily lead article that will capture public attention. "Make all kinds of news your hobby, and be sure you have the freshest and fullest."[47] Greeley also had his newspaper crusade against New York City corruption, especially the "Forty Thieves," the New York Common Council that ran the city, the "meanest, most corrupt, stupid and inoperative" collection of politicians in the world.[48]

In June 1853, the future Lord John Acton, then age nineteen, visited New York to see the Crystal Palace exhibit and obtained an interview with Horace Greeley. Acton was greatly impressed by the *Tribune,* which exceeded the London *Times* in both circulation and printing speed. Acton found it "a Whig paper, but ultra-democratic in every question, without being Democratic." Greeley, he observed, had "taken up a number of hobbies, such as temperance, which he pushes to extravagance." The "half cracked" man in the white linen coat was surely a strange looking apparition who resembled Benjamin Franklin. "He is sincere, though much suspected, for there is so much method in his madness as to make it seem likely that he is a rogue."[49]

By 1853, the *Tribune* was reaching over one hundred thousand readers of Greeley's editorials, feature columns, and the latest news.

The daily paper appeared on the streets every morning except Sunday. The weekly edition came out Wednesday morning. Greeley was especially proud of the weekly, which reached into small towns and rural areas across the country. "We mean that no weekly shall surpass this in giving a full, graphic, and faithful account of what the World is Doing, whereof it is Thinking, and how it is Progressing," he wrote proudly.[50]

News was international as well as national. The *Tribune* covered the Crimean War in some detail. Adam Gurowski continued to edit the contributions of Marx and Engels and to write his own articles on European affairs. Greeley recruited young Bayard Taylor, fresh from his trip on Admiral Perry's expedition to Japan. Taylor was a brilliant linguist, scholar, poet, and traveler. His letters from Japan home to the *Tribune,* reviewed in advance of publication by the admiral himself, were sensational.[51] But the central focus of the paper remained the growing storm over slavery.

The *Tribune* stood defiantly for freedom and against slavery throughout the 1850s. In June 1853, Harriet A. Jacobs, a former slave, wrote letters to the *Tribune* describing in detail the abuses of slavery, including the selling of slave families. Southerners tried to stop or destroy shipments of the newspaper, so copies were mailed in sealed envelopes to agents there. Southern correspondents likewise sent their dispatches North through the post office via agents in Maryland. In 1856, the *Tribune* agent in Harrison County, Virginia, was indicted for inciting slaves to insurrection by distributing the newspaper in the South. Neither the indictment nor the agent ever came to trial, but the message was clear. The *Tribune* was an anti-slavery or abolitionist newspaper not welcome in the South.[52]

By 1854, the *Tribune* building on the corner of Spruce and Nassau Streets housed 220 full-time and 130 part-time staff. Some workers were on regular salaries, some paid by the published line. Reporting to Charles Dana were ten associate editors and forty reporters and correspondents.[53] The *Tribune* was a noisy, dirty, and driven operation, its windows grimy with the soot of the city. The newspaper's name was printed in huge gold letters along the side of the building. Employees called the offices on Printing House Square near City Hall simply "the Rookery." The surroundings smelled of printers ink, glue, leather, hides, sweat, chemicals, and burned paper. The composing room was on the top fourth floor, with skylights, type fonts lying on long tables, and fresh newspaper copy hung on hooks on the wall to dry. Forty compositors worked in "phalanxes" of ten men each. The telegraph chattered away with the latest dispatches from correspondents. The editorial rooms were on the third floor. Here Greeley's crowded office with its roll-top desk and a bronze bust of Henry Clay served as the staff library. The proofreading rooms were on the second floor. Proofreaders sat and mumbled as they read. The latest thirty-foot-high Hoe steam presses roared, hissed, and rumbled in the basement press-room, "white washed, inky, and unclean." Stereotyped plates cast from the original type beds went on the rotary presses. The paper was typeset between dusk and midnight, the scene illuminated by gaslight. Telegraph wires ran into and through the building. There was a constant stream of office visitors at all hours of the day and night. And at dawn, ink-stained and tired men and boys took to the streets to begin distribution of the paper through a network of newsboys, wagons, railway terminals, and offices throughout the city.[54]

So the newspaper prospered, although Greeley himself was in continual need of funds, giving money away to friends, borrowing heavily, or investing unwisely. In July 1854, he wrote a Cincinnati editor that New York was a "broken city," that he owed fifteen thousand dollars to other people, and that he was having to sell his own *Tribune* shares to get out of debt. "Please don't tell anybody how poor I am," he admonished his reader. "The *Tribune* is doing very well now in subscriptions," Greeley wrote a friend in 1855, "though not well in Advertisements, our great source of profit." He was still a "toad under a barrow" as far as his own personal finances were concerned, "owing heavy debts and involved in other people's bad luck." (They wouldn't pay back his frequent loans.) Yet the *Tribune* continued to operate in the black. In 1858, its employees—typesetters and pressmen—gave Greeley a gold watch with twenty-seven links consisting of the letters of the alphabet and the ampersand (&). Attached to a ring were a tiny quill, inkwell, rule, composing stick, and type. In his own company, at least, Greeley found that labor and capital could indeed work in harmony.[55]

But Greeley also thought the *Tribune* was losing its old zest to change the world. "I shall stop taking it soon," he wrote James Pike in July 1858, "if it don't evince a little more reformatory spirit." Despite Greeley's slipping control over his editorial staff, his newspaper was increasingly successful. The *Tribune*'s national-circulation weekly edition now reached some three hundred thousand subscribers, the largest circulation of any newspaper in the world. Throughout the Civil War, Horace Greeley's *New York Tribune* would be considered the leading American newspaper of its time.[56]

In the 1850s, the *Tribune* was an association, a joint-stock company, and a capitalist utopian community in which those shareholders who labored received dividends, as well as salaries. The Tribune Association was in some ways a continuation of Brook Farm and the North American Phalanx, a company of reform-minded and idealistic men seeking harmony in community. They wanted to make the world a better place by working together, rather than as individuals. If Greeley was the philosopher of the *Tribune*, then Charles Dana was its managing director. Greeley wrote most of the editorials, but Dana hired most of the staff. Using the latest printing technology and hiring the best printers, and paying them a fair wage, the newspaper as an association was not simply free to print whatever it wished, but free to profit in the capitalist marketplace. The higher the circulation, the more the advertisements, the greater would be the freedom of those who made the *Tribune* work. The *Tribune* was a corporation that aimed to promote freedom and prevent the corruption of the republic.

FREE STATES: KANSAS-NEBRASKA

In Horace Greeley's day, the states enjoyed freedom from federal government, especially on the issue of slavery. Congress would not even discuss slavery in its halls after the Missouri Compromise of 1820, and it ignored the many abolitionist petitions left at its doorstep. Rather, the country divided itself into free and slave states. Slave States had an unusual preponderance in congressional representation, what Greeley dubbed a southern "slavocracy" ruling in Washington. The federal government seemed too resistant and too weak to launch any kind of assault on slavery even if it wished. But the prospect of new states to be added to the United States as a result of the Mexican War made the slavery issue truly national.

The Kansas-Nebraska Act of 1854 marked a major turning point both in the life of the United States and in the life of Horace Greeley. By allowing settlers in the new territories of the West to decide whether or not their states, if admitted to the Union, would be slave or free states, the Act reversed both the Missouri Compromise and the Compromise of 1850. Free Soil supporters wanted to exclude slavery from the territories entirely. Now Congress was permitting slavery based on the principle of "squatter sovereignty," the votes of citizens settling the new states. The Act also brought together some unlikely political bedfellows, conservative Whigs and radical anti-slavery men, in a common cause—the formation of a new anti-slavery political party with a national base. Radicalized by Kansas-Nebraska, Horace Greeley made final his break with the Whig Party of Seward and Weed, and became a fervent anti-slavery man. "Conservative Unionism and radical Anti-Slavery," he wrote later, "seemed to meet and coincide."[57]

Senator Dodge of Iowa introduced the initial Kansas-Nebraska bill in Congress in December 1853. On March 3, 1854, a revised bill that had been introduced in January passed the Senate by a vote of 37 to 14. The House passed the bill 113–100 on May 22, and President Franklin Pierce signed it into law a week later, on May 30. The Kansas-Nebraska Act was a great victory for Senator Stephen A. Douglas of Illinois, who had plans for a transcontinental railroad that would take the southern route across the country to the Pacific. If Douglas had his way, that railroad would be constructed by private companies and financed by selling public land along the right of way. Congressmen from Missouri, Iowa, and Illinois favored a northern route from Chicago or St. Louis. Southerners favored a route across Texas and through the December 1853 Gadsden Purchase (the future New Mexico and Arizona). The Kansas-Nebraska Act was, among other things, an attempt to buy southern votes by allowing slavery in the territories to be traversed by the railroad. Douglas, in fact, was not the sole architect of the bill, not seeking the presidency at this time and not in favor of slavery in the territories. But he was a symbol of the bill and a proponent of the railroad.

Douglas introduced the bill on the floor of the Senate on January 5, calling for "popular sovereignty." That is, citizens in the territories would decide whether to be slave or free states if admitted to the Union. Greeley promptly dubbed the principle "squatter sovereignty" in the *Tribune*. "What kind of 'popular sovereignty' is it," he asked, "that allows one class of people to vote slavery for another?" He called instead for a new "determined and overwhelming party for freedom" to oppose slavery—what would become the Republican Party.[58]

Kansas-Nebraska galvanized Greeley into action. The *Tribune* fumed for months against the bill as "inebriated political morality," "measureless treachery and infamy," noxious and detestable "infernal rascality," "political dishonesty," and "downright effrontery" to the nation. The bill violated the Missouri Compromise. It breached a contract between North and South on the issue of slavery. It compromised the nation's "principles of freedom." The national battle was now joined between Freedom and Slavery, rather than Liberty and Tyranny. "Freedom's battle was fought and lost in 1850," snarled Greeley, "and the cowards and traitors have all run to the winning side." In May, after the bill finally passed the Senate and House, the *Tribune* listed all Senators and Representatives who voted in favor on the front page of the newspaper—surrounded by a black border.[59]

Although Greeley would claim that he had opposed slavery since he was a teenager in Vermont, he was never an abolitionist, and anti-slavery was not really central to his thinking about freedom until after the Mexican War. He did not join the Free Soil Party in 1848, although he opposed slavery in the territories. He remained a staunch Whig until that party collapsed after the election of 1852. Now he was fully and publicly engaged in the "struggle between Freedom and Slavery for the possession of Kansas." "Slavery is an Ishmael," he wrote, "It is malevolent and malignant." Slavery was the leper of modern civilization. But the American West was "territory consecrated to Freedom." Now the "leprous intruder," slavery, intended to make war upon the "territory of Freedom."[60]

With Kansas-Nebraska, Greeley realized finally that the revolutions of 1848 in Europe were no longer politically significant for American freedom. The new revolution would be in the United States over slavery. True, the Young Americans, including Douglas and George Sanders, were still talking about revolutions in Europe.[61] Sanders, as U.S. Consul in London, even hosted a Washington's Birthday dinner party for the revolutionary exiles of 1848.[62] But in February, the Senate refused 29–10 to confirm Sanders, and he ultimately found his way back to the United States. As Greeley recognized, the revolution of 1848 was over and the revolution to eliminate slavery in the United States was beginning.[63]

Sanders's famous London party helped conceive the Ostend Manifesto to annex Cuba as a slave state from Spain. Northern anti-slavery men had a field day attacking another Southern Democrat plot to extend slavery.[64] But Greeley's only real remaining contact with the European revolutionaries, aside from Sanders, was Adam Gurowski, who continued to write anti-Russian articles for the *Tribune*. Greeley even recommended Gurowski to Weed as an expert on western railroad expansion.[65]

The Kansas-Nebraska Act, Greeley wrote, meant that the time had now come to "struggle earnestly, undauntedly, uncompromisingly for Universal Freedom."[66] America, not Europe, was now the hotbed of revolution in Greeley's mind. "We are in the midst of a revolution," he added, and Kansas-Nebraska was "tantamount to civil war and an open declaration of war between freedom and slavery, to be ceaselessly waged until one or the other finally and absolutely triumphs." "Either the South must put an end to slavery," wrote Greeley, "or the North must adopt it." "My only hope," a friend wrote to James S. Pike, "is the *Tribune*. It is the terror of all the traitorous scoundrels here [in Washington, DC]. It should now be devoted to the exposure of this ungodly infamy."[67] And so it would be.

But the *Tribune* was hardly alone. Abolitionists and anti-slavery men everywhere rushed to denounce the Kansas-Nebraska Act. Theodore Parker warned in a sermon that America might well divide into two nations, a democracy grounded in freedom and a despotism grounded in slavery. "Is America to live or die?" Parker asked rhetorically. Kansas-Nebraska posed the greatest threat to the republic since 1776. America was now "a house divided against itself; of course, it cannot stand."[68]

"We are not one people," raged Greeley, "we are two peoples. We are a people for Freedom and a people for Slavery. Between the two, conflict is inevitable."[69] Kansas-Nebraska had sounded the alarm in the North. Freedom and slavery were incompatible. Either North and South must separate and go their own ways as two separate nations, or the conflict between freedom and slavery must be resolved. If the Democrats were now the party of slavery, there must also be a new party of freedom.

THE PARTY OF FREEDOM

Writing after the Civil War, Horace Greeley characterized the Republican Party as a "child of the Revolution of 1776," born of the unfinished business of the American Revolution, the existence of slavery in a democratic republic. At the "soul of the republic," wrote Greeley, was the "idea of the equality of all men." The Republican Party was significant because it "championed the idea of freedom."[70] Indeed, the emergence of the Republican Party in the 1850s was a complex, but well-known, drama in which Horace Greeley played a leading role.

In the South, republicanism meant *liberty* in the form of states' rights, including the right to individual property in slaves and the right to secede from a compact of states, the Union, if any state thought it necessary to do so. But in the North, republicanism meant *freedom* in the form of free labor for white men and equality of rights. Greeley articulated the free labor ideology of the northern middle-class electorate, grounded in the right to rise or fall depending on one's ability and hard work in the capitalist marketplace. Economically, all white men had the right to make themselves into something better than they were by changing jobs, moving to a new workplace, or migrating west. "All men," as Lincoln put it, "should have an equal chance." "Enslave a man," wrote Greeley, "and you destroy his ambition, his enterprise, his capacity."[71]

The Republican Party emerged gradually out of the ashes of the Whig defeat at the hands of Pierce and the Democrats in 1852. Charles Sumner had been calling for a new anti-slavery "party of freedom" at least since 1848. Now the conscience Whigs began slowly to join hands with renegade Democrats, old Free Soilers, and others to form the new party. Among them were the so-called Know-Nothings, nativist members of the Order of the Star Spangled Banner who opposed immigration and naturalization of foreigners. (Because the order was secret, its members were to "know nothing" if and when queried about its plans.) The Know-Nothings had a particular hatred for Catholics, especially those from Ireland. In July 1854, delegates from thirteen states met and formed the American Party and took a secret pledge not to vote for any foreign-born or Catholic political candidates. In November, the party surprisingly won all but two seats in the Massachusetts legislature and elected forty congressmen. But their triumph was short-lived. The Know-Nothings and the American Party soon drowned in the waters of the slavery issue and the powerful currents moving to organize a new party to defeat the Democrats.[72]

Greeley, as it turned out, abhorred the Know-Nothings and would have nothing to do with a movement that, in part, wanted to oust the New York team of Greeley, Seward, and Weed. The *Tribune,* Greeley promised Pike, would never again mention the Know-Nothings "except to give 'em a devil of a whale."[73]

For a number of years, American politicians and writers had talked about a coming political party of freedom united by its opposition to slavery. Now in 1854, Gamaliel Bailey, an abolitionist, called for a "Party of Freedom" whose purpose would be to "regain possession of the Federal Government, and subvert the Slave Power."[74] Greeley too anticipated a new party that would bring together businessmen, reformers, and anti-slavery men from the remnants of the Whig Party and the Free Soil movement.

Among the disgruntled Whigs that began to meet independently around the country in 1854 was a circle of Greeley's friends in New Hampshire. As early as October 12, 1853, Amos Tuck, a three-term congressman and a friend of Abraham Lincoln, convened a meeting at a hotel in Exeter, New Hampshire. The meeting was private. No records were kept. But apparently those present agreed upon the need to form a new "republican" party. Greeley learned about the meeting two months later when on vacation visiting family and friends in Amherst. He liked the idea, but thought the party needed "some general name" that would carry broad appeal. Greeley agreed that the name "republican" would do the job—"it will sound both Jeffersonian and Madisonian, and for that reason will take well."[75]

In early 1854, Greeley went off to New Hampshire again in search of new political allies for a new party. "New Hampshire is a bad state to move," he complained to James Pike, "and I don't know how to start her." But events were moving elsewhere as well as in New Hampshire that winter. In early March, Greeley wrote an old friend from New York who in 1850 had "gone West" to Ripon, Wisconsin. Alvan Bovay (1818–1903), an attorney and a land reformer, had met Greeley in connection with the "vote yourself a farm" movement in the 1840s. Both were Whig enthusiasts of Charles Fourier and associationism. Bovay saw Greeley again in New York in 1852 and suggested the name "republican" for a new political party. Now Bovay was selling real estate in Ripon, finding his way out of the defunct Whig Party, and trying to organize a new party. "I am a beaten, broken down, used-up politician," moaned Greeley, "and have the soreness of many defeats in my bones." "I am ready to follow any lead that promises northern emancipation," added the editor, "but remember that editors can only follow where the people's heart is already prepared to go." In his reply, Bovay once again recommended the name "republican" for any new party.[76]

Both Bovay and Greeley recognized that the name "republican" would have great appeal across the country, especially in the pages of the *Tribune*. "Greeley of the *New York Tribune* is the right spiritual father of all this region," wrote Emerson during a trip west. "He prints and disperses 110,000 newspapers in one day,—multitudes of them in these very parts [Michigan and Wisconsin]. He had preceded me, by a few days, and people had flocked together, coming thirty or forty miles to hear him speak; as was right, for he does all their thinking and theory for them, for two dollars a year."[77]

Bovay's base in Ripon, Wisconsin, was a small community of about 350 people. Half of them consisted of Fourierists from Kenosha who had established a Phalanx in Ripon. They were radical, anti-slavery, and agrarian in mood and interests. In late March, Bovay convened a meeting of unhappy Whigs, Democrats, and Free Soil men who opposed the Kansas-Nebraska Act. They agreed to adopt the name "republican" for their party, which they would form if the Act passed Congress (as it did). The one-word name suggested a commonwealth, the principle of equality, an earlier Jeffersonian party, and the German *Republikaner* of 1848 (a number of Germans had recently settled in Wisconsin).[78]

Likewise, in May 1854, a number of New York anti-slavery men gathered in the town of Friendship to found a new political party. A. N. Cole, a Free Soil Democrat and the editor of the *Genesee Valley Free Press*, wrote Greeley and asked him to suggest a name. "Call it Republican," the editor snapped back, "—no prefix, no suffix, but plain Republican." The meeting at Friendship adjourned, having called a state convention for October 15 in Angelica. As far as we know, Greeley then first used the name "republican" in the *Tribune* on June 24, 1854, in an article entitled "Party Names and Public Duty." But he had already called for the name on June 16: "We should not care much whether those united were designated Whig, Free Soil Democrats or something else; though we think some simple name like *Republican* would more fitly designate those who had united to restore our Union to its true mission of champion and promulgator of Liberty rather than propagandist of Slavery."[79] Slavery had corrupted the republic. The Republican Party would restore both its virtue and its liberty, now in the name of freedom. Some New York politicians even talked of running Greeley for governor. But when Greeley called on Weed at the Astor House in New York, Weed tactfully said no. Greeley was outwardly cheerful, but inwardly fuming.[80]

That summer, both Michigan and Wisconsin conventions adopted the name "republican," partly in deference to the substantial German voter populations in each state. Germans in fact were beginning to leave the Democratic Party and were looking for a new political home. New York ex-Whigs were planning an anti-Nebraska convention in Saratoga for August. Greeley would draft the party resolutions, although he was not sure he could attend. He supported Seward against a Know-Nothing attack, trying to split him off from Weed, who "thinks I know nothing about politics." Seward indeed won the Senate race in November, backed by Weed's money, in a "scoundrelly canvas" that only revealed the "empty shell of Whiggery," in Greeley's terms. At Saratoga, Greeley's resolutions spoke out strongly for "the sacred cause of freedom, free labor and free soil."[81]

In the meantime, Greeley reconnected with Henry Thoreau. He praised Thoreau's speech "Slavery in Massachusetts" given at Framingham on July 4—at the same event where William Lloyd Garrison had burned a copy of the U.S. Constitution. Greeley reprinted the speech in its entirety in the Tribune. He also helped Thoreau revise eight drafts of Walden, whose printers' proofs arrived in Greeley's office on March 28 and which appeared in print finally on August 9. Thoreau's famous essay, of course, was a long salute to freedom in all its forms—the liberation of the individual, the freedom to live one's life as one wished, self-emancipation, anti-slavery, spiritual liberation, and wildness of the woods. The truly free individual—like Greeley and Thoreau—marched to a different drummer than the rest of society. The Tribune announced the appearance of Walden under "New Publications" on August 9.[82]

Greeley continued his drumbeat against slavery that summer, even as he sought to work his way through the thicket of New York Whig and Republican politics. In September, the Tribune published a letter from a Mississippi slave owner offering to sell Catharine, a mulatto woman in her twenties, into freedom in the North. Greeley responded that northerners had no interest in buying slaves from their "master's control" simply to free them. Rather, he wanted "the overthrow and extermination of the *slave holding system*."[83] Slavery was morally wrong and must perish.

The autumn of 1854 marked a major turning point in Greeley's life. At the age of forty-three, the editor finally broke with his old mentors, Weed and Seward, and moved into the new Republican Party. The break would remain secret until 1860. But Greeley would now find his own way in his own voice.

On November 11, 1854, Greeley wrote a long and pained letter to William Henry Seward in which he announced the "dissolution of the political firm of Seward, Weed, and Greeley." Since their cooperation began in 1837, they had ignored Greeley politically. They had offered him no public office—postmaster of New York in 1840, governor in 1848 and 1854. They had not recognized his "extreme poverty." Seward had humiliated him in a libel case in 1848 with his "needlessly cruel and mortifying" remarks. Weed had tried to read him out of the Whig Party. He had cut off his subsidies for the *Tribune*. "I have no further wish," he wrote, "than to glide out of the newspaper world as quietly and as speedily as possible, join my family in Europe, and if possible stay there quite a long time—long enough to cool my fevered brain and renovate my overtasked energies."[84]

Thus, as the Republican Party was being born, Greeley thought himself on political death row. "My political life is ended," he wrote Seward. His mother, Mary Woodburn Greeley, was paralyzed, almost unconscious, and dying. He spoke of selling out his interest in the *Tribune*. He wanted only to "retire to my little farm [at Chappaqua], there to read and work, and thence to write occasionally for the paper." Like Cincinnatus of the Roman Republic, Greeley wanted to retire from public life and return to his farm—until called back to fight corruption once again. He no longer wanted any "public recognition" from Weed or Seward.[85] He would be on his own.

In fact, Greeley would be born again as an independent editor voicing the concerns and ideals of the new Republican Party. He would help define the party as "a National party, based upon the principle of Freedom." (He would even write a GOP campaign song in 1860 entitled "The March of the Free.")[86] But no party would own him. He would articulate the great battle between Slavery and Freedom in a language liberated from old Whig demands. He would accept no subsidy. He would write exactly as he pleased. He would work to eliminate slavery and give freedmen the vote. In the autumn of 1854, Horace Greeley's political significance was not ending, but beginning.

7

Anti-Slavery Man

INDEPENDENCE

In late 1854, Greeley, forty-three, was exhausted and spent. He had broken with Seward and Weed, and given up on the Whig Party. The *Tribune*, for better or worse, was basically in the hands of Dana and Pike. Molly and the two children were off to London for the winter. Perhaps Greeley could join them in the spring and get some badly needed rest and recreation. But in the winter of 1854–5, Greeley continued to run his paper, and also worked to help organize a new party of freedom, bringing together a disparate coalition of anti-slavery men, former Whigs and Democrats, and eastern manufacturers, all dedicated to protective tariffs and free labor, all united by their opposition to slavery and the South's control of federal government. Eliminating slavery, Greeley believed, would be a long, political, and possibly bloody struggle.

In October 1854, Greeley asked his banker, George Peabody, to help Molly out in England as a "good Samaritan" if anything should "overtake her." Given Molly's continuing ill health and fierce moods, catastrophe might strike at any time, but she survived to see Greeley join her in the spring of 1855. In London, the Young America group was on the wane, and so were the republicans of 1848, many of whom had now gone to the United States.[1]

In April 1855, Greeley arrived in London as a reporter covering another world exposition in Paris—the "paradise of thoughtless boys with full pockets," as he called the City of Light. But Paris was as cold and rainy as London. He visited the exposition and the Louvre Museum. He took Molly and the children to the Swiss alps, where he got lost trying to hike up to a glacier. He haunted the museums of Geneva and Berne. And he got himself arrested by the French police.

Meanwhile, Greeley and his friend P. T. Barnum had both invested heavily in the New York Crystal Palace Exposition of 1853 and lost money in a bankrupt venture. On June 2, 1855, four French policemen showed up at Greeley's hotel in Paris and arrested him. A French sculptor claimed that his statue had been broken or mutilated in New York at the exposition. He demanded $2,500 in damages and got a warrant issued for Greeley's arrest. When Greeley refused to pay, the police took him to Clichy Prison, where he spent the night in cell 139. Amid much publicity, the editor received concerned friends and visitors on Sunday, the following day. The U.S. legation in Paris quickly guaranteed security and payment to the sculptor, and Greeley was released. The lawsuit was finally dropped. But Greeley made the most of the overnight prison episode, which he described at length in the press and in his recollections. "If you are skeptical of the essential worth of Freedom," he concluded, "just allow yourself to be locked up for a while, with no clear prospect of liberation at any specified or definite time."[2]

The Crimean War was still under way. Greeley wrote Dana from Paris that the *Tribune* needed a correspondent there to cover the Anglo-French and Turkish attacks on Sebastopol. "Don't give the editorial boys too entirely to anti-Slavery," he advised. He had sent letters on to the newspaper through the diplomatic pouch, "suspecting that the poke-nose police might otherwise get the first reading, which I object to."[3] Then he was back in London, helping Molly and the children plan for the next winter (she would travel back to Paris, then on to Dresden, then back to New York only in the summer of 1856). By the end of the summer, he was back in New York himself, living a bachelor life and involved in the *Tribune* and the formation of the Republican Party. And he paid a sad visit to Clymer, New York, to visit his family shortly after the death of his mother.

The *Tribune* continued to describe the political contest between freedom and slavery shaping up across the country. "We are two peoples," wrote James S. Pike, after Greeley had left for Europe. "We are a people for Freedom and a people for Slavery. Between the two a conflict is inevitable. A victory will be won against Freedom or Slavery will be driven back over the ruins of its gross usurpations and confined within its legitimate limits under the Constitution."[4]

Both the Whigs and Republicans of New York met simultaneously in Syracuse that September. Weed remained a staunch Whig. The Republicans were a mix of Seward Whigs, Free Soil Democrats, and

Know-Nothings. Greeley shuttled back and forth between the two meetings, desperately seeking fusion and compromise. He also helped draft a common platform emphasizing anti-slavery, gradual emancipation, Free Soil in the territories, and antipathy to Know-Nothing nativists with their exclusion of the foreign-born from politics. "A noble work has been accomplished," Greeley concluded after the meetings, "by the friends of republican freedom at Syracuse. A party has been organized on the basis of opposition to the extension of slavery in this country."[5]

In October, Greeley assigned himself as a *Tribune* correspondent in Washington, "where I shall devote myself to the saving of the Union." He continued to correspond with Weed, offering to speak at Whig gatherings before the November election. He also kept up with what was left of the North American Phalanx in New Jersey after a fire had destroyed most of the farm buildings in April. He solicited articles from Daniel Coit Gilman, future president of Johns Hopkins University, on education in Europe. He hoped for compromise between North and South, even if "perfect harmony" were not possible. Dana continued to run the paper in New York, with or without the consent of the editor on various matters. The Democrats had lost a number of seats in the recent elections for the House of Representatives. Now there was a fight to elect a new Speaker of the House. Greeley immersed himself in the battle to elect Nathaniel P. Banks of Massachusetts, a moderate Know-Nothing and anti-slavery man acceptable to a majority of feuding factions.[6]

During the winter of 1855–6, Greeley's independence became isolating. He was living in Washington, out of touch with New York politics and the *Tribune* head office. His family was off in Europe. He was an increasingly visible, well-known, admired, and hated journalist in the capital. He continued to express his frustrations to Dana. The *Tribune*, he admonished his managing editor, valued facts more than opinions and should stick to the facts. "I hate this hole," he wrote about Washington, "but am glad I came. It does me good to see how those who hate the *Tribune* much, fear it yet more." He urged Dana to stop attacking his political enemies in print. "We must have friends, not only in one party, but in all parties," he chided Dana, "or we can learn nothing." He telegraphed his stories to New York, advised against war with England, and corrected errors he found in the *Tribune* in his absence. "Don't let your people in New York attack persons with whom we are in daily intercourse here unless there shall seem to be an imperative necessity for it," he added. "Stop attacking the Irish and the Jews: I have labored many years to give the *Tribune* a reputation for candor and generosity toward unpopular creeds and races."[7]

Greeley's sense that he was losing control of his own newspaper further isolated him, as did an attack he suffered in January 1856 on a Washington street. An inebriated Arkansas congressman, Albert J. Rust, a Democrat, assaulted Greeley as he strolled down Capitol Hill on his way home to the National Hotel. Rust accosted him, punched him, and knocked him down. No one intervened. Greeley walked back to his hotel on his own, only to find Rust and three or four friends waiting for him. They assaulted him again. Although not seriously hurt, Greeley was deeply shaken and took to his hotel room for several days to recover. "I am too sick to be out of bed, too crazy to sleep, and am surrounded by horrors," the editor wrote Dana.[8]

Rust's assault on Greeley only made him feel further isolated. "Let others denounce or revile Rust," he wrote Dana, "I mean never to speak of him unless obliged to." He would maintain silence on the matter. So should Dana. "I would not publish articles about Rust's assault on me, but especially those that speak of my weakness, inoffensiveness, etc. I do not deserve any sympathy. At all events, I don't wish to beg for it." Dana should not try to make him a martyr. "I must give it up and go home," he wrote Dana. "You are getting everybody to curse me." "You heap a load on me that will kill me," he added, by publishing articles predicting a civil war between North and South. The *Tribune* would soon lose its southern subscribers, or be stopped by the post office. "For God's sake speak truth to me," he demanded.[9]

Greeley was also out of money again. He talked of selling one or two more *Tribune* shares for three thousand dollars each if he could. Washington was getting more and more oppressive. "Did you ever stay in a place where you didn't dare look in a glass when you got up in the morning," he wrote Pike, "for fear of seeing a scoundrel?" In April, he sold two *Tribune* shares for $3,500 each. He advised Dana to stay out of the current budget fight in Albany. He urged him to see John Fremont if he came to New York, but not to commit the *Tribune* to his presidential candidacy. He hoped that Pike would succeed him as Washington correspondent in April, when Greeley planned to return to New York.[10]

Greeley continued to distrust his own newspaper and his managers. "A daily paper," he wrote Dana, "should publish everything as fast as it is ready—if you can't do this, better give up the ghost at once." The newspaper was managed in a "shortsighted spirit." "I am heartsick," wrote Greeley. "The *Tribune* is doomed to be a second-rate paper and I am tired." The "infernal picayune spirit" of the newspaper had now "broken my heart." He was deeply discouraged and disappointed. The paper was not getting out the news fast enough. Dana was editing Greeley's own articles. His salary was still meager. "I am unwell," he finally admitted on April 7, "and tired of this hole."[11]

By spring 1856, Greeley had been out of New York and away from his newspaper for nearly a year. He had broken with Seward and Weed. He no longer depended on their subsidies for his newspaper. He had been physically assaulted in Washington. His family was away in Europe. He needed a new cause, and he would find it in the first Republican campaign for the presidency of the United States.

FREE MEN AND FREMONT

In 1856, America was increasingly a house divided. Could it stand? The men trying to form a Republican Party thought not, unless slavery was eliminated. Now they needed to find a candidate for president. In February of that year, Horace Greeley joined other Republicans in Pittsburgh at the first national organizational meeting of the new party. The assembly quickly resolved to fight any extension of slavery into the new territories of the West, to admit Kansas as a free state, and to oppose the "slavocracy" of the South. There was also talk of building a railroad to the Pacific, thus encouraging trade and emigration to the Pacific Coast. These ideas appealed to the free white settlers of the West, especially the tens of thousands of Germans moving out in search of land. Slavery, after all, would limit opportunity for those too poor to own slaves. Called upon to speak to the assembly, Greeley declined, all too aware that he could antagonize the Know-Nothings and endanger an already fragile coalition.[12]

The Pittsburgh meeting disbanded without nominating a candidate for president, however, although Greeley was disposed toward John Fremont (1813–1890), known as the Pathfinder, a well-known and controversial explorer of the Rocky Mountains and the West. Born in

Georgia of a French father and a Virginian mother, Fremont led four expeditions to the West in the 1840s in search of overland routes to the Pacific. In 1850, the new state of California elected Fremont its first U.S. Senator. But his strong anti-slavery stance denied him reelection. Now he seemed an ideal Republican candidate for president—strongly anti-slavery, a highly visible public figure, and a man of the West.[13]

Greeley now reentered politics with enthusiasm. He said he would work hard for any man who would support "Free Kansas" and restore Freedom to the center of American political life. It was too late to revive the Missouri Compromise, but republicans could work for the "restitution to Freedom of what was lost by its repudiation" in the Compromise of 1850.[14]

In early May, Greeley responded to some republican inquiries about the platform for the forthcoming national convention. The platform should be a broad one, he wrote, encompassing all those whose "animating purpose is the extension of Freedom." The Republican movement, he added, was "defensive, not aggressive." Republicanism was "conservative of Freedom, rather than destructive of Slavery; and its [slavery's] demise will be, not a consummation, but a glorious beginning." Slavery should be ultimately abolished. But the first step would be to stop its extension into the territories of the West. "In this step, all true conservatives, all believers in the doctrines of our Revolutionary Fathers ought to unite."[15] Extending freedom should be the true mission of the Republican Party.

New York Whigs were suspicious of Greeley's motives as he moved into the new Republican Party. Weed wrote Seward that he could never understand Greeley because he did not see the "personal considerations which sway and govern him." Hamilton Fish wrote Weed that he "could not be inspired with confidence in any movement that Greeley controls. With all his ability, he has a crack across his brain that amounts to little short of derangement and will destroy anything which he may be allowed to lead."[16]

By early June, Greeley and the *Tribune* endorsed Fremont, even though Greeley privately considered him to be the "merest baby in politics." The main point was to defeat the Democratic front-runner, James Buchanan of Pennsylvania, whose election would be "prejudicial to the advance of Freedom and Justice throughout the world."[17] On June 17, 1856, the National Republican Convention in Philadelphia nominated John Fremont as its first candidate for president. Greeley promptly ghost wrote a campaign biography of the Pathfinder that came out in late July. According to Greeley, Fremont supported free labor against the Slave Power of the South, and drew strong support among German-American voters. He opposed any "extension of slavery" to the territories. Poet John Greenleaf Whittier, Greeley's cousin, wrote campaign songs for Fremont, whom he praised as the "standard bearer of Freedom." Regarding the upcoming presidential campaign, "there is but one question," wrote Harriet Beecher Stowe, "Freedom or Slavery—for or against."[18]

In the campaign, the Republicans called for Free Speech, Free Press, Free Soil, Free Men, and Fremont. In the South, the Richmond *Enquirer* responded with "free niggers, free women, free land, and Freemont." Greeley compiled *A History of the Struggle for Slavery Extension or Restriction in the United States, from the Declaration of Independence to the Present Day.* He patched most of it together from Adam Gurowski's book on slavery and the work of Richard Hildreth, an associate editor at the *Tribune.* Greeley now emphasized the slavery question rather than land reform. "All the earnest Land Reformers," concluded Greeley, "will vote with us any how."[19]

The Whigs complicated things in November by holding their last party convention in Baltimore and nominating Millard Fillmore for president. Attendance was sparse and few states sent any delegates at all. A Whig pamphlet attacked Greeley as an "avowed socialist" who "dreamed of an earthly millennium" of social reform and "French liberty," rather than a man who left a dying and divided party. He was the "father of the whole movement" creating the Republican Party. "If this party succeeds," grumbled the Whigs, "its success will be monumental of the immortality of Horace Greeley."[20]

But success was not yet to be. Despite Greeley's active campaigning—circulating thousands of copies of his biography of Fremont, trying to woo French Canadian voters in Maine, speaking in New York—the Republicans lost the 1856 election. Greeley thought that if they won, they would make Kansas a free state and show that "Freedom can win in a pitched battle with Slavery." But he admitted that most Americans were not yet anti-slavery. Progress would be slow. The voters proved Greeley's point in November by electing Democrat James Buchanan president with 45.3 percent of the popular vote (1,838,169 votes), compared with Fremont's 33.1 percent of the vote (1,341,264 votes). The Whigs and Fillmore picked up 21.6 percent of the vote.

Had the Whigs joined the Republicans, Fremont would have won. Even if only Pennsylvania's twenty-seven electoral votes had gone to Fremont, the election would have ended up in the House of Representatives, where the Republicans could have won.[21]

"I think we have no reason to be discouraged," Greeley wrote Schuyler Colfax, "we have made a great beginning, and I trust we have helped Kansas by putting all the States west of yours [Indiana] under the government of our friends. I am tired and sore, and a little inclined to rest and quiet, but Kansas will be free."[22]

The election revealed surprising Republican Party support among German-Americans throughout the West. Many German immigrants wanted land and opposed slavery; others were militant abolitionists. Fremont himself had recruited dozens of Germans as botanists, cartographers, topographers, artists, and geologists for his western explorations. Carl Schurz, a Forty-Eighter, was organizing the party in Wisconsin. Gustav Koerner, a friend of Abraham Lincoln, was doing the same in Illinois, as were Hermann Kiefer in Michigan, J. B. Stallo in Ohio, and Friedrich Kapp in New York. Francis Lieber advised Seward how to win over German voters in New York. Schurz thought that the whole election resembled the "disastrous breakdown of the great movement for popular government on the European continent in 1848." The 1856 Republican platform, he wrote later, "sounded to me like a bugle-call of liberty. . . . Thus the old cause of human freedom was to be fought for on the soil of the new world."[23]

The Republicans failed to elect Fremont in 1856, but made their name as a party of the future. With Whig support, they would have won the election. Lincoln and others believed that German support was significant, true or not. The question of the day was clearly whether freedom or slavery would triumph in a single nation. "Three hundred years ago," thundered Theodore Parker in Boston, "our fathers in Europe were contending for liberty. . . . The question laid over by our fathers is adjourned to us for settlement."[24] The question was: slavery or freedom? The answer was being fought over in Kansas.

BLEEDING KANSAS

Horace Greeley and the *Tribune* played a major role in placing "bleeding Kansas" at the center of the debate over freedom and slavery in the 1850s. The widely read newspaper trumpeted the rhetoric of free Kansas against the "slavocracy" in Washington and the "border ruffians" of Missouri, a slave state. Kansas was the new battleground of a world-wide struggle to replace liberty and slavery with freedom and emancipation, the first battle of the Civil War, some thought. As a territory of the expanding West, Kansas also offered a republican utopia for free white labor, and no slaves with which to compete. If Kansas should join the republic as a free state, corruption might be conquered. If Kansas joined as a slave state, the republic faced more corruption, factionalism, and even civil war.

The struggle for freedom in Kansas pitted two concepts of freedom against each other: first, the exclusion of slavery, and the admission of Kansas to the Union as a free state; second, the freedom of the citizens of Kansas to decide whether or not they wished the state to be slave or free. Northern abolitionists and anti-slavery men advocated the first concept, while southern slave owners advocated the second under Stephan Douglas's concept of "popular sovereignty." Greeley and other northerners wanted Free Labor and Free Soil in a free state. Kansas became the first battleground of the war between Slavery and Freedom, a land where friends and enemies of slavery became engaged in a bloody contest. Pro-slavery men from Missouri crossed over to vote in Kansas elections. Anti-slavery men from the Northeast moved in with their families to ensure Free Soil. New England emigrants to Kansas boasted that their forefathers had "sought liberty on the *Mayflower*" and now they would seek "Freedom and Happiness" in Kansas.[25]

In the 1850s, Greeley was involved with abolitionists Eli Thayer of Massachusetts and Moses Grinnell of Iowa in organizing the emigration of free whites and their families to Kansas. Thayer came to New York in May 1854, and persuaded Greeley to help find investors in a company for "the great cause of freedom." Thus was born the Emigrant Aid Company of New York and Connecticut. Going West now took on new meaning. Settling Kansas would not only relieve the pressure on eastern cities, but extend freedom to the territories. The goal was to settle half a million farmers, mechanics, and artisans on the prairie. Settlers would purchase land for $1.25 an acre and be given Sharps rifles for self-defense. (Christian Sharps was a Swiss immigrant who patented his accurate, short-barrel carbine rifle in 1848 in Hartford, Connecticut.) In the end, the company aided only two thousand or so settlers, one-third of whom probably returned home. Unless such emigration were encouraged, wrote the *Tribune*, "we believe that there are at this hour four chances that Kansas will be a slave state to one that she will be free."[26]

In October 1854, the first appointed governor of Kansas, John W. Geary, arrived in the state, ordered a census, and scheduled the first election for a legislature. Border ruffians from Missouri promptly crossed over to vote for slavery, and the first Kansas legislature did adopt a slave code. Free-state men rejected that legislature and organized their own in Topeka in 1855. The Topeka legislature then produced a constitution that excluded slavery (and free blacks) from the state, while applying for admission to the Union as a free state. There were thus two rival governments in Kansas, one free and one slave, both illegal, and both beginning to arm themselves for open warfare.

The *Tribune* led the agitation against slavery in Kansas. Dana's staff, the "friends of freedom," were now raising money, organizing emigration, and shipping rifles. The Emigrant Aid Company in the autumn of 1855 managed to procure a large mountain howitzer in New York at the state arsenal, thanks to the efforts of Greeley and Frederick Law Olmsted, then a young reporter for the rival *New York Times.* The howitzer was privately owned, but Olmsted, with Greeley's (unfulfilled) promise of aid, managed to purchase it and some shells and canister for $480. The howitzer finally made its way to Kansas, as did hundreds of rifles in boxes labeled "Bibles"—the famous "Beecher Bibles," after the minister Henry Ward Beecher.[27]

While Greeley was off in Europe and Washington in fall 1855, Dana and Pike continued to ratchet up the *Tribune* rhetoric about Kansas. "The cause of freedom in Kansas," wrote Pike, "has no longer any hope from any source but the stalwart arms and sure rifles of the people of the Free States. Let them not be wanting!" Greeley protested from Washington that the *Tribune* line on Kansas was leading "every traitor and self-seeker" to view him now with a "demoniac hatred." One of the pro-slavery Kansas Volunteers threatened to whip him. Greeley warned Dana against "plotting treason and inciting insurrection," losing valuable southern subscribers.[28]

But Dana persisted. In 1854, he had sent a young *Tribune* firebrand, a Scot named James Redpath, twenty-eight, to Kansas as a reporter and agitator. Redpath had made a three-month journey through the South in 1854, publishing his articles as *The Roving Editor* in 1859.

He abhorred slavery as a moral evil, and wanted to foment a slave insurrection. He then helped get men and weapons into Kansas from Iowa and New England. Later, on January 12, 1856, Redpath addressed a free-state rally in Lawrence, where feelings ran high on both sides, and predicted civil war. By summer 1856, Redpath was a commissioned officer in the volunteer army of the Free State of Kansas, where he met John Brown.[29] "The Second American Revolution," he announced, was about to begin.[30]

In early 1856, Dana went off to Kansas to see for himself what was going on. Greeley admonished him to omit from the paper anything that was "impelled by hatred of the South" or a "desire to humiliate that section." Yet he also wanted to make Kansas "as prominent as possible" to ensure a "decisive triumph" for the anti-slavery cause.[31]

On May 20, 1856, a pro-slavery mob sacked and burned Lawrence. Two days later, South Carolina representative Preston Brooks nearly beat Senator Charles Sumner to death with a cane on the floor of the U.S. Senate for Sumner's speech "The Crime against Kansas." Sumner had insulted one of Brooks's relatives, attacked slavery, and praised Massachusetts for its "fixed resolve for freedom everywhere, and especially now for freedom in Kansas."[32] Two days after that, abolitionist agitator John Brown and four of his sons hacked five men to death with broadswords at Pottawatomie in front of their families. By December, the civil war in Kansas had killed over two hundred people and cost two million dollars in property damage.

Greeley was outraged. He wrote a friend that he would probably not return to Washington when the Kansas question came up again, because "I shall stand a very good chance to get killed there." In his own massive history of the struggle to restrict slavery from the American Revolution to the present, he called slavery a "domestic despotism" that contradicted the country's original "spirit of liberty." He serialized a novel entitled *The Kansas Emigrants* by his friend Lydia Maria Child, a Boston abolitionist busy sending supplies and weapons to Kansas. Charles Dana spoke out against "bleeding Kansas" at a Free Soil rally in New York. He assured the Emigrant Aid Company that he was helping to provide "money and facilities for transportation" to get emigrants and their families to Kansas. The *Tribune* office openly collected funds for Kansas, but Greeley also criticized Thayer for delays and inefficiencies in his organization and for the "ridiculous war" in Kansas. He was "heartsick" that emigrants could not get out of New York.[33] And he wrote that a civil war between freedom and slavery would happen within the next four years.[34]

In March 1857, the U.S. Supreme Court upheld the legality of slavery in the case of a slave named Dred Scott. Scott claimed his freedom because his owner had moved him from a slave state (Missouri) to a free state (Illinois). U.S. Chief Justice Roger Taney held that a slave, ex-slave, or descendant of a slave was not an American citizen, but the property of an owner. Because Congress was constitutionally required to protect property, it could not prohibit slavery in the territories. Thus the slave owner's constitutional rights to liberty and property under the law superseded the freedom of the slave, who was not a citizen, but a thing. Anti-slavery men and women everywhere were outraged.[35]

Greeley wrote that Taney's decision carried as much moral weight as a majority vote in "any Washington bar room." The decision was bad law, "southern sophism cloaked with the dignity of our highest court." Slaves might be sold on Bunker Hill and in front of Faneuil Hall in Boston, while slave ships might now "land their dusky cargo at Plymouth Rock." The *Dred Scott* decision was a collection of "false statements and shallow sophistries" put together to support a foregone conclusion, and a "fatal blow to the rights and liberties of all." Even the individual states could only establish and strengthen slavery within their borders. The *Dred Scott* case, wrote Greeley, meant that "the Star of Freedom and the stripes of bondage are henceforth one. American Republicanism and American Slavery are for the future synonymous."[36]

Greeley's personal life fared no better than freedom in Kansas or slaves did after the *Dred Scott* decision. Still grieving for his lost son Pickie, Greeley's son Raphael, age six, died of the croup. Molly gave birth to another daughter in late March. "I ought to be thankful for this gift," he wrote, "but am not." He prayed to God that he might soon "rejoin my brave and beautiful boys in Heaven." Then in April, his brother Barnes's wife died in Clymer, New York. And he was yet again in financial trouble—his father owed him thousands, his brother Barnes hundreds, as did several others. He asked his old friend Augustus Allen of Clymer to vote his Erie Railroad stock proxy at a meeting in July.[37]

To complicate matters further, Thomas McElrath went bankrupt in the financial panic of 1857 and lost hundreds of thousands of dollars worth of railroad stock himself. He consequently had to sell off his *Tribune* stock and resign as the president of the Nassau Bank. Richard Hoe, the printing-machine manufacturer, growled that McElrath had "no one to blame but himself." Hoe promised that he would continue to do business with the *Tribune*. But the newspaper itself lost advertising and subscribers that year. Greeley had to default on a five-thousand-dollar loan he owed his friend Peter Cooper because his own loans were still outstanding. "Nobody pays us," he wrote Cooper, "or we would not ask an hour's indulgence."[38]

Greeley remained active on behalf of Kansas nonetheless. The *Tribune* continued to serve as custodian of money contributed on behalf of the National Kansas League, but Greeley was reluctant to disburse the money because Eli Thayer delayed moving emigrants west, and refused to come to New York to help organize emigration there. Greeley criticized Thayer for creating a "ridiculous mess." "For Humanity's sake," he wrote Edward Hale, "do tell the people now waiting how they are to get to Kansas." James Redpath remained active, helping bring more emigrants to Kansas and editing his own newspaper there, the *Herald of Freedom*.[39] But the project to encourage New Englanders to "go West" to Kansas languished.

In 1857, a group of pro-slavery delegates to a convention at the town of Lecompton, Kansas, produced a new constitution for the state. But the December referendum was rigged, the free-state men boycotted it, and it showed over six thousand votes for a slavery constitution. The January 1858 election, however, produced a decisive defeat of slavery: 10,226 voted against the Lecompton Constitution, and only 138 for it. Yet President Buchanan supported Lecompton as an indicator of popular sovereignty, and asked Congress to admit Kansas to the Union as a slave state. In March 1858, the U.S. Senate voted to accept the Lecompton Constitution, but the House of Representatives rejected it. Kansas voters also rejected the Constitution for a second time in August by a vote of 11,300 to 1,788. Kansas voters had overwhelmingly rejected slavery, but the federal government supported it, and federal troops were sent to guard the polls. The smell of gunpowder remained in the air.[40] The corruption of the republic, warned Greeley, would soon "reap the whirlwind."[41]

Horace Greeley entered the battle for Kansas on the side of freedom and against slavery. He and his newspaper participated in that battle editorially, monetarily, politically, and even militarily, through the Emigrant Aid Company, shipping men and weapons to Kansas. The battle for freedom in Kansas was violent and bloody in 1857. But it was also a war of principles, freedom against slavery, principles grounded in Greeley's Universalist belief in freedom for all men.

UNIVERSALIST FREEDOM

Precisely at the time he was involved in Kansas, Horace Greeley reiterated his deep Universalist faith in universal salvation for all—sinners and saints, slaves and slaveholders alike. In May 1858, he spoke on the "Christian Spirit of Reform" in New York and linked Christianity and other religions with the good life. Christianity was the enemy of all the wrong, abuse, and injury of mankind—slavery, war, alcohol, polygamy, and evil. Christianity meant "Absolute Justice, Absolute Morality, impelled by Universal Love." Freedom meant a moral obligation to reform the world and make it a better place.[42]

He continued to attend the Orchard Street Universalist Society church in New York City, where he listened to the sermons of Thomas Sawyer, then Thomas Lake Harris, and finally Edward H. Chapin. Chapin railed against slavery. "We have many practical elements of freedom here at the North," Chapin noted, "but how long shall we be permitted to retain and use them, if the tendencies of the last few years are carried out?"[43]

The Universalist *Christian Messenger* praised Greeley's views. "On the subject of Freedom and Slavery," noted the journal, "Mr. Greeley goes for the largest amount of Freedom that is possibly attainable."[44] Likewise, Greeley published articles in Universalist periodicals throughout the 1850s. The world was witnessing a struggle between good and evil, he thought. Intemperance, war, vice, crime, and poverty were everywhere. The challenge was to "Christianize" the industrial and social relations of humankind through reform. Greeley's reform impulse, in Kansas as elsewhere, reflected his faith in all those who "truly love God" and try to "enlighten and serve their fellow men."[45]

His own age and the death of five of seven children made Greeley more deeply religious than ever. Death and immortality, meeting one's children again in heaven, would be better than living life as a prisoner with a "decaying" body and mind. Greeley truly believed that an "everlasting home" awaited all of us in the "boundless universe" of heaven. God in his infinite wisdom directs some children to die young, so that we may "know them and greet them as children in a Better Land." Heaven would not be heaven, thought Greeley, "unless peopled, in good part, by children."[46]

Greeley also maintained an interest during the Kansas years in Universalist education. He helped lay the cornerstone of St. Lawrence University in Canton, New York, in June 1856. Colleges and universities, he argued (he had never attended one), should educate the whole person, mind, body, and soul, for a life of service and labor. Education should produce complete men, practical men, men like Benjamin Franklin, Daniel Boone, and George Washington.[47]

Family tragedy also turned Greeley toward spiritualism. Like his father, Zaccheus Greeley, his brother Barnes and his wife, Molly, were both spiritualists, seeking especially to reach their own dead children. Molly claimed that a spirit voice had helped her find a misplaced catalogue in the house. She thought she was in touch with Pickie and Raphael. Horace was more skeptical, but intrigued. Much of spiritualism, he wrote a friend in 1858, was "humbug" and a "swindle." But there was still "some foundation for the claim of spirit intercourse" and communication with the dead, he thought. As to the spiritualists themselves, he wrote Theodore Parker, "I regard them, in the true spirit of a Rational Christian, as in part dupes and gross squanderers of time, but not (generally) imposters, and with scarcely more absurdities in their creed than have most of us." The spirit rappings he had observed, he felt, were "not generally simulated," but had some meaning behind them. Molly remained fascinated by rappings and accepted their spiritual origin. She talked daily with her dead Pickie. "I am skeptical," wrote Greeley to his friend Emma Newhall, but thought there might well be some kind of "magnetic telegraph" connection to the unseen world.[48]

It is at this time that the Greeleys fell under the spell of the British spiritualist Thomas Lake Harris. In 1845, Harris turned up in New York City and set up his First Independent Christian Society. Greeley, Emerson, George Ripley, and Henry James were among his admirers, as were many Swedenborgians. The Greeleys joined his congregation, while retaining their Universalist memberships as well.[49] Harris subsequently moved west to establish a commune at Brocton, New York, on Lake Erie, where he developed "the Use," a method of reaching

God through deep-breathing exercises. He encouraged manual labor. He ministered to many ill women. He demanded obedience as "Father Faithful."

Greeley's flirtation with Thomas Lake Harris remained a passing fancy, rather than a life-changing commitment. He had always been interested in spiritualism, was a deeply believing Christian Universalist, and relished new ideas. A friend's sister followed Harris west and later married him.[50] Neither Greeley nor Molly accepted Harris's prophetic authoritarianism and cultist utopia. But even as Greeley influenced national events, he flirted with a spiritualist cult. "Greeley," Bronson Alcott wrote his wife in New Hampshire after visiting Greeley, "is as simple in his greatness as a child, and a sound, sensible, good man: perhaps the most influential power just now in the whole Country."[51]

Greeley's Universalism and interest in things spiritual were a vital part of his quest for American freedom, the moral gyroscope that directed all of Greeley's reform efforts to save the world. Greeley held that gyroscope closely, of course, and let only a few of his closest friends, several of them women, into his world of spirituality. "I need you," he wrote one of those lady friends in October 1871, "as the one woman who can understand and appreciate my reveries concerning the Unseen World."[52] Behind the very public world of the *Tribune* and Greeley's efforts to reform this world lay an abiding interest in the higher and unseen world that animated moral law and anticipated another world beyond death. True freedom was not simply earthly, but divine, reflected in political events even in faraway Kansas and Illinois.

ILLINOIS DEBATES: SLAVERY VERSUS FREEDOM

In 1858, Illinois joined Kansas as a battleground in the war between slavery and freedom. Here a leading Democrat, Stephen A. Douglas, faced a former Illinois congressman and railroad attorney, Abraham Lincoln, in the race for a U.S. Senate seat held by Douglas. To the consternation of Lincoln and most Republicans, Horace Greeley supported Douglas, a Democrat, against Lincoln, a Republican. Why? Many have attributed Greeley's support for Douglas simply to his erratic and inconsistent political behavior. But in fact, Greeley's consistent strategy that year was to divide the Democrats by backing an anti-Lecompton man who had broken with his party and his president, which would help elect a Republican president in 1860. Strategically, Greeley had his eye on the next presidential election, when his old mentor William Henry Seward would probably be the front-runner. Lincoln was an unknown figure outside Illinois. Tactically, Greeley thought defeating Lincoln and returning a renegade Senator to divide the Democrats in Washington was a perfectly reasonable strategy.

Illinois in 1858 was in "the West." The state's population doubled between 1850 and 1860, so that Illinois was the fourth most populous state by the time of the Civil War. The percentage of foreign-born voters, mainly Germans, increased from thirteen to nineteen percent during the 1850s. The Germans were generally opposed to slavery and in favor of free labor and free land, so it is not surprising that Lincoln was close to a number of Germans in Illinois—John G. Nicolay, a young newspaper man working for the *Missouri Democrat*, Gustav Koerner, a Belleville attorney, and Dr. Theodore Canisius, editor of the *Illinois Staats Anzeiger* (of which Lincoln was part owner) in Springfield.[53]

At forty-five, Stephen A. Douglas—the "Little Giant"—was a nationally known politician in 1858, energetic, bold, pugnacious, diminutive, and dedicated to the Manifest Destiny of the United States to expand its territory and influence world affairs. In 1848, the Little Giant supported the European republics and urged American recognition. Douglas despised England and thought America should have the right to intervene in Europe on behalf of republican governments there. George N. Sanders and his *Democratic Review* supported Douglas in his run for the presidency in 1852, when he lost the nomination at Baltimore to Franklin Pierce. After the defeat, Douglas returned to the U.S. Senate from his home state of Illinois, where he now faced reelection.

Greeley had no enthusiasm for Douglas until 1858. In 1856, Greeley described Douglas as a "criminal" who "sells out free territory to be coerced and blackened with the hideous crime and curse of African slavery." This was a bit unfair, since Douglas himself was not pro-slavery, but only favored state sovereignty in the matter. But when Douglas broke with President Buchanan and the Democrats by opposing the pro-slavery Lecompton Constitution in Kansas, Greeley saw an opening. In December 1857, Greeley made secret arrangements through his Indiana friend, Schuyler Colfax, to call upon Douglas regarding his upcoming Senate campaign.[54]

The moment was opportune. Pro-slavery southern Democrats hated Douglas for proposing popular sovereignty and opposing slavery in Kansas. "Douglas has broken the back of the Democratic Party," Greeley wrote Colfax, "it will hold him responsible for the loss of Kansas and will never forgive him—never!" To support Douglas and thereby to divide the Democrats seemed politically astute, and the *Tribune* began moving in this direction. Lincoln was mystified and annoyed. "What does the New York Tribune mean by its constant eulogizing, and admiring, and magnifying [of] Douglas?" he asked a Republican friend. Had Republicans in Washington decided that they could best promote the party cause by sacrificing Lincoln to Douglas in Illinois?[55]

Greeley had known Lincoln ever since they met in Chicago in 1847. They had served together briefly in the U.S. Congress. They shared a Whig interpretation of politics and economics, a love for Henry Clay, an enthusiasm for the new Republican Party, an antipathy to slavery, and a commitment to freedom. Lincoln, an attorney, had special respect for liberty under the law. Protecting the liberty bequeathed by the founding fathers, now the "proud fabric of freedom," was mandatory.[56]

The Kansas-Nebraska Act of 1854 transformed Lincoln from a lover of liberty into an advocate for freedom. Like Greeley, Lincoln became convinced that slavery and freedom were completely incompatible in a republic, and that slavery was a matter of right versus wrong, a moral evil that must be eliminated. Until this point, Lincoln had focused on railroads, banking, and the right of all Americans to rise or succeed in life. Now he understood that slavery subverted the dream of economic progress. On October 5, 1854, in a speech at Peoria, Illinois, Lincoln promised that "the theory of our government is Universal Freedom. 'All men are created free and equal,' says the Declaration of Independence. The word 'Slavery' is not found in the Constitution." The U.S. Constitution might safeguard liberty for some, but the Declaration of Independence promised freedom for all. All "lovers of liberty" must unite to save the Union. All "friends of freedom" must support universal civil liberties based on the Declaration. Slavery and freedom were simply incompatible in the republic. If slavery persisted, wrote Lincoln, "I shall prefer emigrating to some country where they make no pretense of loving liberty—in Russia, for instance, where despotism can be taken pure, and without the base alloy of hypocrisy."[57]

After many months of hesitation, Lincoln helped found the new Republican Party in Illinois in February 1856. He supported Fremont in his campaign for the presidency by giving more than fifty speeches in Illinois. He spoke out against slavery in the territories. And he took note of the large number of German immigrants in Illinois who were completing their five-year naturalization period and preparing to vote.

Through his young law partner, William Herndon, Lincoln also became aware of the abolitionist rhetoric of Unitarian minister Theodore Parker in Boston. Herndon passed Parker's sermons along to Lincoln, who read and annotated many of them. He also advertised Parker throughout Illinois, considering Parker and Lincoln common allies in the "battle of Freedom," seeking government "of all the people, by all the people, for all the people." In October 1855, Herndon wrote Parker that Illinois republicans were organizing themselves for the great struggle with slavery, adding that Douglas was a liar and an alcoholic. But in his response, Parker wrote, "in 1860 comes the real struggle between North and South. Freedom and Slavery! I think not before."[58]

Greeley also admired Parker, if not as fervently. In 1853, he sent Parker a three-volume biography of Seward and asked him to review it for the prestigious *Westminster Review*. A year later, Greeley wrote the Boston minister that most Americans were not yet in favor of eliminating slavery, and that anti-slavery would be most productively pursued through the existing major parties, not another Liberty or Free Soil effort.[59]

After Kansas and the *Dred Scott* decision, Herndon believed a bloody civil war was coming. "The issue is," he wrote Parker, Freedom or Slavery—War in time or Peace." He sent Lincoln's speeches on to Parker and other Boston abolitionists, and reminded Parker that "I am for Freedom, Liberty!"[60]

In early 1858, the Lincoln-Douglas campaign to elect a state legislature that would choose the next U.S. Senator from Illinois began in earnest. Lincoln complained to Herndon that Greeley was now supporting Douglas in the *Tribune*. "I like Greeley," he wrote, "think he intends right, but I think he errs in this hoisting up of Douglas, while he gives me a downward shove." Someone should "put a flea in Greeley's ear" and set him straight.[61]

On his way to Boston to recruit Lincoln supporters, Herndon stopped off in New York. He wrote Lincoln that he had seen Greeley for twenty minutes, and that the editor "evidently wants Douglas sustained and sent back to the Senate." Greeley also told Herndon that the republican standard was too high and that they needed "something practical." Herndon was now suspicious of Greeley. In Boston, Herndon told Parker that Greeley was going to "lower the Republican flag" to support Douglas in Illinois. He had harmed the party there with his pro-Douglas editorials. "Greeley is not fit for a leader," concluded Herndon. "He is capricious, crotchety, full of whims, and as wrong-headed as a pig."[62]

That spring, the rift between Greeley and the Lincoln campaign deepened. Herndon accused Greeley of wanting to "sell us out in Illinois without our consent to accomplish some national political purpose." By late April, Herndon wrote Parker that "our boys here did not like Greeley's course but all is o.k. now." Greeley temporized. "We *know* that Mr. Lincoln will prove an excellent Senator if elected," he wrote in the *Tribune* in mid-May, "we *believe* Mr. Douglas cannot henceforth be otherwise." The *Chicago Democrat* promptly accused Greeley of making a secret deal with Douglas. Greeley promised Herndon that he was not trying to instruct Republicans in Illinois in their "political duties," then urged them to "paddle your own dugout." Herndon told Parker that Greeley seemed determined to split the Democrats by supporting Douglas, "though he sacrifice the Republicans in Illinois." Lincoln also believed that Greeley was supporting Douglas not because of any secret arrangement but simply because Greeley thought a Douglas victory would help the Republicans in the presidential election of 1860. The candidate still admired Greeley as a man "incapable of corruption or falsehood."[63]

In June, Lincoln and Douglas began their famous series of seven debates across Illinois that would last until mid-October. In his famous "House Divided" speech at Springfield on June 17, Lincoln announced that the United States could not exist half slave and half free, using biblical language well known to his audience. When the Republican convention nominated Lincoln a few days later, Greeley printed his speech in the *Tribune* and called it "concise and admirable." But he still feared that a Lincoln victory would drive Illinois Democrats into a position of "virtual subservience to the Slave Power" in the South. Greeley also rejected Douglas's attack on Lincoln's idea that either slavery or freedom must ultimately prevail in the Union. The founding fathers, asserted Greeley, would "hold with Mr. Lincoln on this point, not with Mr. Douglas." Herndon found Greeley's comment "clear and helpful," but reminded him that Illinois Republicans were now in a "hot canvas" against Douglas and the Democrats.[64] Yet Greeley and the *Tribune* basically ignored the rest of the Lincoln-Douglas debates in favor of a possible Greeley run for governor in New York.[65]

Herndon continued to rail against Greeley. He wrote Parker that the editor was harming Illinois Republicans by supporting Douglas, and that Greeley and Douglas had an "arrangement" of some sort. Greeley was either treacherous or indifferent in this election, and was "daily playing into the hands of the pro-slavery camp." Greeley was "acting a great-dog," Herndon wrote Parker. "Who would know by Greeley's paper that a great race for weal or woe was being fought all over the vast world-wide prairies of Illinois? Who would. It is strange indeed."[66]

On November 2, 1858, the Illinois legislature elected Douglas Senator 54–46, despite the fact that Lincoln had won the popular vote. "Mr. Douglas," wrote the *Tribune*, "has achieved a great personal triumph." Herndon went east to Boston again to discuss his political future with prominent abolitionists and Republicans, and continued to blame Greeley, in part, for Lincoln's defeat, noting that "his silence was his opposition." Greeley, Herndon concluded, was a "natural fool" in his "hearty Douglas position." Greeley responded that he had simply been unable to write any pro-Lincoln editorials that would have been "lucid or satisfactory." The Republicans had gained twenty-five seats in Congress in the recent elections in the three states contiguous to Illinois. "Your course may prove wiser in the long run," Greeley told Herndon, "but ours vindicates itself at the outset."[67]

Herndon's judgment on Greeley was mixed. He found Greeley to be conservative and timid. "He is willing to agitate for an idea during its abstract state, but he shudders when it is about to concrete itself amidst living events, human conditions, social, religious, or political. He *will not do* for a great leader of America's present events." Yet, for all that, Herndon found Greeley to be "an honest man and I still like him somewhat."[68]

Lincoln thought his political career was at an end. He might have made some mark on behalf of "civil liberty," but now he would simply "sink out of view." Herndon had not given up, however. He returned from Boston with a trunkload of Parker's sermons for Lincoln to read. Lincoln did indeed read one sermon entitled "The Effect of Slavery on the American People" and underlined in pencil the phrase "government of, by, and for the people."[69]

Greeley remained convinced that he had pursued the right course in Illinois in 1858, even though he believed that Douglas personally was a "low and dangerous demagogue" and unlikely to be elected U.S. president. Douglas had helped divide the country over slavery by his "hateful scheming and reckless legislation." He was a "great political sinner" and a "walking magazine of mischief." Yet Illinois Republicans continued to believe that Greeley and Douglas had schemed and plotted prior to the election. Both Greeley and Douglas denied the charge. Their only political agreement, Greeley asserted, was that both opposed the pro-slavery Lecompton Constitution in Kansas. Lincoln believed him. "Greeley, I think," Lincoln wrote a friend, "will not tell a falsehood; and I think he will scarcely deny that he had the interviews with Douglas in order to assure himself from Douglas's own lips, better than he could from his public acts and declarations, whether to try to bring the Republican party to his support generally, including his reelection to the Senate. What else could the interviews be for?" Greeley was incorruptible, he was "serving the Republican cause," and he was "now pulling straight with us."[70] Both Lincoln and Greeley were mending fences.

Greeley's support of Douglas against Lincoln in 1858 was consistent with his intent to weaken the Democratic Party and elect a Republican president in 1860. In retrospect, many thought Greeley should have supported Lincoln. But Lincoln was still a political unknown in the East. Greeley wanted to win the election, not support a particular candidate prematurely. Ultimately his support in 1860 would guarantee Lincoln's nomination and assist his election. But for now he emphasized his broad republican strategy for freedom, and recalled the republicanism of 1848 in Europe. He introduced Jesse White Mario (1832–1906), an Italian republican, when she lectured on the Risorgimento and the cause of Italian freedom in New York. He joined George N. Sanders and other notables trying to raise money for Mazzini.[71] And he began to think of a trip west along the line of a projected transcontinental railroad, one of Douglas's pet projects. For the first time in his life, Greeley would "go West," if only on an adventurous excursion, not simply to Illinois and Kansas, but to Colorado and California.

CALIFORNIA OVERLAND

In early 1859, Horace Greeley decided at last to take his own advice and "go West." He had no intention of settling there, of course, since he was well established in New York. But, at the age of forty-eight, he wanted to see the West for himself. The railroad men were talking of a transcontinental route again and fighting over southern and northern alternatives. Greeley had long thought a transcontinental railroad was "imperative and inevitable."[72] Now he wanted to see where and how such a railroad would expand the empire of freedom.

Talk of a transcontinental railroad went back to the 1830s. In 1844, Greeley suggested diverting half of the Navy's budget to build it, creating new jobs and giving westerners higher prices for their goods and produce. The federal government could sell public land along the proposed routes to help settle the West. After the discovery of gold in California in 1849, Greeley was even more excited about the project. A Pacific railroad would be the "grandest enterprise of the age," would quadruple the number of families going west, and would provide a moral alternative to slavery, uniting a divided nation. The railroad would help settle the West, open up Pacific markets, bring the wealth of California east, carry the mail at reasonable postal rates, transport troops and supplies if needed, and employ thousands. The federal government, he felt, should finance the entire project, which was essential to the "unity and dignity of the republic" and would be worth more than the Mexican War and "a dozen Cubas."[73]

In January 1859, gold turned up in Colorado, as well as California. The news spread like wildfire. The financial panic of 1857 had encouraged gold fever in hopes of profits during times of inflation and unemployment. A red-bearded Georgian prospector named John Hamilton Gregory had established his "diggings" that spring in a canyon near Clear Creek, Colorado, and now Denver was overflowing with new fortune-hunters. Greeley, along with two other journalists, Albert D. Richardson of the *Boston Journal* and Henry Villard of the *Cincinnati Commercial,* decided to go West and publicize the new discovery. Greeley's old newspaper friend, Jonas Winchester, now the state printer of California, had told him of the gold rush in 1849. Now Greeley wanted to see for himself what the West had to offer.[74]

He originally planned to go back to Europe. Molly and the children had spent a dreary winter in Dresden, corresponding only with Greeley, whom she scolded for one thing or another, and "all absorbed in the pettiest, meanest cares." Now Greeley talked of going to England, France, Switzerland, and Holland. But by April, his plans had changed. "I have business in California," he wrote a friend, "which may put me on the Overland Trail next month." Molly was "in bad health and failing." A trip west offered an escape from family troubles, a chance to unite the anti-Lecompton Democrats and Republicans in Kansas, a way to promote the railroad, and an opportunity to observe the settlement of the frontier.[75]

On May 9, Greeley boarded a train in New York City and headed west via Buffalo, Cleveland, and Chicago. By May 20, he was in Lawrence, Kansas, speaking to local Republicans. His observation to Charles Dana was grim: "Rain—mud most profound—flooded rivers and streams—glorious soil—worthless politicians—lazy people—such is Kansas in a nutshell." He arrived in Denver after a jolting ride on one of the very first stagecoaches from St. Joseph, Missouri. The fare was $175, the baggage limit twenty-five pounds. By June 6, he was in the sprawling new town of Denver, Colorado, where he met Albert Richardson and Henry Villard. Two days later the three journalists headed for Gregory's diggings and the sight of gold. Greeley spoke to a meeting of miners to great applause. They were a jealous, violent, and feuding lot, eager to stake claims, ignore whatever laws might exist (very few), and impress the eastern gentlemen. They even "salted" a streambed with gold flakes for Greeley to pan himself. He promptly reported to the *Tribune* that he had found a gold mine—"the richest and greatest in America." The miners roared with laughter at the thought of a new gold rush based on a salted mine.[76]

Albert Richardson and Henry Villard would cross Greeley's path many times in the future. Both would become *Tribune* correspondents. Villard was a Bavarian-born journalist who covered the Lincoln-Douglas debates in Illinois a year earlier, and later wrote for German-language newspapers and recruited Germans to the Republican Party. He would later marry William Lloyd Garrison's daughter (1866), and become president of the Northern Pacific Railroad.[77]

But for the moment, young Villard had joined the mob of gold hunters headed for Gregory's Gulch, and had run into Greeley at the Denver House in Denver. Denver House, the local hotel, was actually a log cabin with a canvas roof, no floors, ceilings, or walls, no mattresses or pillows, but a well-stocked bar and gambling tables. The place was both noisy and filthy. Greeley himself arrived in dramatic fashion, carried off his stagecoach with a bad leg, injured when buffaloes overturned the coach on the journey west. After ten days in Denver, Greeley had had enough. He headed for Salt Lake City on a route that followed the Overland Trail through Laramie, Wyoming, South Pass, and Fort Bridger, Colorado.

By mid-July, Greeley was in Salt Lake City, where he conducted the first newspaper interview ever held with Brigham Young. Young had led the Mormons (Church of Latter-Day Saints) to Utah in 1847 and formed the state of Deseret (Honeybee) as a kind of theocracy. The territory of Utah emerged from the Compromise of 1850. Young had simply ignored the orders of federal officials and judges, so that in 1857, President Buchanan had to send in federal troops to assert control. The Mormon War of 1857–8 was bloody and savage. It had just ended when Greeley arrived in Salt Lake City.

Greeley's two-hour interview with Young was a major media event. With other Mormons present, Greeley asked penetrating questions about Mormon theology, eternal punishment, opposition to infant baptism, polygamy, and the divine justification for slavery in Mormon eyes. He then telegraphed the results to the *Tribune*. He also attended two services in the Tabernacle, finding them poorly prepared and rambling. Greeley disagreed with most of the precepts of the Mormon church, especially polygamy. As far as he was concerned, the Mormons could have Utah, and Brigham Young could be governor.[78]

From Utah, Greeley headed across Nevada to Placerville, California, then to Sacramento and San Francisco. On the way to Placerville, Greeley rode in a stagecoach with the legendary driver Hank Monk. Greeley asked Monk to speed up so he could attend a welcoming committee meeting at 5:00 p.m. "I'll get you there," promised Monk, driving the next eleven miles downhill and over rocks in fifty-three minutes. "I am not particular for an hour or two," cried out the regretful and shaken Greeley. "Horace," yelled back Monk, "keep your seat!

I told you I would get you there by five o'clock and by G—— I'll do it, if the axles hold!" And he did.[79]

Republicans in San Francisco welcomed Greeley as a prophet and a celebrity. He plumped for a railroad across the country to that city, praised California farmers for their agricultural and irrigation techniques, urged reform of old Spanish land-title laws as a way to break up large landholdings, and visited the Fremonts at their home in Mariposa. He also supported fruit-growing, mining, and the formation of industrial and trade associations. And he condemned the "rascals and ruffians" who denied Native Americans their rights. The *San Francisco National*, a Democratic paper, on the other hand, attacked Greeley as an "arrant demagogue and detestable factionist," as well as a "political incendiary and criminal zealot."[80]

On September 5, 1859, Horace Greeley left San Francisco and returned home on the steamship *Golden Age* via the swampy Isthmus of Panama. Greeley found it a "hard passage" with crowded accommodations, buzzing insects, and rain.[81] Another ship, after running aground on Key West, delivered him to New York on September 28. He was exhausted but elated by his adventures. He had "gone West" and returned safely.

On his western trip, Greeley was pleased to discover that Republicans were making gains in local elections. But he also knew that the next presidential election would be crucial for the Republicans. "Look out for a financial and political tornado in 1860," he concluded.[82]

Greeley's overland trip west convinced him that a transcontinental railroad was essential to the nation. He preferred the northern route he had just traversed, and estimated its cost at fifty million dollars, or seventy-five thousand dollars a mile. Only federal financial aid would make such a project possible. A Pacific railroad would mean "national industry, prosperity, and wealth." "My long, fatiguing journey was undertaken," he wrote, "in the hope that I might do something toward the early construction of the Pacific Railroad; and I trust that it has not been made wholly in vain."[83] He continued to support such a railroad until it was completed in 1869.

The Hank Monk story became a legend. Richardson later called it "apocryphal." Greeley himself reportedly said later that "there was not a damned word of truth in the whole story." The humorist Artemus Ward repeated it often. In March 1866, a New York congressman angered by a Greeley editorial read Ward's version to the entire House of Representatives. Mark Twain in *Roughing It* (1872) tells a hilarious version of the story, a story repeated in identical words by every passenger he met on a trip west:

> I can tell you a most laughable thing indeed, if you would like to listen to it. Horace Greeley went over this road once. When he was leaving Carson City he told the driver, Hank Monk, that he had an engagement to lecture at Placerville and was very anxious to go through quick. Hank Monk cracked his whip and started off at an awful pace. The coach bounced up and down in such a terrific way that it jolted the buttons all off of Horace's coat, and finally shot his head clean through the roof of the stage, and then he yelled at Hank Monk and begged him to go easier—said he wasn't in as much of a hurry as he was a while ago. But Hank Monk said, "keep your seat, Horace, and I'll get you there on time!"—and you bet you he did, what was left of him.[84]

Apocryphal or not, the Hank Monk story became part of the Horace Greeley legend. And its essential truth—that Horace Greeley was in a hurry to go West—was memorable. Now Greeley returned to New York only to find that the tornado was already in the wind in the form of John Brown's raid.

FREEDOM'S MARTYR: JOHN BROWN

Horace Greeley never advocated breaking civil law to achieve freedom in the name of some higher moral law. The moral law certainly governed his thoughts on reform. But his non-violence and respect for the law kept him from rebellion, sedition, or insurrection. In matters of conscience, he sought to reform the republic, but never to overthrow it or break its laws. On the matter of breaking the law in the name of conscience, other *Tribune* staff members were more radical than Greeley.

Greeley had scarcely recovered from his long trip west when abolitionist John Brown attempted to raise a slave insurrection in Virginia. On October 16, 1859, Brown and nineteen followers crossed the Potomac River from Maryland to Harper's Ferry, Virginia, intending to seize federal weapons at the arsenal and incite rebellion. Trapped in a fire-engine house by angry townspeople, they held off a siege until overwhelmed by U.S. Marines led by Robert E. Lee and J. E. B. Stuart. Ten men died, including two of Brown's sons. Five men escaped. The rest were captured. On October 31, a Virginia court convicted Brown of treason. Brown was hanged on December 2.

John Brown's raid sharpened the conflict between freedom and slavery, made Brown a martyr in the eyes of his supporters, and made most southerners identify Brown with the anti-slavery Republican Party. Some blamed Greeley and the *Tribune* for inciting the raid. Lincoln and Seward immediately disavowed Brown's actions. Greeley was more ambivalent. Thinking Brown and the others had all been killed, he wrote that "they died for what they felt to be right, though in a manner which seems to us fatally wrong." Slavery, Greeley averred, had killed Brown. After Brown's execution, the editor wrote that "history will accord an honored niche to Old John Brown."[85]

Linking Greeley and the *Tribune* to John Brown's raid was plausible. The newspaper had been beating the war drums against slavery since the furor over "bleeding Kansas." "We hate slavery generally," wrote the *Tribune* in April 1859, "and desire its extinction." But Greeley recognized that most Americans were not deeply opposed to slavery—he estimated a million anti-slavery men nationwide—and doubted that they would elect an anti-slavery president in 1860, when he thought the Republicans would be "horribly beaten." Would other means be necessary? Certainly James Redpath, the *Tribune* reporter in Kansas, believed in slave insurrection and was well acquainted with John Brown. So was Richard J. Hinton, another *Tribune* man. John Kagi, one of Brown's followers, had worked for the *Tribune* at one time. Even Greeley admitted after the fact that he had given seven hundred dollars to further Brown's cause through yet another *Tribune* reporter, Hugh Forbes.[86]

At forty-five, Hugh Forbes was an aging English soldier of fortune, another one of those radical republican adventurers washed up on American shores by the waves of European revolutions in 1848–9. A former Cold Stream Guards officer, the rich and cantankerous Forbes had fought with Garibaldi and his Red Shirts in Italy in 1849. Only British intervention freed Forbes from an Austrian jail cell after he was captured. After fleeing to New York, Forbes edited an Italian daily newspaper, joined the *Tribune* as a translator, and gave private fencing lessons. In 1853, he published a *Manual of the Patriotic*

Volunteer, a guerilla-warfare manual describing the "art and science of obtaining and maintaining liberty and independence." Freedom and slavery opposed each other, he noted, "as light and darkness." The revolutionary leader must be a "sound republican."[87]

In January 1857, the alcoholic and unpredictable Forbes met Brown in New York and agreed to train his "troops" for a fee of one hundred dollars a month. Brown quickly advanced him six hundred dollars, and Greeley gave Forbes another twenty dollars when he left New York to fight for freedom in Kansas. But instead of going to Kansas, Forbes went to Tabor, Iowa, where Brown and his sons were trying to organize themselves as a military force for Kansas. Finding no recruits or weapons of note, Forbes was soon bored and frustrated. By November, Forbes was back in the East trying to get more money from Senator Charles Sumner and two of Brown's New England supporters, Frank Sanborn and Samuel Howe. He also tried to sell news of Brown's operation to Greeley, who ignored him as another "lunatic."[88]

In May 1858, Forbes tried to convince Boston, New York, and Washington anti-slavery men that Brown had plans to make a "dash at Harper's Ferry" with several hundred emancipated slaves. They thought he was bluffing, viewing Forbes as a hothead, madman, malicious traitor, and villain. Forbes then left for Paris, and the plan was delayed a year. But Brown and Forbes's plan would be carried out.[89]

Hostile critics blamed Greeley and his newspaper, in part, for the entire John Brown fiasco. Had the *Tribune* not helped enflame the political tinder of anti-slavery lying across America, especially in Kansas and Illinois? Was Greeley not responsible for the hotheads who wrote and acted in his name? Didn't supporters of the raid, including Forbes, all write for the *Tribune*? Weed in his newspaper reported rumors that letters from Greeley were found in Brown's carpet bag (they turned out to be one business memorandum regarding Brown's subscription to the *Tribune*). Greeley promptly canceled a trip west to Iowa because of the "angry, troubled look of the political sky." He predicted that Brown's raid would drive the Slave Power to new outrages and bring on what Seward called the "irrepressible conflict" of civil war. He admitted that he had given seven hundred dollars to Brown through Forbes, and that Forbes and other Brown supporters had *Tribune* connections. But he claimed to have had no knowledge of the plan.[90]

Brown's raid, thought Greeley, would drive a useful wedge between North and South, help defeat Douglas and the Democrats, and "help us nominate a moderate man for President on our side." He told Emma Newhall that he was working hard, eating and sleeping rarely, and had no time to read books.[91] Nevertheless, Greeley's employees maintained their sympathies for Brown and his cause. Redpath wrote an instant adulatory biography of Brown, and signed a contract with Thayer and Eldridge of Boston while his hero languished in jail. Royalties would go to Brown's family, Redpath promised. When the book came out in January 1860, Redpath defended Brown as a man who resisted the Slave Power in accordance with the Higher Law. Brown was "the latest and our bravest martyr to the teachings of the Bible and the American Idea." Redpath compared Harper's Ferry to Bunker Hill, Brown to Cromwell. By May 1860, Redpath had sold forty thousand copies of his book, ultimately seventy-five thousand, huge numbers for the period. At the same time, Redpath was fending off arrest warrants issued when he ignored summonses to testify before the Mason Committee of Congress investigating the John Brown raid.[92]

Brown's men were prepared to break the law in the name of a higher law to eliminate slavery. Men talked of civil war between North and South. "What ends are to be attained," asked James Mason of Virginia addressing Samuel Gridley Howe, a Brown supporter, on behalf of the Select Committee of the U.S. Senate investigating Harper's Ferry, "by promoting anti-slavery sentiment? What is the object in view?" Howe answered: "The promotion of freedom among men, the same object as the fathers of the Revolution."[93]

The *Tribune* reporter present at Brown's hanging in December wrote that Brown had paused on his way to the gallows to kiss an African-American woman holding her baby in her arms. In 1884, an Irish-American painter, Thomas Hovenden, immortalized the scene in his painting *The Last Moment of John Brown*.[94] The powerful image of the Old Testament prophet kissing a Negro child reminded all Americans of the moment when freedom turned to violence against slavery. For Horace Greeley, Brown's martyrdom for freedom required sympathy, but not more violence.

8

Civil Warrior

NOMINATING LINCOLN

In the wake of John Brown's raid, the presidential election of 1860 put the Party of Freedom and an anti-slavery man in the White House. Horace Greeley, rumbling westward by train that May to attend the Republican convention free-for-all in Chicago, had anticipated this moment for four years. He had worked consistently for a Republican victory, even when supporting Douglas against Lincoln in Illinois. He recognized that his old patron and current enemy, William Henry Seward, was the front-runner for the Republican presidential nomination. (Seward even rented a cannon to salute his expected victory on his front lawn in Auburn, New York.) Greeley himself supported the aging and forgotten Edward Bates, a future U.S. attorney general from Missouri, but he would ultimately play a crucial role in nominating the man he helped defeat in Illinois in 1858, Abraham Lincoln, by delivering the Bates votes.

"Lincoln," wrote the Norfolk, Virginia, *Day Book*, in 1860, "the wild political despot of the West, whose head has been crazed by the doctrines and isms of Horace Greeley, has proclaimed to those who had patience to hope better things of him, that they must hope no longer."[1] Many believed that Lincoln was Greeley's puppet and that his election would mean civil war.

"I lack faith," Greeley wrote a friend in April 1859, "that the anti-slavery men of this country have either the numbers or the sagacity required to make a President. I do not believe there are a hundred thousand earnest anti-slavery men in this State, or a million in the Union." The abolitionists, he thought, were actually helping support slavery by alienating moderate anti-slavery voters. He assumed that Seward or Chase would get the Republican nomination, and did not think the Republicans could win in 1860. "But let her drive," he concluded.[2]

Greeley and Lincoln approached the problem of slavery and Union from two different angles. Greeley wanted slavery to disappear, even at the cost of Union. Lincoln wanted the Union to survive, whether or not slavery was eliminated. Both preferred a Union without slavery. Ohio Republicans praised Greeley for fighting for the "cause of Human Freedom." Lincoln wrote in 1859 that "he who would be no slave, must consent to have no slave. Those who deny freedom to others, deserve it not for themselves."[3] Understanding the distinction in emphasis between Greeley and Lincoln is crucial to understanding Greeley's behavior before and during the Civil War.

As the Republican convention approached, Greeley remained committed to the moderate and safe candidate, Bates, but admitted that he would support whoever won the nomination. He praised Lincoln as "a man of the people, a champion of free labor, of diversified and prosperous industry." He sat with Lincoln on the platform when Lincoln gave his address at Cooper Union on February 27, 1860, criticizing slavery and warning of the instability of a divided nation. On a cold, snowy evening, fifteen hundred people paid twenty-five cents to hear the future president speak. Greeley himself spoke briefly and may have met Lincoln at the *Tribune* office later that evening to go over page proofs of the address prior to publication. The newspaper helped make Lincoln a national, rather than local, politician by publishing his remarks at Cooper Union for an American audience. "No man," Greeley wrote, "ever before made such an impression on his first appeal to a New York audience." In the coming weeks, Lincoln would repeat his speech many times across New England, where he was virtually unknown. Lincoln, like Greeley, continued to anticipate a Seward nomination, but other New England Republicans were beginning to take a hard look at Lincoln as a serious candidate.[4]

The Republican convention met in Chicago in mid-May 1860 at the Wigwam, a wooden convention center downwind from the stockyards and resonating with the sounds of Illinois farmers brought in to support Lincoln. German delegates convened separately at the Deutsches Haus, seeking to get "Dutch planks" in the party platform, which Greeley helped write. The platform supported the abolition of slavery, a new homestead law, the admission of Kansas to the Union as a free state, the construction of a Pacific railroad, and a commitment to the principles of the Declaration of Independence that "all men are created equal." Greeley, ostracized in New York and formally a substitute delegate from Oregon, remained committed to Bates as a former Whig who could win over both northern and southern voters.[5]

The convention began on May 16. Weed—the "king of the lobby" —held court at the Tremont Hotel, where rumors spread that he had a "corruption fund" of more than four hundred thousand dollars at his disposal. Presumably he was ready to buy Seward the presidency if that was what it took. "We expect to nominate him [Seward] on the first ballot," boasted Weed. Greeley roamed the streets and smoke-filled rooms attacking the corruption rampant in Albany, trying to stop Seward. "Anyone but Seward!" was Greeley's cry to state delegates within sound of his voice. Bates remained Greeley's candidate, and Greeley controlled forty-eight delegates pledged to support him on the first ballot.[6]

Seward looked strong. The *Tribune* predicted a first-ballot Seward victory, but observed that "Mr. Lincoln of Illinois, however, is rising in prominence." Lincoln wrote a friend that he could not endorse Seward's Higher Law doctrine of freedom, but agreed that an "irrepressible conflict" over slavery was imminent. On the first ballot, Seward came out ahead (173.5 votes) but did not have a majority sufficient to nominate (234). Lincoln ran well, with 102 votes, 7 out of 10 from New Hampshire. Lincoln closed the gap on the second ballot, then won on the third ballot only when Greeley threw the support of his 48 Bates votes behind Lincoln.[7]

Once Lincoln was nominated, Greeley supported him fully. In an editorial entitled "Honest Old Abe," the editor praised Lincoln to the skies and promised that his election was "a thing that can be done." There was "no truer, more faithful, more deserving Republican than Abraham Lincoln." Bates might have been the "wiser choice," given his appeal in the South, but Lincoln had won fair and square. Nominating Seward would have been "inadvisable and unsafe." Henry Raymond at the *Times* dredged up Greeley's old 1854 letter to Seward breaking off relations, and claimed that Horace Greeley was the man primarily responsible for Seward's defeat. Greeley challenged Raymond by printing the letter in entirety in the *Tribune* for all to see. Seward and Weed got their revenge by denying Greeley Seward's Senate seat the following year in favor of Ira Harris. Joshua Giddings also criticized Greeley for being "rabid against Seward." New Hampshire Republicans criticized Greeley for delaying and seriously jeopardizing

Lincoln's nomination by supporting Bates. But Greeley maintained that he had "discharged a public duty" at Chicago.[8]

Another Republican, John D. Defrees, wrote that "Greeley slaughtered Seward, and saved the party. He deserves the praises of all men, and gets them now. Wherever he goes he is greeted with cheers." Supporting Edward Bates until Lincoln was in a position to overcome Seward appeared in retrospect to be a brilliant Greeley strategy. "The agony is over," Bates wrote Greeley on May 26, "there is no political future" for himself. "My hearty thanks," he added, "for all you have done to raise my reputation in the country."[9]

After the convention, Greeley returned to New York to get the *Tribune* behind Lincoln. He printed thousands of copies of Hinton Rowan Helper's anti-slavery *The Impending Crisis of the South* (1857), whose statistics showed that slavery was inefficient and wasteful, as well as immoral, and retarded economic progress. Greeley produced a Republican political guidebook with his brother-in-law, John Cleveland, providing speeches, platforms, and voting statistics, including the election returns for each state since 1840 and votes for president since 1824. He hoped to run for Senator in New York, anticipating Seward's departure for Washington if and when Lincoln was elected, but Weed and Seward rejected him.[10]

The election results confirmed Greeley's hopes and predictions. The Democrats had met in April in Charleston, South Carolina, nominated Stephen A. Douglas for president, and alienated party members from the South who wanted a pro-slavery nominee. The southerners met on June 18 in Baltimore and nominated their own candidate, John Breckinridge of Kentucky. As Greeley predicted, Douglas thus split the Democratic Party in two. In the November 6 election, Lincoln received thirty-nine percent of the popular vote, but a clear 180-vote majority in the electoral college. He carried all eighteen free states by decisive margins. Douglas received only twelve electoral votes, Breckinridge seventy-two—all from southern states.

Lincoln's election produced a cabinet position for Seward (Secretary of State), but not Greeley. "It is said Greeley wants to be Postmaster General," Joshua Leavitt wrote Salmon Chase, but his appointment to any place in the cabinet would "ruin the administration." "I would like to go to the Senate," Greeley wrote Beman Brockway shortly after the election, "and would not like to go into the cabinet." He was "overwhelmed with daily cares" and recognized that he could "do nothing to make myself U.S. Senator."[11]

On February 5, 1861, Greeley visited Springfield, Illinois, to give a lecture. The president-elect called on him at his hotel that afternoon, and the two men talked for several hours. Greeley at that point urged no compromise with the South, whose states were beginning to secede from the Union. Greeley gave Lincoln some advice on cabinet appointments. (Lincoln was appointing a number of German friends who helped elect him, and also named Bates his attorney general.) More importantly, Lincoln helped convert Greeley from a man convinced that the South should secede from the Union to a Union man committed to emancipation of the slaves.[12] Secession was in the air, and all Americans were struggling with questions of freedom and slavery, answers to which threatened to disunite the nation and bring about civil war.

DISUNION: "LET THEM GO IN PEACE!"

Horace Greeley abhorred the idea of war, especially civil war. Committed to the ideal of freedom, he struggled in the winter of 1860–61 with how freedom related to the individual states in the Union. Some people thought that the Union was a compact of states, any one of which had the right to secede from that Union. Virtually all states at one time or another had considered secession. The states of New England did so at the Hartford Convention in 1814. South Carolina did so in 1832, but over the tariff, not slavery. Other people, including Abraham Lincoln, thought that the Union was a creation of "we the people" of the United States, not the individual states. Federal power superseded states' rights. Secession threatened the Union, but also seemed consistent with freedom, the freedom of a state to secede from that Union.[13]

Abolitionists had long argued for disunion under the slogan of "no union with slaveholders." They preferred a North without slavery to a Union with slavery. "Liberty with or without Union—Liberty at any rate," wrote Wendell Phillips. Phillips believed that disunion was God's will and the stepping-stone to freedom. New England antislavery men endorsed disunion by a large majority in the 1840s, and opposed "union at the expense of the colored population of the country." "Let me have liberty and Union, if we can," said one Maine congressman, "but liberty without Union rather than Union without liberty."[14]

The *Tribune,* often in James S. Pike's editorials, held to a disunionist position throughout the 1850s. Editorials argued that the Union should be "a thousand times shivered" rather than let the South "plant slavery on free soil." Disunion was the lesser of two evils. "Of the two evils, Disunion or Slavery Extension, we prefer the former of the two perils, we consider the latter the more imminent." At the time of the Kansas-Nebraska debate, Pike wrote that he would much rather belong to a "peace-loving, art-developing, labor-honoring, God-fearing confederacy of twenty millions of Freemen, rather than to a filibustering, war-making, conquest-seeking, slavery-extending union of thirty millions, one-sixth of them slaves. If this be treason, make the most of it."[15]

Greeley was not so sure. "When we are ready to dissolve the Union for Liberty's sake," he wrote Pike, "the South will not let us do it. . . . So let us off on disunion for the present." If Pike really wanted disunion, added Greeley, he should "keep still and let events ripen." Greeley himself did not want disunion as much as "the ascendancy of Liberty." He supported state independence only when it implied antislavery. He objected to Pike's disunion articles. But as early as 1856, Greeley argued that if and when the South decided on secession, the southern states should go in peace. "If they choose to go," he wrote, "let them go." As far as Greeley was concerned, "Slave States and Free States tells the story, and no one can misunderstand it."[16]

Like most Americans, Greeley was trying to reconcile two strands of freedom—the freedom of states to terminate a compact among states, and the freedom and equality of all people embodied in the Declaration of Independence. He believed that the South would, in the end, not really secede from the Union. He scorned compromise with slave states, and remained committed to private property, liberty under the law, land reform, and the elimination of slavery. And he watched as southern states began to secede, beginning with South Carolina on December 20, 1860, followed by Mississippi, Florida, Alabama, Georgia, and Louisiana in January, and then Texas in February. Secessionists too used the liberal rhetoric of liberty, rights, and freedom even in defense of slavery and property. "Freedom," argued one secessionist, "is not possible without slavery."[17]

Tribune correspondents Charles Dana, Adam Gurowski, and James S. Pike, in the meantime, continued to push the disunionist line on Greeley and the paper, over which he now had but limited control. Gurowski called Greeley "an ass" for refusing to come out in favor of disunion, and remained a thorn in the side of both Greeley and Lincoln, who believed Gurowski was the only man really capable of assassinating the president.[18] The *Tribune* continued to support disunion even after Lincoln's election. States had a right to secede from the Union. The South should be permitted to "go in peace." The federal government should not use military force to compel southern states to remain in the Union. The North needed to pursue a strategy of patience and "masterly inactivity." "Let them nullify, secede, form a new Southern Republic, or do what they will, we shall still be glad that Lincoln is elected." "Can you compel them to send members to Congress?" asked the *Tribune* on November 30, 1860. "Can you make them accept federal offices? Can you prevent their tarring and feathering those who do? If not, how idle to talk of subduing them."[19]

In December, the Senate proposed a compromise solution: the Missouri Compromise would be reenacted and extended to the Pacific; the federal government would indemnify owners of fugitive slaves who escaped to the North; squatter sovereignty would be allowed in the territories regarding slavery; slavery in the District of Columbia would be protected by Congress. Seward and Weed favored compromise and presented petitions in support. Greeley opposed any compromise with slavery, even to save the Union. In the end, the so-called Crittenden Compromise (after Senator John J. Crittenden [1787–1863] of Kentucky) was defeated twice by the Senate on January 16 and March 4, 1861. In December, Greeley went up to Pittsfield, Massachusetts, to give a lecture on "America West of the Mississippi" and returned to keep up the drumbeat for the "right of secession." The right of self-government, he wrote, justified America's secession from Great Britain in 1776; "we do not see why it would not justify the secession of Five Millions of Southrons from the Federal Union in 1861." The right of self-government applied even to those who denied freedom to slaves. "We shall feel constrained by our devotion to Human Liberty to say, let them go!"[20]

Five days later, Greeley wrote Abraham Lincoln opposing any "nasty compromise" with the South. "I fear nothing, care for nothing, but another disgraceful back-down of the free states," he wrote. He did not believe that a state could secede from the Union "any more than a stave may secede from a cask." Yet a few days later, on December 26, Greeley wrote Lincoln that any political community had the right to "maintain a national existence" and should not be forced to stay in the Union. On December 28, the *Tribune* editorialized that any southern seizure of federal property (such as forts) would be an act of "treason." The principle of self-government seemed to justify secession, but the principle of property rights under the law implied that the South had no right to seize federal property of any kind. By early January 1861, the *Tribune* had shifted its position and encouraged the North to "resist aggression" by the "rebels."[21]

The shift in *Tribune* editorial policy in the winter of 1860–1 from disunion to support for the Union against secession requires some explanation. Some historians have accused Greeley of inconsistency or even duplicity in supporting, then rejecting, secession as a "fictitious alternative to frightened Northerners" that Greeley knew simply would not work. Others have found him to be a consistent and principled opponent of slavery who saw the Union as a means, not an end, contrary to Lincoln.[22] He also wanted to avoid war at all costs. Yet the fact that Horace Greeley did not have full control over his newspaper that winter cannot be underestimated. He permitted Pike, Dana, and Gurowski to pursue a disunionist line that he himself could not truly accept. Once he regained editorial control after Christmas, he wrote Lincoln and began to argue against secession as well as compromise. His own position may not have changed as much as historians have thought, once we realize that many *Tribune* editorials were not his own work. He remained a staunch Union man as long as the Union was committed to eliminating slavery. It is also entirely possible that he still hoped for Seward's Senate seat and was behaving accordingly.

In January 1861, the *Tribune* vigorously championed the Union cause. Union was a common brotherhood, dividing people into "only two classes—loyal citizens and traitors." Secession was both revolution and treason. In New York, Greeley was rumored to be supporting the Lincoln administration and even hinting at some patronage opportunities, so much so that Lincoln was moved to disavow Greeley's words and actions in a private letter to Thurlow Weed. Lincoln felt "kindness" toward Greeley, he wrote, but did not want his name used in connection with either state patronage or the New York Senate seat vacated by Seward. Apparently Weed had told Lincoln that *Tribune* stockholder and New York state representative Benjamin F. Camp was claiming that Lincoln supported Greeley's appointment to the Senate and that, if elected, Greeley would dispense ample patronage to his friends. Lincoln undoubtedly clarified the matter for Greeley in their meeting the following day in Springfield, when Greeley urged Lincoln to stand firm against the South. Greeley also urged him to appoint Salmon P. Chase and Schuyler Colfax to the cabinet. Lincoln demurred.[23] In the meantime, Ira Harris, a New York supreme court justice, accepted Seward's Senate seat, and Weed and Seward had their revenge on Greeley.[24]

After Greeley's Springfield visit with Lincoln, the *Tribune* continued to support the incoming Republican administration. There should be "no concessions" to the South that would "ruin" the Republican Party and desecrate its "banner of Freedom." On February 16, Greeley —wearing his trademark white linen coat and carrying a yellow bag with his initials on it in large letters, along with a red, white, and blue blanket—unexpectedly boarded the presidential train at Girard, Ohio, near Erie, Pennsylvania, as it wended its way toward Washington. Both President and Mrs. Lincoln gave him a cordial welcome in the president's car, and he got off the train at Erie. "His arrival and departure were altogether so unexpected," wrote the president's secretary, young John Hay, "so mysterious, so comical, that they supplied an amusing topic of conversation during the rest of the journey." Two days later, Greeley joined the train again at Buffalo and rode in it as far as Albany.[25]

The *Tribune* now favored civil war, rather than compromise. The federal government must either treat southern secession as a "revolution" and recognize southern independence, or "confront it as treason, and put it down by the military forces of the loyal states." The *Tribune* favored the second position. The question was not whether "Freedom or Slavery" would guide the federal government, but "whether we shall have a federal government at all. If so, it must be by prompt, decisive action."[26]

In the midst of secession and on the eve of civil war, Greeley attended Lincoln's inauguration in Washington on March 4, 1861, a bright and warm day. Sitting behind the president on the inaugural platform, Greeley listened to Chief Justice Roger Taney administer the oath of office and contemplated the possible assassination of the new president, who had sneaked into town via Baltimore one night with police protection. But the inauguration went off without a hitch. "The federal government of the United States," wrote the *Tribune* the next day, "is still in existence with a Man at the head of it." Lincoln exhibited great "earnestness of purpose" and the "courage to enforce it." But a week later, the paper predicted a coming war between "civilization and barbarism, between light and darkness, between falsehood and truth, between vice and virtue, between freedom and despotism, between Christian faith and infidelity."[27]

By late March, Greeley was in a fighting mood. William Russell, a journalist from the London *Times*, visited him in New York and found him to represent "the nastiest form of narrow minded sectarian philanthropy, who would gladly roast all the whites of South Carolina in order that he might satisfy what he supposes is a conscience but which is only an autocratic ambition which revels in the idea of separation from the South as the best recognition of its power." Greeley promptly urged Russell to go South and see the slave pens and auction blocks for himself.[28]

When southern forces fired on Fort Sumter on April 15, 1861, the result was war. "Fort Sumter is lost," wrote the *Tribune*, "but freedom is saved." After a long struggle over compromise or conflict, secession or Union, Greeley, like most in the North, was now part of a chorus singing the battle cry of freedom. Only later, when he ran for president in 1872, would his enemies remind him of his temporary support for the freedom to secede from the Union. Once the war started, he became a fervent Union man. "There is no more right of a State to secede from the Union," he wrote shortly after the battle of Bull Run, "than to establish an absolute monarchy and make Mormonism the exclusive religion." Secession was a form of treason. A year later, the *Tribune* editorialized that "we utterly deny, repudiate and condemn the pretended Right of Secession."[29] But for a brief moment, Horace Greeley had believed that peaceful secession might be a form of freedom preferable to civil war.

BATTLE CRY OF FREEDOM: "ON TO RICHMOND!"

Horace Greeley, like many northerners, recognized that the South was not entirely a "slavocracy" and that men on both sides of the Mason-Dixon line were Americans fighting for liberty. Both Jefferson Davis and Abraham Lincoln called for liberty. Southerners fought for their liberty against northern tyranny, for "southern rights and southern liberty," for "liberty and independence," or for "life, liberty and property." They also fought for the right to keep slaves, whether they owned them or not. Northern boys fought for Liberty and Union. Both sides invoked 1776 and the founding fathers. Whether they used the words *liberty* or *freedom,* they believed they were fighting to preserve the inheritance of the American republic.[30]

Freedom was a favored word in the North, where the abolition movement and the immigrants from 1848 European revolutions helped fuel the fires of anti-slavery sentiment. Many linked the American Civil War with the national liberation movements in Italy, German, Hungary, and Poland. Freedom, wrote Gustav Struve, a Forty-Eighter, "is the magic word which is filling the United States of North America with immigrants, even during the terrible civil war going on at present." The Cincinnati *Volksfreund* called for "union and freedom." "We are Germans," wrote the St. Paul, Minnesota, *Staatszeitung,* "and in German loyalty are prepared to defend our American home as the blessed place of freedom."[31]

Greeley became an instant supporter of war when it was declared. When President Lincoln called up seventy-five thousand state militiamen, Greeley called for five hundred thousand. "Freedom is not another word for anarchy," he wrote. The federal government should occupy Maryland, march on Richmond, proclaim martial law in the South, and arrest Jefferson Davis. Yet he supported Lincoln throughout the summer of 1861, emphasizing "preservation of the Union" over "destruction of slavery." Secession should be "crushed out by blood and fire if necessary."[32]

Greeley and the *Tribune* received considerable criticism for urging Lincoln and the Union army onward to a premature battle at Bull Run in July. For weeks, the newspaper ran headlines crying "Forward to Richmond!" a slogan coined by a stringer named Fitz Henry Warren. Warren was an Iowa abolitionist who entertained radical republicans of all sorts in his suite at the Willard Hotel in Washington. Again, Greeley had little control over his own newspaper, especially since on May 18 he had gashed himself in the knee with an ax while cutting wood at his Chappaqua farm. The next day, Greeley wrote Lincoln recommending that the "War for the Union" be "prosecuted with emphatic vigor." In Greeley's absence, Warren wrote in the *Tribune* that "On to Richmond!" represented the "voice of the people." From June 26 through July 6, the *Tribune* ran the bold, italicized headline "Forward to Richmond! Forward to Richmond! The Rebel Congress must not be allowed to meet there on the 20th of July! By that date the place must be held by the National Army!"[33]

In February 1863, Greeley claimed responsibility for urging a Union advance, but disavowed the headline, blaming it on overzealous subordinates. "The war cry 'Forward to Richmond!' did not originate with me," he wrote in his memoirs, "but it is just what should have been uttered, and the words should have been translated into deeds." He did favor, however, an aggressive and immediate military operation against the Confederacy. During Greeley's convalescence from his wood-chopping accident, Simon Cameron, Lincoln's new Secretary of War, wrote him asking his help in achieving the "sympathy and confidence of the public" toward the war effort and inviting him to Washington. Greeley declined the offer, being immobile. By July 1 he recovered sufficiently to host Senator Charles Sumner for breakfast (milk, bread, and cold meat) in New York, where the two men talked politics for an hour.[34]

On July 20, 1861, Confederate troops badly routed Union forces at Bull Run (Manassas) in Virginia, south of Washington. The *Tribune* initially claimed a "brilliant Union victory." Greeley only learned of the defeat from Henry Villard's report in the rival *New York Herald*. "We have fought and been beaten," wrote Charles Dana, predicting the imminent resignation of Lincoln's cabinet. The press quickly blamed Greeley and the *Tribune* for egging on the unprepared troops of Union General George McClellan to a humiliating defeat. The *Herald* assaulted the "ferocious Jacobins" at Greeley's newspaper who had "brought on war by headlines." Warren promptly resigned his position at the newspaper. Greeley retired to his bed with "brain fever."[35]

Greeley was devastated and contrite. "I wish to be distinctly understood," he wrote, "as not seeking to be relieved from any responsibility for urging the advance of the Union grand army into Virginia, though the precise phrase 'Forward to Richmond!' is not mine, and I would have preferred not to iterate it. I thought that that army, one hundred thousand strong, might have been in the rebel capital on or before the 20th instant, while I felt that there were urgent reasons why it should be there if possible." Henceforth, the *Tribune*'s policy would be to "rouse and animate the American People for the terrible ordeal which has befallen them."[36]

On July 29, Greeley wrote a pained letter to Abraham Lincoln pouring out his emotions. He had not slept for seven nights. He wanted to die, but knew he probably would not, "because I have no right to die." Lincoln was not a "great man," wrote Greeley, "and I am a hopelessly broken one." Bull Run had been an "awful disaster." "If the Rebels are not to be beaten," he moaned, "then every drop of blood henceforth shed in this quarrel will be wantonly, wickedly shed." He prayed that Lincoln would "decide quickly" what to do, and would let Greeley "know my duty." He proposed a peace conference or an armistice to avoid hostilities. He signed the letter "yours, in the depths of bitterness." The puzzled Lincoln set the letter aside in his desk drawer for future reference.[37]

It is fairly likely that Greeley suffered a nervous breakdown, or bad depression, after Bull Run, as he had after Pickie's death and would after Molly's death in 1872. He was in "scorching, black despair," he wrote Lincoln, viewing himself as quite detached from the *Tribune,* as if he were not responsible for its words. Greeley regretted that his own newspaper had gone "quite so fast or as far as it did." He slept no more than an hour a night for several weeks, and felt himself "quite broken down." On August 17, he wrote a friend that "the hour is very dark" but that he had not lost his "faith in God." The war would be a battle for "liberty and law" now, and would be won. More important, Greeley now realized that the battle would not be for Union alone, but against slavery. "However the end may be postponed and obscured," he wrote, "*this infernal Rebellion seals the doom of slavery.*" As his and the nation's crisis passed, he would "stay about the *Tribune,*" but he recognized after Bull Run that he was now "done as a politician."[38]

Adam Gurowski was equally despondent after Bull Run. He asked Pike to ask Salmon P. Chase to get him a job as a translator at the State Department, which he did. Gurowski promptly left for Washington, assailing Lincoln privately as a "pighead" with a "crew of nonentities" in his cabinet who refused to move against slavery. The Civil War in America was but an extension of the revolutions and wars in Europe since 1830, including the "general events of 1848."[39] But he lauded the foreign-born volunteers who signed up to fight.

Left: Mary Woodburn, Horace Greeley's "republican mother." (Library of Congress, Prints and Photographs Division, LC-USZ62-9057)

Below: Horace Greeley's birthplace and childhood home near Amherst, New Hampshire. (Author's photograph)

Left: Artist's conception of Horace Greeley arriving in New York City (1831). (James Parton, *Life of Horace Greeley*, New York: Mason Brothers, 1855, hereafter Parton)

Below: Episcopal Church, where Horace Greeley married Mary Youngs Cheney in Warrenton, North Carolina (July 1836). (Ann K. Williams photograph)

Left: Horace Greeley Daguerrotype (1840s). (Library of Congress, Prints and Photographs Division, LC-USZ62-8776)

Below: The staff of the *Tribune,* c. 1848. Seated from left to right: George Snow, Bayard Taylor, Greeley, and George Ripley. Standing from left to right: William Henry Fry, Charles A. Dana, Henry J. Raymond. (Library of Congress, Prints and Photographs Division, LC-USZ62-8777)

Left: "One of the People's Saints for the Calendar of Liberty" (1852), with Louis Kossuth aiding Liberty against Austria's throne and altar. (Library of Congress, Prints and Photographs Division, LC-USZ62-89603)

Right: The "Hank Monk Schottish," composed in honor of Horace Greeley's legendary stagecoach ride (1859). (Bancroft Library, University of California, Berkeley)

Top: Currier & Ives cartoon satirizing the anti-slavery orientation of the Republican platform of 1860. At left, abolitionist editor Greeley (left) grinds his New York *Tribune* organ as candidate Abraham Lincoln (center, riding on a wooden rail) prances to the music. William H. Seward stands next to Lincoln, holding a wailing black infant. To the right of Seward are two other New York editors friendly to the Republican cause, Henry J. Raymond of the *New York Times* and James Watson Webb of the *New York Courier and Enquirer*. (Library of Congress, Prints and Photographs Division, LC-USZ62-14226) *Bottom*: New York draft riots (July 1863). (Library of Congress, Prints and Photographs Division, LC-USZ62-16601)

"Pioneers of Freedom" (1866), showing Horace Greeley with abolitionists W. L. Garrison, Charles Sumner, Henry Ward Beecher, Wendell
Phillips, Henry Wilson, and Gerrit Smith. (Library of Congress, Prints
and Photographs Division, LC-USZ62-111195)

Cartoon of Horace Greeley bailing Jefferson Davis out of prison and saving him from being hanged on a sour apple tree (1867). (Library of Congress, Prints and Photographs Division, LC-USZ62-90681)

Top: Greeley, Colorado (1872). (Denver, CO, Public Library, item x9071)
Bottom: Liberal Republican presidential campaign poster for Greeley (1872).
(Library of Congress, Prints and Photographs Division, LC-USZ262-90657)

"Most of the foreigners who came to serve here," wrote Gurowski, "came with the intention to fight for the sacred principle of freedom, and without any firm views whatever of career and advancement."[40]

After Bull Run, Greeley's political star dimmed. Republican Thaddeus Stevens criticized his lack of "backbone." Greeley, grumbled Gurowski in December, was "no more fit for a Senator than to take command of a regiment."[41] But by early 1862, Greeley's personal and political demons seemed exorcised. He predicted to Schuyler Colfax that the war could be won within three months with proper leadership. "If the rebels are not whipped by June, they never will be," he wrote. On January 2, Greeley gave a lecture at the Smithsonian Institution in Washington and was "loudly cheered." Lincoln and Chase were in the audience. Greeley called for the confiscation of all rebel property, including slaves, and demanded an end to slavery. The audience cheered and stamped its feet for more than a minute after he had finished his lecture. "It was a surprise for Old Abe," a friend wrote Colfax, "for he turned quite pale and sunk down in his chair, as much as to say: 'Let me out of here.'"[42]

Greeley's dilemma after Bull Run was considerable. He certainly had his reputation to repair, and he was politically weakened. But he also had to continue to function as editor of the most widely read newspaper in the nation. Two questions confronted him: How free was the American press to criticize its government during wartime? And how fast should the North move on the question of emancipating the slaves? On both issues, Greeley would soon prove to be a continuing thorn in Lincoln's side.

A FREE PRESS AT WAR

Wars have never been kind to freedom of the press. A free press can give aid and comfort to the enemy. It can weaken political leadership and undermine the war effort. But it can also help mobilize the public behind the war. Both Lincoln and Greeley recognized the vital importance of the press in wartime. Both president and editor respected, feared, and needed each other. Throughout the Civil War, they engaged in a combined effort to redefine the limits of freedom as it concerned the world of American journalism.

From the outset of the war, both North and South used the press to gain information about the military movements of the enemy. An army of reporters, dubbed the "Bohemian brigade" for their independent behavior and appearance, followed the armies wherever they went. The telegraph carried instant news from the front to the home front. Lincoln made almost daily trips to the telegraph office in Washington to find out the latest news from the front. In the North, the federal government immediately took over the telegraph lines leading out of Washington and began to impose censorship on war news through the War Department. Both McClellan and Lincoln pleaded with the press to keep secret the information they received about troop movements. The reporters, in turn, were generally ignorant about all matters of military strategy and tactics. Like their papers, they were actively partisan in their politics. Using the heroic language of chivalry, they often produced ignorant and outmoded dispatches. They therefore came to depend on official news briefings provided by the War Department.[43]

Charles A. Dana once received the following battle report from a *Tribune* reporter in the early days of the war: "To God Almighty be the glory! Mine eyes have seen the work of the Lord and the cause of the righteous hath triumphed." Wrote Dana in reply: "Hereafter, in sending your reports, please specify the number of the hymn and save telegraph expenses."[44]

New York City had seventeen daily newspapers at the beginning of the war. Only five of them, including the *Tribune*, remained loyal to the Lincoln administration throughout the conflict. Nine were proslavery, of which five were "Copperhead" (pro-Confederate Democrats). New York City citizens had voted two to one against Lincoln in 1860, and they would do so again in 1864. Lincoln badly needed Greeley's support in the city. He made certain to give *Tribune* staffers a good share of patronage appointments—Thomas McElrath to the New York customs house, J. E. Harvey as minister to Portugal, and James S. Pike as minister to the Netherlands, to name a few. Lincoln also utilized Greeley's good friend Schuyler Colfax to communicate with Greeley and the *Tribune*.[45]

During the war, the *Tribune*'s Washington office became the nerve center of war information. Here in a small, one-story brick building on F Street across from the Willard Hotel gathered the newspaper's main reporters—Samuel Wilkeson, Harvard graduate Adam S. Hill, and Greeley's young Colorado friend, Henry Villard—and a daily crowd of politicians, officials, and army officers seeking, or disseminating, news. Sam Wilkeson was under the protection of Lincoln's first Secretary of War, Simon Cameron, from Pennsylvania, known for procuring lucrative army contracts for his friends back home. Wilkeson would send Cameron flattering articles from the *Tribune,* and Cameron in turn would send Wilkeson inside information and copies of his notes to the telegraph censor, H. E. Thayer, with instructions to leave Wilkeson's dispatches untouched and to send them "as they are written and signed by him."[46]

At first, Greeley intended to maintain his freedom to "denounce the whole Administration should it take a course which seems inconsistent with principle and the public good." But this was before Bull Run. After the battle, *Tribune* circulation plummeted—the weekly edition circulation dropped by twenty-five thousand subscribers within a few months, and the daily edition circulation remained about the same. The still heartsick Greeley ceased to print maps, reduced page size, and used cheaper newsprint. Nevertheless, subscriptions continued to drop off by another thirty thousand as of the spring of 1862. Many dropped subscriptions belonged to McClellan's soldiers massing outside Washington. Greeley realized that both national security and public safety required the press to postpone or limit its "discussions and criticisms with regard to the conduct of the war."[47] Supporting the Lincoln administration was both a political and an economic necessity if the *Tribune* wished to retain its readership.

By autumn 1861, the *Tribune* had come out squarely in favor of limiting press freedoms in time of civil war, citing the constitutions of both New York State and the United States. The press should not publish seditious libel nor give aid and comfort to the enemy. Freedom of the press was "clearly recognized and solemnly guaranteed" in law, but "all who would exercise it are authoritatively notified that abuses of it will subject the offenders to punishment." Any "honest discussion" of public policy was appropriate. But criticism of government actions should not lead to "an attack upon a Government's existence." The government should tolerate criticism of its own actions, but suppress any newspapers that supported the "rebellion." Press criticism was in the interest of the "triumph of the Republic" in the war effort.[48]

In the winter of 1861–2, Lincoln and Greeley appear to have come to a secret agreement regarding official information and freedom of the press. The go-between was Robert John Walker (1801–1869), former U.S. Senator from Mississippi, Secretary of the Treasury under President James Polk and governor of Kansas. Walker was a rare southern Union supporter who had manumitted his own slaves in 1838. Greeley greatly admired Walker and even hoped he might replace Seward as Secretary of State. In 1861, Walker joined forces with James R. Gilmore (1822–1903), a retired New York cotton broker doing business in the South, and occasional *Tribune* writer, to publish the *Continental Monthly*, an anti-slavery journal pressing Lincoln toward emancipation. In April 1861, Walker and Simon Cameron arranged an interview of Lincoln with Gilmore. Lincoln asked Gilmore about the South's likely intent during the Fort Sumter crisis. Shortly afterwards, Greeley asked Gilmore if he could provide Lincoln's "policy views" from time to time. Gilmore said he could not, but could perhaps get them from Walker. Greeley promised to help fund the *Continental Monthly* if Gilmore and Walker could feed him information from the White House and cabinet meetings. Walker favored a "good understanding" with Greeley on behalf of the president because "we can keep him from going off on tangents, and I can give you, from time to time, information that will be of value to him."[49]

On November 21, 1861, Lincoln wrote a letter to Walker asking that he have Gilmore bring the contents of this letter to Greeley's attention. The arrangement of giving news to Greeley "meets my unqualified approval," wrote the president, "and I shall further it to the extent of my ability, by opening to you—as I do now—fully the policy of the government,—its present and future intentions when formed—giving you permission to communicate them to Gilmore for Greeley." Lincoln went on to say that he had the "utmost confidence in Mr. Greeley," who was a "great power" in the land. "Having him firmly behind me," added Lincoln, "will be as helpful to me as an army of one hundred thousand men." Now the government could use the *Tribune*'s columns "when it is desirable to feel of, or forestall, public opinion on important subjects." Gilmore promptly took the letter to New York the next day to show the delighted Greeley, who called Lincoln a "wonderful man." Greeley and Gilmore agreed on the understanding, and Walker reported the Gilmore-Greeley conversation back to Lincoln. The *Tribune* would henceforth refrain from attacking the administration as long as Lincoln continued to feed him inside information. The arrangement would remain confidential. The president felt that Greeley would now be "my mouthpiece," although Greeley should keep the arrangement secret and "I must not be known to be the speaker."[50]

During the winter of 1861–2, Greeley began pushing in public for emancipation. "What in the world is the matter with Uncle Horace?" Lincoln supposedly asked *Tribune* correspondent Homer Byington, "Why can't he restrain himself and wait a little while?"[51]

But Greeley remained typically independent. The new Secretary of War, Edwin M. Stanton, in early 1862 wrote Greeley asking him to credit all military victories to the men in the field.[52] Despite his arrangement with Lincoln, Greeley privately asserted his right to "denounce the whole administration" whenever he thought it contradicted the "public good." He campaigned to remove McClellan from the Army of the Potomac for failing to comply with Lincoln's orders. He wrote a biography of Andrew Johnson, a Union Democrat recently appointed military governor of Tennessee, a "gallant and fearless champion of Order and Liberty, Law and Right." Yet he also held his tongue publicly on a number of matters, including emancipation.[53]

In March 1862, the *Tribune* underwent a major crisis when Greeley fired his longtime managing editor, Charles A. Dana, who had been with him since the Brook Farm days. The board accepted Dana's resignation and sale of his twenty shares of stock on March 29, 1862. According to Dana, either "I must leave or he [Greeley] would." Although Greeley later denied it, he probably forced Dana out because Dana hired too many radical journalists, including Karl Marx, whom Dana dropped as a foreign correspondent after continuous pressure from Greeley. On learning of Dana's resignation, Marx wrote Engels, "so that old jackass with the face of an angel seems to have been behind it all." Dropping him from the newspaper was undoubtedly a "rotten trick of Greeley's and McElrath's." The board then replaced Dana with Sidney Howard Gay (1814–1888), a Boston abolitionist and editor of the *National Anti-Slavery Standard*.[54]

Dana also believed that he was fired because he was too much in favor of the Union war effort, whereas Greeley continued to seek peace at virtually any price and to focus on emancipation. Despite their differences, Greeley recommended Dana for a newspaper job in Philadelphia as a man of "talent, verve, energy, and the best sort of principle," but Dana landed on his feet in Washington shortly thereafter, first auditing war claims for the War Department, then as Assistant Secretary of War under Stanton, who used him to report on U. S.

Grant's activities as a commander in the West.[55] The reports were clearly favorable.

Lincoln himself defended Greeley's press freedom in the spring of 1862. Greeley had criticized Lincoln's friend and bodyguard, Ward Lamon, the federal marshal for the District of Columbia, because Lamon was holding slaves in jail until their owners came to claim them. The slave owners were behind southern lines and generally unavailable. In April, a federal grand jury in Washington indicted Greeley for the "malicious libel of public officers," that is, Lamon, who threatened to go to New York and bring Greeley down to a Washington jail himself. The case languished in the courts until December, when Lincoln quietly intervened to have it dropped. "I thank you heartily for your imposition," Greeley wrote Lincoln, "in the libel case. I can't spare the time for such a trial in Washington." The trial never happened, and Lamon remained in office.[56]

In May 1862, Congress finally approved the long-awaited Homestead Act and a bill to underwrite a railroad to the Pacific, two of Greeley's favorite projects. Shortly afterwards, Lincoln signed into law charters for the new Union Pacific and Northern Pacific Railroads. For years, drought, crop failure, financial panics, and low wheat prices had led reformers to push for free homesteads in the West. Now any citizen over twenty-one could get 160 acres of public land if he were willing to cultivate and improve it for five years. (By 1870, homesteaders had settled fourteen million acres in the West). Greeley called the Homestead Act "one of the most vital reforms ever attempted" and predicted an era of "Peace, Prosperity and Progress." Again, he urged young people to go West and make a new home. Anyone could now own a farm in the "land for the landless" program. "Go West," he cried, "and grow up with the country!"[57]

The Union cause had stalled in the spring and summer of 1862. Greeley severely criticized Grant for Union failures at the Battle of Shiloh on April 6–7. Union officers exemplified "utter inefficiency and incompetency, if not downright treachery." Confederate officers were better strategists. Union generals were criminally negligent. Grant himself was unprepared. "Your paper," Grant wrote to *Tribune* correspondent Albert Richardson, "is very unjust to me."[58] Greeley was equally critical of General George McClellan, typically inactive, supposedly because of the inflated estimates of Confederate troop strength by Alan Pinkerton's informants. McClellan, thought Greeley, was "certainly a fool" and "probably a traitor." He was also a Democrat.[59]

On matters of freedom of the press, Greeley and Lincoln remained wary allies throughout the rest of the war. In June 1863, shortly before the battle at Gettysburg, Greeley chaired a meeting of newspaper editors in New York to protest the government's arrest of Clement Vallandigham, a Copperhead politician from Ohio. The meeting produced a joint resolution that freedom of the press included the right to "criticize freely and fearlessly the acts of those charged with the administration of the Government."[60] The press should also have the right to campaign actively against Lincoln's reelection if they so chose. Many editors chose not to attend the meeting, and no organization resulted. But it reflected the ongoing tension between government policy and press freedom in wartime.

The relationship between press and government could also be symbiotic. Secretary of War Stanton encouraged Greeley to provide him with any "important facts" that might reach him regarding the war effort. *Tribune* managing editor Sidney Gay suggested that correspondent Henry Villard let General William S. Rosecrans in Chattanooga read his dispatches before he sent them, in hopes that Rosecrans would be more inclined to share information with the newspaper. (Villard rejected the idea, refusing to become Rosecrans's "mouthpiece.") In fact, Villard did succeed in getting considerable confidential information from Rosecrans after the battle of Chickamauga. John Nicolay, Lincoln's young personal secretary at the White House, on occasion sent Greeley stories that Lincoln wanted published. In return, Greeley agreeably asked Nicolay to send him "anything of public interest you may at any time have to publish." Greeley maintained that he simply wanted to publish "all the truth I can get and as few falsehoods as possible."[61] He also wanted to sell newspapers and protect his own paper's freedoms.

In general, the U.S. government respected freedom of the press remarkably well in wartime. Only on one occasion, in May 1864, during the Wilderness and Spottsylvania Courthouse battles, did the government suspend twenty-one newspapers, but only briefly, for releasing secret war information. Censorship orders normally came from the War Department or military commanders in the field. Lincoln did shut down the *New York World* that same month for publishing a bogus presidential proclamation calling for six hundred thousand more troops. He had the editor and publisher jailed, but released them two days later. Few shared the desire of James S. Pike, now a diplomat in the Hague, to "suppress" any northern newspaper that opposed the war effort.[62]

Greeley himself earned the criticism of a free press throughout the war, especially newspapers sympathetic to the Democratic Party or the South. He attacked *Harper's Weekly* for its lukewarm support of the war effort, dubbing it the "Weakly Journal of Civilization." *Harper's* responded by assaulting Greeley after Bull Run, publishing cartoons ridiculing Greeley for telling the generals how to run the war, and showing him in a lunatic asylum in chains. They also portrayed him as African-American, an abolitionist, and Lincoln's puppet master.[63] Freedom of the press meant that Greeley got as good as he gave throughout the war.

Suppression of press freedoms was rare during the Civil War. Greeley and other editors continued to enjoy the right to criticize the Lincoln administration as long as they refrained from giving aid and comfort to the enemy. In 1862, it became clear that Greeley's main bone of contention with Lincoln had to do with slavery. A war for the Union made sense for Greeley only if it guaranteed emancipation. The challenge was to push Lincoln into emancipating slaves without compromising the fight for the Union. If Lincoln favored a Union with or without slavery, Greeley favored emancipation with or without the Union. Only emancipation would join their varying conceptions of republican freedom together in a common effort.

EMANCIPATOR

Emancipation of the slaves as free men lay at the heart of Greeley's concept of American freedom by the time of the Civil War. "Liberty is today the cement of our political edifice," he wrote as the war began; "it is slavery alone that distracts and would destroy the nation." "Do you ask how to put down the rebellion?" he asked at the beginning of 1862. "Destroy slavery. Do you ask how to prevent European intervention? Destroy slavery."[64]

Greeley's anti-slavery was longstanding. His views fell somewhere between the old Whig enthusiasm for returning blacks to Africa under a reverse colonization program and the new evangelism of the abolitionists who favored an immediate end to slavery, even at the cost of Union. He was in all but name a Free Soil man, seeking to prevent any extension of slavery into the territories and new states being added to the Union. Lincoln believed in gradual, compensated, and voter-ratified emancipation before the war. But that was too slow for Greeley, even though he shared the view that slavery was withering away. He believed that slavery was a political and economic problem, as much as a moral one. He could not quite bring himself to share the Higher Law doctrines espoused by his political enemy, William Henry Seward, now Lincoln's Secretary of State.

Greeley was a particular enthusiast of the anti-slavery work of Hinton R. Helper, published in 1857 as *The Impending Crisis of the South*. Helper compiled a wealth of economic statistics to show that slavery was diminishing in the South and that northern free labor far surpassed southern slave labor. Slavery was both morally wrong and economically inefficient. Slaveholders would actually profit by emancipating their slaves. Helper predicted slavery's demise by 1876. He claimed to speak for southern men who held no slaves and supported the Republican Party. He defended Greeley as a friend of the South who had been misrepresented. "I earnestly hope to see it [slavery] prosecuted," Helper wrote, "with energy and zeal, until the Flag of Freedom shall wave triumphantly alike over the valleys of Virginia and the mounds of Mississippi." The Tribune Association published Helper's book, and the newspaper endorsed it. By 1860, the book had sold 140,000 copies. The Tribune Association reprinted it that year as a compendium of selections and shipped in into the South in "bales, bags, boxes, and barrels."[65]

By 1862, Greeley understood that the Union superseded emancipation as a northern war objective. Yet he continued to press for emancipation. He supported freeing slaves who fled across the lines to join the Union army. He criticized Lincoln for countermanding General Fremont's order of emancipation in the West. The South should be given thirty to sixty days to lay down their arms. Otherwise, the president should proclaim their slaves freemen. Carl Schurz, Republican minister to Spain, returned to Washington and urged Lincoln to emancipate the slaves before the European powers began to recognize the Confederacy. Thus, the *Tribune* welcomed Lincoln's March 1862 proposal for compensating those states of the Confederacy that emancipated their slaves, even though abolitionists roundly attacked the proposal for not going fast enough. Greeley also praised Lincoln when he abolished slavery in the District of Columbia in April, calling the president and Tsar Alexander II of Russia, who had recently freed his serfs, leaders in the worldwide struggle for "Man's Emancipation." They would be remembered "as long as Freedom is dear to the human heart." Lincoln wrote Greeley a letter stating that emancipation should be urged "persuasively, and not menacingly, upon the South." Greeley responded that the country would only tolerate Lincoln's "go slow" approach to emancipation as long as people understood that "things are going ahead."[66]

On July 5, 1862, Abraham Lincoln showed James Gilmore the first draft of his forthcoming Emancipation Proclamation. Gilmore routinely showed White House dispatches to Sidney Howard Gay at the *Tribune* for possible publication and helped "soften Mr. Greeley's wrath on several occasions." "What is he wrathy about?" asked Lincoln. Gay communicated that Greeley still wished the president would move more quickly on emancipation. Greeley was already pushing for a proclamation of emancipation that would encourage slaves to flee to the North to receive a "certificate of freedom and protection." Such an action would "immensely weaken the Rebels at once." Slaves should be encouraged to fight for the Union. "The Freedom or Slavery of a race," promised Greeley, "hangs on the results of the war."[67]

On July 13, 1862, Lincoln read the first draft of his preliminary proclamation to William Henry Seward and Gideon Welles, Secretary of the Navy. Both were dumbfounded and confused. But Lincoln's motives were clear—to arm slaves to fight for the North, to prevent foreign recognition of the Confederacy as an independent nation, and to create havoc behind enemy lines. Emancipation would be a military measure of limited scope but profound impact. Four days later, Congress passed the Second Confiscation Act, emancipating all slaves of owners in armed rebellion against the United States, whether those slaves were fugitives, prisoners, or simply abandoned. The next day, Walker and Gilmore called on Lincoln to discuss whether or not to inform Greeley of the impending proclamation. They decided to do so, but not before Greeley had launched his own proclamation in the pages of the *Tribune*. The delay may have been due to the mixed reaction Lincoln got on July 22 when he broached the idea of emancipation to his assembled cabinet.[68]

In early August, Greeley wrote friends that he was discouraged because the government was moving so slowly on emancipation. Why should he support the Union until emancipation was central to its war policy? "I do not feel like making a war speech," he wrote, "till the Government toes the mark on the Slavery question." He would volunteer for the war effort himself, he said, probably in the Commissary, if he were only in good health. "Bad as our generals are," he complained, "I think our Commissaries have thus far sacrificed more men then they have." Disease and bad food were taking more casualties than enemy fire.[69]

On August 19, 1862, Greeley sent his famous letter to Lincoln, printed the next day in the *Tribune* as the "Prayer of Twenty Millions." In it, he demanded that the president execute the law with regard to nine points related to emancipation. An "immense majority" of Americans, he claimed, now wanted emancipation. His generals were disregarding the confiscation acts. Lincoln was listening too much to "fossil politicians" from the border states. The president was too cautious in his policies and statements on the matter. The very same day, Gilmore belatedly delivered the news about the draft Emancipation Proclamation to Greeley. But it was too late. Every *Tribune* reader in the country now had Horace Greeley's views on emancipation before Lincoln's. "We have fought wolves with the devices of a sheep," thundered the editor. It was time now to "fight slavery with liberty."[70]

Lincoln's response to Greeley's prayer would become much more famous than the prayer itself. In a letter to Greeley telegraphed to the *Tribune,* Lincoln promised that he would try to save the Union either "without freeing any slave" or "by freeing all the slaves" or by "freeing some and leaving others alone." Emancipation for Lincoln was simply a way to "save the Union." Lincoln added that he hoped personally for a day when "all men everywhere could be free." Greeley grumbled that Lincoln had not really answered his "Prayer," had prepared his response in advance, and simply wanted to get his own views before the public. "But I'll forgive him everything," promised Greeley, "if he'll issue the proclamation."[71]

Rival newspapers were not so charitable. The Washington *National Intelligencer* found Greeley's "Prayer" to be "arrogant, dictatorial, and acrimonious." The *New York Times* called it a "bold assumption." The main difference between Lincoln and Greeley was that the president "must be governed by his own sense of oath, honor, and duty, as to the time and manner of his actions," whereas the editor "wishes to substitute his conscience for Mr. Lincoln's."[72] But Greeley stood firm.

Greeley continued to argue with the president. "Let it be proclaimed tomorrow from the White House that every slave fleeing to us from the Rebels is thenceforth a free man, and the knell of Treason will have been sounded," wrote the editor. Traitors could not legally hold slaves under American law. Lincoln should obey the laws of the North and free the slaves of the South. Greeley's goal was "Freedom for All," not merely the survival of the Union. Saving the Union required that "you may promptly and practically realize that Slavery is to be vanquished only by Liberty." "As to Old Abe's letter," wrote Greeley to a friend, "I consider it a sign of progress. I have no doubt the Nation will get on the right ground at last; I only fear it will get *under* the ground previously. It is time to fight with both hands now."[73]

In September 1862, after the bloody Union victory at Antietam, Lincoln decided the time was right to move on the issue of slavery. Antietam produced some twenty thousand casualties in one day, more than twice all previous American casualties in all previous wars. "The Rebels are upon us," wrote the *Tribune*, "the life and death of the Union is a question not of months, but of days." The European powers stood ready to recognize the Confederacy. On September 11, Greeley addressed the annual state fair in Rutland, Vermont, and decried the war for destroying man's natural state—peace and industry. The war would be worth the cost only if it helped achieve "the stately fabric of impartial and universal Freedom!"[74]

On September 22, Lincoln finally made public his Emancipation Proclamation, to take effect on January 1, 1863. Greeley immediately called the proclamation a "great boon of Freedom." He applauded Lincoln for his action. "Henceforth and forever," Greeley told Gilmore, "we shall be a free people." "It is the beginning of the end of the Rebellion," wrote the *Tribune*, "the beginning of the new life of the nation. GOD BLESS ABRAHAM LINCOLN!" The South, thought Greeley, could now move from the "semi-barbarism of a medieval age" to the "light and civilization of the Nineteenth Christian Century." The "emancipation of a race" was truly a "sublime" event.[75]

Lincoln's war for Union was now also Greeley's war for emancipation. The two purposes were one. Union now meant "Liberty for All" and the end of slavery. The war would continue, but the Union would win. North and South would some day walk hand in hand toward a relationship of "fraternal concord." America was now the "legitimate child and foremost champion of Human Freedom."[76] Peace was in sight. Greeley proposed to Lincoln that there be a general amnesty for rebel soldiers, immediate emancipation, and money for those southern states that emancipated their slaves. "All this," he promised Lincoln, "will cost less than to prosecute the War through 1863."[77]

Nevertheless, the war continued, even as emancipation took effect. On January 1, 1863, Lincoln proclaimed, "all persons held as slaves within any State or designated part of a State, the people whereof shall then be in rebellion against the United States, shall be then, thenceforth and forever free." In other words, immediate emancipation applied only to the states of the Confederacy on the grounds of "military necessity." Fugitive and freed slaves would be "received into the armed service of the United States," mainly as guards and sailors. "From that date," wrote Greeley later, "the war for the Union became, what in essence it had necessarily been from the outset, a struggle for freedom to all." The *Tribune* praised emancipation as a "new base of freedom," even calling the proclamation a "Proclamation of Freedom." The newspaper published it two days running, adding its opinion that Lincoln should now move to free the slaves in every state of the Union, not just the Confederacy.[78]

When Greeley attended a mass rally of African-Americans in New York City at Cooper Union shortly after the Emancipation Proclamation, there was "immense cheering" for the *Tribune* and "tremendous cheering" for Greeley. Please tell the president, Greeley told John Nicolay a few days later, that "his message fully satisfies the expectations of his friends, and is received with general enthusiasm."[79] But Greeley's rivals and critics were less sanguine. Thurlow Weed wrote Lincoln a letter saying that Greeley "possesses the power to ruin our country." Adam Gurowski told his friends that Greeley was "an ass, a traitor, and a coward."[80]

But Greeley's support of emancipation made him a popular voice in the North that spring. When William Lloyd Garrison attended an anti-slavery meeting at Cooper Union in May, he resisted the crowd's calls for him to speak. "Then calls were made for Horace Greeley, who came forward and made a few remarks in his queer-toned voice and a very awkward manner." The crowd applauded, and Garrison also spoke briefly. Greeley continued to bombard the White House with suggestions and recommendations for appointments. "In God's good time," he wrote Senator Charles Sumner, "this is to be a land of real freedom, where equal rights and equal laws shall banish rebellion, treason, and riot, and all manner of kindred diabolisms." Emancipating the slaves was a brilliant stroke on Lincoln's part, politically and morally. "They now know that Union means Freedom, and they are uneasy, excited, anxious, vigilant and insubordinate."[81]

The Emancipation Proclamation and the "Prayer of Twenty Millions" brought Lincoln and Greeley closer together on the war effort. Holding the country together and freeing the slaves were now parts of a single campaign. But Greeley would remain a nuisance for Lincoln, even as the two men cooperated. They agreed on the general aspirations of freedom, but disagreed on the boundaries of personal liberty.

PERSONAL LIBERTY MAN

Horace Greeley had always been committed to personal liberty as a citizen's right under any free republican system of government, in wartime as in peacetime. Yet in 1863, the battle cry of freedom was endangering personal liberty. How much individual liberty should Americans sacrifice in the name of collective freedom? Shortly after Antietam, Lincoln suspended the legal right of *habeas corpus,* which guarantees Americans against illegal imprisonment by the government. The suspension covered anyone disloyal to the Union, seeking to evade the draft, or giving aid and comfort to the enemy. The army had already begun arresting "disloyal" persons in areas under its jurisdiction. The *Tribune* promptly expressed its concern over the arrests, but added, "we would not deprive the government of the power to make them in a crisis like the present." The newspaper warned that existing constitutional safeguards should not be "debauched and broken down."[82] But numerous arrests followed Antietam, and Americans feared for their own civil liberties.

The central test case of personal liberty during the Civil War involved Clement Vallandigham, an Ohio congressman and leader of the Peace Democrats. Many so-called Peace Democrats supported slavery, the South, and peace at any price. Republicans called them Copperheads. In January 1863, Vallandigham wrote a letter to Greeley saying that he was still a "true Union man," not a secessionist, and recognizing that Greeley was not the disunionist he at times appeared to be. Emancipation, Vallandigham claimed, should be abandoned as a war aim. The Union should be restored with slavery permitted. The immediate goal was a peace between North and South, perhaps using mediation by the European powers to achieve harmony and reunion. "You can do much," Vallandigham wrote Greeley, "but it will require great moral courage. Do nothing against Peace in the *Tribune*; but do what you desire to do for it, *first outside.*"[83]

Vallandigham's approach to Greeley caught the editor at a bad time. He was still euphoric over emancipation. Molly was yet again sick at home. He was engaged in a libel suit at the *Tribune.* Moreover, Vallandigham's letter appeared in the press, and tarred Greeley with the brush of a Peace Democrat. "Your suicidal course on the subject of the war," wrote a friend, meant "every Republican in both houses [of Congress] is denouncing you" for "shaking hands with Vallandigham." Greeley's entire political career was going down in "shame and ignominy."[84] How could he be so unpatriotic?

On May 1, 1863, as the war dragged on, Vallandigham made an inflammatory speech in Mt. Vernon, Ohio (where "Dixie" had been composed), claiming that the war did not intend to save the Union, but to free blacks and enslave whites. General Ambrose Burnside charged him with violating Order Number 38 forbidding declarations of sympathy for the enemy in time of war. He arrested Vallandigham, court-martialed him, and sent him to prison in Cincinnati. Although Lincoln never actually signed any order suspending Vallandigham's rights, Secretary of War Stanton issued a general order stating that "in the judgement of the president, public safety requires the suspension of the writ of *habeas corpus* in the case." Lincoln then commuted the sentence to banishment to the Confederacy (Tennessee) toward which Vallandigham was so sympathetic.

Coming at the time of the Union defeat at Chancellorsville, the response to the arrest of a civilian by military authorities for exercising his right of free speech was dramatic. In Dayton, Ohio, a crowd of some six thousand burned newspaper offices, cut telegraph lines, and destroyed a bridge. Troops arrived from Columbus and Cincinnati to restore order. Authorities arrested thirty ringleaders and closed all bars and liquor stores in town. The *Tribune* admitted that Vallandigham was a "Pro-Slavery Democrat of an exceedingly coppery hue. His politics are as bad as bad can be." But the newspaper editorial went on to note that federal and state constitutions did not permit prosecution of individuals for "perverse opinions, nor unpatriotic speeches." Vallandigham had a legal right to speak his mind. Sending him South was "the worst joke Mr. Lincoln has yet made." "We pray the President to pardon him and turn him loose," concluded the paper.[85]

Two months later, the Peace Democrats of Ohio nominated Vallandigham for governor (he lost the election). He subsequently escaped from Tennessee to Canada, then returned to Ohio where he held his tongue and was not arrested again. After the Battle of Gettysburg and the draft riots in New York City in July 1863, Lincoln issued a proclamation suspending the writ of *habeas corpus* in the interest of "public safety" during a time of "rebellion." No citizen would enjoy full constitutional rights until the end of the war. Military officers did not have to turn over anyone in custody to a civil court judge, but could hold them in prison indefinitely.[86]

Greeley now praised Lincoln's suspension of personal liberty in the interests of future national freedom. In 1863, guarantees of that liberty were "in the hands of traitors, the two-edged sword of treachery and craft pointed at the heart of the nation." The president had "courageously and wisely" suspended a basic constitutional right by deciding that "the liberty of the few, if need be, shall be sacrificed for the moment, in order to preserve the liberty of all for all time to come." Freedom in the long run required suspension of individual liberty in the short run. In time, the "loyal North" would realize that the president had employed his "unalterable resolve" in order to "save this imperiled Republic."[87] Without the republic, freedom of any kind —including personal liberty—was surely doomed.

Greeley also welcomed the president's State of the Union address at the end of the year, when he announced a Proclamation of Amnesty and Reconstruction once the war was over. All those in rebellion against the United States could receive pardon and amnesty if they signed a loyalty oath. All slaves, not just those in the Confederacy, would be freed. The *Tribune* praised Lincoln for recognizing that even those in rebellion might in time choose a "speedy return to loyalty and peace."[88]

Greeley continued to support Lincoln on the matter of personal liberty throughout the rest of the war. He retained his working relationship with the White House, even when chastised for making errors in news reporting or "reckless misstatements and unfounded imputations of your Washington correspondent," as John Hay put it. When Vallandigham returned from Canada in June 1864, Greeley wrote that it would be a "great mistake" to arrest him again. He agreed with "sensible Republicans" that the best idea was simply to "let him alone." Lincoln did so. The voting public would decide his fate. "His running for governor last year," wrote Greeley, "was worth fifty thousand votes to the Unionists of Ohio." Vallandigham contin-ued to write Greeley letters urging "conciliation and pacification" to end the war.[89] Both men probably agreed with Lincoln that, when peace came, it should be without malice and with clemency. But peace was still a long way off.

Although both Greeley and Lincoln agreed that, in time of war, personal liberty might be suspended in the name of freedom, neither man was comfortable with the suspension of civil rights, as the Val-landigham case indicated. The war continued, as did the redefinition of freedom, most notably in Lincoln's Gettysburg Address.

GETTYSBURG AND A NEW BIRTH OF FREEDOM

In June 1863, Horace Greeley went up to Havana, New York, to dedi-cate the new People's College. He offered a resolution to the board that they thank President Lincoln and Congress for signing and pass-ing the Land Grant College Act, the origin of our current state college and university system.[90] But the idyll passed quickly. A week after his visit, Greeley was overwhelmed by news of the massive three-day bat-tle raging in the southeastern Pennsylvania town of Gettysburg.

Greeley recognized immediately that the Battle of Gettysburg was a turning point in the Civil War, the beginning of the end of the war. On July 4, he wrote that there was reason to hope that a Union victory at Gettysburg would "date anew the birth of American Indepen-dence." That day was "the darkest Fourth of July which has dawned upon us since the commencement of our national existence," but also the brightest. Until this point, Americans could "hardly talk of liberty without laughing in each other's faces." The Constitution and the Declaration of Independence had become a "rare joke" because of the existence of slavery. Today, amid the carnage of the battlefield, Gree-ley wrote, "let our martyrs be freshly remembered." Americans might well be distracted by matters of policy, he claimed, but never by "doubts of principle." Human equality and freedom were no longer a "dubious or dishonest experiment." A nation founded on great ideas would lead the way to universal freedom. The God of Battles was surely on the side of "Justice, Humanity, and Freedom," and had given a great victory to the Army of the Potomac. "The Republic," he concluded in Periclean words foreshadowing Lincoln's a few months later, "whom its [the army's] valor preserves, wreathes its living heroes with imperishable garlands, and mourns amid its joy the gallant dead, who died that the nation might live."[91]

No sooner was the battle over when New York City was engulfed in the flames of civil disorder. In March, Congress enacted a conscription act drafting all eligible men between the ages of twenty and thirty-five for military service. On June 11, the first names in the draft lottery were drawn. The next day, Greeley wrote Stanton that most people did not support the draft. Military pay should be increased. The rich should not escape the draft by paying for substitutes. "The burdens of the war must be made to fall upon property where they justly belong."[92] But such was not to be the case. On July 11, one week after the Battle of Gettysburg, draft riots overwhelmed New York City.

A Republican mayor, George Opdyke, had recently succeeded a Democrat, Fernando Wood. On Saturday, July 11, over one thousand names for the draft were drawn in the Ninth District without incident. But on Sunday, crowds around hotels and bars began to assault draft officials and offices. By Monday, excited crowds gathered on every street corner, looting and burning draft offices. Speakers in Printing House Square denounced Greeley and the *Tribune* for supporting emancipation and the war. A mob appeared in front of the newspaper's offices, singing "Hang Horace Greeley to a Sour Apple Tree" to the tune of "John Brown's Body." Despite Greeley's admonition to avoid bloodshed, newspaper staff members brought muskets, pistols, and rifles from the Governor's Island armory into the second floor and laid them out on a table in case of emergency. Sidney Gay and James Gilmore decided to sleep in their offices that night.[93] No one had much faith in the few militia in the city who had not been sent to Gettysburg, nor in their commander, eighty-year-old Major General John E. Wool.

Out in the streets, the situation was much worse. Mobs killed soldiers and draft officials, and hanged on lampposts any African-Americans they could lay hands on. They beat policemen, looted stores, burned warehouses, ripped up rails, cut telegraph lines, and stopped horse cars and omnibuses in the street. By 7:00 p.m. Monday evening, the *Tribune* offices were closed and shuttered. A noisy crowd surrounded the building, throwing stones and calling for a lynching of Horace Greeley, "the nigger's friend." Five policemen arrived but were quickly overpowered. At some point, a few mob members entered the building, breaking off gas burners, overturning desks and tables, and lighting fires in wastebaskets. Somehow, Greeley and his staff made it through the night.[94]

On Tuesday, July 14, the situation worsened. An infuriated mob burned the Colored Orphan Asylum on Fifth Avenue near 46th Street. The *Tribune* wrote of "not simply a riot, but the commencement of a revolution." Gilmore took a cab to the Brooklyn Navy Yard and returned with bombs, hand grenades, and fifty forty-pound artillery shells with fuses. One hundred and fifty men of the 8th Long Island Regiment, armed with muskets and rifles, occupied the *Tribune* building, setting up bales of paper as barricades. A howitzer capable of firing grapeshot and canister appeared on the second floor.[95] Still, the building remained secure, and Greeley got his paper out that night listening to the mob howl outside in the rain.

On Wednesday, July 15, the riots continued. The *Tribune* blamed Copperhead agitators and warned the mobs not to attack the building, by now armed to the teeth. Up in Chappaqua, Molly Greeley and her two daughters, Ida and Gabrielle, were surrounded by drunken mobs threatening to kill the entire Greeley family. The farm manager sent them off to safety with a nearby Quaker family, then laid a circle of gunpowder around the outside of the house in case the mob attacked. Someone warned patrons of a nearby tavern that "Horace Greeley is a peace man, but Mary Greeley will fight to the last." The mob arrived that night, howled at the house, and dispersed.[96]

The *Tribune* charged that license to riot was undermining law and liberty. The civil authorities were "complaisant." The army was "weak" in putting down the riots. The racist violence directed against African-Americans was part of a "slaveholders' rebellion," a Confederate diversion. The mobs were organized. In Greeley's view, the "traitors of the North" had deliberately planned the riots. By Friday, stores and businesses reopened, and cars and stages began to run again in the streets. Two regular army regiments arrived from Gettysburg. The Common Council appropriated over two million dollars to help pay for substitutions. Order returned to the city. "Wise or unwise," wrote the *Tribune* on July 18, "laws are laws, and must be obeyed."[97] Lincoln and the federal government should enforce the draft laws as they saw fit.

The New York draft riots went beyond the boundaries of freedom. They were treasonous acts of mob violence, probably fomented by the enemy. "I was in no wise harmed by the mobs," Greeley wrote a friend, "though they must have hurt their throats bawling at me. I did not stop at the office during the evenings, but was here during the days and went in and out cautiously, but without fear. They did not know where to find me nights."[98] In the end, the riots cost more than one thousand lives, injured thousands more, and caused over three million dollars in property damage. Greeley was shaken by the events. But he and his family were safe, and the *Tribune* did not miss a single edition.

In November, Lincoln came to Gettysburg to say a few words at the opening of the new federal military cemetery where so many Union soldiers were now buried. His few immortal words completely eclipsed the real "Gettysburg Address," a long-winded account of the battle by Massachusetts orator Edward Everett. Lincoln summarized, in telegraphic language, the transition from liberty to freedom espoused by both European and American republicans of the day.

Garrison and the abolitionists had long contrasted the *liberty* of the founding fathers and the American Revolution with the *freedom* promised by the emancipation of slaves everywhere. The "true union for freedom" lay in the future. "We see what our fathers did not see," said Garrison in 1856, "we know what they did not know." Greeley often made the same point. "Eighty-six years ago this day," wrote Greeley on July 4, 1862, "the representatives of our fathers, in Congress assembled in Philadelphia," had produced the U.S. Constitution. The fathers had fought for the equal and inalienable rights of man. But America had not been "faithful to the principles thus boldly enunciated." They had failed to abolish slavery, "our national sin." Now we were engaged in a "furious civil war" to pay for that sin. "God save the Republic!" concluded Greeley.[99]

Abolitionists and republicans had also long spoken of government "of, by, and for the people." The phrase may go back to the Middle Ages. Daniel Webster used it often in his speeches, as did Theodore Parker in his sermons that William Herndon passed along to Lincoln out in Illinois. Lincoln marked one particular passage from an 1858 Parker sermon: "democracy is direct self-government, over all the people, for all the people, by all the people." "A democracy," said Parker in Boston in 1850, "that is, a government of all the people, by all the people, for all the people, of course, a government of the principles of eternal justice, the unchanging law of God; for shortness' sake, I will call it the idea of Freedom."[100] Louis Kossuth and Giuseppe Mazzini had expressed the same idea in similar words since the 1830s.

Lincoln's audience was undoubtedly as familiar with his Periclean style of rhetoric as they were with his republican political ideas.[101] They surely noticed that he described America as a "nation conceived in liberty" at the beginning of his brief remarks, but ended with a call for a "new birth of freedom" in the future. As his audience knew well, *liberty* was for some and *freedom* for all. Lincoln was grounding his remarks not in the Constitution that tolerated unspoken slavery, but in the Declaration of Independence that declared all men free and equal. The founding fathers had defended liberty against British tyranny. The current generation must defend freedom against American slavery.

The *Tribune* reporter at Gettysburg, Joseph L. Gilbert, heard the address. He then consulted Lincoln's delivery text (handwritten notes) at the platform after Everett's oration. (Scholars still argue about various texts of the address and accounts of what Lincoln said that day.) The *Tribune* ran its own full account of the Gettysburg ceremonies on November 20, 1863, including Gilbert's reported text. The newspaper ran it again the following day. On November 26—the first proclaimed Thanksgiving Day—Greeley welcomed Lincoln's "Proclamation of Freedom," as he called the Gettysburg Address. Lincoln had predicted a "new birth of freedom." "Be it ours also to ask," wrote Greeley, "that the fear of the Lord, even for His mercies, may keep Rulers and People humble and faithful to that end." Adam Gurowski was more cynical, writing in his diary that Lincoln spoke "with one eye to a future platform and to re-election."[102] But that was another matter.

A few months later, Lincoln reiterated his distinction between *liberty* and *freedom* in a letter to Governor Michael Hahn, newly elected in liberated Louisiana. Hahn had proposed that voting rights be extended to freedmen. This did not happen. Lincoln supported Hahn's proposal, saying such rights "would probably help, in some trying time to come, to keep the jewel of liberty within the family of freedom." Freedom was something bigger and broader than liberty. One month later, Lincoln noted in his address to a Sanitary Commission Fair in Baltimore that "the world has never had a good definition of the word liberty, and the American people, just now, are much in want of one. We all declare for liberty; but in using the same *word* we do not all mean the same *thing*."[103] Francis Lieber had been saying this for years in his political theory writings. By distinguishing publicly between *liberty* and *freedom*, Lincoln was providing new language for the second American Revolution, the elimination of slavery.

Horace Greeley had written much the same thing as Lincoln said that day at Gettysburg, but in his own slangy, homespun language. He too had long distinguished the liberty of gentlemen from the freedom of all, including slaves. He also recognized that his generation had to complete the work of the revolutionary fathers. A bloody and prolonged Civil War was the price of freedom. "We are to go through this war," Greeley wrote on July 4, 1864, a year after Gettysburg, "to preserve the inheritance bequeathed us, to save the Republic—that is what our fathers taught us."[104] Lincoln could not have said it better.

Both Lincoln and Greeley realized that Gettysburg had transformed the war into a mythic event of historic proportions. Lincoln's address reflected a deep sense of the unfinished business of history, as well as the debt to those who had gone before and sacrificed so much that the nation might live. A few days after the battle, publisher O. D. Case of Hartford, Connecticut, visited Greeley and suggested that he begin writing a "history of the rebellion." Greeley was a journalist, not a historian. But he was sorely tempted. Now that the war for the Union was also a war for freedom, he was more comfortable with the idea. "In fact," he wrote much later, "not till that war was placed on its true basis of a struggle for liberation, and not conquest, by President Lincoln's successive Proclamations of Freedom, would I have consented to write its history." The draft riots in New York provided further evidence that a popular history of the war was a good idea. So did the liberal compensation promised by the publisher and the chance to write a full-scale historical critique of slavery for the literary marketplace even before the war was over. The book would sell by subscription. Greeley needed money, as usual, and the time was right. He would produce his own "Gettysburg Address," a history of the Civil War in two volumes to be entitled *The American Conflict*.[105]

A few weeks after Gettysburg, Greeley set to work. He hired a secretary and began to haunt New York libraries—the Public Library, the Astor Library, and the Mercantile Library. Collecting and compiling a massive amount of material, he churned out a chapter every three or four days. By April 10, 1864, he had completed the first volume and dedicated it to his British radical republican friend John Bright. The first volume covered the period up to 1861 (the title said 1860–1864) and emphasized the long struggle to eliminate slavery in the United States. Much of it consisted of long quotations from documents. Much of the prose was flowery and ornate. For example, after Bull Run, "the nation, flung headlong to the earth, and temporarily paralyzed by her fall, rose at length with a truer appreciation of the power, the purpose, and the venom of her foes, and a firmer resolve that they should be grappled with and overcome."[106] But within a few months, the book produced ten thousand dollars in royalties for Greeley. By 1867, volume one had sold 125,000 copies, an enormous number for the period. Horace Greeley had written a bestseller.

"Greeley, the historian, is the same as Greeley the war leader," grumbled Adam Gurowski. His Civil War history would "sell well," but "almost on every page the politician pierces through." Greeley had omitted much, including many political leaders and virtually all mention of foreign relations. Former president James Buchanan grumbled later that the editor was "incapable of becoming a discriminating and unbiased historian. Accuracy is certainly not his forte." But the *Atlantic Monthly* gave the book a good review, finding the author "vigorous and discriminating" and the book "never dull, never languid," but also damning it with faint praise: "Mr. Greeley has written nothing better." The editor, the review concluded, had "an instinctive passion for Freedom." John Bright in England was also delighted with the book, and thanked Greeley for dedicating it to him.[107]

Greeley's history of the Civil War was but one among many history-by-the-pound lavish volumes that came out during and after the war. He admitted later that he had not conceived the idea until after Gettysburg and the merging of emancipation and Union into a single war aim that Greeley could accept. Sales dropped precipitously for volume two in 1867, when Greeley helped bail Jefferson Davis out of prison. Greeley made continuous complaints to his editor—he had not received reimbursement for his research expenses, the price was too high, the editing was careless, the book should come out sooner rather than later, and so forth. But overall, the history was a grand success.

Greeley reported in 1868 that he had received $12,947.73 in 1867 and $15,074.77 in 1868 for the two volumes, a princely sum at the time for any publishing project. "I still live," he told his publisher.[108]

By 1870, Greeley had sold 225,000 copies of *The American Conflict*. By comparison, a competitor in the field of popular, bulky, illustrated histories of the Civil War, Thomas P. Kettell, had sold only 120,000 copies of his *History of the Great Rebellion* (1865). Both figures were impressively large for the period. Greeley might have done better but for the Jefferson Davis affair. "It has taken a great deal longer for the storm to blow over, caused by the Davis Bail Bond, than I anticipated," he wrote O. D. Case in 1870, "and the fruitless efforts we made the first year to overcome it cost us a good deal of money."[109]

Horace Greeley's foray into history was a natural outcome of the great proclamations of freedom of 1863—Lincoln's Emancipation Proclamation and the Gettysburg Address. Both Lincoln and Greeley recognized the historical importance of the moment. The tide of a bloody civil war had turned, and a "new birth of freedom" was at hand, fulfilling the unfulfilled promise of liberty made by the fathers. What Lincoln had done as a rhetorical legal brief, Greeley did as popular history. Both men realized the historical importance both of Gettysburg and of the transformation of liberty into freedom.

9

Unionist

PEACEMAKER

Peace and freedom were intertwined in the mind of Horace Greeley as republican virtues. Domestic harmony in America required peace among industrious neighbors and fellow employees, protected by government tariffs from unfair foreign competition. Harmony abroad meant peace with foreign neighbors. Large government expenses on an army and navy were unnecessary if harmonious political and social relations could be maintained. Greeley abhorred the Civil War as he had abhorred the Mexican War and, before that, the War of 1812. The American conflict to put down a treasonous rebellion should end in peace and harmony, returning the republic to its state of virtue.

Greeley's desire for a mediated peace settlement went back to the early days of the Civil War. "I have no faith in wholesale bloodshed," he wrote his future managing editor, Sidney Gay, "to *no definite end*. It is our duty to fight so long as we may with a rational hope of success —no longer."[1] His enemies accused him of being a Secessionist or a Copperhead. His friends knew better. Horace Greeley intended simply to save the republic from committing suicide.

Greeley became intrigued by the idea of a peace settlement mediated by European powers immediately after the Emancipation Proclamation. In January 1863, Greeley approached Henri Mercier, the French minister of Napoleon III in Washington, about such a settlement. The second Union defeat at Bull Run in late summer 1862 made European intervention plausible. But the Union victory at Antietam ended prospects for European recognition of the Confederacy. Seward rejected Mercier's suggestions of mediation. Yet Peace Democrats favored a settlement after doing well in the November elections. In January, Vallandigham attacked Lincoln's war policies as a "most bloody failure," urging a restoration of the Union with slavery.[2]

Greeley's enthusiasm for peace at this time derived in part from the influence of William Cornell ("Colorado") Jewett. Scion of a prominent Portland, Maine, family with gold mining interests in Colorado, Jewett sympathized with the idea of a peace settlement and was just back from a trip to Europe and Canada, where he had described his peace plans to Queen Victoria and other European rulers. A Peace Democrat, Jewett proposed to introduce Greeley to Mercier. The editor agreed, but told Jewett he would only consider negotiations with accredited authorities of the Confederacy, a Confederate "willingness to make peace," and arbitration by a neutral third-party nation supportive of republican principles. The last point, of course, excluded arbitration by England, France, or Russia. Jewett told Mercier that Greeley's support in the pages of the *Tribune* could be "decisive." Greeley then promised his friend Henry J. Raymond, editor of the *New York Times*, that as far as peace was concerned, he, Greeley, would "drive Lincoln into it."[3]

On January 2, 1863, Greeley wrote a letter to Jewett that he published in the *Tribune* only later in May. In it, he reiterated his points that a negotiated peace must be authorized by the Confederate government in Richmond, that the Confederates would have to take the initiative, and that the arbiter must be a republic, not a monarchy. Greeley then went off to Washington to see Mercier, who regretted that the *Tribune* had distorted the French position on peace negotiations. Greeley averred his "good intentions," then left to see Lincoln and Charles Sumner. He also visited Jewett, who promised Mercier that Greeley would "through his journal place France right." Greeley now supported the French plan for mediation, noting in the *Tribune*, "it is almost impossible to make a good war or a bad peace." He reported that the policy of the Emperor of France in proposing mediation was "wholly friendly to the United States," and was inspired by a desire to see the Union "re-established upon a basis of mutual concession." Emperor Napoleon III, no republican, was nevertheless acceptable as a friendly mediator. Henry Raymond promptly attacked Greeley for "violating the law by dealing with the representative of a foreign state."[4]

In the meantime, Jewett sent a petition to both houses of Congress asking for an armistice and mediation with the South. Greeley was supporting the same line in the *Tribune*. Charles Sumner, in particular, was displeased with this action, and had moved that the U.S. Senate postpone indefinitely Jewett's petition. The motion carried easily. A month later, Thurlow Weed accused Greeley of trying to negotiate with the Confederacy. Greeley responded only that he was "not averse to peace through mutual submission to the arbitration of our differences." He continued to criticize Sumner's rigid stance on the matter and to support arbitration by an "impartial" European tribunal as a way to peace. In May, Greeley called the earlier negotiations with Jewett and Mercier "in effect a fraud."[5]

In May 1863, there was another peace feeler. Colonel James F. Jaquess, a Methodist minister from Illinois serving in Tennessee under General Rosecrans, proposed a peace mission to the South through the Methodist Church. He sent a letter to that effect to President Lincoln through the good auspices of James R. Gilmore. He proposed to come to Washington and talk to Lincoln about the scheme. Lincoln wired Rosecrans that Jaquess should not come to Washington. He did, however, grant Jaquess a furlough so that he might travel in the South, but "he cannot go with any government authority whatever." Jaquess then went to Richmond, but Jefferson Davis refused to see him because he was not an authorized representative of the United States. Gilmore also proposed peace terms "on the basis of the abolition of slavery" to his friend Zebulon Vance, governor of North Carolina, but to no avail.[6] With the carnage at Chancellorsville, then Gettysburg and Vicksburg, talk of peace subsided.

Charles Sumner wrote Greeley that mediation was a possibility, and that "like you, I loathe and detest war." But the *Tribune* that autumn noted that Lincoln wanted peace as much as anyone, as did his cabinet officers. For now, Greeley recommended that Lincoln be left "unfettered" to make a peace in his own way, and the war raged on.[7]

On March 1, 1864, Colonel Ulrich Dahlgren led a daring cavalry raid on Richmond. Dahlgren was the son of Rear Admiral John A. Dahlgren, a close friend of Lincoln. But the affair went awry, Dahlgren was killed, and his men captured. Seized papers suggested that Dahlgren's men planned to kill Jefferson Davis and his entire cabinet, thus decapitating the Confederacy. Widely published in the press, North and South, the Dahlgren Papers seemed to the Confederate leaders to justify a new and unorthodox "black flag" terrorist war against the North, including northern cities, bases, and prisoner-of-war camps. Under verbal orders from Davis, Colonel Thomas H. Hines of Kentucky began to organize a massive campaign against the North based in Canada. The plan was to influence northern opinion against the war, free Confederate prisoners, undermine the Union war effort, and aid peace candidates in the coming elections of November 1864. To support the effort, Davis chose Jacob Thompson, a former U.S. Secretary of the Interior from Mississippi; Clement C. Clay, a former U.S. Senator; and James P. Holcombe, a law professor from Virginia, already in Canada on Confederate business. Thompson began to dispense a million dollars in gold authorized by Davis and the Confederate Congress in Richmond, money that he placed in an account with the Bank of Ontario in Montreal. Thompson and Clay left Richmond and sailed north up the Atlantic coast past the gauntlet of Union ships. Holcombe went to Halifax, Nova Scotia, to organize Confederate prisoners who had escaped from northern incarceration. Hines was to go north and confer with Holcombe and northern peace advocates in Canada before launching his operations. The center of Confederate intrigue was Niagara Falls, where tourist hotels on both sides of the border allowed for lenient border crossings and meetings.[8]

A key player in the Confederate offensive in the North in 1864 was George N. Sanders, Young American, former editor of the *Democratic Review,* and Greeley's fellow journalist from New York City. Sanders was tall, debonair, and friendly, a bearded man never lacking in money or women. He was an enigmatic and enthusiastic political schemer whose volatility was exceeded only by his bombastic rhetoric. He revered the European heroes of 1848. In 1858, Sanders campaigned for Stephen A. Douglas and publicly supported the attempted assassination of Emperor Napoleon III. Hines disliked Sanders. Clay was too old and infirm to pay much attention as Sanders worked the crowd at Confederate dinner parties in Montreal. We know that Greeley and Sanders met personally on at least one occasion in 1855. John Hay claimed that the two men were intimate friends. Since 1857, Sanders had also served as the U.S. Navy purchasing agent for New York harbor, working out of an office at the Brooklyn Navy Yard, requisitioning money and paying contractors for their work. Sanders ultimately moved south to work for the Confederacy. In summer 1862, Davis sent him to Europe to seek British and French military aid. On June 1, 1864, Sanders arrived in Montreal from Paris to work for Jacob Thompson. He became the unofficial intermediary between Confederate agents in Canada and Peace Democrats in the United States. Sanders and Colorado Jewett began to set up meetings for northern politicians with Clay and Holcombe to influence the impending presidential elections. On July 12, 1864, Sanders sent Jewett off to New York to see Greeley on the matter of opening peace talks.[9]

Summer 1864 was another critical moment in the seemingly endless bloodbath between North and South. Grant's armies, licking their wounds after bloody battles in the Wilderness, Petersburg, and Cold Harbor in Virginia, were lodged in a rabbit warren of trenches around Richmond and Petersburg. The Army of Tennessee was trying to prevent General William Sherman from moving toward Atlanta. The siege of Charleston was proving indecisive. Jubal Early and his Confederate raiders had entered Maryland and threatened to attack Washington. Confederate war supplies from Europe continued to get through the northern coastal blockade. There was general war weariness in both North and South. Lincoln's first term in office would end in November. The time was right for a peace settlement to become a national political issue, to divide the Republican Party, and perhaps to overturn the Lincoln administration.

Greeley was eager for peace, and on July 5, 1864, George Sanders wrote his friend Samuel Tilden, a rising Democrat politician in New York, and told him he had joined Clay and Thompson in Canada. They hoped to settle the war "with honor to both sections" of the country. (Tilden may have told Greeley that a southern delegation in Canada wished to visit Washington, confer with the president, and negotiate a peaceful settlement to the war.) The very same day, Jewett wrote Greeley from Niagara Falls that he had met Sanders and that "two ambassadors of Davis & Co. are now in Canada, with full and complete powers for a peace." Sanders urged Greeley to come to Niagara Falls and help arrange safe passage for Confederate agents to Washington. "Will you come here?" Jewett wired Greeley the next day, "parties have full power."[10] Greeley took the bait.

Lincoln was clearly not going to appear in public to be an opponent of peace. At the same time that Sanders was approaching Greeley through Jewett and Tilden, Lincoln authorized James Gilmore and Jaquess to pass again through Union lines to the South on their own Methodist peace effort. On July 7, Greeley wrote Lincoln a letter and enclosed the telegram from "our irrepressible friend," Colorado Jewett. Greeley doubted that the Confederates in Canada had "full powers" from Davis to negotiate, but thought peace talks would be reasonable if (1) the Union was restored, (2) slavery was abolished, (3) all rebel soldiers could receive an amnesty, (4) the Union would pay $400 million to each slave state to compensate them for emancipation, (5) southern states would again have representation in Congress, and (6) a constitutional convention would ratify and amend any peace treaty. "I do not say a just peace is now attainable," wrote Greeley, "although I believe it to be so." He urged Lincoln to provide safe conduct for rebel negotiators from Niagara Falls to Washington. "Our bleeding, bankrupt, almost dying country also longs for peace," he added, and "I beg you to invite those now at Niagara Falls to exhibit their credentials and submit their ultimatum."[11]

The enclosed telegram from Jewett to Greeley said that George Sanders had assured Jewett that two "ambassadors" of the Confederate government were in Canada with "full and complete powers for a peace." Either Greeley should come to Niagara Falls, or the Confederate agents should receive a safe conduct to go to Washington.[12]

Lincoln was too shrewd to fall for the ploy. He agreed to receive a Confederate delegation under safe conduct, with Greeley in tow, if and only if "you can find any person anywhere professing to have any proposition of Jefferson Davis in writing, for peace, embracing the restoration of the Union and abandonment of slavery." Such a piece of paper, obviously, did not exist. Greeley remained optimistic, even though he had seen no Confederate credentials authorizing their mission. He did not want to be Lincoln's agent, nor did he want Lincoln to appear to be resistant to an early peace. On July 12, Sanders wrote Greeley that he, along with Clay and Holcombe, would be the three "authorized" agents to travel to Washington. Greeley wrote Lincoln the next day that a "reliable source" (Sanders) had identified three agents. He hoped Lincoln would find a way to "terminate this wholesale slaughter if a basis of adjustment can be mutually agreed upon."[13] A serious peace effort would have public relations benefits at home and abroad.

Lincoln responded that he was "disappointed" in Greeley's communication. He was expecting a delegation, not a letter, and a delegation agreeing to his terms. He would send his trusted young secretary, John Hay, up to New York with an answer. Hay left the White House at 11:00 a.m., took the fast train and boat to New York, and presented Greeley at six o'clock the next morning a letter from Lincoln stating, "I not only intend a sincere effort for peace, but I intend that you shall be a personal witness that is made." Hay wrote in his diary that "he didn't like it, evidently: Thought he was the worst man that could be taken for the purpose." But Greeley reluctantly agreed to go to Niagara Falls himself as the president's witness. "Although he thinks some one less known would create less excitement," Hay wired Lincoln, "and be less embarrassed by public curiosity, still he will start immediately if he can have an absolute safe conduct for four persons to be named by him."[14] Lincoln agreed to let Hay write out the safe-conduct document. Greeley grumbled, "I want no safe conduct. If they will catch me and put me in Fort Lafayette it will suit me first rate." But he agreed to go—"I will start tonight." On July 17, Greeley boarded a train for Niagara Falls, and Hay returned to Washington. Hay wrote in his diary about Greeley that "he was all along opposed to the President proposing terms."[15]

As luck would have it, on July 17, Gilmore and Jaquess arrived in Richmond and had an interview with Judah Benjamin, Secretary of State of the Confederacy. Jefferson Davis was unwilling to interview them as private citizens without authorization to negotiate, but he did meet briefly and informally with them. As expected, Lincoln's terms were unacceptable.[16]

On the same day, Greeley arrived in Niagara Falls and received a note from Clay and Holcombe saying that they were "not accredited" by Jefferson Davis, but merely "in the confidential employment of our Government." Greeley wired Lincoln on the eighteenth that he had met the Confederate agents and "do not find them so empowered as I was previously assured." The Confederates still wanted safe conduct to Washington, then Richmond. Lincoln, after checking with Seward and Hay, told Hay to take the next train to Niagara Falls and deliver written instructions to Greeley. After yet another exhausting train ride, Hay arrived at the International Hotel in Niagara Falls at 11:30 a.m. on the morning of July 20.[17]

Greeley recognized immediately that Lincoln's written terms would be quite unacceptable to the Confederates. "Saw Greeley at once at the International Hotel," wrote Hay in his diary. "He was evidently a good deal cut up at what he called the President's great mistake in refusing to enter at once into negotiations without conditions." Greeley regretted that Lincoln had shown his hand first. Greeley and Hay climbed into a carriage and went over to Clifton House to meet Sanders in the lobby, and then Holcombe. (Clay was out of town.) A curious crowd promptly gathered around the famous Greeley. "Major Hay," said the editor to Sanders and Holcombe, "has come from the President of the United States to deliver you a communication in writing & to add a verbal message with which he has been entrusted." Hay passed Lincoln's note to Holcombe. Holcombe said he would wire Clay and "inform you in the morning" of the outcome. "I expect to be blackguarded for what I have done," sighed Greeley, although he was later talkative and pleasant on the way to dinner with Hay. The two men parted and left, Greeley for New York City and Hay for Buffalo, then Washington.[18]

On July 22, Lincoln gave his cabinet a blow-by-blow description of the "(pretended) attempt to negotiate for peace," in the words of Attorney General Edward Bates. Lincoln read all the letters to and from Jewett and Greeley. Bates found the president "green enough" for being "entrapped" into such conversations with the enemy, but found his letters "cautious and prudent." (Bates found Jewett to be a "meddlesome blockhead" and a "crack-brained simpleton.") Cabinet members all held their tongues about Greeley, not wishing to appear in a *Tribune* lampoon. Greeley, thought Bates, was "cunningly seeking to make a pretext for bolting the Baltimore nomination" of Lincoln for his second term as president. The president, Bates feared, was "afraid of the Tribune" and could not afford to "have them as an enemy." On the same day, Greeley wrote in his newspaper that rumors and inaccuracies were flying about the Niagara Falls meeting. He himself had never taken part in any negotiations that were not authorized by Lincoln. He had no intention of violating any laws regarding dealings with the enemy in time of war.[19]

The northern press promptly attacked Greeley for a foolish, if not treasonous, attempt to negotiate with Confederate agents in Canada. Greeley denied any wrongdoing, claimed that the talks might have helped move the nation toward peace, and blamed Jewett for the fiasco. Greeley had supported the "best possible peace" on the basis of "Universal Freedom." He talked of a "Northwest Conspiracy" of "McClellan militiamen"—McClellan was the likely Democratic nominee for president—planning to overthrow the government in Washington by legal and illegal means. He denied James Bennett's charge that he favored disunion of North and South. He even persuaded Lincoln to agree to the publication of all letters exchanged regarding the Niagara Falls conversation.[20]

Much of the furor surrounding Niagara Falls was related to the upcoming presidential elections in November. "Does anyone doubt," asked Lincoln, that the only thing the Confederate agents were authorized to do was to "assist in selecting and arranging a candidate and a platform for the Chicago convention [of the Democrats]?" He compared Greeley during a cabinet meeting to "an old shoe—good for nothing new, whatever he has been." Greeley, like an old shoe, was "so rotten that nothing can be done with him. He is not truthful; the stitches all tear out." But Greeley continued to bombard the White House through John Nicolay with news of Confederate emissaries in New York, plans for a prisoner exchange, and proposals to "stop this useless carnage" on the battlefield, even after the fall of Atlanta to Sherman's army on September 1.[21]

In October, Sanders and Clay turned to violence by launching a Confederate attack on the northern Vermont town of St. Albans. Inspired by a similar, but failed, raid on Calais, Maine, in July, the Confederates rode into town firing pistols and giving rebel yells before robbing the local banks of some $175,000 in gold, securities, and cash. They even tried to burn down the town. A posse captured seven of the raiders that night in Canada and brought them back to St. Albans for trial. By October 23, fourteen were in custody. Sanders later served as a witness for the defense, claiming that the captured Confederate raiders were soldiers, not civilian bandits. He also disbursed funds to defense lawyers and may even have suborned witnesses. The raiders were ultimately released, and Sanders returned to Montreal, where he stayed in a room at St. Lawrence Hall a few doors away from an actor and Confederate sympathizer, John Wilkes Booth.[22]

After Lincoln's reelection, Greeley continued to push for a negotiated peace with the Confederacy. The federal government should at least offer to receive Confederate envoys, he wrote Francis Blair, U.S. Postmaster General and a friend of Lincoln. Shortly after Sherman took Savannah (December 22), in fact, Lincoln gave Blair a pass across the lines to go south to Richmond, where Blair spoke with Jefferson Davis on January 12. "I am working hard (sub rosa)," Greeley wrote his attorney, Isaiah Williams, "for the earliest endurable peace."[23] He would continue to do so until the guns were silenced at Appomattox.

Horace Greeley was a man of peace, as well as a man of freedom. His participation in Lincoln's peace feelers in the summer of 1864, roundly criticized at the time, was part of a much larger peace effort by both North and South, weary of the bloodletting. He did not know at the time that he was a dupe of Confederate agents in Canada, including his old friend George N. Sanders, operating under direct orders from Jefferson Davis to wreak havoc in the North in revenge for the Dahlgren raid and in anticipation of presidential elections. When Greeley ran for president in 1872, critics would remind him of his peace negotiations with Sanders. "I did nothing then that I am ashamed of now," responded Greeley. Sanders likewise disavowed his role and his supposed influence on Greeley. "The meeting with Mr. Clay, Mr. Thompson, myself and Mr. Greeley," Sanders recalled, "was a proper attempt to bring about a peaceful end to a horrible war."[24] But in the summer of 1864, neither the war nor presidential politics showed any sign of abating. As Lincoln observed, any talk of peace in 1864 was intimately connected to the coming election.

REELECTING LINCOLN

Political elections were central to democracy and to Greeley's evolving concept of American freedom. Without representative government and free elections, the virtuous republic could not survive. The electorate was free to make choices and to vote for or against those choices, even amid the rough-and-tumble election politics of the nineteenth century. Horace Greeley believed that presidents should serve for only one term of four years, and that Abraham Lincoln should not be reelected in November 1864. But when Lincoln received the nomination, as in 1860, Greeley stood with his party and his president despite his earlier political maneuvering.

Presidential election politics began even in January 1863, when Lincoln issued the Emancipation Proclamation. The *Tribune* duly noted that "malignant Copperheads" and Democrats of all stripes in the North were opposed to the Lincoln administration and the war effort. So were some Republicans. The war was increasingly expensive in blood and money. The war must end within six months, Greeley wrote Treasury Secretary Salmon P. Chase, to avoid national bankruptcy, a "financial collapse and a Copperhead revolution."[25]

In May 1863, in the wake of Chancellorsville, Greeley dispatched his friend James R. Gilmore as a *Tribune* correspondent to Tennessee to try to persuade a successful Union general, William Rosecrans, to run for president. Greeley told Gilmore that if Rosecrans was agreeable to running for president, he, Greeley, would "go personally to Lincoln and force him to resign," in favor of Vice President Hannibal Hamlin of Maine, a radical anti-slavery man. Hamlin would make Rosecrans the commanding general of all Union armies, and a viable presidential candidate. Justly suspicious of Greeley, Rosecrans would only reply, "my place is here" with the army. Lincoln, added the wise general, was "in his right place," and Greeley was "mistaken about Mr. Lincoln."[26] The plan came to nothing.

After Gettysburg, Greeley thought Salmon P. Chase might be a good candidate. "If in 1864 I could *make* a candidate," Greeley wrote Chase, "you would be my first choice." But Greeley also thought that Generals John Fremont, Benjamin Butler, or Ulysses S. Grant would make good candidates, even though Lincoln had "done well" as president. Grant, in particular, was capable of "smoothing the path from Slavery to Freedom" as president. Yet Greeley continued to defend Lincoln's program of war for the Union and emancipation for the slaves as "the true programme for saving life and staunching the wounds of our country."[27] Greeley also participated in the presidential boomlet for John Fremont, the Pathfinder, who planned to make the Confederacy pay for the war, reduce amnesty terms for rebel soldiers, and abolish slavery throughout the entire country, not just behind enemy lines. At a Fremont meeting in Cooper Union, Greeley proposed that national political conventions be delayed until after Grant's summer campaign season was over, that presidents serve only one term, and that he would support any Republican nominee but believed that Fremont was best for "sustaining Freedom."[28]

As the Republican convention in Baltimore scheduled for May approached, Lincoln was both amused and concerned about Greeley's support for other candidates. He said he was gratified by the *Tribune*'s "kindly spirit in its criticism." But he also pulled out of his desk drawer Greeley's anguished letter of July 29, 1861, after Bull Run, for John Hay to "decipher." Hay promptly declared the letter "the most insane specimen of pusillanimity that I have ever read." John Nicolay told Lincoln that editor James Bennett, Greeley's rival, would pay ten thousand dollars for the letter. But Lincoln, retying the letter with red tape and putting it back in his drawer, said only, "I need ten thousand dollars very much but he could not have it for many times that."[29]

Despite Greeley's opposition, the Republican convention in Baltimore nominated Lincoln overwhelmingly (484–22) for president. The Battle of the Wilderness was raging. Ahead lay the slaughter at Cold Harbor. For a time, Greeley broke ranks and joined radical Midwest Republicans and Germans opposed to Lincoln and favoring John Fremont. Schuyler Colfax, Wendell Phillips, Frederick Douglass, and other abolitionists also refused to endorse Lincoln. Greeley helped arrange a third-party convention of "radical democracy" in Cleveland at the end of May, but attendance was sparse. Even Greeley himself did not attend. The group nominated Fremont for president, but the nominee withdrew in September and threw his support behind Lincoln. In early June, Greeley arrived at the White House to call on the president, but Lincoln understandably refused to see him.[30]

During the bloody summer of 1864, Greeley still refused to support Lincoln and preferred Fremont. In August, he predicted a Lincoln defeat in November, favoring Grant, Butler, or Sherman as the best candidate. Lincoln himself thought he could not be reelected. Greeley's old Fourierist friend Albert Brisbane wrote from Buffalo that "strong reactions are setting in, in favor of the Democrats and against the war." Prices were rising, and gold bonds were unavailable at any price. "Something must be done," wrote Brisbane. On August 30, Greeley attended a meeting of influential Republicans in New York City that decided to send a delegation to Washington to urge Lincoln to withdraw from the race. (Francis Lieber and Charles Sumner refused to sign, but Greeley apparently did so.) "We must save the Government from the Copperheads," Greeley wrote a friend, "for I see no difference between their triumph and that of the outright Rebels."[31]

Then Sherman took Atlanta on September 2, probably guaranteeing the election of Lincoln. Greeley and Fremont both boarded the Lincoln bandwagon. In September, Greeley still predicted a McClellan victory in New York City—no surprise to anyone. (His prediction would turn out to be correct.) In October, the French historian and admirer of the American republic Eduard Laboulaye wrote a long letter to the *Tribune* pronouncing, "to vote for Lincoln is to vote for Union and Liberty." Defeat of the South would bring about "freedom of the people," the end of slavery, and "an example still greater than the War of Independence."[32] Lincoln's reelection promised universal freedom.

In November, Greeley urged his readers, "by your love of Liberty and hate of wrong and oppression," to vote for Lincoln for president. Many did so. So did seventy-seven percent of voting Union soldiers. Lincoln beat General George McClellan by 212 to 21 in electoral votes, and in the popular vote garnered 2,219,924 votes to McClellan's 1,814,228. To Greeley's surprise, Lincoln even won in New York State and Connecticut, where soldiers' votes may have made the difference. (McClellan won in every New York *city* except Rochester.) Greeley was, in the end, pleased by Lincoln's reelection. "We hold that these people," he roared, "have just decided, in the election of Lincoln and [Andrew] Johnson, "that the NATION SHALL LIVE and THAT SLAVERY SHALL DIE—so much, and no more." The election promised victory for "the Union with Universal Freedom."[33]

That winter passed quietly for Greeley, if not for the country. He complained about not having finished the second volume of his Civil War history, even though the war had not yet ended. He delighted when Sherman took Savannah. Molly was sick with a "terrible cough" and looked "as thin as a weasel." Ida was being safely educated at a convent in Paris. And Greeley was badgering financier Jay Cooke about the new 7-30 U.S. war bonds being issued to help finance the war. Cooke helped the government sell seven hundred million dollars worth of the 7-30 notes in 140 days that winter and the next spring, all in all a grand success. Greeley urged Treasury Secretary William Pitt Fessenden to support government contracts for the Navy cutter proposed by two friends. When the war finally ended at Appomattox in April 1865, Greeley rejoiced with the rest of the country. "We are a nation," he wrote in the *Tribune*, "no longer divided against itself, but one, indivisible, united, free."[34]

Horace Greeley did not support Abraham Lincoln for reelection in 1864, as in 1860, until it was obvious that his nomination—and Union victory—was apparent, if not assured. He connived with Peace Democrats, Confederate agents, and foreign diplomats to try to end the war and to replace Lincoln with another Republican. But these were tactical political maneuverings, and he remained true to Republican principles of freedom. Once Lincoln was renominated, Greeley worked hard for his reelection. And he looked forward to a postwar republic where the Union would be reunited and slavery abolished. Much as he criticized Abraham Lincoln, Greeley was as shocked as anyone by his political murder.

TYRANNICIDE

Killing a tyrant has a long history in western republican political thought. An unjust ruler does not deserve to rule. Therefore, tyrannicide is a just act. A republic can also degenerate into tyranny if its citizens do not remain virtuous and active. Undoubtedly the actor John Wilkes Booth, when he cried "Sic semper tyrannis!" after shooting Abraham Lincoln on Friday, April 14, 1865, at Ford's Theater in Washington, thought he was killing a tyrant. Like most Americans, Horace Greeley was horrified at the assassination of the president. But he was also anxious, for Greeley had a long relationship with one of the men initially implicated in the plot to kill Lincoln, George N. Sanders.

In his history of the Civil War, Greeley wrote that Lincoln was a victim of a "conspiracy of partisans of the rebellion," but not of the Confederate leadership in Richmond. John Wilkes Booth was the "animating soul" of the conspiracy, "one of the many badly educated, loose-living young men infesting the purlieus of our great cities."[35] But recent scholarship suggests that the Confederate leadership was in fact involved in the Lincoln murder. Triggered by the abortive Dahlgren raid on Richmond in March 1864, Jefferson Davis had unleashed a campaign of counter-terror on the North, of which one scheme was to kidnap or kill the president of the United States. Davis may have known nothing of the specifics of any such plan, but he verbally authorized Confederate operations in the North and in Canada that helped produce the Lincoln assassination.

Political assassination was in the air in the 1850s and 1860s. On January 14, 1858, Felice Orsini and three accomplices tried to kill Napoleon III and Empress Eugenie when they attended the opera in Paris. All were tried and executed for the crime. Two years later, Abraham Lincoln remarked, "Orsini's attempt on Louis Napoleon and John Brown's attempt at Harper's Ferry were, in their philosophies, precisely the same."[36] Lincoln himself feared assassination at his first inauguration and thereafter.

In early 1864, even before the Dahlgren raid, the *Tribune* ran a series of articles by an anonymous correspondent telling of Confederate spies, agents, and raiders plotting against the North. Some planned to kidnap Lincoln. The newspaper claimed that this was all the work of Copperheads and Peace Democrats. The Democratic press called the reported plots a hoax. (The author of the *Tribune* articles was a journalist, Sanford Conover, convicted of perjury after the war.) James W. White, a friend of Greeley, wrote the editor that he had heard from General Benjamin Butler of a northern plan to kidnap Jefferson Davis and blow up the Tredegar Ironworks in Richmond. Moreover, Confederate agents planned to start a Yellow Fever epidemic in the North by distributing infected clothing in northern cities at public auctions. By the late summer of 1864, there were perhaps one hundred or so Confederate agents—the "Confederate Canadian Cabinet," as one wag put it—lodged in hotels in Montreal. Among them were John Wilkes Booth and George Sanders, the latter photographed at Niagara Falls in July with Captain Thomas Hines, the major planner of terror operations against the North. Booth was deeply upset by the failure of Greeley's Niagara Falls peace negotiations, blaming the failure on Lincoln. That autumn, he met with two disgruntled Confederate veterans in Baltimore in a plot to kidnap Lincoln and hold him for ransom in Richmond until the federal government released Confederate prisoners in the North.[37]

In October 1864, the *Tribune* reported Advocate General Joseph Holt's comment that he fully anticipated the "cold-blooded assassination of Union citizens" by Confederate agents in the North. Booth arrived in Montreal, may have met Clay and Thompson, as well as Sanders, who stayed in the same hotel with Booth. Plans to capture or kill Lincoln abounded, especially after the failed St. Albans, Vermont, and Calais, Maine, raids. On November 25, Confederate agents set fire to New York hotels, shops, and Barnum's museum, some thirty-two buildings in all. They also planned to blow up the Croton Reservoir.[38]

The *Tribune* bemoaned Booth's deed, and Greeley was as shocked as anyone by the murder of Lincoln. But he was elated that the war was over and that slavery had been eliminated, or nearly so, from the land. He thought the cries for vengeance against the South were un-Christian and misguided. Like Lincoln, he favored "malice toward none, and charity toward all." He hoped to see the South transformed by free labor. He urged magnanimity and generosity on Lincoln in his dealings with the South. Yet he also remained sharply critical of Lincoln. Indeed, Greeley had prepared an anti-Lincoln editorial on the very night that Lincoln was shot. When news came of Lincoln's shooting (he was still alive), Sidney Gay, the managing editor, refused to run Greeley's editorial. Greeley reprimanded Gay.[39] But the editorial did not run.

During the mournful days following Lincoln's murder, Greeley joined in the eulogies to the dead president. A depraved assassin, he told a Universalist assembly, had taken the life of "the kindest heart." Although Greeley refused at first to join the "extravagant and preposterous laudations on our dead President as the wisest and greatest man who ever lived," he was genuinely shocked and saddened by Lincoln's death. "Few graves," he wrote, "will be more extensively, persistently visited, or bedewed with the tears of a people's prouder, fonder affection, than that of Abraham Lincoln."[40]

By the end of April, Booth had been shot dead in a Virginia barn while trying to escape, and his fellow conspirators were in custody. In addition, on May 2, President Andrew Johnson signed a proclamation offering monetary rewards for other suspects in the Lincoln murder case, including Jefferson Davis ($100,000), Clay, Thompson, and George Sanders ($25,000 each). The sensational list initiated a search for conspiracies that has not yet ended. "Jefferson Davis an Accomplice," ran the *Tribune* headline. The newspaper also published a letter from George Sanders, still in Montreal, asserting that Johnson's proclamation was a "burning lie" and that he, Sanders, had "no acquaintance whatever with Mr. Booth, or any of those alleged to have been engaged with him." Greeley was skeptical of a plot by rebel leaders to kill Lincoln. Political assassination was "not an American custom," he noted, and the charge was improbable. "Let us patiently and candidly scrutinize the forthcoming facts before passing judgment," he urged his readers. At the same time, he argued that Booth was "the tool of more cunning men than himself" and that the assassins resembled the Canada Confederates who organized the St. Albans raid, the plots to release Confederate prisoners in the North, and the burning of northern cities.[41]

Greeley also criticized Secretary of War Edwin Stanton for submitting the arrested accomplices of Booth to a secret military, rather than civil, court for trial. Greeley charged Stanton with violating the Constitution. Personal freedom was a constitutional right and it was time to restore the "privilege of *habeas corpus*." Stanton was sufficiently annoyed by Greeley's criticism to threaten the *Tribune* with a lawsuit because the newspaper was attempting to "incite assassins to finish their work by murdering me." On May 10, Jefferson Davis surrendered to federal troops in Georgia. Clement Clay had also surrendered. Both were imprisoned in Fortress Monroe near Washington to await trial. (On July 21, Johnson's cabinet voted to try Davis for treason in a civil court, but not for assassinating the president; the charges were never actually brought.) The *Cincinnati Times* meanwhile pilloried the "vagabond Sanders" for being not only a Rebel, but a Red Republican and a "friend of Orsini." Sanders was allegedly "the accomplice of a dozen plots and counter-plots of murder and revolution" since 1848, and the "itinerant peddler of infernal machines and rusty carbines." He was a perjurer, an assassin, and a "cunning, unprincipled and ready" rowdy. "No doubt he employed Booth, and was the authorized agent of Davis."[42]

By the autumn of 1865, Stanton no longer believed in a conspiracy to kill Lincoln beyond that of Booth and his associates, most of whom had been hanged after a military trial that summer.[43] Jefferson Davis was languishing at Fortress Monroe. George Sanders returned to Europe from Canada, where he lived until his return to the United States in 1872, the year of Greeley's death. No charges were ever brought against him, and he died in New York City on August 13, 1873. Although Sanders escaped prosecution, he lived out his remaining years under a cloud of suspicion. If not directly implicated in Lincoln's murder, Sanders was deeply involved in the machinations of Confederate agents in Canada after the Dahlgren raid. He certainly knew Clay and Thompson, and he may have known or met Booth in Montreal. He may also have been involved in an earlier September 1864 plot to kidnap Lincoln. Greeley was certainly eager to disassociate himself from his old friend and from the violent legacy of the European revolutions of 1848 that Sanders represented. Orsini had failed to kill Napoleon III, but Booth had succeeded in killing Lincoln. Tyrannicide in the name of liberty had failed to stem the revolutionary push toward universal freedom that both Lincoln and Greeley had helped engineer. The Civil War was over. It was time to redefine the meaning of freedom yet again.

The Civil War began as an attempt to save the Union from the right of secession claimed by states. It ended with the promise of freedom for all Americans (adult males, at least) and the emancipation of slaves. Lincoln wanted to save the Union. Greeley wanted to emancipate the slaves. After Lincoln's two "proclamations of freedom" in 1863, these two purposes were united in one. Throughout the war, Greeley continued to criticize Lincoln for his cautious policy on emancipation, his minimal attempts at peace, and his violation of civil rights in wartime. He sought to limit Lincoln to one term as president. He connived with Peace Democrats and lobbied for political appointments for his friends. But he also offered unsolicited advice to the president, printed what Lincoln wanted in the pages of the *Tribune*, and kept in touch with the White House regularly through the president's secretaries, John Hay and John Nicolay. Greeley lobbied for peace, but followed Lincoln's instructions when he witnessed peace feelers in action. Both Greeley and Lincoln emerged from the Civil War as major American icons. Now Lincoln was gone, and the Republican Party had become an institutional power. With the elimination of slavery, liberal republicanism was on the wane. But the philosopher of the *Tribune* remained active as a conscience and critic of the newly powerful Republican Party, a party that was quite distinct from the radical reform movement against slavery that he had helped to lead to victory.

RECONSTRUCTING FREEDOM

America in 1865 was vastly different than in 1860. The nation was exhausted by a bloody, fratricidal struggle between North and South. Telegraph and railroad lines snaked across the country, linking tiny hamlets and big cities together in a network of transport and communication. The federal government had surpassed the individual states in power and authority. Westward expansion continued to threaten the existence of Native Americans. The South was in ruins, and the North was bleeding from its wounds. Horace Greeley and the *Tribune* were still preeminent in the changing world of journalism. But there were many new people and voices now, and the world had grown ever more competitive. Reconstructing the South was at the top of the political agenda. Could Reconstruction mean both the reunification of white southerners with the United States and the integration of freed black slaves into southern society, and, in so doing, change the meaning of freedom? Greeley thought so.

The *Tribune* remained a Republican fixture in the Democratic city of New York, and in the nation. The newspaper continued to occupy a cramped, dingy series of offices and to encourage democratic thinking and participation in all its affairs. But a new generation of journalists was taking over the paper. Greeley remained editor, but also continued to depend on his ever more numerous staff. George Ripley, Charles T. Congdon, and Bayard Taylor were around from the old days, and Sam Wilkeson still ran the Washington office. But Charles Dana had moved on to the War Department, and Henry Villard to the railroad industry. A number of "Greeley's young men" born in the 1830s were finding their way into the world of journalism. In 1868, Ohio journalist and war reporter Whitelaw Reid, thirty-one, arrived at the *Tribune* from the *Cincinnati Gazette*. Greeley had urged him for two years to consider the position of managing editor, and he finally accepted the offer. By 1870, the virtual editor of the *Tribune* was Whitelaw Reid.[44]

The newspaper world had changed significantly. For one thing, there were more newspapers than ever before, some 150 in New York City alone by 1870. The telegraph brought news from around the nation and the world in minutes, not days. The railroad distributed newspapers overnight to millions of people. Production was faster and more efficient. The rotary Hoe press of the 1840s could turn out a thousand copies of a newspaper in a single day. By 1870, the new presses could produce twenty thousand copies an hour. The Tribune Association continued to manage the paper as a joint-stock enterprise. Indeed, most newspapers now had dozens of partners, thousands of shareholders, and hundred of printers, editors, and other staff. The role of the individual editor, including Greeley, was greatly diminished. Newspapers were no longer country affairs turned out by editors on hand-cranked presses, but urban high-technology big businesses. Circulation and advertising were becoming more important than editorial opinion, and newspapers reflected public attitudes more than they shaped them. "The people buy newspapers mainly to learn what they want to know," Greeley complained to Isaiah Williams, "rather than what they ought to know, and the fact must be always kept in mind."[45]

One of Greeley's new young staffers was a Missouri writer named Samuel Clemens. In June 1867, the *Tribune* hired Clemens as a foreign correspondent. He was to write two articles each week on his trip to Egypt and the Middle East. He would receive forty dollars for each column of type. In November and December, he dutifully filed reports from Paris, Jerusalem, and Cairo under the new pen name "Mark Twain." What Twain later called "my first notoriety" and what became *Innocents Abroad* was a result of Horace Greeley's continuing willingness to hire young people of strong opinions and independent thought. Greeley was so pleased that he kept Twain on as Washington correspondent for a congressional term. "I have solemnly yielded up my liberty," Twain wrote a friend, "for a whole session of Congress —enrolled my name on the regular *Tribune* staff, made the *Tribune* bureau here my headquarters, taken correspondences for two other papers and one magazine." That winter, Twain also talked about purchasing some Tribune Association shares at seven thousand dollars a share.[46]

After the war, Greeley continued his limitless activity. He sold six of his fifteen shares in the Tribune Association at $6,500 per share. He purchased wild lands in Virginia (more on that later), stock in various companies—mining, desiccated eggs, photo-lithography—and continued to loan money to anyone who came his way, hat in hand. (Many, like Poe and Gurowski, never paid him back.) "I ran away from New York," he wrote Isaiah Williams in 1868, "to get rid of the beggars, who wanted to devour me. When the blockade of winter is raised, I will hasten back. But I needed deliverance from their importunities. I have been too much in New York for my own good."[47] He became less and less involved in New York politics, and spent more time at Chappaqua, where he had bought a second house in 1864 (in Molly's name), and then a third, "Hillside House," in 1871.

Greeley actively participated in Reconstruction and the "second American Constitution" after the Civil War. Over a five-year period, Congress enacted into law a series of acts that prevented states from legally abridging the rights of any citizen, including life, liberty, or property, without due process of law, forbade slavery in the United States, and gave Congress the right to make certain that states did not abridge the right to vote on account of race, color, or previous slave status. "Liberty's nation," as the poet Walt Whitman wrote, was giving birth to "Freedom, completely arm'd and victorious and very / haughty, with Law on one side and Peace on the other."[48]

Greeley campaigned hard for peace, justice, and freedom after the war. He favored amnesty toward the defeated South "on the single condition of acquiescence in Universal Freedom," as he put it. He greeted Appomattox as a moment of peace, Union, and liberty. "What we ask," he wrote on the day the president was shot, "is that the President say in effect, 'Slavery having, through rebellion, committed suicide, let the North and South unite to bury the carcass, and then clasp hands around his grave." The federal government should pursue a policy of "mercy and magnanimity" toward its former Confederate enemies, as long as they abandoned slavery. The great significance of the North's victory, he wrote a friend, was "the triumph of republicanism and free labor."[49]

Free labor remained central to Greeley's concept of American freedom. He welcomed President Johnson's call for peace and justice in administering the defeated Confederacy. He was elated at the adoption of the Thirteenth Amendment to the U.S. Constitution eliminating slavery or "involuntary servitude." The editor campaigned vigorously on behalf of the newly emancipated slaves' right to vote. He feared Chinese immigration now, not for reasons of racism or xenophobia, but because coolie labor was the new form of slavery. "We have four million degraded Negroes in the South," he wrote, "and if there were to be a flood-tide of Chinese population . . . with no knowledge of free institutions or constitutional liberty . . . we should be prepared to bid farewell to republicanism and democracy."[50] Yet Chinese (and Irish) labor would soon be essential to one of Greeley's favorite projects, the transcontinental railroad.

In the spring of 1866, Greeley lost patience with his old friend and political ally President Andrew Johnson. He and Johnson had worked hard together for years to get a Homestead Bill through Congress. He had even written a brief biography of Johnson during the war. In April 1866, however, Johnson declared the rebellion against the Union officially concluded. He then vetoed a number of congressional Reconstruction measures, including universal suffrage in the District of Columbia. Johnson's intention to keep the southern states "unreconstructed and unrepresented" was, Greeley wrote, "deplorable."[51]

But Greeley's enthusiasm for freedom remained undiminished. He spoke at shipyard rallies in New York on behalf of an eight-hour day for workers. He basked in the warmth of old abolitionist Lewis Tappan's praise of his work—"twenty-five years [of] arduous labor in the cause of humanity." He maintained his workaholic ways, muttering to his friends of overwork, headaches, and "rheumatic complaints." He tried to tend to the ailing Molly, who "needs more attention than I am able to give her." And he listened to Anna Sanders complain that her husband, now in European exile, had been unfairly accused of complicity in Lincoln's murder. Greeley advised her not to have her husband return until Johnson had withdrawn his "shameful proclamation offering a reward for Jefferson Davis etc. as assassins of Mr. Lincoln." George Sanders, Greeley felt, should have turned himself in to the federal government and demanded a jury trial. But any return to the United States now was dangerous for him. The North, wrote the *Tribune,* should pardon all southerners and readmit the southern states to the Union as long as they agreed to civil rights and suffrage for all African-Americans and former slaves.[52]

In the winter of 1866-7, Greeley tried his hand at politics again, running for the New York U.S. Senate seat. He promptly hurt himself by advocating "universal amnesty" for rebel leaders, including Jefferson Davis. Trying Davis for treason might have seemed like a good idea a year ago, he wrote, but to do it now would result in "far more evil than good." He also strongly supported African-American suffrage, hardly a way to appeal to Democratic voters in New York. "*We cannot elect Greeley,*" wrote Sam Wilkeson, "His universal amnesty article has killed him. How *could* he publish that suicidal editorial? How *could* he do it?" Despite his defeat, Greeley doggedly held to his position that freedmen in the South should enjoy universal manhood suffrage. The federal government should not "force Negro suffrage on the South at the point of the bayonet, but suffer her to unite with us in pacifying the country and fixing forever one uniform rule for suffrage throughout the Union." Greeley's convictions would clearly not elect him to the Senate. "I have probably now no chance of election," he wrote a friend, "if I ever had—but the Rebels will always find me on the platform of Universal Amnesty and impartial suffrage if they honestly seek me there."[53]

In many ways, time was catching up with Greeley, whose message no longer seemed as relevant as it had before the war. His father, Zaccheus Greeley, was now in his eighties and "utterly disabled," living with his brother Barnes. His sister Esther was in Paris, another sister in a Paris convent. His wife was an invalid. "I am growing old fast," Greeley wrote his cousin Lavinia Phelps. Greeley contributed fifty dollars to a testimonial for the aging William Lloyd Garrison, urged business students to work hard and avoid borrowing or lending money, and welcomed Charles Dickens on his second trip to the United States, presiding at a fancy dinner at Delmonico's Restaurant. He rejected his enemy William Henry Seward's offer of a diplomatic post in Vienna.[54]

Greeley remained skeptical about gaining real freedom for former slaves in the South. He welcomed the idea of the Bureau of Refugees, Freedmen and Abandoned Land (Freedman's Bureau) created by Congress in March 1865. Indeed, Greeley often published Freedman's Bureau dispatches verbatim in his newspaper. But he knew that dealing with four million freed slaves and their families was a monumental task for the War Department, which headed the Bureau. The Bureau was a mixed success, encountering widespread white resistance through "black codes" to any attempts at land reform or political participation. There was not enough land to go around for slaves to become landowners overnight. Johnson's amnesty proclamations meant, in practice, the restoration of the white man's rule in the South, and undercut the Freedman's Bureau from the outset. For generations, the *Tribune* noted, the slaves had looked for a "Man of Universal Freedom." But freedom was not so easy to come by. "It is necessary to define this word [freedom]," admitted Oliver Otis Howard of Maine, head of the Freedman's Bureau, "for it is most apt to be misunderstood." Under Reconstruction, the word *freedom* meant an end to slavery, equal rights for all citizens, the right to sing freedom songs, free migration to the cities (where "freedom was free-er"), the reunification of families divided by the war and slavery, free land for male freedmen, freedom of religion for African-American churches, free education for children. Freedom was the key to economic autonomy and political suffrage, the only real defenses against the white man's power. The end of slavery, observed Greeley in the *Tribune*, meant the "annulment of our one great legalized tyranny," the broken chains of a legislative act which "set them free."[55]

Greeley shared many of the racist proclivities of his era, and he was not optimistic about the long-term efforts of the Freedman's Bureau. African-Americans, he told a friend in 1870, were an "easy, worthless race, taking no thought for the morrow." They must be stimulated to self-reliance. "So long as they look to others to calculate and provide for them, they are not truly free." But he welcomed the Fourteenth and Fifteenth Amendments giving African-Americans full citizenship in the "battle for Universal Freedom." That freedom would take a long time and a lot of hard work. "The Millennium is not here," he observed, "and not likely soon to be."[56]

Greeley undertook his own Reconstruction experiment by purchasing some land for freedmen in North Carolina. Ike Bean had been a friend of Greeley since the editor came to New York in 1831. A

Buffalo attorney and farmer, Bean moved to Norfolk, Virginia, during the Civil War and ran a store. In 1865, Bean offered to purchase some land in Yonkers, New York, with Greeley. The gullible Greeley gave Bean three thousand dollars toward the land, to be owned jointly by Greeley and Bean. A few months later, Bean asked Greeley for another three thousand dollars, this time for twenty-five hundred timbered acres near Norfolk. Greeley gave him the money in government bonds in return for Bean's thirty-nine shares of stock in the Atlantic Iron Works of Norfolk. The land was actually in North Carolina, eight miles south of the Virginia border and on the edge of the Great Dismal Swamp, where some seventy thousand slaves had fled to safety.[57] The plan was to form a joint-stock company along associationist lines to harvest the timber and make lumber, employ freed slaves to cut and clear the forest, and give the freedmen the cleared land to farm on their own.

In 1866, Bean purchased a four-mile-square tract of land from Hatchett Taylor, a business associate with whom he had traded cotton and other goods across enemy lines during the war. The land was known as the Tadmore Tract. Bean then formed the South Mills Company to run the project. Greeley received stock certificates representing a quarter interest in the business. A few months later, Bean's store in Norfolk went bankrupt. He then asked Greeley to give him yet another three thousand dollars, but the editor declined. In 1867, Greeley turned sour on the company and got his attorney, Isaiah T. Williams, to sue Bean to recover his six thousand dollars. "He has had that property three years," wrote Greeley, "by virtue of my money!" A year later, Greeley discovered that Bean had never actually purchased the farm in Yonkers at all. The editor sent an agent south to Norfolk in 1868 to check on the land and timber project. The agent reported back to Greeley that he owned a swamp. Greeley filed a complaint, the sheriff of Westchester County arrested Bean and held him on eight thousand dollars' bail, and in 1869 Bean went on trial for fraud in New York Superior Court of Westchester County.

The trial revealed that the South Mills Company owned 150 acres of swamp land worth perhaps $7.50 an acre because of the cypress timber on the land. At issue was whether Greeley's six thousand dollars had bought him one-half, or the entirety, of the land, which neither Greeley nor Bean had ever seen. Greeley had surrendered the first deed for the land for a second deed in August 1868. In the end, Bean apparently settled out of court with Greeley. But in early 1872, Greeley was still complaining to Isaiah Williams about "that dismal swamp tract" and urging him not to drag the editor through yet another trial, nor pay any additional taxes on the land. The whole murky affair remained somewhat unresolved until Greeley's death.

The Great Dismal Swamp fiasco revealed Greeley's continuing connection with the South, especially North Carolina. The South Mills Company was a Reconstruction version of Greeley's continuing search for ideal community, in this case, for an enterprise that would make former slaves into productive and self-reliant citizens. Ike Bean was yet another shrewd deal maker who took advantage of the editor. The entire episode illustrated Greeley's ongoing search for a definition of freedom that depended upon corporate initiative and individual contributions. But the North Carolina joint-stock company failed both economically and politically to help freedmen find their own way to freedom. Freedom without land or money, as Greeley recognized, was not really freedom at all.

Horace Greeley believed in freedom for his enemies as well as his friends. Even former traitors and rebels had rights under the law, once they had mended their ways. In 1867, Greeley committed political suicide by co-signing a bail bond to free former Confederate President Jefferson Davis from a federal military prison. Many northerners wanted to bring Davis to trial for treason, or, as William Lloyd Garrison said, to hang him from a sour apple tree. But Greeley's sense of Christian charity and fairness toward all prevailed. Even former traitors and enemies deserved the rights of a free man.

Since his capture by Union troops in May 1865, Jefferson Davis had languished in chains and solitary confinement at Fortress Monroe south of Washington. Both Davis and Clement Clay, a suspected conspirator in the Lincoln assassination, occupied adjacent cells and were held without bail. Indicted for treason, they were held without any specific charges framed against them.

Before the war, Greeley and the *Tribune* had sharply criticized Davis, then Secretary of War, for his talk of disunion and even secession. Davis, charged Greeley in June 1854 at the time of the Kansas-Nebraska crisis, had in his speeches "incited rebellion" against the federal government, and might even be "organizing treason." Six years later, Davis would lead the Confederate states out of the Union. After his arrest and incarceration, however, Greeley urged amnesty.

Why, he asked in 1866, was the government keeping Davis in prison without charges and "at public cost"? In general, Greeley supported pardons for all former Confederate leaders, including Clement Clay and Governor Zebulon Vance of North Carolina. In December 1865, Greeley advised Clay's wife to seek a pardon or parole from President Johnson, which Clay received a few months later. Month after month, Greeley complained in the pages of the *Tribune* that Jefferson Davis was being imprisoned illegally. He should either be put on trial or released from jail. In May 1866, he urged his friend Salmon P. Chase, Chief Justice of the Supreme Court, to oversee a U.S. Circuit Court hearing on Davis in Richmond. But Chase refused to issue a writ of *habeas corpus*, and the judge, John C. Underwood, a New York friend of Greeley, denied Davis's request for bail.[58]

Greeley was unrelenting, especially after Assistant Secretary of War Charles A. Dana, his former *Tribune* colleague, ordered Davis manacled and fettered in May 1866. Davis would not be tried, Greeley argued, so "let's have an end to this shame." He should be released on bail. Davis's wife, Varina, wrote Greeley a few months later asking for his intervention. Her husband was "patiently, uncomplainingly fading away" and losing physical strength. He was "greatly exhausted." Would Greeley get enough signatures to persuade President Johnson to release him from his "arbitrary imprisonment"? Greeley continued to urge that Davis be let out on bail. "You are powerful with your party," Varina Davis wrote the editor. "Can you not restore us, dear Mr. Greeley, to our little ones?"[59]

In May 1867, the Davis issue came to a head. In December, the Supreme Court ruled that military tribunals could not try civilians in time of peace in areas where civil courts existed, such as in Richmond. On Johnson's authority, former president Franklin Pierce visited Fortress Monroe on May 8 and ordered Davis turned over to federal marshals, who took him to Richmond and housed him under guard at the Spotswood Hotel. On May 11, he sailed up the James River while crowds along the banks threw flowers and cheered. There was more cheering in Richmond. On May 13, in a tense, packed courtroom, Judge John C. Underwood set his bail at $100,000. Horace Greeley, abolitionist Gerrit Smith, Cornelius Vanderbilt, and ten Richmond businessmen posted the bail bond. Greeley personally guaranteed twenty-five percent of the bond should Davis violate his parole. He also attended the hearing, noting that he had never seen or met Davis until that day in court. Greeley and Davis were introduced briefly and greeted each other. The federal marshal ordered the court to release the prisoner. The South celebrated. That night, Jefferson Davis took the steamboat to New York, and then on to Montreal to join his children.[60]

Greeley may well have preferred to try Davis for treason. Johnson and Stanton probably wanted him hanged. But Greeley understood that the charge might fail legally in court, even though Davis could be indicted. He returned from Richmond to New York with the anguished outrage of northern public opinion against him. "I seem only to reap abuse," he wrote a friend, "where others find fame and wealth." President Johnson called Greeley "a sublime child . . . all heart and no head . . . like a whale ashore." Subscriptions to the second volume of his Civil War history declined precipitously. Thirty members of his Union League Club in New York called for a meeting to expel him as a member. The Club consisted of eight hundred mainly Republican businessmen who had supported a Loyal Publication Society, recruited black soldiers, and raised money for hospital work during the war. He called them "narrow-minded blockheads" and dared them to act. They did not. He urged that all rights of American citizens be restored to southerners. He called for "freedom of the blacks" and reunification of the Republic. "The public has learned," he wrote, "that I act upon my convictions without fear of personal consequences."[61]

The Union League Club episode was particularly distasteful for Greeley. On May 16, the Club informed him in writing of a called meeting regarding his conduct in the Davis matter. The letter encouraged Greeley to attend the meeting and "be heard on the subject." This he wisely refused to do. Instead, he wrote a long open letter citing the need for reconciliation, not enmity, between North and South. There should be universal amnesty, not hangings and executions. In signing the bail bond for Jefferson Davis, concluded Greeley, "I did more for freedom and humanity than all of you were competent to do." He urged them to expel him. But the called meeting of two hundred men to consider Greeley's "mistake" and "error of judgment" considered his long record of patriotism and service to his nation. Members also noted that Greeley had a "larger following" than the Union Club of New York. "To remonstrate with him," the Club concluded, "was to make the matter worse." The Club then failed to pass a resolution to "disapprove" of Greeley's bailing out the "chief enemy of the Republic." The majority resolution said only that "there is nothing in the action of Horace Greeley, relative to the bailing of Jefferson Davis, calling for proceedings in the Club."[62]

Greeley persisted in his campaign for universal amnesty toward the South. The war was over. The Union had been saved. Slavery was eliminated. The North should extend a "warm hand" to the South and "restore the era of good feeling while we rebuild the waste places of our common country." Congress, not Andrew Johnson, represented the people of the republic. And Congress, not the president, should declare a general amnesty. He urged his old friend Rebecca Whipple not to worry about the Davis scandal. On Christmas Day, 1868, President Johnson did indeed proclaim a general amnesty, short-circuiting the potentially divisive trial of Jefferson Davis for treason. In February 1869, Davis's attorney filed a request to release the bondsmen from their obligation, and the case was closed.[63] Jefferson Davis was a free man.

WOMEN'S RIGHTS MAN?

Women's rights were a critical aspect of any concept of universal freedom, but not necessarily in the eyes of nineteenth-century men. Under the law, American women were largely considered subjects of men. They had few rights to hold or inherit property, sue in court, divorce, or vote. State laws varied, of course, but the idea of women's rights was both novel and revolutionary. Women often seemed closer to slaves, the property of men to be acquired or disposed of at will. Even women involved in the anti-slavery movement quickly discovered that they were more easily seen than heard. The movement for women's rights, in fact, probably began in 1840 when female delegates to the World Anti-Slavery Convention in London discovered that they could neither speak nor hold a seat in the auditorium.

Inspired by the 1848 European revolutions, a group of like-minded men and women met at Seneca Falls, New York, that year and declared, "all men and women are created equal," and thus deserved equal rights under the law. Grounded in the natural-rights theories of John Locke and the Enlightenment, the trans-Atlantic campaign for women's rights reached its peak between 1848 and 1856 under the leadership of Elizabeth Cady Stanton, Lucretia Mott, and Susan B. Anthony. Horace Greeley was one of the movement's few male supporters in the press.[64]

Women always played a crucial role in Horace Greeley's life. His benevolent and hard-working mother, Mary Woodburn, was more important in his upbringing than his failed, alcoholic father, Zaccheus Greeley. His two sisters, his wife Molly, and his close friend Margaret Fuller also played central roles in his life. He corresponded with, hired, and supported female journalists and correspondents. He welcomed anthologies by women writers and poets. In 1849, he co-signed a handbill urging women to "go West" and marry Forty-Niners seeking gold in California. Yet he also repudiated the "rightful equality of the sexes in political privileges and social conditions." Instead, he respected the "tacit compact" between men and women whereby they lived in separate "spheres of action," public and private.[65] In politics and business, women should yield to men out of deference. Try as he might to respect the equal rights of women, Greeley could not bring himself to support their right to vote.

After Seneca Falls, Greeley admitted that women someday should enjoy the right to vote. "However unwise and mistaken the demand," he wrote in the *Tribune*, "it is but the assertion of a natural right and as such must be conceded." He allowed Elizabeth Cady Stanton to publish her ideas in his newspaper. (The Stantons were regular *Tribune* subscribers.) Stanton considered Greeley "one of our most faithful champions." He joined her in trying to found a co-educational college in Seneca Falls in 1851. Greeley urged the nascent Republican Party to support women's right to vote if and when they should demand it, because voting was a "natural right, however unwise or unnatural the demand."[66]

Greeley also fought for the rights of women to speak in public. When the World Temperance Convention met in New York in 1853 and excluded women, he supported a walkout and called the convention an "Orthodox White Male Adult Saints' Convention." In a letter to the Women's Rights Convention later that year, he recognized "the right of women to choose her own sphere of activity and usefulness." Women "ought not to be satisfied" with current laws on marriage property and inheritance. "Women alone," he wrote, "can in the present state of the controversy, speak effectively for Woman, since none others can speak with authority or from the depth of a personal experience."[67]

Greeley continued to speak on behalf of women throughout the 1850s. In his address to the tenth National Women's Rights Convention at Cooper Union in May 1860, he was eloquent in defense of women. Yet he still defended monogamous marriage and opposed extending the right to vote to women prematurely. Stanton was not amused. "Let us all hope," she wrote, "that all wisdom does not live, and will not die, with Horace Greeley. I think if he had been married to the New York Herald, instead of the Republican Party, he would have found out some Scriptural arguments against life-long unions, where great incompatibility of temper existed between the parties." In time, Greeley and Stanton drifted apart. She advised him in 1864 to refer to her as Elizabeth Cady Stanton in his editorials. He responded by calling her Mrs. Henry Stanton.[68]

True republicanism and universal freedom, as women's rights advocates were quick to agree, logically required equal rights for women, including the right to vote. Susan B. Anthony pointed this out to the managing editor of the *Tribune*, John Russell Young, in 1866 when the paper refused to support the Equal Suffrage Convention in New York. How could Greeley and the *Tribune* support voting rights for black freedmen after the Civil War and not voting rights for white women? How could they ignore the campaign for women's suffrage in Kansas now under way? How could Greeley not support his friend, Elizabeth Cady Stanton, in her run for office in New York's Eighth Congressional District? Yet Greeley's position remained unwavering —women should get the right to vote "whenever a majority of our women shall indicate their deliberate choice to be enfranchised."[69] But how could they indicate their opinion without the right to vote in the first place? Greeley did not say.

In 1867, the State of New York held its decennial Constitutional Convention. Greeley was a delegate from Westchester County. One hundred and sixty representatives met in Albany to discuss taxation, finance, black suffrage, women's suffrage, judicial appointments, bribery, education, canals, home rule for municipalities, and dozens of other issues. The convention met from June 1867 through February 1868 and exhibited continuing division and rancor over political issues held over from the war. (In November 1869, the voters actually rejected the revised constitution.) Greeley also served as chair of the committee on women's suffrage. Anthony and Stanton, eager to present the chair with a petition on behalf of women's rights, had Molly Greeley sign her name at the top of the list—as "Mrs. Horace Greeley." Molly was now fifty-five, an invalid, returning from years of absence in Europe (most recently for seven months), and somewhat paranoid from the prescribed opiates doctors advised her to take. Anthony and Stanton dragged Molly along with them to see Greeley at the *Tribune* offices shortly before the convention began. They presented him with the petition signed by twenty-eight thousand men and women to remove the word "male" from the New York State Constitution.[70] Greeley thanked them, but did not support their petition.

When Greeley's committee refused to recommend voting rights for women, he became a pariah in the eyes of the women's movement. Removing the $250 property qualification for voting for black males undoubtedly rubbed salt in female wounds. So did the fact that the convention endorsed the Greeley committee recommendation by a vote of 125 to 19. "The Convention," Greeley wrote to his attorney Isaiah Williams in August 1867, "is killing me. I never before worked so hard to so little purpose." When Elizabeth Cady Stanton encountered Greeley in the streets of New York shortly after the vote, she told Susan B. Anthony to "prepare for a storm." "Good evening, Mr. Greeley," said Stanton. You two, replied Greeley, are "about the best maneuverers among the New York politicians." Why, he asked, had they substituted "Mrs. Horace Greeley" for "Mary Cheney Greeley" on the petition? They refused to answer.[71]

Despite his cool relations with his former friends in the women's movement, Greeley remained their supporter. Anthony criticized him for not reviewing their new journal, *The Revolution*, in his newspaper. Yet the *Tribune* was forthright in its endorsement of a referendum on women's suffrage in Kansas a few months later. "If the great body of the women of Kansas wish to vote," the paper declared, "we counsel the men to accede them the opportunity." Still, Greeley distrusted the "experiment" of female suffrage in the West, where women had the right to vote in places. Future president James Garfield was delighted that Greeley had "exposed" Stanton's claim that women should have equal voting rights. Yet, when the flamboyant Virginia Woodhull announced in 1871 that she would run for public office, the *Tribune* waxed eloquent on her behalf for the "courage of her opinions."[72]

In principle, Horace Greeley wanted women to share in the blessings of American and universal freedom. Women should have the same property and inheritance rights under the law as men. They should have equal opportunity in employment, as he had provided them at the *Tribune.* Yet when it came to the practical politics of voting rights for women, Greeley weighed in on the side of the male majority. On the issue of women's suffrage, Greeley was not ahead of his time, but in tune with it, even though he sympathized with the women's rights movement and allowed its leaders space in his newspaper. He recognized that equal rights for women were coming in the future, and would form an equal part of American freedom. The time was just not yet right.

10

Liberal Republican

Republican freedom required limits on executive power, including the execution of foreign policy. Citizens not only needed to elect their ruler, but to be able to remove that individual. Illegal activities, in particular, could result in removal by impeachment. In America, citizens and their elected representatives have the right to put the president on trial for "high crimes and misdemeanors" if he break the law or violates the Constitution. The impeachment trial of President Andrew Johnson provided a unique test of American freedom. So did the expansion of the American empire in the years after the Civil War under the continuing direction of William Henry Seward. And typically Horace Greeley was involved in both cases of abuse of power.

Andrew Johnson, a southern Democrat, had replaced the anti-slavery Hannibal Hamlin as Lincoln's vice president in 1864. Once president, Johnson tried to slow down or undercut many congressional initiatives to help with Reconstruction of the South. Both radical Republicans and liberal Democrats were among his many critics. From the outset, an unelected Democratic president and a Republican Congress provided a recipe for crisis. Talk of impeachment began almost as soon as Johnson took office, but became serious only in the summer of 1867.

Greeley had been concerned about the widening gap between the president and Congress for some time. His English friend John Bright warned him against impeaching Johnson. But by early 1867, Greeley believed that the country was "within thirty days of a fresh civil war." An "impending tornado" was coming, he predicted, and he would himself "probably go with the party of Progress rather than of Reaction." That summer, Greeley testified before a congressional committee about bailing out Jefferson Davis, saying that he would have preferred a trial and claimed he knew of no link between Davis and the Lincoln assassination.[1]

On August 12, 1867, Johnson fired Secretary of War Edwin Stanton when he refused to resign, replacing Stanton with the reluctant Ulysses S. Grant. Johnson thus violated the Tenure of Office Act that protected federal officials against such an eventuality. In November, the Senate Judiciary Committee voted 5–4 to impeach Johnson for a variety of high crimes and misdemeanors—pardoning traitors, making money in Tennessee by illegally selling railroad bonds, trying to prevent ratification of constitutional amendments, and so on. In January 1868, Grant resigned and the Senate voted to reinstate Stanton, setting up a constitutional conflict between the president and Congress. On February 21, 1868, Johnson, in defiance of Congress, named Lorenzo Thomas interim Secretary of War. Stanton, however, refused to vacate his office. On February 24, the House of Representatives voted in favor of impeachment, accusing Johnson of violating Reconstruction acts and obstructing Congress.

Greeley had an opinion, as always. The *Tribune* characterized Johnson as a master of political cunning whose strength lay "entirely in peccadilloes." But Greeley doubted that Johnson could be impeached. "When Congress concludes to impeach him for petty misdemeanors," he wrote, "it will find plenty of them. But if it waits for high crimes, he will serve out his term in feverish peacefulness, and empty feints." He admitted there was a national crisis, but believed Johnson would weather the storm—as he did. Greeley favored impeachment, however, once the House of Representatives had made its intentions clear. The "salvation of this country" was at stake. The president was responsible for breaking the law, and "Congress must assume the responsibility of impeaching him." Johnson's actions were "treachery," and his administration was "evil." He wanted to restore the Rebels to power in the South, to defy Congress, and to violate the Constitution. Constitutional liberty required the impeachment of Andrew Johnson and the triumph of Republican institutions. "Free America," promised Greeley, "will show the world."[2]

On March 5, Johnson's trial opened in Washington. "A great nation," wrote Greeley, "is as much on trial as the President." The white-haired editor attended some of the sessions himself, many with his daughter Ida. He wished America a "speedy delivery from Mr. Johnson." The president must execute the laws, not be above the laws.

The *Tribune,* he promised Thaddeus Stevens, intended to "keep up a steady fire on the impeachment question till the issue is decided." "We will have to take Grant for President," Greeley wrote Rebecca Whipple, "he is far from my choice, but I hope he will be right at heart." On May 16, Johnson avoided impeachment by one vote in the Senate. A second Senate vote on May 26 also failed. Johnson remained in office, and the radical Republicans lost political face.[3] The push for equal rights and freedoms for freedmen in the South was coming to an end.

Greeley thought Johnson deserved to be impeached. The verdict, he wrote, was tainted. Johnson had been "morally condemned" by thirty-five Senators, one vote short of the two-thirds majority needed. Greeley thought bribes secured Johnson's acquittal and suspected Thurlow Weed. He praised Stanton as the last member of the Lincoln administration to remain "true to freedom."[4] Impeachment had failed, so that the Republic remained in danger of corruption.

Greeley also criticized executive abuse of power in foreign policy, still under the direction of his nemesis, Secretary of State William Henry Seward. Greeley remained a protectionist rather than an expansionist. He had no desire to extend the "empire of liberty" at the expense of other nations. Universal freedom was not part of America's "manifest destiny," as the Young Americans had claimed. In April 1867, Seward persuaded the Senate to ratify a treaty with Russia selling Alaska to the United States for seven million dollars. Greeley promptly accused Seward of covering up failures at home by acquiring "a luxury we are in no condition to afford." Alaska was "an expensive continent of ice" full of "rocks and Esquimaux." He dubbed it "Walrussia." "On paper it is a wonderful country; on ice it is what is generally called a big thing." Again, he suspected he saw Weed's hand in the whole business and mocked Seward's large "Russian treaty dinner parties" in Washington. When Congress finally agreed to the purchase of Alaska in July 1868, Greeley complained that President Johnson should not have taken possession of "Mr. Seward's hard bargain" before Congress had approved the purchase.[5]

In early 1869, Greeley again attacked the purchase of "Seward's icebox." He charged that Russian embassy officials in Washington had lobbied and bribed journalists and congressmen to sell the deal to the public. The "swindling" of Americans with Alaska had bought only "uncivil polar bears and walruses," nothing more. The cost of acquiring Alaska, he predicted, would be high.[6]

Nor was Greeley pleased with American attempts to acquire the islands of Cuba and Haiti from Spain after the Civil War. He had long opposed the revolutionary leader Narciso Lopez for keeping four hundred thousand blacks enslaved in Cuba while fighting for "liberty." He knew that southerners had wanted to buy the island as another slave state. Nor was he very pleased with former *Tribune* reporter James Redpath's Haitian Bureau of Emigration, which tried to export American slaves to Haiti in a scheme supported by Lincoln. Slavery on the sugar plantations of Haiti was as evil as slavery on the cotton plantations of the American South.[7]

Greeley became more interested in Cuba in 1868, however, when an island rebellion broke out against Spanish control. Rebels attacked island garrisons, captured the city of Bayamo, and recruited thousands of guerilla followers. Stories of torture and murder abounded. Cuba declared itself a republic in April 1869. The American press generally supported the rebels. Greeley's old friend Cassius Clay of Kentucky promptly formed a Cuban Aid Society. Greeley was vice president, Charles A. Dana the treasurer. The group planned to send relief supplies and medicines, to lobby for American recognition of an independent Cuba, and to emancipate Cuban slaves. Dana chaired a mass meeting to support the rebellion. In March, the House of Representatives passed a resolution sympathetic to the rebels. By October 1869, Greeley and other New York supporters of a free Cuba had disbursed a million dollars in aid. Greeley wrote President Ulysses S. Grant in early 1870 urging him to recognize "Cuban patriots" in their conflict with the "Spanish nation." American ships soon arrived in Cuba with volunteers, weapons, and supplies. Greeley now urged action and intervention.[8] But a few months later, he cautioned that congressional support of Cuban self-government might lead to war, which would be undesirable.[9]

Greeley also continued to support Irish freedom from Great Britain in these years, but not to the point of armed intervention. In May 1870, a group of radical Fenians took trains to St. Albans, Vermont, and made a raid into Canada. The so-called Battle of Eccles Hill was a comic affair, but caused considerable resentment north of the border. The Fenians (after Finn MacCumhol, an ancient Gaelic warrior) had organized in Dublin in 1858 as a secret society of Irish republicans. They soon gained support among the Irish-Americans of New

York and other eastern cities. By 1865, the Fenians claimed ten thousand members across the United States. Many were veterans of 1848, the American Civil War, and the Troubles in Ireland. Canada provided the closest British target for Irish rage. Because Seward supported Fenian schemes against British Canada, Greeley naturally opposed them.[10]

In the spring of 1866, Fenians tried to seize Campobello Island in the Bay of Fundy near the Canadian border. American and British warships arrived soon thereafter, seized Fenian arms, and dispersed the men without making any arrests. Troops under General George Meade began patrolling the border. A month later, fifteen hundred Fenians crossed into Canada from St. Albans, Vermont, and Buffalo, New York, where General Grant was visiting. Again, American troops arrived on the scene. Fenian hopes that Seward and President Johnson would intervene on their half were dashed. One Fenian complained that the U.S. government was impeding their "onward march to freedom." About a dozen Fenians and British-Canadian soldiers died in the fighting.[11]

Greeley had no love for Irish-American violence, especially since so many involved were Democrats, old Copperheads, or anti-black racists. Still, he supported Ireland's right to freedom. The Irish surely deserved as much "liberty and opportunity" as the freedmen, since there were "natural, inalienable rights, not of superior races, but of every race." He blamed Johnson for the Fenian fiascos in Canada, citing his "weak policy" that "failed to satisfy Irishmen, Americans, and Canadians." One of the Fenian leaders, John C. O'Brien, wrote Greeley to thank him for his "able and convincing articles on Irish affairs" in the *Tribune*. The editor had provided significant aid for "the cause of Irish liberty," O'Brien added.[12]

Both Johnson and Seward were men who had befriended Horace Greeley in the past, but now stood condemned for their roles in the corruption of the republic by abusing their power at home and abroad. Johnson had as president tried to defy Congress and the Constitution. In Greeley's mind, he deserved to be impeached. Seward had stayed on too long after the Civil War as Secretary of State, and embraced interventionist policies that could lead to war. Greeley remained a republican citizen in search of virtue, and he found it not in Washington, DC, but in a bourgeois utopia in Colorado.

BOURGEOIS UTOPIAN

Horace Greeley's vision of American freedom was grounded in the middle class. Although he supported workers and the labor movement throughout his life, he was not a socialist, but a capitalist. Yet he also abhorred the speculation and corruption rampant in capitalist society. A virtuous republic, he believed, could only be saved by virtuous citizens who were neither rich nor poor, but bourgeois, middle-class, hard working, and self-reliant. Classes were fluid, not static. Any worker had the right to rise by dint of free labor into the middle class. Any rich man could lose his fortune in a minute through bad investments or bad fortune and become middle-class. For Greeley, middle-class citizens were the backbone of the republic, the guardians of freedom, the repository of virtue, the engine of reform, and the enemy of corruption.

The "crabgrass frontier" of the suburban home and its well-kept lawn and gardens was another alternative to going West, an escape from poverty, prostitution, and crime to virtue and domesticity. Greeley had his own frontier farm at Chappaqua. He also became involved in the Industrial Home Association of John Stevens, a New York merchant tailor who wanted to transform urban rent-paying workers into land-owning suburbanites. In 1854, Stevens founded a planned community called Mt. Vernon on farmland in Westchester County. Reflecting other intentional communities, Mt. Vernon also offered quarter-acre lots for sale to workers wishing to escape the city. Greeley and the *Tribune* supported the project.[13]

In 1869, Greeley and a group of New York friends decided to establish a planned community called the Union Colony in Colorado as an alternative to industrial capitalism and eastern cities. Nathan Meeker, a former Fourierist and old friend of Greeley, identified twelve thousand acres of land on the Cache la Poudre River, four miles upstream from the Platte River, in eastern Colorado north of Denver. In 1844, Meeker and his wife had joined the Trumbull Phalanx in Ohio, related to Brook Farm and to Greeley's North American Phalanx, one of many intentional communities founded in that era. Meeker, an Oberlin College graduate and an abolitionist, served for several years as auditor, teacher, librarian, poet, and historian of the colony until it collapsed. He also grew fruit and vegetable crops and later joined the *Tribune* during the Civil War as a war correspondent.

Greeley, who had corresponded with Meeker since the mid-1840s, had met him in 1860 in connection with Lincoln's presidential campaign. Greeley liked Meeker's articles. In 1865, the editor named Meeker agricultural columnist, replacing Solon Robinson, who had retired to Florida. Entranced by the idea of a planned community in the West, Meeker went to Colorado, Wyoming, and Utah in 1869 to explore the territory.[14] Over dinner, Meeker presented Greeley with his plan. Greeley, captivated as usual by a new idea, agreed to support him in the *Tribune*.

The idea was to create in the western desert a bourgeois utopia grounded in the principles of associationism, mutual cooperation, harmony, and freedom. The town would ban the sale or production of all alcoholic beverages and become the third temperance town in the United States, after Vineland, New Jersey, and Evanston, Illinois. There would be, in Greeley's words, "no fences and no rum." The colony would be a corporation and joint-stock company. The new association would purchase land from the Denver Pacific Railroad at five dollars an acre. A grid of streets for the town would be laid out in advance without any common land. Individual investors and homeowners would build on lots in town and have larger tracts (40, 80, or 160 acres) outside of town on which to farm. They would all be "temperance men, and ambitious to establish a good society." Most would be Christians of all denominations. There would be no poor and no unemployed. Nor would there be any slaves, Germans, Irishmen, or southerners if Meeker had his way. The result would be a western version of a New England town along the lines of Greeley's own hometowns—Amherst, New Hampshire, and East Poultney, Vermont.[15] Meeker proposed that the town be named after Greeley.

The Union Colony town would be dry in more ways than one. Water was a scarce resource in the West, and irrigation a necessity. Greeley, Colorado, which would have five hundred homes within a year and two thousand inhabitants by 1879, became a model for settling the West and maintaining public control over water. Industrial capitalism might not encourage shared resources, but associationism would do so. Thus, a new generation of pragmatic, middle-class associationists established a mixed socialist-capitalist economy where water was a public utility and land was privately owned. Greeley was among the very first towns to create water laws that regulated private consumption and established public control of river water. The community was founded on principles of freedom and self-reliance, but that freedom did not include any private right to exploit or own water resources at the expense of others.

On December 4, 1869, the *Tribune* ran an ad for Meeker's proposed Union Colony, not yet named after Greeley. Meeker would be the president of the new association, Greeley the treasurer. They wanted "intelligent, educated and thrifty" men of good character to join them. Three thousand answered the call within a week. On December 23, an organizational meeting in Cooper Union enrolled 438 young men, mainly farmers, craftsmen, artisans, and small-businessmen. Greeley chaired the meeting. "I would advise no one who is doing well," he warned, "to leave his business and go West unless he is sure of bettering his condition." Despite this warning, several hundred other men joined in the next few weeks. Each supposedly paid a five-dollar membership fee, and another $150 for land and equipment to begin farming and building a home. Members had to agree to improve their land within a year. Fifty-nine men actually came up with the money. By February 1870, a locating committee had purchased one hundred thousand acres of undesirable land from the railroad and organized the Union Colony of Colorado as a state corporation. The colony was also registered in New York as a joint-stock company.[16]

Within a month or two, the Union Colony had received nearly one hundred thousand dollars, held by the *Tribune* cashier at Greeley's office. Meeker put up most of his own money and borrowed more. Greeley warned Meeker that food and housing would be the most important concerns for the next five years, along with building, fencing, soil tilling, and irrigation. Irrigation was crucial and should improve on the Mormon system. By May 1870, Meeker promised to provide irrigation water to all colonists and began constructing water ditches. Colonists would buy perpetual water rights subject to public control. The colony would be known as the town of Greeley, and would have its own newspaper, the *Tribune*. "The whole country," wrote the *New York Tribune*, "is treeless, covered with grass, and in sight of the proposed town, 1,500 head of Texas cattle are now feeding."[17] The town was conveniently on the Denver-Pacific Railroad line between Denver and Cheyenne, Wyoming. With the completion of the transcontinental railroad in May 1869, rail traffic in Greeley was guaranteed to increase.

Greeley himself purchased two lots in the new town and, as treasurer of the association, was supposed to invest its funds, but never received specific instructions in that regard. Throughout 1870, he fended off Meeker's frequent requests that he come out for a visit. Then, on October 12, he made his one and only visit to the town that bears his name. Houses flew American flags. The entire population of several hundred people turned out to welcome him at the railroad depot, gave three cheers, and listened to him speak before the *Tribune* office. He praised the town's new irrigation system, urged herding rather than fencing livestock, and criticized cattlemen for violating property boundaries. He urged the town to build a gigantic fence around its land. He inspected the irrigation ditches. He hoped there would be ten thousand acres under cultivation within the next year. And he praised the new settlers of the town as "sober, industrious, intelligent moral men."[18]

But the situation in many ways was difficult. Greeley knew that the West was a place of "savage solitude and bleak desolation" where the desert, wolves, and Native Americans threatened the security of new settlers daily. Only two hundred of the more than four hundred nominal settlers had yet made it to Greeley. The town had no money to refund those who did not come. (Greeley could never balance the books anyway.) Greeley had to loan Meeker another thousand dollars to keep him afloat. The setting of the town was barren prairie. One visitor from Illinois described "a baker's dozen of slab shanties, as many tool chests, a great ditch, and twenty acres of prickly pears—on a barren, sandy plain, part and parcel of the Great American Desert, midway between a poverty-stricken ranch and a prairie-dog village on two sides; and a poverty-stricken ranch and a prairie-dog village on the other. It is bounded chiefly by prickly pears."[19]

The enthusiastic Greeley was undaunted. The town's facilities for cheap and extensive irrigation were excellent. The population was hard working, sober, and of high character. There were no "blacklegs, grogsellers, nor any class which aims to get rich by speculating on the needs or pandering to the vices of others." There was no drinking and no gambling. The town's leaders were men of integrity who did not indulge in cabals, demagoguery, or intrigue: that is, politics. "We have no whiskey dens, no beer shops," the *Greeley Tribune* wrote, "no gambling halls nor billiard saloons; no rows; no street fights; very little profanity is ever heard; the Sabbath is almost universally observed, and people generally mind their own business."[20] Greeley, Colorado, was a virtuous town in a virtuous republic dominated by free white men.

Greeley's close friend and fellow Universalist P. T. Barnum soon joined the colony, visited the town, and purchased a lot. In May 1871, he opened the two-story Barnum's Hotel, which housed some of his friends, illegitimate children, and relatives. He owned two farms outside the town and a vacant lot for circus performances downtown. He visited again in 1872 and 1876, acquiring eleven lots in Greeley before selling them off in the 1880s.[21] The town might lack sin, but it would have entertainment.

Greeley himself declined to go West. New York was his home. His family was no utopia, and he felt responsible. Molly was constantly in poor health, mentally and physically, and daughters Gabrielle and Ida had to nurse her. Greeley himself complained about ill health, even as he continued his lecture tours. And he warned others that life in the West was not romantic, but arduous. Summers were hot and winters hard. "I say to all who are in want of work, Go West! But what can you do? Cook? Plow? Mow? Master new skills. Work hard. Then go take up your family, and Go West!" He complained to Meeker about his usual lack of funds. But he still believed in Meeker and the Union Colony as a "good investment for my children."[22]

Greeley, Colorado, required farming skills to survive. So Greeley published his own ideas on agriculture in 1871 in a book entitled *What I Know about Farming*. Farming was a miserable part of his childhood —mindless, monotonous, and hard—that he romanticized in old age. "I should have been a farmer," he wrote in his memoirs. But he was more of a suburban gentleman than a farmer, a man whose outdoor hobbies were not part of earning a living at all. (He could afford a full-time farm manager.) In Chappaqua, he tried raising clover, rye, beets, carrots, and turnips. He prided himself on his corn and oats, as well as his apple orchard. In his book, Greeley recommended cooperation, irrigation, technology, drainage, fertilizer, and agricultural fairs as means of improving the land for cultivation. He predicted the coming of electricity and steam-powered plows and tractors to rural areas. Good farming was a "paying business," although Greeley himself never made it so.[23]

Mark Twain frequently poked fun at Greeley for his supposed expertise on farming and agriculture in connection with the Union

Colony. In April, Greeley sent Twain a copy of his new book. "If you will really betake yourself to farming, or even to telling what you know about it," wrote Twain, "rather than what you *don't* know about mine, I will not only refrain from disparaging criticism, but will give you my blessing."[24] Worse yet, Twain satirized Greeley's notoriously unreadable handwriting.[25]

After his October 1870 visit, Horace Greeley made no more trips to the bourgeois utopia in Colorado that bore his name. With Greeley's death in late 1872, his daughters sued Nathan Meeker for the fifteen hundred dollars Meeker owed the editor. Having no money, Meeker sold his forty-acre plot in Greeley and agreed to become the Indian Agent of the White River Agency in Wyoming. There he tried unsuccessfully to transform the Utes into productive farmers. They believed farming was woman's work. In September 1879, a band of Utes killed Meeker and ten others in the so-called Meeker Massacre. It was a nightmare end to a utopian dream.

In time, Greeley, Colorado, ceased to be an intentional bourgeois-Christian community and became another western town, the county seat of Weld County. Aside from the colonists who settled there, the main beneficiaries were the railroad land agents who sold land they considered worthless. By 1879, the town had two thousand inhabitants. A year later, Greeley ceased to exist as a joint-stock corporation and became simply a town with a branch of the state university.

Horace Greeley foresaw from the outset the danger of a Hobbesian war of all against all for scarce water in the arid West. Farmers told tales of how the rivers dried up and the plants turned brown. Colorado courts filled with lawsuits over water rights. By the 1880s, irrigation laws in many areas placed water in the hands of state-appointed commissioners.[26] Associations to farm and irrigate the land established limits on individual freedom. No one could have a right to water at the expense of his neighbor. In this way, the town of Greeley became not a bourgeois utopia, but a balanced experiment in the rights of private individuals and the need for public administration. The town of Greeley survived not simply by virtue of hard work and private enterprise, but by limiting individual freedom to consume a scarce resource. Freedom had its boundaries, as Greeley himself had always known.

Greeley was a bourgeois utopian in the sense that he sought an idealized community that would enhance freedom for the expanding and fluid American middle class. Any hard-working men of good character willing to improve their land and property could qualify for his utopia. Farming was central to his vision. Both his farm at Chappaqua and his planned town in Colorado reflected the ideals not only of Horace Greeley, but of the emerging American suburb.

CORRUPTION FIGHTER

All his life Horace Greeley had fought corruption within the republic, and after the Civil War, corruption meant the administration of the eighteenth president of the United States, Ulysses S. Grant. Grant was a good general surrounded by corrupt men who put private gain ahead of public interest. He wanted to achieve a lasting peace, pay back war debts in gold (not the easily printed paper Greenbacks), and extend the vote to freedmen through what would become the Fifteenth Amendment to the Constitution (1870). But during his first administration, corruption ran rampant. The spoils system encouraged officeholders to reward supporters with political appointments of one kind or another. Financial buccaneers and speculators Jay Gould and Jim Fisk tried to corner the gold market in 1868, when Grant was frequently seen in public with them. In September 1869, Grant ordered the U.S. Treasury to sell off gold, and the financial bubble burst, so that investors lost millions of dollars. Some blamed Grant. In St. Louis, the Whiskey Ring bribed tax collectors to purchase tax stamps at a fraction of their high Civil War value. More than one hundred Treasury officials were convicted of bribery. In New York, the Tweed Ring got rich on government contracts. Grant's Secretary of War, William Belknap, accepted bribes from the corporations licensed to trade on Indian reservations. Unknown until 1872, a financial corporation known as the Credit Mobilier operated as a dummy construction company for the transcontinental railroad. Nearly half of the fifty million dollars raised from the federal government and shareholders for the railroad was diverted into the pockets of the Credit Mobilier promoters. Money governed Republican politics, and "Grantism" became synonymous with corruption.

Corruption was rampant at both the federal and state levels of government. The Republican Party had lost its sense of purpose. The old radicals of the anti-slavery days were now retiring from politics. A new generation of machine-politics men was putting politicians above parties. Rival factions were fighting for control of party organizations. Voting fraud was everywhere. The republic was in danger.

The moving spirit behind the Liberal Republican movement that emerged to fight corruption and oppose the reelection of Grant in 1872 was a German Forty-Eighter named Carl Schurz (1829–1906).[27] Schurz was a melting-pot politician, an immigrant who had transformed himself from German into American citizen, and his political credo from *Freiheit* into *Freedom*. Schurz, a Prussian, became involved in the 1848 revolutions as a university student in Bonn, and eventually had to flee Germany as a radical republican. In 1852, he left for the United States, where he became a journalist, an abolitionist, and the leader of Germans joining the new Republican Party in Wisconsin.

Schurz helped shape the immigrant debate over slavery and freedom throughout the Midwest in the late 1850s. He campaigned vigorously in 1858 for Lincoln's Senate race against Douglas, and in 1860 for Lincoln's campaign for the presidency. His reward for Lincoln's victory was the post of U.S. Minister to Spain, then the rank of Brigadier General in the Union army during the Civil War. He saw action at Second Bull Run, the Wilderness, Gettysburg, and Chickamauga.

Schurz believed deeply in American freedom. Shortly after his arrival in the United States, he wrote a friend in Germany, "here you see the principle of individual freedom carried to its ultimate consequences." America had no barriers to individual freedom. Freedom did not mean anarchy, as it did in monarchical Europe, but the only way for men to "know themselves" and see themselves "as they really are." In Illinois, Schurz made contact with Gustav Koerner, the future governor of the state, and Friedrich Hecker, another Forty-Eighter active in emerging Republican Party politics. When Schurz returned to London for a visit in 1855, he told his friend Kinkel that a major battle was under way in the United States between freedom and slavery. "The slaveholder," he said, "fears the propaganda of freedom, because he does not know how far it may go. Even the mere word of *freedom* has to him a dangerous and ambiguous sound."[28]

By 1860, Schurz was eagerly defining "Americanism" for other German immigrants in his accented English. The 1848 revolutions had crushed liberty in Europe, he noted. But freedom was alive in the United States, where slavery would soon be abolished and liberty was inseparable from equal rights. Self-government required constant practice. Liberty for all meant freedom, a "truly American idea." At the Chicago convention that year, Schurz at first supported Seward as the Republican nominee for president. He then joined Greeley's Bates supporters in switching to Lincoln on the third ballot. From that point on, Schurz played a crucial role in winning Lincoln supporters from among the new German voters of the Midwest.[29]

As a brigadier general, Schurz commanded a number of German units during the war. Many of his officers were also Forty-Eighters, some of whom had served in Italy under Garibaldi. Schurz continued to be an avid Republican, praising the Emancipation Proclamation and the Gettysburg Address as extensions of the "universal principle" of freedom embodied in the Declaration of Independence. After the war, he joined B. Gratz Brown, a former U.S. Senator from Missouri, in urging universal amnesty for all former Confederate soldiers. For a time, Schurz edited a German-language newspaper in St. Louis before being elected to the U.S. Senate in 1869.[30]

Greeley and Schurz had a somewhat difficult relationship that went back to 1867, when Greeley published in the *Tribune* an account of the Battle of Chancellorsville (1863) that gave little credit to Schurz and his Germans, many of whom fled the battlefield. Schurz objected, and Greeley printed Schurz's own account of the battle. Then both men got caught up in the campaign to elect Grant president. "Horace Greeley alone in the *New York Tribune*," Schurz wrote his wife, "appears cracked as usual. He has already done us great harm, but I hope that by the beginning of the presidential campaign we may be able to tame him."[31]

After the Civil War, old party alignments began to break up. Reconstruction divided conservative and radical Union men, southern and northern Democrats, abolitionists and anti-slavery reformers. Liberals began to drift away from the powerful and increasingly business-oriented Republican Party. In September 1871, Schurz decided to launch a third party to fight corruption and to oppose the reelection of Grant. He chose the name "Liberal Republican" and grounded his new party on civil service reform, tariff reduction, lower taxes, and no additional land grants to the railroads. He also advocated local self-government and "property and enterprise"—code words for white supremacy—in the South. The Liberal Republicans were an odd collection of anti-Grant men: New England patricians, agrarian radicals, civil service reformers, anti-slavery veterans, old Free Soilers, free traders, and protectionists. Their only real bond was a distaste for Grant and his corrupt administration. They wanted liberal reform without Grant, the politicians, and the big businessmen. They also wanted reconciliation with the "best men" of the South. Many of them were politicians forced out of office by the Grant machine. And, with the election of 1872 looming on the horizon, the Liberal Republicans needed a presidential candidate.

Greeley had dutifully supported Grant for president in 1868, but was increasingly disenchanted with the new Republican Party of money and big business. "We have chosen our president," Greeley wrote a friend, and thus "secured the country against a fresh civil war." Grant was a man of "good sense and moderation" who would make the former Rebels behave "sensibly."[32] But in 1872, Greeley began to have his own presidential aspirations grounded in the liberal republicanism of his past.

In 1872, Horace Greeley was among the most famous, and most easily recognized, Americans of his day. His *Recollections of a Busy Life* revealed a plain-speaking man of the people who had risen to fame, if not fortune. "It seems as if I should never have less work," wrote Greeley regarding his latest book on the tariff, "but rather more until I sink under it." Greeley was a man of courage and eminent good sense, not the philosopher he imagined himself to be, but neither the fool others criticized him for being. He also continued to lust after public office and to hobnob with wealthy Republicans like Jim Fisk.[33]

In November 1869, Greeley ran for New York State Comptroller and lost. He outpolled the rest of the Republican ticket, except for General Franz Sigel, who cornered the German vote. In 1870, he ran again for Congress from his Sixth District in New York City, although he was ill and could not make any speeches. Again, he lost. Yet many, including Greeley himself, continued to think of him as presidential material, especially in an age of corruption, because of his fame as an editor and his reputation for honesty.

In December 1869, Greeley dedicated his *Essays Designed to Elucidate the Science of Political Economy* to his hero, Henry Clay. In it, he noted that the most essential human activity was labor. Protection of free labor through tariffs was a central government responsibility. Virtually every adult male was a nascent capitalist, whether he knew it or not. Capital and property were the basis of freedom. Capitalists and workers had a common interest in production and should not be in conflict. Free Trade was a cruel illusion that crushed the individual worker economically by placing him in competition with cheap foreign labor. Workers deserved a fair and just wage. Cooperation and association were keys to industrial efficiency. Only association could rescue labor from "dependence, dissipation, prodigality and need" and lead labor to "forecast, calculation, sobriety, and thrift."[34] Production was more important than the distribution of profits, whether to the rich or the poor. Greeley's attack on Free Trade and defense of Protection contained no new ideas. But the book helped remind Schurz and other politicians of Greeley's republican ideology and political availability.

Some politicians, however, remained wary of Greeley. Grant's supporters in the New York Republican Party, led by Roscoe Conkling, were suspicious of a temperance man, protectionist, old reformer, and moralizer still active in Universalism.[35] Moreover, Grant, like Lincoln, feared Greeley because of his enormous influence on public opinion. "Mr. Greeley," Grant wrote John Russell Young, "is an honest, firm, untiring supporter of the Republican Party. He means its welfare at all times. But he is a free thinker; jumps at conclusions; does not get the views of others who are just as sincere as himself, in the interest of the party that saved the country, and now wants to pay its honest debts, protect its industries, and progress to a prosperous future, as well as himself." Grant may have also sensed a potential rival for the presidency. When Grant and Greeley met at a funeral in Washington on December 10, Grant took Greeley off in his carriage for dinner and the evening.[36] Grant talked about naming Greeley to a diplomatic post in Santo Domingo. Perhaps the president could buy off the editor by making him an envoy to a black republic. Greeley remained unimpressed.

He was also exhausted. Molly and Ida were again out of the country, staying on the Isle of Wight off the coast of England. Gabrielle was attending a convent school north of New York City. His old *Tribune* friend Beman Brockway was concerned for the editor's health. He advised Greeley to take a vacation. "Get away from the *Tribune* for a year or two, recruit, leaving the young men now about the concern to run it. Better to do that than to kill yourself off, and then take final leave of the glorious *Tribune*."[37] But Greeley was not about to stop.

Greeley, now almost sixty, began the year 1871 with a flurry of political activity. He supported the claims of the Choctaw Indians to

U.S. bonds promised them by treaty. He wrote an article for *Wood's Household Magazine* advising young men to believe in God, learn a trade, stay in good health, avoid alcoholic beverages, be a good citizen, avoid borrowing money, and never despair. These maxims undoubtedly had a political purpose, because the first inklings of a Greeley-for-president boom were beginning to appear in New York. Greeley reiterated his one-term philosophy for presidents, directing it against Grant as he had against Lincoln. He had Whitelaw Reid confirm that Senator Charles Sumner would not be a presidential candidate. He reminded *Tribune* readers that he would never refuse any duty "which my political friends shall see fit to devolve upon me." And he began to formulate positions on civil service reform and general amnesty toward the South.[38]

Carl Schurz wanted national Liberal Republican Party organizations established in each state. Although he denied any desire to break up the Republican Party, by the end of the summer he was calling himself a Liberal Republican and organizing clubs of the "best men" from both parties across the country. Greeley was intrigued, and went off on a speaking tour to Texas and other southern states in May to test the waters of a Republican presidential run. He called for national reconciliation and universal amnesty for Confederate veterans, urged agricultural improvement using irrigation and steam plows, and noted that the freedmen were "working better than expected." He attacked the new Ku Klux Klan as an "execrable" organization, and announced that he "believed in Human Progress." Enthusiastic crowds greeted him everywhere he went. Liberal Republicans in New York City feted him upon his return. Again, he spoke of reconciliation of North and South, attacked the Klan as cowardly traitors, and supported federal Enforcement acts that guaranteed free elections in the South. Post–Civil War America needed to move from strife to harmony. His friend Cassius M. Clay of Kentucky supported him in his speeches in the Midwest. In June, a Greeley Club was organized in New York to support him for president.[39]

By autumn 1871, Greeley was openly declaring himself a Republican candidate for the presidency. He was still a party member in good standing, and the Liberal Republicans were not yet nationally organized. Josiah Grinnell hosted a dinner in his honor in Chicago. Independent Republican newspapers in the Midwest began to support his candidacy. He told Wisconsin Republicans that he would be a candidate before the 1872 Republican National Convention—"not that I want the nomination, but I hope to develop sufficient strength in that convention to force Grant off the track and to nominate Schuyler Colfax." But the Colfax ploy fooled no one, least of all Grant. "Mr. Greeley," Grant wrote a friend, "is simply a disappointed man at not being estimated by others at the same value he places upon himself. He is a genius without common sense. He attaches to himself the fawning, deceitful and dishonest men of the party. . . . His judgment will not do to trust, and I have come to doubt his intentions."[40]

But Greeley's intentions were clear. He wanted to be president of the United States, preferably Republican, and if not, Liberal Republican. Yet he also wanted to rest. "My sixtieth Christmas," he wrote a friend at the end of 1871, "is going soberly and with abundance of work. I am no richer, unless in friends, for my last ten or twelve years of hard work; and I begin to long for quiet and rest. I have hardly known what home meant for years, and am too busy to enjoy anything. I most regret the lack of time to read books. I hope I shall not die so ignorant as I now am."[41] Molly and Ida were still away. He attended Christmas services that year with his close friend P. T. Barnum.

Greeley was having second thoughts in early 1872. "I heartily wish my name had never been connected with the Presidency," he wrote the Springfield, Massachusetts, *Republican.* "I see plainly that it can only result in vexation and misapprehension. And I shall never shape and groove my opinions to make myself acceptable to any party."[42] He was, as always, an independent.

When Carl Schurz gathered a Liberal Republican convention together in Missouri in late January, the leading candidate was not Greeley, still an active Republican, but Benjamin Gratz Brown (1826–1885). Brown was forty-five, a Kentuckyian, Henry Clay Whig, and Yale graduate who had served in the Missouri legislature since 1852. Brown was anti-slavery, radical Republican, free labor, and a favorite of the German community in St. Louis, where he edited the *Missouri Democrat.* In 1863, Missourians elected him to the U.S. Senate on a platform of "Freedom and Franchise" for the freedmen of the South. (Brown also favored the "free principles" of "free thought, free speech, and free ballot.") Unlike Greeley, he opposed high protectionist tariffs. Brown retired from the Senate in 1868, and Schurz replaced him. In 1870, Brown was elected governor of Missouri. By 1872, Brown thought of himself as a likely Liberal Republican candidate for president of the United States.[43]

There was only one problem: Brown was a notorious alcoholic. His nickname was "Boozy Brown." He drank in public, and garbled his speeches. The Liberal Republicans of Missouri were united against Grant. They could call for a national convention in Cincinnati in May on a platform of universal amnesty, universal suffrage, tariff reform, civil service reform, and an end to the spoils system. But they could not, with straight faces, support Benjamin Gratz Brown.

Greeley, learning of the anti-protection mood of the Missouri convention, protested that the tariff issue was one "the *Tribune* can never abide no matter who may be the rival candidates for President." He continued to attack the Grant administration for its corruption, especially on charges of bribery and fraud at the New York Customs House. But Greeley himself had plenty of enemies, among them the former abolitionists who remembered his past. "Greeley," wrote William Lloyd Garrison to a friend, "was never in harmony with us, but in his *Tribune* often treated us very shabbily, and to this day has not outgrown his contempt for our movement." The essence of Greeley, wrote Garrison, was his "compromise between God and the Adversary [Satan]."[44] Yet Greeley believed he was a man of principle, not compromise, and as much on God's side as the abolitionists.

On February 3, 1872, a group of his friends celebrated Horace Greeley's sixty-first birthday at Alvin Johnson's home on West 57th Street, where Greeley now boarded.[45] Johnson was a fellow publisher and an old friend. Several hundred invited guests attended the festive occasion. Carriages thronged the street. Fresh flowers and evergreens adorned each room. There was no wine, but plenty of singing. Among the guests were the writer Bret Harte, Mark Twain, John Hay, and Greeley's old friend P. T. Barnum. Edward Chapin was there from Greeley's church. The elegant Whitelaw Reid came with other *Tribune* staff, including George Ripley.

Reid now thought Greeley could be nominated and elected as a Liberal Republican, if not a Republican, and explored the possibility with Schurz and Sumner. Others criticized him for leaving the Republican Party. Except for Reid and his *Tribune* supporters, Greeley had no formal organization to back him. He wrote Josiah Grinnell urging him to send a strong delegation to the Liberal Republican convention in Cincinnati and work against "Grant's fifteen or twenty brothers-in-law, nephews, and cousins which he has appointed to office." "Speak plain," he added, "and the people will hear."[46]

By April 1872, Greeley had won the support of sixty-four of sixty-eight New York delegates to the Liberal Republican convention. Most, including Schurz and Sumner, thought his nomination unlikely and ludicrous, but Reid did not. The Liberal Republicans had real strength in the Midwest: Missouri, Ohio, Wisconsin, Indiana, Illinois, and Kansas. In New York City, Greeley told a mass meeting at Cooper Union on April 12 that the Grant administration was corrupt and that he would "go forward with the non-office-holding Republicans to the Cincinnati convention and its consequences."[47] Greeley was, in fact, popular from Maine to California, as one man put it, and had support from both businessmen and workers. He was the classic reformer, appealing to white southerners, as well as blacks and freedmen. He was well known and trusted. He spoke his convictions, whether against slavery, for protectionism, or on principle.

The most likely slate at Cincinnati initially was David Davis, an Illinois judge and friend of Lincoln, for president, and Greeley for vice president. Other possibilities included the New England patrician Charles Francis Adams, Benjamin Gratz Brown (if sober), George Julian, and Lyman Trumbull. Schurz was out of the picture because he was foreign-born. He chaired the proceedings instead. Davis led Greeley by fifty-one votes on the first ballot. On the second ballot, Gratz Brown threw Greeley his ninety-five votes, and Greeley led by two votes. Then Adams became the front-runner, leading by fifty-one votes on the fifth ballot. Finally, after a carefully planned "spontaneous" demonstration for Greeley organized by Reid, Greeley won handily on the sixth and final ballot, and a noisy rally for the colorful editor in the white coat followed. "The Hall was filled," wrote one eyewitness, "with a mechanical preordained, stentorious bellowing. Hoary-haired, hard-eyed politicians, who had not in twenty years felt a noble impulse, mounted their chairs and with faces suffused with a seraphic fervor, blistered their throats hurraying for the great and good Horace Greeley. The noise bred a panic. A furor, artificial at first, became real and ended in a stampede."[48]

Horace Greeley's nomination for president of the United States was neither fluke nor fraud, as some charged at the time. Greeley had broad national appeal. John Greenleaf Whittier called him "one of the most popular men in the United States." He was a man of high moral character, sharp intellect, and principles. He was not an abolitionist, but an anti-slavery man. He supported the right of secession, peace during wartime, universal amnesty after the war, and reconciliation of North and South. His protectionism was well known and unpopular, but tolerable. Schurz tried to persuade Greeley to withdraw after the first ballot, but subsequently climbed on the Greeley bandwagon. Despite Schurz's attempts to nominate Adams, Gratz Brown had turned his Missouri delegates over to Greeley on the condition that he have second place on the ticket, which he did. Greeley promptly tried to mollify Schurz, especially since he knew German-American voters would dislike him for his temperance as much as for his protectionism. "I am sure you have ever meant to do the right," Greeley wrote Schurz, "though your judgment on important points differs widely from that of . . . Horace Greeley."[49]

Whitelaw Reid, managing editor of the *Tribune,* was the real engineer behind Greeley's victory at Cincinnati. At thirty-five, Reid was unflappable, energetic, smart, and tactful. He supported amnesty toward the South and sought the support of southern whites in the coming election. In the past, he had supported Henry Clay, John Fremont, Abraham Lincoln, and Salmon P. Chase—as had Greeley. Reid believed that political parties had only a twenty-year life span, and that the time was right for a new Liberal Republican party. He telegraphed Greeley daily from Cincinnati about the convention. He kept up the morale of the Greeley men even as Schurz worked against them. He shaped the Greeley-Brown coalition around a platform of amnesty for the South, civil service reform, a one-term presidency, and no comment on the tariff question. He spoke frequently on Greeley's behalf, especially to newspaper editors. In the end, Reid's political skill won the day. Horace Greeley would not have won the nomination without him.[50]

Carl Schurz was naturally disappointed. Most German newspapers opposed the Greeley nomination. Free Traders began to melt away from the Liberal Republicans. Rival reform tickets sprang up across the country. The Republicans unanimously re-nominated Grant in Philadelphia in June. But in July, the Democrats, meeting in Baltimore and lacking a viable candidate with national appeal, overwhelmingly nominated Horace Greeley for president of the United States, making him the first nominee of two political parties. Schurz came over to his side. In the summer of 1872, the improbable had become plausible—Horace Greeley might yet be the next president of the United States.[51]

Greeley would run strongest in the South. Within days of his nomination, a pamphlet appeared in Lynchburg, Virginia, urging southern voters to support Greeley as a man of principle who endorsed both Peace and Union. The author, a Democrat, urged both whites and blacks to forget and forgive past transgressions. Greeley could unite black freedmen and white southerners in a successful overthrow of the corrupt Grant administration. Greeley was a great editor who wielded enormous moral power throughout the country. He supported the "true theory of republican liberty" and the "right of self-government under the Declaration of Independence." Throughout his lifetime, he had shown "unimpeachable consistency" in his support of liberty, freedom, and independence for all. He had fought for peace during the war and urged amnesty toward the South afterwards. He had freed Jefferson Davis from prison. And he supported "equivalent," if not equal, education for black children in the South.[52]

Greeley's appeal in the South, of course, would help doom him in the North. But no one knew that for certain in the hot summer of 1872. At a time of widespread corruption in the republic, Horace Greeley appeared to be a man of virtue who could win the U.S. presidency as an incorruptible republican.

THE INCORRUPTIBLE REPUBLICAN

Horace Greeley once made the famous comment that he never knew in 1872 whether he was running for the presidency or the penitentiary. The comment ignores the seriousness of Greeley's candidacy. The incorruptible and popular newspaper editor was taking on a corrupt Republican administration, in defense of freedom. He was one of the first presidential candidates to travel the country speaking on his own behalf, rather than rocking on his front porch awaiting election returns. In May, he made clear that he understood the difference between white and black races but that "I trust the time will come when no man's color will exclude him from any church or religious organization whatever," nor from politics. He wrote a friend that he thought Andrew Johnson's Reconstruction policy was wrong because it left former slaves "uncared for." Greeley spoke out for a more just and equitable system of taxation. He continued to defend tariff protection, even though many Liberal Republicans opposed it. He overworked himself as usual.[53]

Greeley certainly had his supporters. Josiah Grinnell in Iowa observed that "the farmers are turning to the man with the great brain, the warm and honest heart, who for forty years has by his example, dignified labor, and in every sense has dignified the American name." But abolitionist Gerrit Smith thought Greeley's election would be a great success for the Democratic Party, which was scheduled to meet in July, would turn Greeley himself into a Democrat, and would elect a Democratic Congress. Theodore Tilton published a favorable pamphlet on Greeley's record on amnesty toward the South. But on May 22, Congress preempted the issue by passing its own Amnesty Bill, succumbing to Liberal Republican pressure, but also eliminating one of the party's major platform planks. "If I should die before the election or be beaten therein," Greeley wrote a friend, "please testify for me that I do not regret having braved public obsession when I thought it was wrong and knew it to be merciless."[54]

Greeley had his instant detractors as well. Many attacked his past views on secession, the South, paying off war debts, and "clasping hands across the bloody chasm" after the Civil War. His nomination by the Democrats, probably without Greeley's active participation, further alienated old Republican and anti-slavery friends. Abolitionist Lydia Child, who had known Greeley since North American Phalanx days in the 1840s, found him "woefully deficient in many elements of character essential to such a responsible office." He had once been a "loud-spoken herald of freedom." Now he was simply a "tool in the hands of Southern despots, and their unprincipled allies, the Democrats." She preferred Sumner, Colfax, or even Grant to Greeley. The historian George Bancroft predicted that Greeley would attract "all the worst elements in our society"—rogues, Catholic priests, and "friends of disorder" in the South. He was simply the "stalking horse of the Secessionists." Hamilton Fish of New York found Greeley "erratic, uncertain, violent in his temper and unwise in his judgment." Even Carl Schurz went off and tried to organize a second Liberal Republican convention in New York in June, but nothing came of it.[55]

There was real irony in the fact that the Democrats, meeting in Baltimore on July 9–10, also nominated Horace Greeley for president. All his life, Greeley had thundered against the Democrats for their corrupt ways. But he also had consorted with Democrats in New York and elsewhere throughout his career—including John O'Sullivan, George N. Sanders, Andrew Johnson, and Clement Vallandigham. Greeley himself was not in Baltimore, but graciously accepted the Democratic nomination—the first time a candidate had been nominated by two separate parties.[56] In retrospect, Greeley came off as an opportunist, rather than the man of principle he had claimed to be.

Reactions to the dual nomination were mixed. Abolitionist Gerrit Smith opposed the "Cincinnati-Baltimore platform" as inadequate to support the rights of freedmen in the South, as Grant was doing. William Lloyd Garrison spoke of political corruption and called Greeley "a man without any fixed principles" and a "first-class political demagogue" who was "smitten with imbecility." Greeley's friend Beman Brockway thought that Greeley had divided the Republicans before the Democratic nomination, but that afterwards the Greeley movement was headed "plainly nowhere." Even a Greeley supporter found the editor to be an "illbred boor, and although a sort of inspired idiot, neither a scholar, statesman, or gentleman." Republican newspapers charged that Greeley had cut a deal with the despised Democrats even before his nomination at Cincinnati. Some Democrats switched to Grant, rather than vote for their old enemy and lifelong critic.[57]

Greeley cheerfully ignored such carping. He gave speeches from Maine to Texas, sometimes in a lecture hall, sometimes from the rear of a railway train. He spoke up to fifteen or twenty times a day. One listener found his speeches to be "marvelous, impromptu oratory, convincing in their simplicity and integrity." The Liberal Republican Party had banners with pictures of Greeley and Gratz Brown, with an eagle clutching a streamer that read, "Liberty, Equality, and Fraternity, Universal Amnesty and Impartial Suffrage." The Tribune Association put out a collection of Greeley's favorite jokes and campaign songs. Grant, in the meantime, recognizing that he was a poor speaker, spent most of his time at his summer home.[58]

The Greeley *Campaign Songster* set the tone for his campaign, grounded in his republican principles of freedom, peace, national unity, and reconciliation (his protectionism was not widely shared). Greeley himself appeared in the songs as the man in the white hat, the Apostle of Freedom, the Friend of Freedom, the Evangelist of Peace, the Wise Man of the East, the White Coat Statesman, the Old White Coat Philosopher, and "the constant friend of freedom for the black man and the white." Another song reminded listeners, "Our leader is a statesman, an honest farmer too." Like Cincinnatus at his plow in the Roman Republic, Horace Greeley would reluctantly leave his home and farm to save the republic in time of need. "Doctor Greeley," as one song put it, would heal the "sickened body politic." Finally, the "Greeley Marseillaise" trumpeted, "For Freedom and for Greeley!"[59]

But Greeley's personality and fame as a fearless editor and reformer, more than his political philosophy, made him a serious candidate. He symbolized virtue over corruption, reform over reaction, reconciliation over revenge, generosity over greed. In late July, Greeley thought he might even be in the White House "with time to hang up my hat." Rutherford B. Hayes wrote in his diary, "I have just now a feeling that Greeley will be elected." General William Sherman hoped Grant would win, "though several shrewd judges insist that Greeley will be our next President." Senator Charles Sumner thought that the "best Republicans" were now supporting Greeley, a man with a "large head and heart." Sumner finally endorsed his candidacy because "unquestionably the surest trust of the colored people is in Horace Greeley." Greeley thought his prospects for election were good, and wrote his daughter Gabrielle on July 28, "I guess we shall all go to Washington next winter." But he urged her not to "put on any White House airs" yet.[60]

In August, the campaign heated up. Despite the weaknesses that Gratz Brown brought to the ticket, Greeley felt hopeful and upbeat. Former president Andrew Johnson came out publicly for Greeley and called him "an honest man, and above a bribe." Three thousand printers cheered him and sang "Hail to the Chief!" at Jones Wood Amusement Park in New York. But state elections in North Carolina produced a safe majority for the Republican Party. Hayes now thought Grant, not Greeley, would be reelected. Francis Lieber saw in the Greeley nomination only "presumptuous mediocrity and inanity" indicative of the "concubinage between Republicanism and Democracy." A Greeley victory, thought Lieber, would mean states' rights, financial ruin, more bloodshed, and federal assumption of the Confederate debt.[61]

The Republicans took the counter-offensive with a series of insulting pamphlets and cartoons aimed at Greeley. These accused Greeley of being a secessionist, a pacifist, a traitor, disloyal, cowardly, unqualified, erratic, favoring miscegenation, a friend of Tammany Hall, a supporter of the Ku Klux Klan, a Democrat, and a supporter of Free Love. Such labels and distortions found a ready audience in Republican, abolitionist, feminist, and racist circles where distrust of Greeley and Liberal Republicanism already ran high. The most famous and effective critic of Greeley was Thomas Nast, a young Bavarian cartoonist who had fought for freedom in Italy with Garibaldi and in his twenties become a regular contributor to *Harper's Weekly*. Nast satirized Andrew Johnson, Tammany Hall, the Tweed Ring, and now Greeley. "Two things elected me," Grant said later, "the sword of [General Phillip] Sheridan and the pencil of Thomas Nast." His cartoons showed the Sage of Chappaqua offering bail money to Jefferson Davis, cheering himself, trying to steal Grant's shoes, throwing mud on Grant, acting as the monkey of an organ grinder (Whitelaw Reid), whitewashing Tammany Hall, and clasping hands with John Wilkes Booth across Lincoln's grave.[62]

In early September, Greeley's campaign was still running strong. Throughout the month, he gave nearly two hundred speeches in New Jersey, Pennsylvania, Ohio, Kentucky, and Indiana. Greeley, one observer wrote, "travels about in his white coat like the Candidate in the worst old Roman days, soliciting votes for himself and playing humble to the multitude, a style never before exhibited by a Presidential aspirant." Charles Sumner was now praising him in public for his "amazing industry" and "rare intelligence" in defense of the "liberal cause." The poet Whittier told some African-American voters that either Grant or Greeley would do, but that Greeley had "nobly distinguished himself as the advocate of human rights irrespective of race or color." Greeley represented the "cause of freedom."[63] The Republicans were increasingly concerned about the editor's popularity.

Then, on September 4, the Credit Mobilier scandal rocked the nation. Charles A. Dana's *New York Sun* charged that the railroad company had bribed politicians with shares of stock in a massive profit-sharing scheme that went back a number of years. Reid picked up the story for the *Tribune*. For weeks, newspaper readers were mystified and scandalized by mounting evidence of corruption in high office. Vice President Schuyler Colfax, James A. Garfield, and James G. Blaine were all linked to the scandal. Blaine called Greeley a "slanderer." In 1868, Greeley had accused Erie Railroad officials of raking off profits from the company. But Greeley himself was linked to the scandal by an earlier stock purchase of the Northern Pacific Railroad, stock that some claimed Greeley received in return for his favorable coverage of the project in the paper.[64] The scandal, fueled no doubt by pre-election fever, may have hurt Greeley as much as it hurt Grant, who was linked to the scandal through his political friends.

As the election approached, Greeley's position worsened. In October, the abolitionists continued to hammer away at him for his lenient policy toward the South, his support for Democrats, and his talk of paying off the Confederate war debt. Andrew Johnson spoke on his behalf in Tennessee, assuring African-American voters that Greeley had "written and done more for you than all others combined." But Molly was now seriously ill with dropsy and water in her lungs, and Greeley spent most of late October at her bedside at the home of his close friend Alvin J. Johnson. The family physician and Ida kept a daily and nightly vigil. After a political rally near Chappaqua on October 12, Greeley effectively ceased to campaign any longer. His old friend and rival Seward died on October 10. His sister Esther was sick after helping the family out at Chappaqua. He wrote Nathan Meeker, Rebecca Whipple, and Margaret Allen that he did not think Molly would make it through the month. "My sky is darkened in many ways," he wrote, "my wife is going at last."[65] Molly died on October 30, and Greeley was devastated.

The election compounded personal grief with political disaster. Grant won handily, taking 55.6 percent of the popular vote to Greeley's 43.8 percent, or 3,597,132 votes to 2,834,079 votes nationwide. Voter participation was over seventy percent. Greeley won the border states and the South: Texas, Missouri, Kentucky, Tennessee, Georgia, and Maryland. Grant won the rest. No northern state, including his native New Hampshire, went for Greeley. The Republicans had the money, the party machinery, and the federal officeholders. The Liberal Republicans had an inept campaign machine and an exhausted candidate. Grant was a national hero, and Greeley an uncertain risk. Three-quarters of the abolitionists voted for Grant, and not enough southern whites or freedmen voted for Greeley. Women's suffrage supporters paid Greeley back for his earlier lack of support for their cause. "I had rather see Beelzebub President," wrote Elizabeth Cady Stanton, "than Greeley."[66]

At age sixty-one, Greeley was despondent and defeated. "We have been terribly beaten," he wrote a friend in New Hampshire, "I was the worst beaten man who ever ran for the high office. And I have been assailed so bitterly, that I hardly knew whether I was running for President or for the Penitentiary. In the darkest hour of my suffering my wife left me, none too soon, for she had suffered too deeply and too long. I laid her in the ground with hard, dry eyes. Well, I am used up." Greeley felt "beyond tears" now. When Josiah Grinnell visited Greeley in New York after the election, he was "shocked by his limp, bony hand, sunken eye, and wan expression. The voice was off-key, tremulous and low, and I ventured to express admiration for his speeches. . . . I hoped that he would soon find rest."[67]

By mid-November, Greeley felt the end was near. He began dictating his last thoughts on paper. "Truly ruined beyond hope," he wrote, "I desire before the night closes its jaws on me forever, to say that, though my seeking for president has placed me here, it is not the cause of my ruin."[68] He was politically and financially bankrupt. Others had stolen money from him. He had failed to provide for his family. Now he could not sleep, he was delirious, and his body and brain were feverish. On Tuesday, November 12, he stopped coming to his office. His family physician, Dr. Krackowitzer, recommended that he be moved to the asylum of Dr. George S. Choate, who lived near the Greeley farm in Chappaqua. He moved on Thursday, November 20. There, the editor took to his bed and waited for the end. On Wednesday, November 27, he began to fail rapidly. He slept poorly, gestured meaninglessly, and muttered things to himself. By Friday, he was nearly unconscious, suffering chills and fever, asking for water. He died on November 29 with his daughters and Whitelaw Reid at his bedside.

Charles Sumner and many others thought Greeley's presidential campaign had killed him. Others thought he was simply broken by Molly's death. We will never know. But we do know that Greeley, as a believing Universalist, accepted his fate. "God is the same everywhere," he wrote in 1856, and is "more merciful and benignant than I can imagine." His time had come, and he knew it. "We leave his praises," wrote his beloved *Tribune*, "to the poor whom he succored, to the lowly whom he lifted up, to the slave whose back he saved from the lash, to the oppressed whose wrongs he made his own."[69]

The incorruptible Greeley was, in the end, no match for the corruptible Grant. But the philosopher of the *Tribune* ran a hard campaign, largely on his own, and forced his former Republican Party to bury him. His defeat in 1872 was also the defeat of liberal republicanism, that movement toward universal freedom that animated his mind and spirit. Like the European immigrants from across the Atlantic who joined him in that movement, Horace Greeley wanted liberty and equality for all, and called it freedom. Even his opportunistic flirtation with the Democrats did not divert him from that dream.

11

Conclusion

Freedom's Champion

THE LEGACY

Horace Greeley's most famous legacy was probably his injunction to "Go West, Young Man!" Millions did, of course. Whether or not Greeley ever said these exact words, generations of school children recited or remembered them. Westward expansion in search of land and freedom constituted one of the major trends in American history. Greeley both articulated and reflected that trend. But he also fused European and American ideas of freedom into a single republican philosophy grounded in free labor and the right to rise or fall by dint of one's own hard work.

Horace Greeley's immediate legacy was an empty place at the table in American homes, especially where the *Tribune* was gospel. Widespread national sadness and grief followed his passing. His political defeat and death shocked the country. For decades he had served as the voice of the people, the conscience of republicanism, and the advocate of universal freedom. Now he was gone. Vice President Schuyler Colfax, his old friend, was "shocked" by the news of his death, but treasured twenty-five years of "earnest friendship and glorious leadership." His cousin, the poet John Greenleaf Whittier, called him "the educator of the people in liberty, temperance, integrity, and industry, uniformly taking the side of the poor, enslaved, or suffering of every color and nationality." Bayard Taylor was "shocked and stunned" by the editor's passing. "This sudden ending, after all the vile and cruel abuse poured upon him through the campaign," noted Taylor, "was really tragic." James Garfield also found Greeley's death "pathetically tragic."[1]

Elements of both comedy and tragedy abounded in Greeley's life. His tragic flaw, perhaps, was his principled conscience that compelled him to think independently and say what was on his mind at all times. His eccentric dress and mannerisms often made him seem slightly ridiculous. The *Atlantic Monthly* characterized his run for the presidency as "an uprising of office-seekers under the lead of an erratic, unstable, and ill-advised philanthropist." Abolitionist Lydia Child opined cruelly that "to die was the most fortunate thing that could have happened to him."[2] But carping critics had dogged Greeley throughout his famous life. Most Americans suffered a genuine loss and sadness at his death.

Many believed Horace Greeley to have a financial legacy too. Greeley often seemed like a banker, freely loaning money to strangers and con-men who came his way. But how much money was he really worth? Was Greeley a man of fortune as well as virtue? In his first 1857 will, Greeley had left nearly everything to Molly, including the farm at Chappaqua, and five thousand dollars to each of his two daughters, Ida and Gabrielle. His three sisters—Arminda Greeley, Esther Cleveland, and Margaret Bush—were to receive one thousand dollars apiece. His farm on the New York line in Erie County, Pennsylvania, would go to his spiritualist brother Barnes. Smaller amounts of money were earmarked for the Universalist church, his old friend O. A. Bowe, and two colleges—People's College (later Cornell University) and Universalist College (later St. Lawrence University). He seems to have made another will in September 1863. In 1871, Greeley redid his will, leaving most of his property to Ida and Gabrielle, including his book royalties. Molly would get Chappaqua and half of his *Tribune* shares, in addition to the two she already owned herself. Barnes would continue to use the farm during his lifetime, but it would then go to Ida.[3]

On November 9, 1872, following Molly's death, the despondent Greeley created a new will that gave all his property to Ida, "one half to be used at her own discretion in the education and support of her sister Gabrielle." He also bequeathed his gold watch, given him by the Typographical Union, to Gabrielle. When Thomas Rooker saw him at his office two days later, Greeley seemed distraught and unbalanced. Shortly afterwards, he apparently sold his six *Tribune* shares to Alvin Johnson for about thirty thousand dollars, intending that it go to his daughters. He also asked John R. Stuart, a Tarrytown friend, to sell the Chappaqua farm, and sold Johnson eighty acres of woodland in New York; a five-hundred-acre farm in Buckingham County, Virginia;

forty-five acres of land in Greeley, Colorado; and ten acres in Madison, Connecticut. Despite selling off his land and stocks, Greeley had little net worth except on paper as he approached the end.[4]

In December, Greeley's various wills were contested in court. Ida signed an agreement to support Gabrielle until she reached the age of twenty-one. An old Greeley family friend, "Auntie" Susan Lampson, testified at a hearing on December 18 that Greeley had signed yet another will on his deathbed. Dr. Choate, a nurse, Ida, and Whitelaw Reid were also there. Isaiah T. Williams, Greeley's attorney, who had witnessed the 1871 will, challenged the supposed last will and urged that it not be admitted in court. On December 30, the court summoned Alvin Johnson, Samuel Sinclair (publisher of the *Tribune*), and Samuel Wilkeson (former Washington correspondent of the paper) to testify regarding whether the 1871 or 1872 will should be probated. Wilkeson promptly wrote his friend Jay Cooke, the financier, that he had been subpoenaed and had to testify. He knew he would be asked about the value of Greeley's Northern Pacific Railroad stock because of its possible link to the Credit Mobilier scandal. Wilkeson suggested ten thousand dollars. Cooke said, "don't swear too hard about anything."[5]

Greeley's brother Barnes sought to acquire ownership of his farm, occupying some hundred acres in western Pennsylvania. Zaccheus Greeley had settled on the land in 1824 and improved it to the point where he had title to the land—originally 370 acres, of which he sold one hundred acres to his son. But Horace Greeley actually held the deed, established only in 1860, and subsidized his father and brother annually with cash donations. Barnes wanted the land for himself, rather than Ida. Once it became clear that very little money was actually involved, Barnes Greeley, Arminda Greeley, and Margaret Bush gave up all claims to the estate.

In February 1873, the matter came to court again. Isaiah Williams accused Whitelaw Reid of false allegations about the supposed deathbed will, which disinherited one of the daughters, and threatened to sue Reid. By now, Greeley's estate (bonds, stock shares, promissory notes, book royalties, and cash) was estimated at more than two hundred thousand dollars. Unfortunately, most were "doubtful assets," that is, money owed Greeley by others. Despite complications, the 1871 will was finally settled only on the morning of December 14, 1877. Most of Horace Greeley's estate ended up with Ida and Gabrielle—as he had intended. But after settling debts and expenses (Dr.

Choate's bill, the water taxes in Greeley, Colorado, etc.), the estate of $206,084.25 had become an estate of $2,589.28. "The assets of the deceased," concluded the Westchester County court, "are for the most part worthless."[6]

There was one bright spot, however. For years, Greeley had befriended Cornelius Vanderbilt, grandson of the Commodore, an epileptic gambler, and the black sheep of the family endlessly spending his inheritance. When the Commodore cut him off and banished him from his home, Greeley loaned him thousands of dollars. After the senior Vanderbilt died in 1877, Ida and Gabrielle received a check for sixty thousand dollars in payment for their father's considerable generosity.[7] For a time, attorneys for Ida and Gabrielle also tried to collect on notes held by their father for Nathan Meeker out in Colorado. But Meeker perished at the hands of the Utes, and the notes were forgiven.[8]

There were many monuments to Greeley's memory. The greatest monument, of course, is the *Tribune*, now the *Herald Tribune*, still an American's friend from home when traveling abroad. In early 1873, the Typographical Union met to plan a monument to him at Greenwood Cemetery in Brooklyn, where he was buried, to memorialize "the training of his hand, the grandeur of his brain and the largeness of his heart." The idea was to build a twelve-foot-high statue out of Maine granite. Five hundred people attended the unveiling on December 4, 1876. Bayard Taylor praised Greeley as a son of granite New Hampshire and observed that "his political course, from first to last, was determined by the operation of the same unchanging principles." In February 1874, the cornerstone for the new *Tribune* building in New York was laid.[9]

In 1888, Horace Greeley Post 577 of the Grand Army of the Republic, consisting mainly of printers, campaigned for a statue of the editor, sitting in a chair and holding a newspaper, to be erected in Manhattan's City Hall Park. Five thousand people attended the unveiling on May 30, 1894. Congressman Amos J. Cummings summed up Greeley's lifelong struggle for universal freedom: "A sincere republican, he had fought tyranny at every point. In the revolution of 1848 he had seen a second bow of promise to mankind. Italy, Hungary, France, Germany, downtrodden Ireland—the world itself—were to be redeemed. When monarchists triumphed and Kossuth, Garibaldi, Schurz, Meagher and other patriots were fugitives, his purse was always open to them."[10]

At Greeley's death, only two daughters remained of his and

Molly's seven children, five of whom died prematurely. In 1875, Ida married an attorney, Nicholas Smith of Kentucky, who opposed slavery and had freed his own slaves during the Civil War. They had three children, Nixola, Ida, and Horace. The elder Ida died in childbirth in 1888. Gabrielle married Frank M. Clendenin, rector of St. Peter's Church in the Bronx, in 1891 and bore four children, of whom only one, named Gabrielle, survived. Gabrielle the mother died in 1937 at the age of seventy-nine, seven years after her husband.

The tributes to Greeley persisted. In February 1911, an appreciative audience in New York celebrated the centennial of Greeley's birth with music and speeches. In August 1947, Vermont dedicated the Horace Greeley Memorial Highway from the New York state line through Poultney, East Poultney, and on to East Rutland. It remains a beautiful, if winding, tribute to one of Vermont's favorite sons. Fourteen years later, on February 3, 1961, the U.S. Postal Service issued a Horace Greeley postage stamp in its "Famous Americans" series. In Chappaqua, New York, there is a Greeley Avenue and a Horace Greeley High School. Greeley, Colorado, and its *Tribune* continue to reflect his memory. Many babies were named after Horace Greeley, including Hitler's finance minister Hjalmar Horace Greeley Schacht (1877–1970), as was the liberty ship *Horace Greeley*, launched in 1924.

Greeley once imagined ten thousand towns like Greeley, Colorado, dotting the American landscape. These bourgeois utopias would be incubators of freedom, islands of virtue in a republic always on the verge of corruption or tyranny. There were not ten thousand, but there were a number of towns named Greeley—in Colorado, Kansas, Missouri, Nebraska, Kentucky, South Carolina (Greeleyville), and Pennsylvania. Most have fewer than one thousand residents. There is also a Greeley Dam in Arizona and a Greeley Point in Wyoming.[11] Horace Greeley lives on in small-town America in a way he could never have imagined.

The ancient Greeks had a small statue called the *Silenus* that opened up, like a Russian *matrioshka* doll, to reveal yet another statue inside. The outer statue was but the appearance of an inner, hidden reality. The exterior human visage hid something divine, a virtue, inside. Perhaps that is ultimately Horace Greeley's legacy, that we all carry deep within ourselves the same republican virtue, a longing to explore and define the limits of human freedom and to protect that freedom, not only for ourselves, but for all.

HORACE GREELEY AND AMERICAN FREEDOM

Horace Greeley exemplified a struggle to define freedom in America before and after the Civil War as a universal good better than the liberty that tolerated slavery. Republican citizenship required liberty under the law if citizens were to be virtuous. But between about 1830 and 1870, the worldwide debate over slavery charged the words *liberty* and *freedom* with very different meanings. The Second American Revolution transformed the liberty of the revolutionary generation's struggle for independence from the tyranny of Great Britain into the freedom of all people in a world where slavery was largely abolished. Liberty under the law for white men of property gave way, if slowly, to freedom under the moral law for all men and women. Lincoln recognized this exquisitely when he spoke at Gettysburg of a nation "conceived in liberty" whose future would see a "new birth of freedom." He knew his audience and he knew his language.

Greeley was thus involved in a trans-Atlantic conversation about the meaning of freedom that included abolitionists, economists, politicians, journalists, and businessmen. The failed republican revolutionaries of 1830 and 1848 in Europe admired the American dream of a free society, and the American Civil War demonstrated the fragility of that dream. Corruption, tyranny, and anarchy always stalked the virtuous republic. Freedom was a fragile social construction that tried to balance the rights of all individuals against one another. Freedom was thus always in danger.

The word *republican* in these years also had radical connotations unknown to us today. Republicans were anti-slavery men who favored land reform, a free press, free labor, and free movement. Some drifted toward liberalism, others toward socialism, still others toward conservatism. But republicans belonged to a party of reform, of change, and of progress. They abhorred the status quo.

Horace Greeley may have looked like an apparition, a man of eccentric habits dressed in an old linen coat that made him look like a farmer who came into town for supplies. Inside lurked a prodigious intellect, with tremendous moral values, a photographic memory, and a true love of words. Greeley's apparently erratic changes of mood, behavior, and political stance masked a principled and consistent strategy of freedom. The Liberal Republican movement of which he was a part lasted from about 1848 to 1872, and overlapped with the

Democratic movement Greeley claimed to despise. Greeley's search for the definition and limits of American freedom was lifelong and transcended political parties. He was consistent and uncompromising in that search, even as he adjusted his tactics to fit an ever-changing political environment. "It is a lamentable spectacle," he wrote in the *Tribune* in 1867, "to see men whose best days of manly maturity and mental power were devoted to the cause of freedom departing from consistency in their old days, to the disheartening of those upon whom the better example of their early life might exert an inspiriting influence."[12]

Greeley's republican ideology was grounded in the freedom of individuals to improve their status in life, rather than simply protect their personal liberty and property. Freedom meant both improvement and reform of society. Greeley himself worked hard, lived a Spartan existence, avoided alcohol and tobacco, and was thrifty, but was generous to a fault to the poor, to charities, and to an army of would-be borrowers. He was an "instinctive Puritan" and a born reformer, an optimist and a moralist crusading against evil wherever he found it—slavery, capital punishment, polygamy, the oppression of women, land speculation, corruption, and censorship. He believed that the "struggle for Freedom" was merely part of the human struggle with "darkness and evil." He wanted to make the world a better place where all might be saved.[13]

Greeley was in a larger sense the father of American middle-class republican thinking about the nature of freedom. Born in small-town America, he combined the highly competitive life of an urban journalist with nostalgia for rural life and farming. His life at Chappaqua reveals an early suburbanite, a man who never actually went west, but moved out of the corrupt city, commuting daily from his home to his office. His family life was hardly a bourgeois utopia, but rather a dystopia of dying infants, lost money, long absences, constant illnesses, and a depressed and unstable wife. But his daughters idolized him as a kind and gentle man whose criticism of others stopped at the front door and would not enter the house. Greeley always imagined a better world for families other than his own.

Many compared Greeley to Benjamin Franklin. Franklin too began life as a printer, edited journals and newspapers, was a vegetarian, and loved pithy one-liners of the sort that fill *Poor Richard's Almanac*. He believed that God helped those who helped themselves, that industry, perseverance, and frugality brought success, that America was a land of free labor, that work was a virtue and laziness a vice, and that time was money. Unlike Greeley, though, Franklin owned slaves. Nevertheless, Greeley admired Franklin enormously. "I love and revere him," he wrote in 1871, "as a journeyman printer, who was frugal and didn't drink; a *parvenu* who rose from want to competence, from obscurity to fame, without losing his head; a statesman who did not crucify mankind with long-winded documents or speeches; a diplomatist who did not intrigue; a philosopher who never loved, and an office-holder who didn't steal."[14]

Horace Greeley grounded freedom in religion, as well as in law, land, and labor. Throughout his political life, the editor was an active Christian, a Universalist who believed that all—not an elite—could in the end be saved. "I believe God's truth is higher, wider, deeper, and longer than all our creeds," he wrote, "and includes what is best in each of them." Perhaps Greeley's religiosity enabled him to make tactical and political compromises in the name of a higher goal. The world was a moral universe that exhibited a constant struggle between good and evil. Christianity was a vital religion, but had no claim on exclusive truth. "My creed," he wrote, "is very thought. I think Jesus of Nazareth was sent by God to enlighten and save our race; but precisely what or who He was beyond this I do not know." Throughout his life, he maintained what he called his "cheerful faith" in an "All-Wise and All-Loving God" who sent Jesus of Nazareth to be his messenger on earth.[15] Many historians have ignored Greeley's religious side in favor of his journalism and his politics. Yet his Universalist religion of success underlay his ideas of freedom.

Greeley was not simply the quintessential Yankee, or a northern New Englander, but an American. He was, in many ways, a national liberal republican seeking union as well as freedom. But he was also a man of the world, drawing on international freedom movements to shape his vision of American freedom. European ideas and experiences informed Greeley's search for American freedom. Locke's ideas on land improvement guided his reform strategy. He devoured Thomas Carlyle's and Thomas Young's writings on land reform, Lord Brougham's "higher law" speeches against slavery, Charles Fourier's ruminations on harmony and association, and Mazzini's and Kossuth's oratory on republican government of, by, and for the people. He traveled to Europe twice himself, and welcomed the flood of German and Irish immigrants inundating the country. He favored independence for Ireland, Italy, Germany, and Poland. He sent Charles Dana and Margaret Fuller to Europe to cover the revolutions of 1848, and hired a number of radical Europeans to write for the *Tribune*—Karl Marx, Adam Gurowski, James Redpath, Henry Villard, and Carl Schurz. He realized that both 1848 and the American Civil War were part of a world-wide liberal republican struggle for freedom. "The struggle now raging in America," as New York congressman Roscoe Conkling put it in the spring of 1863, "is only the old battle for human rights transplanted from the Old World to the New."[16]

But freedom meant more than human rights, and Horace Greeley was an important and consistent, if not original, thinker regarding the nature of freedom. Through the *Tribune,* he became a friendly guest in the homes of small-town America. He spoke, and listened to, the language of ordinary people. His words reached across the land to anyone who would take the time to read them. He was an optimist of faith, vision, and morality who "wore no disguises." "The age needed him," wrote one contemporary after his death, "such as he was, and the age made him thus."[17] The age struggled to define and achieve an American freedom, and so did Horace Greeley.

In that sense, Greeley was a gatherer, transmitter, and reflector of ideas, a kind of switchboard operator for international republicanism. He picked up ideas wherever he found them—temperance, Anti-Masonry, pacifism, associationism, land reform, protectionism, antislavery, spiritualism, and political reform. He transmitted them to a broad reading public through his newspaper editorials, interviews, and opinions. And his own thinking and writing reflected the popular ideas and language of his day. He listened and learned before he thought and wrote. And he made the *Tribune* into one of the most influential and widely read newspapers of his age. Horace Greeley was in conversation with America.

In the end, Greeley's evolving definition of American freedom was grounded in association as much as the individual. Without hard work, money, and investment, individual liberty under the law meant little. Greeley's many associations enabled the combined efforts of many investors to produce more than they might have individually, whether at the *Tribune*, Red Bank, New Jersey, or Greeley, Colorado. These were bourgeois utopias open to hard-working shareholders who took advantage of the opportunity to rise above their class origins. Unlike Marx, Greeley believed in class harmony, not class conflict. Class origins were not a prison nor an excuse, but a springboard to success, and associations were corporations that paid dividends to their investors in proportion to their investment and their labor. True freedom, economic freedom from want and poverty, required association, not state intervention or simple legal protection.

Greeley's version of American freedom, then, incorporated responsibility more than license. Freedom meant the opportunity to improve oneself and society through social and economic labor and reform. The individual was responsible to the community. Freedom therefore carried with it the responsibility to improve society, not simply to better oneself. Freedom was an investment as well as a dividend. And freedom, like universal salvation, was open to all in equal measure. Freedom was central to the American dream of equal opportunity, and Horace Greeley was freedom's champion.

Notes

NOTES TO THE PREFACE

1. *Sun*, November 30, 1872. *New York Tribune* (hereafter *Tribune*), November 30, 1872. Citations are normally to the daily, not weekly or semi-weekly, edition of the newspaper.

2. On New York City in 1872, see especially Edwin G. Burrows and Mike Wallace, *Gotham: A History of New York City to 1898*, New York: Oxford University Press, 1999.

3. *New York Times*, November 30, 1872, 4, and December 2, 6.

4. *Tribune*, December 4, 1872, 1. *New York Times*, December 4, 1872. City Hall was a French Renaissance brownstone building constructed in 1811 on the site of an old African American burial ground for victims of the cholera of 1770. Greeley's body lay in state in the Governor's Room, next to a chair used by John Quincy Adams and a mahogany table used by George Washington.

5. The description of Greeley's funeral comes from the *Tribune*, December 5, 1872, and the *New York Times*, December 5, 1872, 4. See also Joseph Bucklin Bishop, *Notes and Anecdotes of Many Years*, New York: Scribner's, 1925, 43.

6. On Greeley's habits and general appearance, see especially James Parton, *Life of Horace Greeley*, New York: Mason Publishers, 1855, 421–33, and on his speaking, 331–2.

7. Beman Brockway, *Fifty Years in Journalism*, Watertown, NY: Daily Times Printing and Publishing House, 1891, 152, also 71–2 and 98–9.

8. James R. Gilmore. *Personal Recollections of Abraham Lincoln and the Civil War*, Boston: L. C. Page and Company, 1898, 205.

9. Glyndon G. Van Deusen, *William Henry Seward*, New York: Oxford University Press, 1967, 564. George Templeton Strong, *The Diary of George Templeton Strong, 1820–1875*, New York: Macmillan, 1952, Volume 4, 459.

10. Iver Bernstein, *The New York City Draft Riots: Their Significance for American Society and Politics in the Age of the Civil War*, New York: Oxford University Press, 1990, 169.

11. Brockway, *Fifty Years*, 30.

12. *Tribune*, December 9, 1872, 5.

13. Horace Greeley Papers, New York Public Library (hereafter HGP-NYPL), reel 3, 670.

14. *Tribune*, December 4, 1872, 4.

NOTES TO THE INTRODUCTION

1. Hannah Pitkin, "Are Freedom and Liberty Twins?" *Political Theory*, Volume 16 (November 1988), 523–52.

2. Orlando Patterson, *Freedom, Vol. 1: Freedom in the Making of Western Culture*, New York: Basic Books, 1991.

3. Christopher Hill, *Liberty against the Law*, London: Penguin Books, 1996, 273–97. See also David Underdown, *A Freeborn People: Politics and the Nation in Seventeenth-Century England*, Oxford: Clarendon Press, 1996, 132; and A. S. P. Woodhouse, ed., *Puritanism and Liberty*, London: Everyman Press, 1992, 73. On words and meanings, see J. C. D. Clark, *The Language of Liberty 1660–1832*, Cambridge: Cambridge University Press, 1994.

4. Mary Wollstonecraft, *A Vindication of the Rights of Women* (1792) (Carol Poston, ed.), New York and London: Norton, 1975, 37.

5. David Hackett Fisher, *Albion's Seed*, New York: Oxford University Press, 1989, 199–205, 410–18, 595–603, 777–82.

6. A. G. Roeber, *Palatines, Liberty and Property: German Lutherans in Colonial British America*, Baltimore: Johns Hopkins University Press, 1999, *passim*.

7. Thomas Pangle, *The Spirit of Modern Republicanism: The Moral Vision of the American Founders and the Philosophy of Locke*, Chicago: University of Chicago Press, 1988, 117.

8. Michael Kammen, *Spheres of Liberty: Changing Perspectives of Liberty in American Culture*, Madison: University of Wisconsin Press, 1986, 69–70.

9. Eric Foner, *The Story of American Freedom*, New York and London: Norton, 1998. Gordon S. Wood, *The Radicalism of the American Revolution*, New York: Knopf, 1992, 229–43. See also the more recent work by David Hackett Fischer, *Liberty and Freedom: A Visual History of America's Founding Ideas*, Oxford: Oxford University Press, 2005.

10. Guido de Ruggiero, *The History of European Liberalism*, Boston: Beacon Press, 1959, 352, 372. Isaiah Berlin, *Four Essays on Liberty*, Oxford: Oxford University Press, 1997.

11. Leonard Krieger, *The German Idea of Freedom: History of a Political Tradition*. Boston: Beacon Press, 1957. Paul M. Cohen, *Freedom's Moment: An Essay on the French Idea of Liberty from Rousseau to Foucault*, Chicago: University of Chicago Press, 1997, 2–4.

12. On Lincoln's use of classical oratory and political language in crafting the Gettysburg Address, see especially Gary Wills, *Lincoln at Gettysburg: The Words That Remade America*, New York: Simon and Schuster, 1992.

13. Bruce A. Kimball, *Orators and Philosophers: A History of the Idea of Liberal Education*, New York: Columbia University Teachers College Press, 1986, 161.

14. Lawrence M. Friedman, *A History of American Law*, New York: Simon and Schuster, 1985, second edition, 71–77. James Oakes, *Slavery and Freedom:*

An Interpretation of the Old South, New York: Vintage, 1991, 62–79. Emory M. Thomas, *The Confederate Nation: 1861–1865,* New York: Harper, 1979, 45–47, 58.

15. Amartya Sen, *Development as Freedom,* New York: Knopf, 1999, 36–38.

NOTES TO CHAPTER I

1. James Parton, *The Life of Horace Greeley, Editor of the New York Tribune,* New York: Mason Brothers, 1855, 29.

2. Peter Kolchin, *American Slavery, 1619–1877,* New York: Hill and Wang, 1993, 95.

3. John N. McClintock, *History of New Hampshire,* Boston: B. B. Russell, Cornhill, 1888, 532–3.

4. Horace Greeley pointed out that Londonderry, New Hampshire, purchased British broadcloth in 1820 but in 1841 paid seventy percent less for cloth made in nearby Lowell, Massachusetts, because of American protective tariffs. Horace Greeley, "Remarks on Free Trade," *Tribune,* May 1, 1841.

5. Donald R. Hickey, *The War of 1812: A Forgotten Conflict,* Urbana and Champaign: University of Illinois Press, 1989, 309.

6. Horace Greeley, *Recollections of a Busy Life,* New York: J. B. Ford and Co., 1868, 41.

7. Parton, *Greeley,* 33.

8. Lawrence Osborne, "The Little Professor Syndrome," *New York Times Magazine,* June 18, 2000.

9. Horace Greeley to Moses Cartland, April 14, 1845, HGP-LC, Box 1.

10. Greeley, *Recollections,* 46.

11. Gregory P. Lampe, *Frederick Douglass: Freedom's Voice 1818–1845,* East Lansing: Michigan State University Press, 1998, 9.

12. Caleb Bingham, *The Columbian Orator,* New York: Duyckinck, 1816 (18th edition), 65, 240–2, 293–4.

13. Horace Greeley, *What I Know about Farming,* New York: G. W. Carleton, 1871, 23.

14. Greeley, *Recollections,* 60.

15. J. Joslin, B. Frisbie, and F. Ruggles, *A History of the Town of Poultney, Vermont,* Poultney: Journal Printing Office, 1875, 46–50, 89–94, 214–8.

16. "There's something in that towhead," Bliss reportedly told his foreman, "as you'll find out before you're one week older." Parton, *Greeley,* 86.

17. On apprenticeships at this time, see W. J. Rorabaugh, *The Craft Apprentice,* New York: Oxford University Press, 1986, 79–80.

18. Horace Greeley, *Essays Designed to Elucidate the Science of Political Economy,* Philadelphia: Porter and Coates, 1869, 64, 168.

19. Horace Greeley to Moses A. Cartland, April 14, 1845, HGP-LC, Box 1.

20. James Moran, *Printing Presses: History and Development from the Fifteenth*

Century to Modern Times, Berkeley and Los Angeles: University of California Press, 1973, 47, 62, 83.

21. Rorabaugh, *Craft Apprentice,* 76–7.

22. Parton, *Greeley,* 97–8.

23. On the republican tradition in America, derived from Aristotle, Machiavelli, and James Harrington, see especially John G. A. Pocock, *The Machiavellian Moment: Florentine Political Thought and the Atlantic Republican Tradition,* Princeton: Princeton University Press, 1975, 506–52.

24. Parton, *Greeley,* 98.

25. Greeley, *Recollections,* 98–105.

26. Everett S. Stackpole, *History of New Hampshire,* New York: American Historical Society, 1916, Volume 4, 252.

27. James Rorabaugh, *The Alcoholic Republic: An American Tradition,* New York: Oxford University Press, 1979, 151, 181, 194–5.

28. Horace Greeley, *Alcoholic Liquors: Their Essential Nature and Necessary Effects on the Human Constitution,* New York: Brognard, 1849, 5. "Temperance and Law," *Tribune,* February 13, 1852. Gerrit Smith to Horace Greeley, March 17, 1852, HGP-NYPL.

29. On Anti-Masonry, see especially Paul Goodman, *Toward a Christian Republic: Antimasonry and the Great Transition, 1826–1836,* New York: Oxford University Press, 1988.

30. William P. Vaughn, *The Antimasonic Party in the United States, 1826–1843,* Lexington: University Press of Kentucky, 1983, 70. Goodman, *Christian Republic,* 120–46.

31. Amasa Walker, *An Oration Delivered at Stoughton, Mass., July 5, 1830,* Boston: J. Marsh and W. Souther, 1830, 24. Walker was a prosperous Boston shoe dealer, Congregationalist, moral reformer, and temperance and anti-slavery man.

32. *Eaton's Antimasonic Almanac for 1834,* Danville, Vermont, n.d., cited in Goodman, *Christian Republic,* 238, 315n.

33. Goodman, *Christian Republic,* 125–6.

34. William M. Cornell, *The Life and Public Career of Hon. Horace Greeley,* Boston: D. Lothrop & Co., n.d., 60.

35. Horace Greeley to Dick ?, November 19, 1829, HGP-LC, Box 1.

36. John Elmer Reed, *A History of Erie County, Pennsylvania,* Topeka, KS: Historical Publishing Co., 1925, Volume 1, 468.

37. Parton, *Greeley,* 109.

38. Whitney Cross, *The Burned-Over District,* Ithaca, NY: Cornell University Press, 1982, 18.

39. Clymer townspeople shared their recollections of Greeley with a reporter in the *New York Herald Tribune,* April 12, 1925. Judge O. C. Pratt of San Francisco, writing in 1886, remembered Greeley as a young printer who was

"the equal of any of the young men of his time. He was much more polished as a young man than in middle age, and much more polished as a middle-aged man than in his latter days." Although "cross when disturbed," Greeley "always had a noble heart." *Jamestown, New York Journal,* May 14, 1886.

40. Reed, *History of Erie County,* Volume 1, 406.

41. On Greeley's experiences in the context of American apprentices of the time, see Rorabaugh, *Craft Apprentice,* 81–2.

42. Greeley to Bowe, March 11, 1831, HGP-LC, Box 7. Greeley and Bowe corresponded for years afterwards. In 1856, Bowe was still running a country store in East Neifert, Vermont. "His health is still miserable, and he just lives," wrote Greeley to a friend. See Greeley to E. Winchester, May 1, 1856, HGP-NCHS.

43. Greeley to Bowe, April 31, 1831, HGP-LC, Box 7.

44. See Greeley's speech in Erie in 1872 in *Speeches of Horace Greeley,* n.p., 1872, 20.

45. Rorabaugh, *Craft Apprentice,* 83.

46. Parton, *Greeley,* 71, 75. Greeley, *Recollections,* 68–70.

47. Greeley, *Recollections,* 71–74.

48. On Universalism, see Ann Lee Bressler, *The Universalist Movement in America, 1770–1889,* Oxford: Oxford University Press, 2001; Cross, *Burned-Over District,* 323–4; Steven Mintz, *Moralists and Modernizers: America's Pre–Civil War Reformers,* Baltimore: Johns Hopkins University Press, 1995, 23.

49. Russell E. Miller. *The Larger Hope,* Boston: Unitarian-Universalist Association, 1979, Volume 1, 45–6.

50. Michael G. Kenny, *The Perfect Law of Liberty: Elias Smith and the Providential History of America,* Washington, DC: Smithsonian Institution Press, 1994, 17. On the "liberty clause," see Miller, *Larger Hope,* 46.

51. McClintock, *History of New Hampshire,* 527–8. Goodman, *Christian Republic,* 137–8.

52. Greeley, *Recollections,* 86. Horace Greeley to Moses Cortland, April 14, 1845, HGP-LC, Box 1, 5.

53. Greeley, *Recollections,* 103–4.

54. Greeley to O. A. Bowe, November 20, 1831, HGP-LC, Box 7.

55. Richard Eddy, *The Life of Thomas J. Sawyer, and of Caroline M. Sawyer,* Boston and Chicago: Universalist Publishing House, 1900, 295. The 1828 church was originally Dutch Reformed, then Grand Street Chapel, then the Second Universalist Society.

56. Eddy, *Sawyer,* 135.

57. Eddy, *Sawyer,* 232.

58. Eddy, *Sawyer,* 295.

59. Greeley to O. A. Bowe, from Amherst, New Hampshire, September 28, 1832, GLC, 880.

60. Greeley to Moses Cartland, April 14, 1845, HGP-LC, Box 1.

61. Anya Jabour, *Marriage in the Early Republic: Elizabeth and William Wirt and the Companionate Ideal,* Baltimore: Johns Hopkins University Press, 1998, 149–51.

62. Richard Kluger, *The Paper: The Life and Death of the New York Herald Tribune,* New York: Knopf, 1986, 26–7. Greeley, *Recollections,* 94.

63. George D. Lillibridge, *Beacon of Freedom: The Impact of American Democracy upon Great Britain, 1830–1870.* Philadelphia: University of Pennsylvania Press, 1954, 5.

NOTES TO CHAPTER 2

1. F. W. Taussig, *The Tariff History of the United States,* New York: G. P. Putnam's Sons, 1931, 16–24, 63–7.

2. Henry Mayer, *All on Fire: William Lloyd Garrison and the Abolition of Slavery,* New York: St. Martin's, 1998, 97.

3. Michael F. Holt, *The Rise and Fall of the American Whig Party: Jacksonian Politics and the Onset of the American Civil War,* New York: Oxford University Press, 1999, 27–32.

4. Daniel W. Howe, *The Political Culture of the American Whigs,* Chicago: University of Chicago Press, 1979, 78–9.

5. Merrill D. Peterson, *The Jeffersonian Image in the American Mind,* New York: Oxford University Press, 1960, 10, 37.

6. Howe, *Political Culture,* 225–37.

7. Greeley, *Recollections,* 111–2.

8. Whitelaw Reid, *Horace Greeley,* New York: Tribune, 1872, 7.

9. Beman Brockway, *Fifty Years of Journalism,* Watertown, NY: Daily Times Printing and Publishing House, 1891, 16.

10. Don Seitz, *The James Gordon Bennetts,* Indianapolis: Bobbs-Merrill, 1928, 36. Harvey Saalberg, "Bennett and Greeley, Professional Rivals, Had Much in Common," *Journalism Quarterly,* Volume 49, Number 3 (1972), 538–46, 550.

11. Henry Lothrop Stoddard, *Horace Greeley: Printer, Editor, Crusader,* New York: G. P. Putnam's, 1946, 37.

12. Frank E. Comparato, *Chronicles of Genius and Folly: R. Hoe & Company and the Printing Press as a Service to Democracy,* Culver City, CA: Labyrinthos, 1979, 60–1. Greeley did save his account books, only to lose them later in an 1845 fire at the *Tribune.* Greeley, *Recollections,* 97.

13. *New Yorker,* March 26, 1836.

14. *New Yorker,* May 7, 1836.

15. Greeley to B. F. Ransom, May 9, 1836, HGP-LC, Box 1.

16. *New Yorker,* June 18 and 25, 1836.

17. John Russell Young, *Men and Memories: Personal Reminiscences by John Russell Young*, New York and London: F. Tennyson Neely, 1902, Volume 1, 114–5.

18. Henry Clay to John Switzer, May 19, 1831, GLC, 3725.

19. John Greenleaf Whittier, letters to William Ellery Channing, March 24, 1836, and William Lloyd Garrison, April 12, 1834, in John B. Packard, ed., *The Letters of John Greenleaf Whittier*, Cambridge, MA: Harvard University Press, 1975 (hereafter cited as Whittier, *Letters*), Volume 1, 136–7, 144–5.

20. *New Yorker*, July 1834, as cited in Parton, *Greeley*, 162–3.

21. John Greenleaf Whittier, *The Complete Poetical Works of John Greenleaf Whittier*, Boston: Houghton Mifflin, 1892, 48–52.

22. Betty Fladeland, *Men and Brothers: Anglo-American Antislavery Cooperation*, Urbana: University of Illinois Press, 1972, 229. On the anti-slavery mobs, see Leonard L. Richards, *"Gentlemen of Property and Standing": Anti-Abolitionist Mobs in Jacksonian America*, Oxford: Oxford University Press, 1970, 65–71.

23. Mayer, *All on Fire*, 238.

24. Larry Ceplair, ed., *The Public Years of Sarah and Angelina Grimke: Selected Writings, 1835–1839*, New York: Knopf, 1989, 54.

25. Samuel Flagg Bemis, *John Quincy Adams and the Union*, New York: Knopf, 1956, 341–2, 360.

26. *New Yorker*, May 21, 1836. *Cincinnati Whig*, July 19 and 21, 1836; cited in Richards, *"Gentlemen of Property,"* 97.

27. Bernard K. Duffy and Halford R. Ryan, *American Orators before 1900: Critical Studies and Sources*, Westport, CT: Greenwood Press, 1987, 317.

28. William Harlan Hale, *Horace Greeley, Voice of the People*, New York: Harper, 1950, 32. Barbara Goldsmith, *Other Powers: The Age of Suffrage, Spiritualism, and the Scandalous Victoria Woodhull*, New York: Knopf, 1998, 56–8. On the genealogy of the Cheney family, see Charles Henry Cheney, *The Cheney Genealogy*, Boston: Charles Henry Pope, 1897, 279, 332.

29. Horace Greeley, *Recollections*, 103–5. For a more recent description of the Graham diet system, see Susan E. Cayleff, *"Wash and Be Healed": The Water Cure Movement and Women's Health*, Philadelphia: Temple University Press, 1987, 13.

30. On the Graham boarding houses, see Stephen Nussenbaum, *Sex, Diet, and Debility in Jacksonian America: Sylvester Graham and Health Reform*, Westport, CT: Greenwood Press, 1980, 142–4.

31. Logan Uriah Reavis, *A Representative Life of Horace Greeley*, New York: G. W. Carleton, 1872, 182–3.

32. Mary Polk, *The Way We Were*, Winston-Salem, NC: John F. Blair, 1962, 135–6. Polk's book is a history of Warrenton.

33. Greeley to Winchester, July 4, 1836, HGP-LC, Box 7.

34. Helen F. M. Leary and Maurice R. Stirewalt, *North Carolina Research"*

Genealogy and Local History, Raleigh: North Carolina Genealogical Society, 1980, 579.

35. Marriage bond of Horace Greeley, North Carolina State Archives, Raleigh, NC.

36. *New Yorker,* July 16, 1836.

37. Parton, *Greeley,* 166–7.

38. Roderick Nash, *Wilderness and the American Mind,* New Haven: Yale University Press, 1967, 65, 84.

39. Daniel A. Seager, in the Greeley, Colorado, *Tribune,* April 28, 1971, summarizing an earlier article on the incident in *The Trail,* Volume 14, Number 7 (December 1921). See also Richard Kluger, *The Paper: The Life and Death of the New York Herald Tribune,* New York: Knopf, 1986, 53.

40. Josiah B. Grinnell, *Men and Events of Forty Years,* Boston: D. Lothrop, 1891, 86–7, 220.

41. Michael F. Holt, *The Rise and Fall of the American Whig Party: Jacksonian Politics and the Onset of the Civil War,* New York: Oxford University Press, 1999, 63.

42. *New Yorker,* June 19 and September 10, 1836.

43. Stoddard, *Greeley,* 36.

44. *New Yorker,* April 22 and 27, June 3, 1837.

45. *New Yorker,* June 3 and August 19, 1837.

46. *New Yorker,* November 25, 1837. *New York Tribune,* February 2, March 9, July 19 and 21, 1843.

47. *New Yorker,* August 25, 1838.

48. Roy Marvin Robbins, "Horace Greeley: Land Reform and Unemployment, 1837–1862," *Agricultural History,* Volume 11 (1933), 18–41.

49. *New Yorker,* July 16, 1836; July 1 and 8, 1837.

50. *New Yorker,* November 27, 1837.

51. Holt, *Rise and Fall,* 74–8.

52. Thurlow Weed, *Autobiography,* Boston: Houghton Mifflin, 1884, Volume 1, 466. Kluger, *The Paper,* 42.

53. *New Yorker,* December 23, 1837; January 22, 1838.

54. Weed, *Autobiography,* Volume 2, 53–4. Also Greeley to S. Mears and B. F. Ransom, his friends in East Poultney, VT, January 14, 1838, HGP-LC, Box 1.

55. *Jeffersonian,* Volume 1, Number 1 (February 17, 1838).

56. Parton, *Greeley,* 174.

57. Greeley to O. A. Bowe, February 22, 1838, HGP-NYPL. Greeley to Bowe, March 1, 1838, HGP-LC, Box 7.

58. Greeley to Ransom, January 14, 1838, HGP-NYPL.

59. Don Seitz, *Horace Greeley, Founder of the Tribune,* Indianapolis: Bobbs-Merrill, 1926, 75.

60. Holt, *Rise and Fall*, 46.

61. *Jeffersonian*, March 31, 1838. *New Yorker*, March 24 and April 14, 1838.

62. Greeley to Ransom, August 16, 1838, HGP-LC, Box 1.

63. Greeley to Mary ("Mother"), June 22, 1838, HGP-NCHS.

64. Greeley to R. W. Griswold, March 18, 1839, HGP-LC, Box 1. Goldsmith, *Other Powers*, 56–8.

65. Greeley to Ransom, January 26, 1839, HGP-LC, Box 1.

66. Greeley to R. W. Griswold, March 18, 1839, HGP-LC, Box 1.

67. Greeley to Goldsmith Dennison, May 28, 1839, Weed Papers, URL. Greeley to Morgan Bates, May 30, 1839, Bancroft Library, UCB.

68. *New Yorker*, June 27, 1839. Seitz, *Greeley*, 63–4.

69. Greeley to O. A. Bowe, Herkimer, New York, September 8, 1839, HGP-NYPL.

70. Horace Greeley, "The Faded Stars," *Southern Literary Messenger*, Volume 6, Number 1 (January 1840), 49.

71. Horace Greeley, "Adolph Bruner," *The Lady's Book*, December 1839.

72. Kenneth Cmiel, *Democratic Eloquence: The Fight over Popular Speech in Nineteenth-Century America*, Berkeley: University of California Press, 1990, 60–2.

73. Stoddard, *Greeley*, 91.

74. Noah Webster, *An American Dictionary of the English Language*, New York: Converse, 1830, 359 (freedom), 495 (liberty), and 762 (slavery).

75. Webster, *Dictionary*, Springfield, MA: Merriam, 1870, 769 (liberty).

76. Greeley to Webster, December 25, 1837, and Webster to Greeley, December 26, 1837; cited in Stoddard, *Greeley*, 41–3.

77. *New Yorker*, June 2, 1841.

78. Greeley to Webster, March 30, 1843, Noah Webster Papers, NYPL.

79. "Good Manners in Jerusalem," *New York Times*, April 15, 1868.

80. Cmiel, *Democratic Eloquence*, 143–4.

81. Hans L. Trefousse, *Thaddeus Stevens: Nineteenth-Century Egalitarian*, Chapel Hill: University of North Carolina Press, 1997, 63. William Preston Vaughn, *The Antimasonic Party in the United States, 1826–1843*, Lexington: University Press of Kentucky, 1983, 112.

82. Greeley to Weed, May 10, 1839, HGP-LC, Box 7. Greeley to Bowe, November 25, 1839, HGP-NYPL.

83. *New Yorker*, December 7, 1839.

84. Greeley to Stevens, December 10, 1839, Thaddeus Stevens Papers, LC, 01/0276.

85. Greeley to Bowe, December 14, 1839, HGP-NYPL.

86. *Log Cabin*, Number 1, May 2, 1840. See also Greeley, *Recollections*, 129–35.

87. Seitz, *Greeley*, 81, 372. Parton, *Greeley*, 181–2.

88. Greeley to Weed, July 27, 1840, in Weed, *Autobiography*, Volume 2, 84–5. Greeley to Seward, August 8, 1840, HGP-NYPL.

89. *Log Cabin Song Book,* New York: Log Cabin Office, 1840.

90. Eddy, *Life of Thomas J. Sawyer,* 433–4.

91. *Log Cabin,* September 5, 1840.

92. *Log Cabin,* October 24 and 31, 1840.

93. On the campaign of 1840, see Holt, *Rise and Fall,* 112, and, in more detail, Robert G. Gunderson, *The Log Cabin Campaign,* Lexington: University Press of Kentucky, 1957. Also see Ronald P. Formisano, "The New Political History and the Election of 1840," *Journal of Interdisciplinary History,* Volume 23 (Spring 1993), 661–82, and Ronald Zboray and Mary Saracino, "Whig Women, Politics, and Culture in the Campaign of 1840: Three Perspectives from Massachusetts," *Journal of the Early Republic,* Volume 17 (Summer 1997), 277–315.

94. *Log Cabin,* November 9, 1840. *Cincinnati Daily Republican,* October 3, 1840, as cited in Gunderson, *Log Cabin Campaign,* 169.

95. Greeley to Bowe, December 22, 1840, HGP-NYPL, Box 1..

96. Horace Greeley, *Why I Am a Whig,* New York, 1840.

NOTES TO CHAPTER 3

1. See Josiah Bushnell Grinnell's description of New York in 1841 in Charles E. Payne, *Josiah Bushnell Grinnell,* Iowa City, IA: State Historical Society, 1938, 11–2.

2. Horace Greeley, "Thoughts for the Season," *New Yorker,* December 26, 1840.

3. Seitz, *James Gordon Bennetts,* 77. Robert E. Riegel, *Young America, 1830–1840,* Norman: University of Oklahoma Press, 1949, 410.

4. Seitz, *James Gordon Bennetts,* 61–2.

5. Greeley to Bowe, December 22, 1840, HGP-NYPL.

6. Greeley to Weed, January 27, 1841, in Weed, *Autobiography,* Volume 2, 91–2.

7. *New Yorker,* March 13, 1841.

8. Greeley, *Recollections,* 136–8. Reavis, *Greeley,* 15–6, 265. *Log Cabin,* April 10, 1841.

9. Meyer Berger, *The Story of the New York Times, 1851–1951,* New York: Simon and Schuster, 1951.

10. Kluger, *The Paper,* 46–9.

11. Robert Remini, *Henry Clay,* New York: Norton, 1992, 582, n.14. Donald A. Ritchie, *Press Gallery: Congress and the Washington Correspondents,* Cambridge, MA: Harvard University Press, 1991, 37–8.

12. Greeley to Griswold, July 10, 1841, HGP-LC, Box 1. Greeley to Bowe, August 21, 1841, HGP-LC, Box 7. *New Yorker,* September 4, 1841.

13. Weed to Webster, December 18, 1841, in Harold D. Moser, ed., *The Papers of Daniel Webster: Correspondence, Volume 5, 1840–1843,* London: Univer-

sity Press of New England, 1982, 175–6. Greeley to Weed, December 7, 1841, in Weed, *Autobiography*, Volume 1, 468–9.

14. Greeley to Weed, December 15, 1841, Weed Papers, URL. Greeley to Caleb Cushing, December 17 and 29, 1841, HGP-DUL. See also Claude Fuess, *The Life of Caleb Cushing*, New York: Harcourt, Brace and World, 1923, Volume 1, 337–9.

15. Greeley to C. C. Bristol, November 9, 1842, Weed Papers, URL. Greeley to Hubbell, November 16, 1842, WSHS.

16. Irving Wallace, *The Fabulous Showman: The Life and Times of P. T. Barnum*, New York: Knopf, 1959, 43–7, 64–6.

17. Reavis, *Greeley*, 81–2. Allan Nevins, ed., *The Diary of Philip Hone, 1828–1851*, New York: Dodd, Mead and Co., 1927, Volume 1, 726.

18. Bayard Taylor to Mary Agnew, January 29, 1848, in Bayard Taylor, *Life and Letters*, Boston: Houghton Mifflin, 1884, 115. Saalberg, "Bennett and Greeley, Professional Rivals," 538–46, 550. Stoddard, *Greeley*, 133–4. George H. Douglas, *The Golden Age of the Newspaper*, Westport, CT: Greenwood Press, 1999, 15.

19. Greeley to Bayard Taylor, October 11, 1847, in Taylor, *Life and Letters*, 103.

20. Louis Starr, *Bohemian Brigade: Civil War Newsmen in Action*, Madison: University of Wisconsin Press, 1987, 17. Clarence Darrow, *Story of My Life*, New York: Scribner's, 1932, 50.

21. William Roscoe Thayer, *John Hay*, Boston: Houghton Mifflin, 1908, 171–2. Ralph Ray Fahrney, *Horace Greeley and the Tribune in the Civil War*, New York: Da Capo Press, 1970 [c. 1936], 2, 4. On Greeley's Ciceronian rhetoric, see R. Timothy Metz, "Horace Greeley's Rhetoric as Seen in the Light of Cicero's," Master's thesis, Marquette University, 1965, 75.

22. Reid, *Horace Greeley*, 9–10.

23. Horace Greeley, *The Cooperage of the Tribune*, New York: Greeley and McElrath, 1843, 7.

24. *New York Tribune*, December 12, 1842. See also Kluger, *The Paper*, 56–7.

25. *New York Tribune*, December 15, 1842.

26. Greeley, *Recollections*, 157.

27. Greeley, *Recollections*, 145–7.

28. Jonathan Beecher, *Charles Fourier: The Visionary and His World*, Berkeley: University of California Press, 1986, 65, 213, 232, 242.

29. Albert Brisbane, *Albert Brisbane: A Mental Biography with Character Study*, New York: Burt Franklin, 1969 (originally Boston: Arena Pub. Co., 1893), 187. See also T. H. Pickett and F. De Rocher, eds., *Letters of the American Socialist Albert Brisbane to K. A. Varnhagen von Ense*, Heidelberg: Universitatsverlag, 1986, 10.

30. *New Yorker*, January 16, 1841.

31. William A. Linn, *Horace Greeley: Founder and Editor of the New York*

Tribune, New York: D. Appleton, 1903, 80, n.1. Weed, *Autobiography,* Volume 1, 468, Volume 2, 92–3. Weed believed that "Fourierism was among the plausible but fallacious theories the impractibility of which time explodes."

32. Greeley to Weed, February 19, 1842, in Stoddard, *Greeley,* 81.

33. Greeley to Weed, September 10, 1842, in Stoddard, *Greeley,* 87–8.

34. Brisbane to Greeley, 1842, HGP-LC, Box 1. *New York Tribune,* March 1, 1842.

35. Greeley, *Recollections,* 385, 396–400. Bressler, *Universalist Movement,* 305.

36. See Dana's address at the University of Michigan on January 21, 1895, on Brook Farm, quoted in James Harrison Wilson, *The Life of Charles A. Dana,* New York: Harper, 1907, 523–4.

37. Greeley, *Recollections,* 148–50. Stoddard, *Greeley,* 84.

38. Greeley to O. A. Bowe, March 30, 1842, HGP-NYPL.

39. R. W. Emerson to his wife Lydia, March 1, 1842, and to Margaret Fuller, same day, in Ralph L Rusk, ed., *The Letters of Ralph Waldo Emerson,* New York: Columbia University Press, 1939 (hereafter cited as Emerson, *Letters*), Volume 3, 18–9, 23.

40. Greeley to Emerson, May 26 and July 20, 1842, HL, bMS AM 1280, 1249–50.

41. Emerson to Fuller, in Emerson, *Letters,* Volume 3, 20.

42. Greeley to Francis Dana, July 4, 1842, from Watertown, MA, HGP-LC, Box 1. Amelia Russell, "Home Life of the Brook Farm Association," *Atlantic Monthly,* Volume 42 (1878), 458–66, 556–63, especially 556.

43. Stoddard, *Greeley,* 103.

44. Wilson, *Dana,* 40–2.

45. Parton, *Greeley,* 221–2. Reavis, *Greeley,* 75.

46. Greeley to Emerson, November 12 and December 26, 1842, HL, bMS AM 1280, 1251–2.

47. Greeley's motto in Albert Brisbane, *A Concise Explanation of the Doctrine of Association,* New York, J. S. Redfield, 1843, cover and title page.

48. Greeley to Rufus Griswold, February 22, 1843, HGP-LC, Box 1. Greeley to Noah Webster, March 30, 1843, in Stoddard, *Greeley,* 84–5. Greeley to C. G. Collins, April 1, 1843, HGP-NYPL.

49. Octavius Brooks Frothingham, *Memoir of William Henry Channing,* Boston: Houghton Mifflin, 1886, 186–97. *Tribune,* May 13, 1843.

50. On the Religious Union of Associationists, see the papers of James T. Fisher at the Massachusetts Historical Society. Fisher also served as treasurer of the North American Phalanx.

51. Greeley to Emerson, March 21 and May 16, 1843, HL, bMS AM 1280, 1253–4. Greeley to Rufus Griswold, April 6, 1843, HGP-BPL.

52. Stoddard, *Greeley,* 85. *New York Tribune,* April 6 and 13, May 2 and 6, 1843. Other officers of the Sylvania Association were Thomas W. Whitely,

President; J. D. Pierson, Vice President; J. T. S. Smith, Secretary; and A. J. McDonald, Collector. The offices were at 25 Pine Street in New York City.

53. *News Eagle,* Hawley, PA, October 10, 1979.

54. *Tribune,* September 5, 1843. Dolores Hayden, *Seven American Utopias: The Architecture of Communitarian Socialism, 1790–1975,* Cambridge, MA: Massachusetts Institute of Technology Press, 1977, 157–8.

55. Alice Felt Tyler, *Freedom's Ferment: Phases of American Social History to 1860,* Minneapolis: University of Minnesota Press, 1944, 217–9. Franklin Ellis, *History of Monmouth County, New Jersey,* Philadelphia: R. T. Peck and Co., 1885.

56. Seitz, *Greeley,* 120–2. George W. Cooke, *John Sullivan Dwight,* Hartford, CT: Transcendental Books, 1973, 29–30.

57. Seitz, *Greeley,* 128.

58. "Balance Sheet of the North American Phalanx," November 30, 1849, Fisher Papers, MHS.

59. Lydia Child to E. G. Loring, February 6, 1852, Lydia Child Papers, Schlesinger Library, Radcliffe College, A/C 536, 3. *Expose of the Condition and Progress of the North American Phalanx,* New York: Dewitt and Davenport, 1853, an April 2, 1853, response to Greeley's February 8 letter.

60. The "Annual Statement of the North American Phalanx" of January 1, 1854, showed assets and liabilities of some $98,000. A January 1855 statement showed $107,000 despite the fire. Fisher Papers, MHS.

61. Horace Greeley, "The Idea of Social Reform," *Universalist Quarterly,* Volume 2 (April 1845), 136–47.

62. J. S. Dwight to George Ripley, March 16, 1846, Dwight Papers, BPL, Ms. E.4.1 no. 60: "I had quite a talk with Greeley. He wrote upon the paper which I took with me: 'I give up all my stock which I [possess?], and will subscribe besides the first $100 I get which does not belong to someone else."

63. The *Tribune,* August 6 and November 20, 1846, started the debate by publishing another long article by Brisbane in defense of Fourier's ideas.

64. *Tribune,* March 12, 1847.

65. Horace Greeley, "Fourier and His Social System," in J. G. Adams, ed., *Our Day: A Gift for the Times,* Boston: B. B. Mussey, 1848, 128–46. See also Greeley's "Social Reform," in *Rose of Sharon,* Volume 9 (1848), 139–58; and Seitz, *Greeley,* 131–2.

66. Horace Greeley, *Industrial Association,* n.p., 1850, 8, 13, 16, 19, 22.

67. Greeley to Mary Cabet, May 24, 1853, Fisher Papers, MHS.

68. Greeley, *Recollections,* 171–8. Margaret Fuller, *Woman in the Nineteenth Century,* Boston: Roberts Brothers, 1875, x.

69. Greeley, *Recollections,* 178. Greeley to Sarah J. Hale, September 3, 1850, HGP-NYPL. Reavis, *Greeley,* 531.

70. Mary Kelley, ed., *The Portable Margaret Fuller,* New York: Penguin, 1994, 498–9. Elizabeth A. Bartlett, *Liberty, Equality, Sorority,* Brooklyn: Carlson

Publishers, 1994, 105. Perry Miller, *The American Transcendentalists: Their Prose and Poetry*, Garden City, NY: Doubleday Anchor, 1957, 103.

71. Greeley to O. A. Bowe, May 16, 1843, HGP-NYPL.

72. Greeley to Fuller, April 17, 1844, HL, bMS Am 1280.226 (3575).

73. Margaret Fuller to Little Brown, June 3, 1844, in Robert N. Hudspeth, ed., *Letters of Margaret Fuller*, Ithaca, NY: Cornell University Press, 1983–94 (hereafter cited as Fuller, *Letters*), Volume 3, 200–1. Fuller to Maria Rotch, September 25, 1844, in Fuller, *Letters*, Volume 3, 229–30.

74. Margaret to Richard Fuller, October 15, 1844, in Fuller, *Letters*, Volume 3, 235.

75. Julia Ward Howe, *Margaret Fuller (Marchesa Ossoli)*, Boston: Roberts Brothers, 1883, 131. Fuller, *Letters*, Volume 3, 250.

76. Fuller, *Woman in the Nineteenth Century*, 372. Seitz, *Greeley*, 331.

77. Parton, *Greeley*, 256, 258.

78. Fuller to Samuel G. Ward, December 29, 1844, in Fuller, *Letters*, Volume 3, 256.

79. Fuller to Mary Rotch, January 15, 1845, in Fuller, *Letters*, Volume 4, 210.

80. Greeley to Rufus Griswold, January 14, 1845, HGP-BPL. Greeley to Griswold, February 16, 1845, HGP-LC, Box 1. Fuller's letter of March 9, 1845, to Eugene F. Fuller, in Fuller, *Letters*, Volume 4, 213. Arthur Brown, *Margaret Fuller*, New York: Twayne, 1964, 132.

81. Fuller to James Nathan, July 22 and June 24, 1845, in Fuller, *Letters*, Volume 4, 120–2, 135.

82. Fuller to a friend, July 2, 1845, in Fuller, *Letters*, Volume 4, 128.

83. Fuller to Ellis and Louisa Loring, August 2, 1945, and to James F. Clarke, August 14, 1845, in Robert H. Hudspeth, ed., *"My House Is a Large Kingdom": Selected Letters of Margaret Fuller*, Ithaca, NY: Cornell University Press, 2001, 227–9 (from the Wellesley College Library and Massachusetts Historical Society, respectively).

84. Fuller, *Letters*, Volume 4, 177–80.

85. Fuller to Richard Fuller, February 13, 1846, in Fuller, *Letters*, Volume 4, 186–8. Greeley to Schuyler Colfax, February 28, 1846, HGP-NYPL.

86. Fuller to Greeley, March 20, 1846, and to James Nathan, April 25, 1846, in Fuller, *Letters*, 200, 205. Emerson to Carlyle, July 31, 1846, in *The Correspondence of Thomas Carlyle and Ralph Waldo Emerson 1834–1872*, Boston: Houghton Mifflin, 1883, Volume 2, 140.

87. Greeley to Griswold, July 22, 1846, HGP-BPL.

88. Nussenbaum, *Sex, Diet, and Debility in Jacksonian America*, 149–52. Joan D. Hedrick, *Harriet Beecher Stowe*, New York: Oxford University Press, 1994, 177–83. On the Brattleboro spas, see Harry Weiss and Howard R. Kemble, "The Forgotten Water Cures of Brattleboro, Vermont," *Vermont History*, Volume 37 (1969), 165–277.

89. See the article on the Wesselhoeft spa in the *New York Dispatch* of July 7, 1845, taken directly from the *Tribune*.

90. Greeley to Fuller, February 8 and July 29, 1847, in Stoddard, *Greeley*, 110–2.

91. Greeley to Fuller, September 14, 1847, in Stoddard, *Greeley*, 112–3.

92. Richard F. Teichgraeber, *Sublime Thoughts/Penny Wisdom: Situating Emerson and Thoreau in the American Market*, Baltimore: Johns Hopkins University Press, 1995, 200–11.

93. Greeley to Emerson, October 14 and December 10, 1845, and March 17, 1846, HL, bMS AM 1280, 1255–7.

94. Walter Harding, *The Days of Henry Thoreau: A Biography*, New York: Knopf, 1965, 142.

95. Henry David Thoreau, "Walking," in Miller, *American Transcendentalists*, 144.

96. Robert D. Richardson, *Henry Thoreau: A Life of the Mind*, Berkeley: University of California Press, 1986, 131.

97. Thoreau to Helen Thoreau, July 21, 1843, in Walter Harding and Carl Bode, eds., *The Correspondence of Henry David Thoreau*, Westport, CT: Greenwood Press, 1974, 128 (originally New York University Press, 1958; hereafter cited as Harding and Bode, *Thoreau*). Emerson's son, Edward, later remembered hearing Thoreau talk about his visit: "In this visit to New York he [Thoreau] became acquainted with Horace Greeley, who appreciated his work and showed himself always generous and helpful in bringing it to publication in various magazines, and getting him paid for it." Edward Waldo Emerson, *Henry Thoreau as Remembered by a Young Friend*, Boston: Houghton Mifflin, 1917, 13.

98. Harding and Bode, *Thoreau*, 133.

99. R. W. Emerson to William Emerson, December 3, 1844, in Emerson, *Letters*, Volume 3, 268. Channing made fun of Greeley in a letter to Thoreau dated March 5, 1845, in Harding and Bode, *Thoreau*, 162. One critic has noted that "in the long run, Greeley was probably the most valuable professional contact Thoreau ever made aside from Emerson." See Steven Fink, *Prophet in the Marketplace: Thoreau's Development as a Professional Writer*, Princeton: Princeton University Press, 1992, 93.

100. Dwight Thomas and David K. Jackson, *The Poe Log: A Documentary Life of Edgar Allan Poe, 1809–1849*, Boston, G. K. Hall, 1987, 581. Ralph Waldo Emerson, *Journals and Miscellaneous Notebooks*, Cambridge, MA: Harvard University Press, 1960–, Volume 9, 337.

101. Greeley to George R. Graham, summer 1846, in Rufus Griswold, *Passages from Correspondence*, Cambridge, MA: W. M. Griswold, 1898, 207.

102. Greeley to Rufus Griswold, August 25, 1846, HGP-BPL.

103. Greeley to Griswold, December 16, 1846, HGP-BPL.

104. Greeley to Thoreau, August 16, 1846, in Harding and Bode, *Thoreau,* 169–70. Greeley to Thoreau, September 30 and December 16, 1846, in Griswold, *Passages,* 212–3, 217. Greeley to Thoreau, February 5, 1847, in Harding and Bode, *Thoreau,* 173–4.

105. Greeley to Griswold, November 21, 1846, HGP-BPL.

106. Greeley to Emerson, January 26 and September 20, 1847, HL, bMS Am 1280, 1258–9. Thoreau to Greeley, March 31 and May 19, 1848, and Greeley to Thoreau, March 17, April 3, and April 17, 1848, in Harding and Bode, *Thoreau,* 217–9, 222–5. Thoreau to Greeley, May 19, 1848, HGP-BPL. Thoreau to Emerson, May 21, 1848, in Emerson, *Letters,* Volume 4, 83.

107. Harding, *Days of Henry Thoreau,* 213–4, 229. Greeley to Thoreau, May 25 and October 28, 1848, in Harding and Bode, *Thoreau,* 228–9, 231–2. Taylor's recollection appeared in the *Tribune,* August 28, 1875.

108. Teichgraeber, *Sublime Thoughts/Penny Wisdom,* 256–62. *Tribune,* April 2 and June 13, 1849. Harding and Bode, *Thoreau,* 276–84, 292–4, 300–1, 380.

109. Greeley to Emerson, July 27, August 7, and August 14, 1850, HL, bMS Am 1280, 1260–2. Harding and Bode, *Thoreau,* 323–5. Charles Sumner to Samuel Gridley Howe, July 30, 1850, in Beverly Wilson Palmer, ed., *The Selected Letters of Charles Sumner,* Boston: Northeastern University Press, 1990, Volume 1, 304.

110. Greeley to Thoreau, March 4 and April 30, 1856, in Harding and Bode, *Thoreau,* 411, 419, 422–3. Bradley P. Dean, "Horace Greeley and Henry Thoreau Exchange Letters on the 'Spontaneous Generation of Plants,'" *New England Quarterly,* Volume 66, Number 4 (1993), 630–6. Greeley to Thoreau, September 29, 1860, HGP-NYPL.

NOTES TO CHAPTER 4

1. Eric Foner, *The Story of American Freedom,* New York: Norton, 1998, 20–1.

2. John Locke, *Second Treatise of Government,* ed. C. B. Macpherson, Indianapolis: Hackett Publishing Company, 1980, 21, 26 (from Chapter 5, "Of Property").

3. Coy Cross, *Go West Young Man! Horace Greeley's Vision for America,* Albuquerque: University of New Mexico Press, 1995, 53–4.

4. Roy M. Robbins, *Our Landed Heritage: The Public Domain, 1776–1936,* Lincoln: University of Nebraska Press, 1962, 70–1.

5. Cross, *Burned-Over District,* 272.

6. Reeve Huston, *Land and Freedom: Rural Society, Popular Protest, and Party Politics in Antebellum New York,* New York: Oxford University Press, 2000, 204–5.

7. Thomas Carlyle, *Past and Present,* London: Chapman and Hall, 1894, 182–3, 187–9, 229, 245, 241–2.

8. Thomas Carlyle, *Sartor Resartus,* Boston, 1835, in *The Collected Works of Thomas Carlyle,* New York: Greystone Press, n.d., 27, 32, 38, 94, 128.

9. *Tribune,* May 12 and May 16, 1843.

10. Greeley to Thurlow Weed, May 14, 1843, Weed Papers, URL. Greeley to O. A. Bowe, May 16, 1843, HGP-NYPL.

11. Bruce Levine, *Half Slave and Half Free: The Roots of the Civil War,* New York: Hill and Wang, 1992, 159. Sean Wilentz, *Chants Democratic: New York City and the Rise of the American Working Class, 1788–1850,* New York: Oxford University Press, 1984, 336–7.

12. Helene Sara Zahler, *Eastern Workingmen and National Land Policy, 1829–1862,* New York: Columbia University Press, 1941, 36–7.

13. *Tribune,* January 23, 1846. See also John R. Commons, "Horace Greeley and the Working-Class Origins of the Republican Party," *Political Science Quarterly,* Volume 24 (1913), 481–2.

14. *Tribune,* September 6, 12, and 17, 1845. See also Charles W. McCurdy, *The Anti-Rent Era in New York Law and Politics, 1839–1865,* Chapel Hill: University of North Carolina Press, 2001, 168, 223–8.

15. Huston, *Land and Freedom,* 26, 138, 143.

16. *Weekly Tribune,* May 2, 1846; also *Weekly Tribune* of January 3, 1846, and the *Tribune* of February 11 and 18, 1846.

17. Greeley to Schuyler Colfax, February 28 and April 22, 1846, HGP-NYPL; also Huston, *Land and Freedom,* 173, 182–3.

18. *Tribune,* July 31, 1845; January 23 and June 5, 1846.

19. Greeley to Beman Brockway, November 19, 1847, HGP-LC, Box 1. Horace Greeley, *Hints toward Reforms,* New York: Harper and Brothers, 1850, 325. *Tribune,* March 25, 1850.

20. *Tribune,* February 18, March 7 and 13, 1854. Robbins, *Landed Heritage,* 169–82. Also *Tribune,* November 7, 1859, and January 21 and 26, 1860.

21. Henry Carey, *Essay on the Rate of Wages with an Examination of the Causes of the Differences in the Condition of the Labouring Population throughout the World,* Philadelphia: Carey, Lea, and Blanchard, 1835, 45, 59–60, 132, 179.

22. Henry Carey, *Principles of Political Economy,* Philadelphia: Carey, Lea, and Blanchard, 1837, 33, 37.

23. *Tribune,* April 29 and June 21, 1841.

24. *The American Laborer,* Volume 1, Number 1 (April 1842); Volume 1, Number 2 (May 1842), 47; Volume 1, Number 4 (August 1842); Volume 1, Number 6 (September 1842), 1; Volume 1, Number 9 (December 1842), 281; Volume 1, Number 12 (March 1843), 364.

25. Greeley, introduction to William Atkinson, *Principles of Political Economy,* New York: Greeley and McElrath, 1843, iii–xvi.

26. See Edward Kellogg, *A New Monetary System: The Only Means of Securing the Respective Rights of Labor and Property and of Protecting the Public from*

Financial Revulsions, New York: United States Book Company, 1861. Greeley supported Kellogg's ideas in the *Tribune* in 1843.

27. Greeley, *Hints toward Reforms,* 193.

28. George A. Tracy, *History of the Typographical Union,* New York: International Typographical Union, 1913, 109. *Hints toward Reforms,* 335–41. *Tribune,* January 17, 1850. Stoddard, *Greeley,* 134–5.

29. Greeley, "The Dishonor of Labor," November 7, 1853, in Julia Griffiths, ed., *Autographs for Freedom,* Auburn, NY: Alden, Beardsley, and Company, 1854, 194.

30. Greeley to Thomas Dixon, September 22, 1868, HGP-NYPL.

31. Daniel W. Howe, *The Political Culture of the American Whigs,* Chicago: University of Chicago Press, 1979, 39.

32. *Liberator,* January 29 and May 30, 1839. Henry Brougham, *Speeches of Henry Lord Brougham,* Philadelphia: Lea and Blanchard, 1841, Volume 1, 472 (speech of February 20, 1838). Maria Chapman to Elizabeth Pease, August 30, 1838, cited in Clare Taylor, *British and American Abolitionists: An Episode in Transatlantic Understanding,* Edinburgh: Edinburgh University Press, 1974, 66.

33. Louis Filler, *The Crusade against Slavery, 1830–1860,* New York: Harper and Row, 1960, 150.

34. Clare Midgely, *Women against Slavery: The British Campaigns, 1780–1870,* London: Routledge, 1992, 121–53. John McKivigan, *The War against Proslavery Religion: Abolitionism and the Northern Churches, 1830–1865,* Ithaca, NY: Cornell University Press, 1984, 148–9. Betty Fladeland, *Men and Brothers: Anglo-American Antislavery Cooperation,* Urbana: University of Illinois Press, 1972, 185. See also David Turley, *The Culture of English Antislavery, 1780–1860,* London: Routledge, 1991.

35. *New Yorker,* May 6, 1841, 121 (Volume 12, Number 5).

36. *Tribune,* June 10, 1841.

37. Linn, *Greeley,* 144.

38. Parton, *Greeley,* 214. Greeley to O. A. Bowe, April 12, 1843, HGP-LC, Box 7; and Greeley to Bowe, August 21, 1843, HGP-NYPL. David L. Smiley, *Lion of White Hall: The Life of Cassius M. Clay,* Madison: University of Wisconsin Press, 1962, 57.

39. George W. Clark, *The Liberty Minstrel,* New York: Leavitt and Alden, 1845, 58–9, 63–4, 68–9, 80–1, 87, 128–9, 166, 184 (an anti-slavery song book about the "wrongs of slavery, and the blessings of liberty," p. iv). Filler, *Crusade,* 185. Fladeland, *Men and Brothers,* 231.

40. Greeley, *Recollections,* 166.

41. Henry Clay to Epes Sargent, August 7, 1844, Sargent Papers, BPL, Mss. Acc. 361.

42. Greeley to Colfax, November 24, 1842, HGP-NYPL. Greeley to Levi

Hubbell, November 16, 1842, Horace Greeley Miscellany, SC2019, WSHS. Greeley to Solon Robinson, February 4, 1843, Weed Papers, URL.

43. Stoddard, *Greeley*, 77. Linn, *Greeley*, 119–20.

44. Horace Greeley, "The Grounds of Protection," February 10, 1843, in his *Recollections*, 528–53. Greeley, "Facts for Farmers and Mechanics, the Commercial Intercourse of the United States and Great Britain," New York: Greeley and McElrath, 1844; Greeley, "Protection and Free Trade: The Question Stated and Considered," New York: Greeley and McElrath, 1844. *Tribune*, July 2, 1844. Holt, *Rise and Fall*, 166. Godeck Gardwell [Greeley?], *Currency: The Evil and the Remedy*, fourth edition, n.p., 1844. Greeley to Nathan Appleton, August 17, 1844, Appleton Family Papers, MHS, Box 6, asking for statistics on cotton and woolen profits. Greeley, "The Tariff as It Is," New York: Greeley and McElrath, 1845.

45. Horace Greeley, "An Address before the Literary Societies of Hamilton College, July 23, 1844," New York: William H. Graham, 1844.

46. Philip E. Mackey, *Hanging in the Balance: The Anti–Capital Punishment Movement in New York State, 1776–1861*, New York: Garland Press, 1982, 113–4, 122–3, 192–3. *Tribune*, December 11, 1841, and January 8, 1842.

47. Greeley to Weed, May 14, 1846, Weed Papers, URL. *Tribune*, May 16, 1846; March 6, 1847; February 5, 1849.

48. Holt, *Rise and Fall*, 192, 204. *Tribune*, November 6 and 28, 1844.

49. *New Yorker*, October 8, 1836.

50. Holt, *Rise and Fall*, 169. *Tribune*, November 28, 1844, and January 25, 1845. Greeley to Molly Greeley, February 23, 1845, HGP-LC, Box 1.

51. *Tribune*, June 3 and 20, 1845. Greeley to O. A. Bowe, July 2, 1845, in Frederick E. Snow, "Unpublished Letters of Horace Greeley," *The Independent*, Volume 59, Number 2968 (October 19, 1905), 913–4.

52. *Tribune*, November 29, 1845. Greeley to Weed, January 22, 1846, NYHS. Greeley to Colfax, January 22 and April 22, 1846, HGP-NYPL.

53. "What Means This War?" *Tribune*, May 13, 1846. Kluger, *The Paper*, 63–4.

54. Charles Sumner, "Speech against the Mexican War," in *Orations and Speeches by Charles Sumner*, Boston: Ticknor, Reed, and Fields, 1850, Volume 2, 148. Glyndon G. Van Deusen, *Thurlow Weed: Wizard of the Lobby*, Boston: Little, Brown, 1947, 148–9. Harlan Hoyt Horner, *Lincoln and Greeley*, Urbana: University of Illinois Press, 1953, 72.

55. Seward to Greeley, October 12, 1846, HGP-NYPL. Greeley to Henry Clay, November 15, 1846, in James F. Hopkins, ed., *The Papers of Henry Clay*, Lexington: University Press of Kentucky, 1959–, Volume 10, 289–90. Clay to Greeley, June 23 and November 21, 1846, in Hopkins, ed., *Papers of Clay*, Volume 10, 273, 294. Clay to Greeley, November 21, 1846, Clay Papers Project, King Library, United Kingdom, cited in Remini, *Henry Clay*, 682.

56. Greeley to Seward, October 14, 1846, Weed Papers, URL. Charles Sumner to Salmon P. Chase, December 12, 1846, in Edward L. Pierce, ed., *Memoirs and Letters of Charles Sumner*, Boston: Roberts Brothers, 1877 (hereafter cited as Sumner, *Letters*), Volume 1, 180. J. R. Giddings to Greeley, December 24, 1846, Giddings Papers, LC, Volume 1. Sumner to Giddings, December 30, 1846, in Sumner, *Letters*, Volume 1, 183–4.

57. Greeley to Bristol, December 30, 1846, Bristol Papers, URL. Greeley to Weed, January 13, 1847, Weed Papers, URL, and NYHS.

58. *Tribune*, February 8 and 16, and March 9, 1847. Sumner to Giddings, January 20, 1847, in Sumner, *Letters*, Volume 1, 186–7.

59. Seward to Greeley, February 11, 1847, HL, bMS Am 1928 (12). Giddings's speech in Bernard K. Duffy and Halford R. Ryan, *American Orators before 1900: Critical Studies and Sources*, New York: Greenwood Press, 1987, 92. Greeley to Colfax, May 1, 1847, HGP-NYPL. Sumner to Giddings, May 24, 1847, in Sumner, *Letters*, Volume 1, 191.

60. *Tribune*, July 17 and 31, and September 3, 1847.

61. Greeley recalled his trips West in his *Recollections*, 242–7. David Anderson, "Horace Greeley on Michigan's Upper Peninsula," *Inland Seas*, Volume 17, Number 4 (1962), 301–6. O. M. Hyde to Greeley, June 1, 1846, enclosing thirty shares of Green Mountain–Lake Superior Co. mining stock at twenty-four cents per share, HGP-LC, Box 6. Robbins, *Public Lands*, 104. A. P. Swineford, *History and Review of the Copper, Iron, Silver, Slate and Other Material Interests of the South Shore of Lake Superior*, Marquette, MI: Mining Journal, 1876, 37.

62. Greeley to Weed, from Sault Ste. Marie and dated August 25, 1848, NYHS.

63. Robert S. Harper, *Lincoln and the Press*, New York: McGraw-Hill, 1951, 8. David Donald, *Lincoln*, New York: Simon and Schuster, 1995, 115. Mentor Williams, "Horace Greeley and the River and Harbor Convention, 1847," *Inland Seas*, Volume 3, Number 4 (1947), 223. Weed, *Autobiography*, Volume 2, 148.

64. Horace Greeley, "River and Harbour Improvements: The Chicago Convention, November 1847," *De Bow's Commercial Review*, Volume 4 (1847), 291–6.

65. Philip Hone, *The Diary of Philip Hone 1828–1851*, New York: Dodd, Mead and Co., 1927, Volume 2, 823. "I do not usually agree with the opinions of the *Tribune*," wrote Hone on January 11, 1848. "Mr. Greeley is a sensible man and means well, but he is apt to be wild, visionary, and abstracted in his notions about politics and the relative duties of social communities." *Diary*, Volume 2, 835.

66. *Weekly Tribune*, October 30, 1847. Greeley to Beman Brockway, November 13, 1847, in Brockway, *Fifty Years of Journalism*, 115–6. Clay to Greeley, November 22, 1847, in Hopkins, ed., *Papers of Clay*, Volume 10, 378–9.

67. *Tribune,* January 29, 1848. Greeley to Weed, January 31, 1848, NYHS. Holt, *Rise and Fall,* 300–1.

68. C. Peter Ripley, ed., *The Black Abolitionist Papers,* Chapel Hill: University of North Carolina Press, 1992, Volume 2, 76.

69. *Tribune,* January 29, 1848.

70. Theodore Parker, *The Collected Works,* Boston: American Unitarian Association, 1907–13, Volume 7, 211, 260.

71. *Tribune,* March 8, 1848. Greeley to H. S. Weld, March 5, 1848, GLC, 2467. *Tribune,* March 7, 10, 11, and 13, 1848, on the Clay visit to New York City. Greeley to Colfax, April 3, 1848, HGP-NYPL.

72. Greeley to Clay, May 29, 1848, Clay Papers, LC. Oliver Dyer, *Great Senators of the United States Forty Years Ago,* New York: R. Bonner's Sons, 1889, 81–2.

73. Greeley to Joshua Giddings, June 20, 1848, NYHS. *Weekly Tribune,* July 3, 1848.

74. Henry J. Blue, *The Free Soilers: Third Party Politics, 1848–1854,* Urbana: University of Illinois Press, 1973, 121, 293–6.

75. Greeley to Colfax, September 15, 1848, HGP-NYPL.

76. Greeley to Weed, September 22, 1848, NYHS. *Tribune,* September 23, 1848. Hone, *Diary,* September 29, 1848, 855; on the same day, Greeley came out for Taylor in the *Tribune.*

77. *Tribune,* September 29, 1848. Horace Greeley, *The American Conflict: A History of the Great Rebellion in the U.S.A., 1860–1864,* Hartford, CT: O. D. Case, 1864/1867, Volume 2, 199–200.

78. Holt, *Rise and Fall,* 368. Greeley to Thomas B. Stevenson, February 27, 1849, in Holt, *Rise and Fall,* 411. *Tribune,* November 10, 1848.

79. Robert G. Raybeck, *Free Soil: The Election of 1848,* Lexington: University Press of Kentucky, 1970, 309. Greeley to Colfax, November 30, 1848, HGP-NYPL.

80. Richard H. Sewell, *Ballots for Freedom: Antislavery Politics in the United States, 1837–1860,* New York: Oxford University Press, 1976, 216–7. *Tribune,* December 25, 1849; January 9, 1850; February 20, 1850.

81. Greeley to William H. Seward, November 11, 1854, in Weed, *Autobiography,* Volume 2, 150.

82. *Tribune,* November 1, 1848. Greeley, *Recollections,* 215.

83. Greeley to the electors of the Sixth Congressional District of New York, November 8, 1848, in Reavis, *Greeley,* 313–4.

84. Greeley to J. B. Wilcox, December 11, 1848. Linn, *Greeley,* 99–101.

85. *Tribune,* December 22, 1848. Horner, *Lincoln and Greeley,* 55–6. *Congressional Globe,* Volume 20, 108–9, 203, 229, 230, 271, 282, 283.

86. *Tribune,* January 19, 1849. Greeley to Rufus Griswold, January 21, 1849, Griswold Correspondence, BPL, 442.

87. *Congressional Globe,* Volume 20, 371.

88. Greeley to J. G. Brainard, Londonderry, NH, December 25, 1848, Grinnell College Archives. Sewell, *Ballots*, 266. *Congressional Globe*, Volume 20, 605.

89. *Congressional Globe*, Volume 20, 608–10.

90. Greeley to Mott, February 21, 1849, HGP-DUL. Greeley to E. G. Aymer, February 24, 1849, HGP-DUL. Greeley to Bowe, February 28, 1849, HGP-LC, Box 7.

91. Horner, *Lincoln and Greeley*, 51–2.

92. Greeley to John Dickey, a cousin, April 7, 1849, HGP-NCHS.

93. Edmund Tweedy to J. T. Fisher, July 13, 1849, Fisher Papers, MHS, P-412. Greeley to O. A. Bowe, July 25, 1849, HGP-LC, Box 7. Greeley to Colfax, August 2, 1849, Colfax Papers, URL. Greeley, *Recollections*, 428.

94. Greeley to Colfax, August 2, 1849, Colfax Papers, URL.

95. Ann Lee Bressler, *The Universalist Movement in America, 1770–1880*, New York: Oxford University Press, 2001, 77–80, 83–5, 97–125. Thomas J. Sawyer, "The Influence of Cerebral Organization on Religious Opinions and Belief," *American Phrenological Journal of Miscellany*, July 1840, 468–72. Sawyer believed that human problems resulted from bad cerebral organization. Man must develop the faculties of conscientiousness, benevolence, and veneration. See his "On the Abuse and Perversion of Certain Faculties in Religion," *American Phrenological Journal of Miscellany*, July 1841, 517–22.

96. Horace Greeley, "The Unfulfilled Mission of Christianity" (May 4, 1842), in Greeley, *Recollections*, 379–85, citation 382. Also see the *Rose of Sharon*, Volume 4 (1843), 50–8.

97. Horace Greeley, "The Ideal of a True Life," *Rose of Sharon*, Volume 3 (Boston, 1842), 107–12. Greeley to O. A. Bowe, August 21, 1843, HGP-NYPL, where he writes, "I mean to go to the Universalist Convention this year and get resolutions passed advocating my sort of anti-Slavery." Greeley to Bowe, September 24, 1843, HGP-LC, Box 7.

98. Horace Greeley, "Human Life," *Rose of Sharon*, Volume 5 (1844), 9–20. Greeley, "The Idea of a Social Reform," *Universalist Quarterly*, Volume 2 (April 1845), 136–47. Greeley, "Glimpses of a Better Life," *Rose of Sharon*, Volume 6 (1845), 150–60.

99. Greeley, "The Aims of Life," *Rose of Sharon*, Volume 7 (1846), 164–71. Greeley, "Hope for Humanity," *Rose of Sharon*, Volume 8 (1847), 247–63. Greeley, "Universalism and Rationality," *Universalist Miscellany*, Volume 5 (April 1848), 384–8.

100. Herbert Schneider and G. Lawton, *A Prophet and a Pilgrim, Being the Incredible Life of Thomas Lake Harris and Laurence Oliphant*, New York: Columbia University Press, 1942, 4–6.

101. William S. Bailey, "A Boy Who Knew Horace Greeley," New York Herald Tribune, April 12, 1925, Barker Library, Fredonia, New York.

102. For an informative biography of Edward Hubbell Chapin, see Sumner Ellis, *Life of Edwin H. Chapin*, Boston: Universalist Publishing House, 1883.

103. Ellis, *Chapin*, 50, from a poem written by Chapin in July 1837.

104. Slater Brown, *The Heyday of Spiritualism*, New York: Hawthorn Books, 1970, 98–124. Tyler, *Freedom's Ferment*, 81–2.

105. Brown, *Heyday of Spiritualism*, 49.

106. Tyler, *Freedom's Ferment*, 81–2. Goldsmith, *Other Powers*, 55–6. Linn, *Greeley*, 90–1. Cross, *Burned-Over District*, 346–7.

107. *Tribune*, January 18, 1850.

108. Bayard Taylor, *Life and Letters*, Boston: Houghton Mifflin, 1884, Volume 1, 195.

109. Greeley to Bowe, August 25, 1851, HGP-NYPL. Greeley to Emma Newhall, December 29, 1851, HGP-NYPL. Horace Greeley, "Spirit and Matter," *Rose of Sharon*, Volume 13 (1852), 131, 135, 139.

110. Greeley to Thomas L. Kane, October 7, 1852, HGP-NYPL. Horace Greeley, "Modern Spiritualism," *Putnam's Monthly*, January 1853, 59–64.

111. Reavis, *Greeley*, 536.

112. Greeley, *Recollections*, 239.

NOTES TO CHAPTER 5

1. Louis S. Gerteis, *Morality and Utility and American Antislavery Reform*, Chapel Hill: University of North Carolina Press, 1987, 62. Jonathan Sperber, *Rhineland Radicals: The Democratic Movement and the Revolution of 1848–1849*, Princeton: Princeton University Press, 1991, 491.

2. Russell B. Nye, *Society and Culture in America, 1830–1860*, New York: Harper and Row, 1972, 203–4. I. M. Leonard and R. D. Parmet, *American Nativism, 1830–1860*, New York: Van Nostrand, 1971, 32, 55, 124. Roger Daniels, *Coming to America: A History of Immigration and Ethnicity in American Life*, New York: HarperCollins, 1990.

3. T. J. Clark, *The Absolute Bourgeoisie: Artists and Politics in France, 1848–1851*, London: Thames and Hudson, 1973, 26, 83, 129. Matthew Josephson, *Victor Hugo: A Realistic Biography of the Great Romantic*, Garden City, NY: Doubleday Press, 1942, 281–3.

4. Maurice Alguhon, *Marianne into Battle: Republican Imagery and Symbolism in France, 1789–1880*, Cambridge: Cambridge University Press, 1981, 98.

5. David S. Reynolds, *European Revolutions and the American Literary Renaissance*, New Haven: Yale University Press, 1988, 11–2, 14–5, 49. Nye, *Society and Culture*, 14. J. B. Moore, ed., *The Works of James Buchanan*, Philadelphia: J. B. Lippincott, 1908–11 (hereafter cited as Buchanan, *Works*), Volume 8, 33–4.

Eugene N. Curtis, "American Opinion of the French Nineteenth-Century Rev-
olutions," *American Historical Review,* Volume 29 (January 1924), 255. Serge
Gavronsky, *The French Liberal Opposition and the American Civil War,* New York:
Humanities Press, 1968, 38–9. Mayer, *All on Fire,* 379.

6. *Tribune,* March 1, 6, 24, and 29, 1848.

7. Stackpole, *New Hampshire,* Volume 4, 200. Emory Holloway and Ralph
Adimari, eds., *New York Dissected by Walt Whitman,* New York: R. R. Wilson,
1936, 132. For full biographies of Dana, see James H. Wilson, *The Life of Charles
A. Dana,* New York: Harper, 1907, and the more recent Janet E. Steele, *The Sun
Shines for All: Journalism and Ideology in the Life of Charles A. Dana,* Syracuse,
NY: Syracuse University Press, 1993.

8. Wilson, *Dana,* 61–2.

9. *Tribune,* March 28, April 12, 15, and 17, 1848.

10. *Tribune,* July 13, 14, 22, and 26, 1848.

11. Charles J. Rosebault, *When Dana Was the Sun,* New York: McBride, 1931,
43. Wilson, *Dana,* 80–2. Steele, *Sun Shines,* 8.

12. *Tribune,* October 10, 1848. Wilson, *Dana,* 81.

13. Wilson, *Dana,* 89–91, 94–6. *Tribune,* October 9, 1848.

14. Wilson, *Dana,* 159. Parton as quoted in Steele, *Sun Shines,* 29. Kluger,
The Paper, 72.

15. On German concepts of liberty and freedom, see especially Leonard
Krieger, *The German Idea of Freedom,* Boston: Beacon Press, 1957.

16. Gustav Koerner, *Memoirs of Gustav Koerner,* Cedar Rapids, IA: Torch
Press, 1909, Volume 1, 534–9. Carl Wittke, *Against the Current: The Life of
Karl Heinzen,* Chicago: University of Chicago Press, 1945, 46, 167. William H.
Goetzmann, ed., *The American Hegelians: An Episode in the Intellectual History of
Western America,* New York: Knopf, 1973, 162.

17. Stanley Nadel, *Little Germany: Ethnicity, Religion, and Class in New York
City, 1845–1880,* Urbana: University of Illinois Press, 1990, 22, 32.

18. *New York Staats-Zeitung,* January 26 and February 9, 1850. Karl Marx
and Friedrich Engels, *The Communist Manifesto,* Arlington Heights, IL: Harlan
Davidson, 1955, 32.

19. Karl Marx and Friedrich Engels, *Collected Works,* New York: International Publishers, 1982, Volume 6, 463–4.

20. George A. Stevens, *New York Typographical Union Number 6: Study of a
Modern Trade Union and its Predecessors,* Albany, NY: J. B. Lyon, 1912, 205–6,
620–1.

21. Stevens, *Typographical Union,* 219–20, 224–5, 637–8. Greeley, *Hints
toward Reforms.* Greeley wrote in 1853 that strikes were "seldom necessary," a
"waste of time," and productive of "social anarchy." Mutual agreement on fair
wages was better than class conflict. See the *Tribune,* April 13, 1853.

22. Carl F. Wittke, *The Utopian Communist: A Biography of Wilhelm Weitling,*

Nineteenth-Century Reformer, Baton Rouge: Louisiana State University Press, 1950, 193–4. Stevens, *Typographical Union,* 623.

23. Dana to Marx, July 15, 1850, in Morton Borden, "Five Letters of Charles A. Dana to Karl Marx," *Journalism Quarterly,* Volume 36 (Summer 1959), 315. Marx to Wedemeyer, August 2, 1851, in Marx and Engels, *Collected Works,* Volume 38, 403.

24. Marx to Engels, August 8, 1851, and Engels to Marx, August 10, 1851, in Marx and Engels, *Collected Works,* Volume 38, 409 and 419.

25. Engels to Marx, August 21 and 27, 1851; Marx to Engels, August 25, September 13, and October 13, 1851, in Marx and Engels, *Collected Works,* Volume 38, 434, 436, 445, 457, and 475.

26. Engels's articles appeared under Marx's name in the *Tribune* of October 25 and 28, and November 6, 7, 12, and 28, 1851.

27. Engels to Marx, December 3, 1851, and Engels to Jenny Marx, December 18, 1851; Marx to Weydemeyer, December 19, 1851, in Marx and Engels, *Collected Works,* Volume 38, 506, 518, 519. Karl Obermann, *Joseph Weydemeyer, Pioneer of American Socialism,* New York: International Publishers, 1947, 246. *Tribune,* February 27 and March 18, 1852.

28. Dana to Marx, April 20, 1852, in Borden, "Five Letters," 315. Marx to Engels, August 5, 1852, and January 21 and December 14, 1853, in Marx and Engels, *Collected Works,* Volume 39, 145–6, 272–3, 404. Also Marx to Engels, January 29, 1853, in Nelly Rumyantseva, "Karl Marx, Correspondent for the *New York Tribune,*" *Soviet Life,* Number 318 (March 1983), 30.

29. *Tribune,* April 7, 1853. Marx to Engels, June 14, 1853, April 22, 1854, and December 12, 1855, in Marx and Engels, *Collected Works,* Volume 39, 346, 439, 560–1.

30. A. E. Zucker, *The Forty-Eighters: Political Refugees of the German Revolution of 1848,* New York: Russell and Russell, 1950, 166. Engels, "The Real Issue in Turkey," in the *Tribune,* April 12, 1853.

31. *Tribune,* February 8, 1853.

32. Joseph Mazzini, *The Duties of Man and Other Essays,* New York: Dutton, 1907, 78.

33. Joseph Rossi, *The Image of America in Mazzini's Writings,* Madison: University of Wisconsin Press, 1954, 135–6. Clara M. Lovett, *The Democratic Movement in Italy, 1830–1876,* Cambridge, MA: Harvard University Press, 1982, 30–4. E. E. Hales, *Mazzini and the Secret Societies: The Making of a Myth,* New York: Kennedy Press, 1956, 77, 113.

34. Gunther F. Eyck, "Mazzini's Young Europe," *Journal of Central European Affairs,* Volume 17, Number 4 (January 1958), 358, 361, 363, 372. Hales, *Mazzini,* 138–9. Roland Sarti, *Mazzini: A Life for the Religion of Politics,* Westport, CT: Praeger Press, 1997, 57, 109. Rossi, *Image,* 7. Dennis Mack Smith, *Mazzini,* New Haven: Yale University Press, 1994, 15.

35. Smith, *Mazzini*, 24, 33–8, 52–3. Sarti, *Mazzini*, 115–6. Rossi, *Image*, 19–24. On Linton, see especially F. B. Smith, *Radical Artisan: William Jones Linton, 1812–1897*, Manchester: Manchester University Press, 1973, 67, 75.

36. Greeley to Emma Whiting, July 28, 1847, HGP-LC, Box 1. *Tribune*, January 1, 1848. Greeley to Fuller, January 27, 1848, in Stoddard, *Greeley*, 113–5.

37. Greeley to Fuller, April 4, 1848, in Fuller, *Letters*, Volume 5, 83. Stoddard, *Greeley*, 114–8.

38. Whittier to Greeley, August 21, 1849, HGP-LC. Also Whittier, *Letters*, Volume 2, 143–4. Greeley to Fuller, July 23, 1849, in Stoddard, *Greeley*, 119.

39. Emerson to Greeley, July 23, 1850, and August 5, 1850, in Emerson, *Letters*, Volume 4, 219, 225.

40. Greeley, note of May 1, 1852, HGP-NYPL, reel 3, 0515.

41. Gregory Claeys, "Mazzini, Kossuth, and British Radicalism, 1848–1854," *Journal of British Studies*, Volume 28, Number 3 (July 1989), 225–61.

42. Horace Greeley, "Italy," *Rose of Sharon*, Volume 15 (1854), 41, 48.

43. Daniel O'Connell in August 1843, in William Langer, *Political and Social Upheaval, 1832–1852*, New York: Harper, 1969, 242. On Irish emigration to the United States, see Thomas Keneally, *The Great Shame: And the Triumph of the Irish in the English-Speaking World*, New York: Nan A. Talese, 1999.

44. Letter from Greeley to Donald G. Mitchell around 1844, in Stoddard, *Greeley*, 89.

45. Hershel Parker, *Herman Melville: A Biography*, Baltimore: Johns Hopkins University Press, 1996, Volume 1, 299. Greeley's "Ode" was read on January 3, 1844, and later published in *The Penny Magazine*, Volume 1, Number 6 (August 1896). See also C. W. Everest, *The Memento: A Gift of Friendship*, New York: Wiley and Putnam, 1845, 56–8. *Tribune*, April 10, 1844. Letter of Greeley to William Cooney of the Young Friends of Ireland, March 23, 1845, in *Proceedings at the Unveiling of a Memorial to Horace Greeley at Chappaqua, New York, February 3, 1914*, Albany, NY, 1915, 150.

46. Keneally, *Great Shame*, 29. Greeley, in the *New York Courier and Express*, April 24, 1847. Roy M. Robbins, *Our Landed Heritage: The Public Domain, 1776–1936*, Princeton: Princeton University Press, 1942, 104.

47. Cormac O'Grada, *Black '47 and Beyond: The Great Irish Famine in History, Economy, and Memory*, Princeton: Princeton University Press, 1999, 114–7.

48. Ella Lonn, *Foreigners in the Union Army and Navy*, Baton Rouge: Louisiana State University Press, 1951, 202–3. Keneally, *Great Shame*, 152–3. John Belchem, "Nationalism, Republicanism, and Exile: Irish Emigrants and the Revolutions of 1848," *Past and Present*, Number 146 (February 1995), 112, 114.

49. John Campbell, *Theory of Equality; or, The Way to Make Every Man Act Honestly*, Philadelphia: Perry, 1848, 18, 29.

50. Reavis, *Greeley*, 84–5. Parton, *Greeley*, 283–4.

51. *Tribune,* September 4, 9, and 12, 1848.

52. Greeley to Weed, September 18, 1848, NYHS. *Tribune,* October 26 and 28, 1848.

53. *Tribune,* November 21, 1848. Greeley to Hamilton Fish, September 17, 1850, Hamilton Fish Papers, SUNY-SB. Keneally, *Great Shame,* 216–7, 248–53. Robert G. Athearn, *Thomas Francis Meagher. An Irish Revolutionary in America,* Boulder: University of Colorado Press, 1949, 28–9. Paul Jones, *The Irish Brigade,* Washington, DC: Robert B. Luce, Inc., 1969, 33–4.

54. Isser Wolloch, *Revolution and the Meanings of Freedom in the Nineteenth Century,* Stanford, CA: Stanford University Press, 1996, 167–8. *New York Times,* December 20, 1853, on the huge banquet for Mitchell at the Broadway Theater in New York. Both Meagher and Greeley spoke on Ireland's behalf.

55. Donald S. Spencer, *Louis Kossuth and Young America: A Study of Sectionalism and Foreign Policy, 1848–1852,* Columbia: University of Missouri Press, 1977, 25–7, 70.

56. Arthur J. May, *Contemporary American Opinion of the Mid-Century Revolutions in Central Europe,* Philadelphia: Westbrook Pub. Co., 1927, 48, 94.

57. Thomas Meagher to William O'Brien, November 29, 1849, in Athearn, *Meagher,* 35. Thomas Kabdebo, *Diplomat in Exile: Francis Pulszky's Political Activities in England, 1849–1860,* Boulder: University of Colorado Press, 1979, 34–5, 65–8. Ferencz (Francis) Pulszky was an attorney, Hungarian Diet representative, and Undersecretary of State in the Hungarian Republic, who served as Kossuth's emissary and secretary subsequently.

58. *Tribune,* August 4 and 27, 1849, and March 13, 1850. Greeley to Weed, May 27, 1850, NYHS.

59. Claeys, "Mazzini, Kossuth," 244–55. John H. Komlos, *Louis Kossuth in America, 1851–1852,* Buffalo, NY: East European Institute, 1973, 65.

60. Johann George Hulsemann to Daniel Webster, November 20, 1851, in *The Papers of Daniel Webster: Diplomatic Papers, Volume 2, 1850–52,* London: University Press of New England, 1987, 83–4.

61. Komlos, *Kossuth,* 78–80. Kabdebo, *Diplomat,* 78–9. Larry J. Reynolds, *European Revolutions and the American Literary Renaissance,* New Haven: Yale University Press, 1988, 151–61.

62. *Report of the Special Committee Appointed by the Common Council of the City of New York to Make Arrangements for the Reception of Governor Louis Kossuth,* New York: Common Council, 1852, 33, 63.

63. Anne-Marie Taylor, *Young Charles Sumner and the Legacy of the American Enlightenment, 1811–1851,* Amherst: University of Massachusetts Press, 2002, 89. Glyndon G. Van Deusen, *William Henry Seward,* New York: Oxford University Press, 1967, 140. Holt, *Rise and Fall,* 692–7. Charles Sumner, *Speech of the Honorable Charles Sumner of Massachusetts for Welcome to Louis Kossuth,* Wash-

ington, DC: Buell and Blanchard, 1851, 3, 6, 8. Sumner to John Bigelow, November 25, December 13 and 27, 1951, in John Bigelow, *Retrospections of an Active Life*, New York: Baker and Tyler Co., 1909, Volume 1, 122–3.

64. Greeley to William Otis Johnson, Lynn, Massachusetts, December 12, 1851, in the Edes Papers, MHS.

65. Roy P. Basler, ed., *Abraham Lincoln: Collected Works*, New Brunswick, NJ: Rutgers University Press, 1953–5 (hereafter cited as Lincoln, *Collected Works*), Volume 2, 62, 115–6, 118.

66. Komlos, *Kossuth*, 90–3. Anna J. Sanders, diary entry of December 6, 1851, in George N. Sanders Papers, LC, Box 1. Kossuth to Sanders, January 27, 1852, in George N. Sanders, *The Political Correspondence of the Late Hon. George N. Sanders*, New York: American Art Galleries, 1914, 92.

67. P. C. Headley, *The Life of Louis Kossuth*, Auburn, NY: Derby and Miller, 1852, vii, ix, x (Greeley's introduction). That same month, Henry W. De Puy echoed Greeley's sentiments in his *Kossuth and His Generals*, Buffalo, NY: Phinney, 1852, xviii, xix, xx, 361, 406. An even more popular book was *The Kossuth Offering and Family Souvenir: A Gift Book for All Seasons*, New York: Mark H. Newman & Co., 1852, 238.

68. Rossi, *Mazzini*, 136. Komlos, *Kossuth*, 119.

69. Komlos, *Kossuth*, 122–5. Spencer, *Kossuth*, 151. On Kossuth's New England speaking tour, see *Kossuth in New England*, Boston: J. P. Jewett, 1852.

70. Komlos, *Kossuth*, 131, 157–8, 162–3. Sanders had promised Kossuth he would purchase 144,000 old rifles from the War Department. See Rossi, *Mazzini*, 97; also Kossuth to Sanders, July 11, 13, 29, 1852, in Sanders, *Political Correspondence*, 94, 95.

71. Sanders, *Political Correspondence*, 97, 98, 102, 103, 109–13.

72. Kossuth to Greeley, July 30, 1863, HGP-NYPL, reel 2, 0441. Maria Weston Chapman to Mary Estlin, January 24, 1852, in Clare Taylor, *British and American Abolitionists: An Episode in Transatlantic Understanding*, Edinburgh: Edinburgh University Press, 1974, 327.

73. Jerzy Lukowski, *Liberty's Folly: The Polish-Lithuanian Commonwealth in the Eighteenth Century, 1697–1795*, London: Routledge, 1991, 11. Joan S. Skurnowicz, *Romantic Nationalism and Liberalism: Joachim Lelewel and the Polish National Idea*, Boulder, CO: East European Monographs, 1981, 99–100.

74. Skurnowicz, *Nationalism*, 81. Jerzy Lerski, *A Polish Chapter in Jacksonian America: The United States and the Polish Exiles of 1831*, Madison: University of Wisconsin Press, 1958, 25.

75. Charles Congdon, *Reminiscences of a Journalist*, Boston: James R. Osgood and Co., 1880, 237–8. Hale, *Greeley*, 187, 269–70. Henry G. Pearson, *The Life of John A. Andrew, Governor of Massachusetts, 1861–1865*, Boston: Houghton Mifflin, 1904, Volume 2, 25.

76. Adam Gurowski, *Russia as It Is*, New York: Appleton, 1854, ix–xii. The

best biography of Gurowski is L. H. Fischer, *Lincoln's Gadfly, Adam Gurowski*, Norman: University of Oklahoma Press, 1964. See also Andrzej Walicki, *Russia, Poland and Universal Regeneration: Studies in Russian and Polish Thought of the Romantic Epoch*, Notre Dame: Notre Dame University Press, 1991, 158–83.

77. Adam Gurowski, *La verite sur la Russie et sur la revolte des provinces polonaise*, Paris: Delaunay, 1834.

78. Adam Gurowski, *The Turkish Question*, New York: Taylor, 1854, 27. Gurowski's voluminous writings from this period include *La Civilisation et le Russie* (St. Petersburg, 1840), *Pensees sur l'avenir des Polonais* (Berlin, 1841), *Aus meinem Gedankenbuch* (Breslau, 1843), *Ein Tour durch Belgien* (Heidelberg, 1845), *Impressions et souvenirs* (Lausanne, 1846), *Die Letzte Ereignisse in den drei Theilen des Alten Polen* (Munich, 1846), and *Le Panslavisme* (Florence, 1848).

79. Florian Stasik, *Adam Gurowski, 1805–1866*, Warsaw: Panst. Wydaw. Naukowe, 1977, 210, 213–33. See the portrait of Gurowski in Julia Ward Howe, *Reminiscences, 1819–1899*, Boston: Houghton Mifflin, 1900, 220–7.

80. Fischer, *Lincoln's Gadfly*, 55–65. Norman Saul, *Distant Friends: The United States and Russia, 1763–1867*, Lawrence: University of Kansas Press, 1991, 179, 216, 233, 306. Marx to Engels, October 30, 1856, in Walicki, *Russia, Poland*, 174.

81. Gurowski obituary in the *Atlantic Monthly*, Volume 18 (November 1866), 631–2. Marx and Engels, *Collected Works*, Volume 39, 536–7.

82. Parker, *Collected Works*, Volume 14, 356, 478–9, n. 2.

83. Ivan Golovin, *Russia under the Autocrat Nicholas the First*, London: Henry Colburn, 1846, reprinted in New York in 1970 by Praeger publishers, 37, 80. John Glad, *Russia Abroad: Writers, History, Politics*, Tenafly, NJ: Hermitage and Birchbark Press, 1999, 80–1. Linguistically, Russian distinguishes between *svoboda*, the ability to act independently without restraint under the law, and *volia*, the moral power to act freely in fulfilling one's own desires or will without any restraint at all. Russian liberals talked of *svoboda*, while Russian peasants dreamed of *volia*. See V. I. Dal', ed., *Tolkovyi slovar' zhivogo velikorusskago yazyka*, Moscow: Russkii yazyk, 1978, Volume 1, 238–40, and Volume 4, 151–2.

84. P. V. Annenkov, *The Extraordinary Decade*, Ann Arbor: University of Michigan Press, 1968, 166–7. Alexander Herzen, *My Past and Thoughts*, trans. Constance Garnett, New York: Knopf, 1968, Volume 3, 1398. Sidney Monas, *The Third Section: Police and Society under Nicholas I*, Cambridge, MA: Harvard University Press, 1961, 236.

85. Gurowski, *Russia as It Is*, 37, 242–3, 248, 262, 270.

86. Adam Gurowski, *A Year of the War*, New York: D. Appleton and Co., 1855, 19, 62, 63, 109.

87. Ivan Golovin, *Zapiski Ivana Golovina*, Leipzig: Wolfgang Gerhard, 1859, 155–6, 160–1. Diary of Anna J. Sanders, George N. Sanders Papers, Library of

Congress, Box 1, entries for September 22, 27, and 29, 1855. *Tribune*, September 29, 1855. Golovin wrote a letter to the *Tribune*, published September 27, arguing that the "greatest enemy of freedom" was not the recently deceased Nicholas I, but Napoleon III of France. "Wars don't benefit freedom," he added. Sanders replied that Golovin was in the United States to "attack European republicans." He was really a "friend and supporter" of the Tsar.

88. Ivan Golovin, *Stars and Stripes, or American Impressions*, New York: Appleton and Co., 1856, 10, 273–4, 275, 309–10.

89. *Tribune*, March 2, 1850.

NOTES TO CHAPTER 6

1. Theodore Parker, "The Slave Power," May 29, 1850, a speech to the Boston branch of the New England Anti-slavery Convention, in Parker, *Collected Works*, Volume 11, 250.

2. *Tribune*, March 9, 1850. Greeley to Thaddeus Stevens, May 27, 1850, Papers of Thaddeus Stevens, LC, Box 1. Greeley to Thurlow Weed, May 27, 1850, Weed Papers, NYHS.

3. Henry Brougham, *Speeches of Lord Brougham*, Philadelphia: Lea and Blanchard, 1841, Volume 1, 427, 438. Gilbert M. Barnes, *The Antislavery Impulse, 1830–1844*, Gloucester, MA: Peter Smith, 1957 (1933), 29, 32. Janet H. Pease, "The Road to Higher Law," *New York History*, Volume 40 (April 1959), 385.

4. William Henry Seward, *An Autobiography from 1801 to 1834*, New York: Derby and Miller, 1891, 472.

5. Seward to Greeley, February 15, 1850, Griswold Papers, BPL, 950.

6. *Tribune*, March 12, 19, 1850. Van Deusen, *Seward*, 584, n. 11. Greeley to Colfax, HGP-NYPL, roll 3, 809.

7. Greeley, *Hints toward Reforms*, 8, 59, 64, 72, 80, 84. The critical comments on Greeley's book appeared in *Godey's Lady's Book*, Volume 41 (August 1850), 120. The *Southern Literary Messenger* called Greeley the "confident evangelist of a new Saturnian age," an abolitionist and a socialist whose "revolutionary and disorganizing measures" reflected the "social fever of Europe" in 1848 (Volume 17, Number 5 [May 1851], 257–80).

8. *Tribune*, July 23 and 27, 1850.

9. Greeley to Schuyler Colfax, December 26, 1850, HGP-NYPL, roll 3, 830–2.

10. Theodore Parker, "The Chief Sins of the People," sermon given April 10, 1851, in response to the arrest of Thomas Sims in Boston under the Fugitive Slave Law, in Parker, *Collected Works*, Volume 9, 6–8. William Hosmer, *The Higher Law, in its Relations to Civil Government: With Particular Reference to Slavery, and the Fugitive Slave Law*, New York: Derby and Miller, 1852 (reprinted by Greenwood Press, 1969).

11. Greeley to Colfax, December 26, 1850, and February 12, 1851, HGP-NYPL, reel 3, 831.

12. Greeley to Weed, February 26, 1851, NYHS. Greeley to Colfax, April 10, 1851, HGP-NYPL, reel 3, 837.

13. Horace Greeley, *Glances at Europe*, New York: Dewitt and Davenport, 1852, 19.

14. Alfred Plummer, *Bronterre: A Political Biography of Bronterre O'Brien, 1804–1864*, London: Allen and Unwin, 1971, 218–9. Greeley to Edward Riddle, May 29, 1851, Cutting Family Papers, MHS. Greeley, *Glances at Europe*, 83–6, 349. Greeley, *Recollections*, 268–75. Parton, *Greeley*, 348–53. Greeley, *The Crystal Palace and Its Lessons: A Lecture*, New York: Dewitt and Davenport, 1852.

15. On Greeley's European trip, see especially Parton, *Greeley*, 354–66.

16. On the peace congresses of 1848–1851, see Merle Curti, *The American Peace Crusade, 1815–1860*, Durham, NC: Duke University Press, 1929, 166–71.

17. Horace Greeley, "The Crystal Palace and Its Lessons" (November 1851), reprinted in *Hints towards Reforms*, 401–25. On George Peabody, see Franklin Parker, *George Peabody: A Biography*, Nashville, TN: Vanderbilt University Press, 1971; also Greeley to Peabody, August 24, 1852, and January 18, 1859, George Peabody Papers, Peabody Essex Museum (PEM), MSS 181, Box 193, F 3 and Box 195, F3. *Cleveland Plain Dealer*, June 11, 1851. *New York Herald*, May 24, 1851.

18. On American participation in the exhibit, and American attitudes toward it, see Robert F. Dalzell, Jr., *American Participation in the Great Exhibition of 1851*, Amherst, MA: Amherst College Press, 1960.

19. Horace Greeley, ed., *Art and Industry as Represented by the Exhibit at the Crystal Palace New York, 1853–1854*, New York: Redfield, 1853. Horace Greeley to Rebecca Whipple, July 21, 1853, HGP-LC, Box 1. A. H. Saxon, ed., *The Selected Letters of P. T. Barnum*, New York: Columbia University Press, 1995, 71–4. *Godey's Lady's Book*, Volume 48 (March 1854), 274.

20. Greeley, *Art and Industry*, 46.

21. James Fenimore Cooper to William Bradford Shubrich, July 22, 1850, in James F. Beard, ed., *James Fenimore Cooper: Letters and Journals*, Cambridge, MA: Harvard University Press, 1960–8, Volume 6, 208.

22. Greeley to G. P. Prindle, October 3, 1851, HGP-NHS. Greeley to Colfax, February 12, 1851, HGP-NYPL, reel 3, 834. Holt, *Rise and Fall*, 682.

23. Hale, *Greeley*, 145–6.

24. Leonard W. Levy, *The Law of the Commonwealth and Chief Justice Shaw*, New York: Oxford University Press, 1957, 90, 83, 107. On the Shadrach case, see Gary Collison, *Shadrach Minkins: From Fugitive Slave to Citizen*, Cambridge, MA: Harvard University Press, 1997. *Tribune*, November 6, 1851.

25. Stephan A. Myers to John Jay, in *The Black Abolitionist Papers, Volume 6*,

the United States, 1847–1858, Chapel Hill: University of North Carolina Press, 1991, 409.

26. Thomas S. Perry, ed., *The Life and Letters of Francis Lieber,* Boston: James R. Osgood, 1882, 90. On Lieber, see especially Frank Freidel, *Francis Lieber: Nineteenth-Century Liberal,* Baton Rouge: Louisiana State University Press, 1947.

27. Francis Lieber, *Stranger in America,* London: Bentley, 1835, Volume 1, 40–41, Volume 2, 189. Perry, *Life and Letters,* Volume 1, 187.

28. Francis Lieber, *Political Hermeneutics,* Boston: Little, Brown, 1837, 9–10. Francis Lieber, *Manual of Political Ethics,* Boston: Little, Brown, 1838, Volume 1, 205, 207, Volume 2, 2. Lieber's diary entry of August 18, 1837, in Perry, *Life and Letters,* 119–20.

29. Francis Lieber, "American and Gallican Liberty" (1849), in his *Miscellaneous Writings,* Philadelphia: Lippincott, 1880, Volume 2, 369–88. Francis Lieber, *On Civil Liberty and Self-Government,* Philadelphia: Lippincott, 1853, Volume 1, 34, 38, 48–50, 57, 68–84, 277, 304.

30. Greeley to Weed, December 1, 1851, NYHS. Greeley to Weed, December 20, 1851, in Weed, *Autobiography,* Volume 2, 197–8.

31. Horace Greeley, *Why I Am a Whig: Reply to an Inquiring Friend,* New York: Tribune, 1852.

32. Greeley to Colfax, January 20, 1852, HGP-NYPL, reel 3, 905. Greeley to Weed, April 18, 1852, in Weed, *Autobiography,* Volume 2, 216–7. Greeley to Seward, April 20, 1852, HGP-LC, Box 1.

33. Greeley to Pike, May 26 and 29, June 13, 1852, James S. Pike Papers, UMO.

34. Horace Greeley and Epes Sargent, *The Life and Public Services of Henry Clay,* New York: Saxton, Barker, & Co., 1852, 4. John C. Winston Company published another edition in Philadelphia.

35. Wilson, *Dana,* 116. William S. McFeeley, *Frederick Douglass,* New York: Simon and Schuster, 1991, 172–3. Linn, *Greeley,* 163.

36. Charles Sumner, *"Freedom National, Slavery Sectional": Senate Speech to Repeal the Fugitive Slave Bill,* Boston: Ticknor, Reed, and Fields, 1852, 14. The *Tribune* printed a summary of Sumner's speech on August 27, 1852. Eric Foner, *Free Soil, Free Labor, Free Men: The Ideology of the Republican Party before the Civil War,* New York: Oxford University Press, 1970, 76, 83. Louis Gerteis, *Morality and Utility in American Antislavery Reform,* Chapel Hill: University of North Carolina Press, 1987, 52, 55.

37. David Donald, *Charles Sumner and the Rights of Man,* New York: Knopf, 1970, 149, 234, 274.

38. Larry J. Reynolds, *European Revolutions and the American Literary Renaissance,* New Haven: Yale University Press, 1988, 139, 150. Larry Gara, *The Presidency of Franklin Pierce,* Lawrence: University Press of Kansas, 1990, 26–7, 35.

39. *Tribune*, September 11, 1852. Parton, *Greeley*, 376–7. Holt, *Rise and Fall*, 754–5.

40. Charles Sumner to William Seward and to Joshua Giddings, November 6, 1852, in Sumner, *Letters*, Volume 1, 373.

41. *Tribune*, November 30, 1852.

42. William Ellery Channing, *The Works of William Ellery Channing*, New York: B. Franklin, 1970, 615.

43. Greeley to Bayard Taylor, January 13, 1849, in Taylor, *Life and Letters*, 41. Of 100 shares in 1851, Greeley owned 25, McElrath 25, Snow 10, Strebeigh 10, Bayard Taylor 5, Charles Dana 5, Rooker 5, Samuel Sinclair 3, Hall 2, and George Ripley 1. James S. Pike, *First Blows of the Civil War: The Ten Years of Preliminary Conflict in the U.S. from 1850 to 1860*, New York: American News Co., 1879, 87–8.

44. Linn, *Greeley*, 69–70.

45. Greeley to Colfax, April 9, 1850, HGP-NYPL, roll 3, 812. Comparato, *Chronicles of Genius and Folly*, 263, 282.

46. Pike, *First Blows*, 41, 50. Jane Swisshelm to Horace Greeley, March 8, 1850, HGP-DUL. Greeley to Pike, April 24, 25, and 27, 1850, Pike Papers, UMO. Ritchie, *Press Gallery*, 43–6. On Samuel Sinclair, see *Centennial History of Chautauqua County*, Jamestown, NY: Chautauqua History Co., 1904, Volume 1, 350.

47. Greeley to William Davis Gallagher, March 6, 1851, HGP-URL.

48. *Tribune*, November 8, 1853. On corruption in these years, see Mark W. Summers, *The Plundering Generation: Corruption and the Crisis of the Union, 1849–1861*, New York: Oxford University Press, 1987, 138–50.

49. S. W. Jackman, ed., *Acton in America: The Journal of Sir John Acton, 1853*, Shepherdstown, England: Patmos Press, 1979, 7, 12, 24.

50. Greeley to R. Hoe and Co., August 18, 1853, in Comparato, *Chronicles of Genius and Folly*, 98.

51. F. G. Notehelfer, ed., *Japan through American Eyes: The Journal of Francis Hall, 1859–1866*, Princeton: Princeton University Press, 15–6. Taylor later collected his letters to the *Tribune* as *A Visit to India, China, and Japan in the Year 1853*, New York: G. P. Putnam, 1855.

52. *Tribune*, June 19, 1853. Linn, *Greeley*, 167–8. Bernard A. Weisberger, *Reporters for the Union*, Boston: Little, Brown, 1953, 49–50. See also Weisberger's "Horace Greeley: Reformer as Republican," *Civil War History*, Volume 23 (March 1977), 5–25.

53. Ritchie, *Press Gallery*, 48. Parton, *Greeley*, 385.

54. Emmett Crozier, *Yankee Reporters, 1861–5*, New York: Oxford University Press, 1956, 16–20.

55. Greeley to William Schouler, July 30, 1854, William Schouler Papers,

MHS. Schouler, a friend of Seward and editor of the Boston *Atlas,* had moved to Cincinnati to edit the *Gazette* there. Greeley to E. Winchester, January 29, 1855, HGP-NCHS. The story of the watch and chain is in Stoddard, *Greeley,* 135–6.

56. Greeley to James S. Pike, July 7, 1858, Pike Papers, UMO. Douglas, *Golden Age of the Newspaper,* 56–7

57. Greeley, *Recollections,* 293.

58. *Tribune,* January 5, 1854.

59. *Tribune,* January 5, 6, 10, and 30, February 2, 3, 13, and 17, March 15 and 28, May 12, 1854.

60. *Tribune,* January 11, 1854. Greeley, *Recollections,* 281–8.

61. Greeley to George N. Sanders, January 7, 1854, Simes Collection, HL. On Sanders, see William A. Tidwell, *April '65: Confederate Covert Action in the American Civil War,* Kent, OH: Kent State University Press, 1995, 18–37. Gunter Moltmann, *Atlantische Blokpolitik im 19 Jahrhundert: Die Vereinigten Staaten und der deutsche Liberalismus wahrend der Revolution von 1848/49,* Dusseldorf: Droste Verlag, 1973, 346–9.

62. Amos Ettinger, *The Mission to Spain of Pierre Soule, 1853–1855,* New Haven: Yale University Press, 1932, 315–20. Rossi, *Mazzini,* 91, 96. David Shengold, "From the Other Shore: Aleksandr Herzen on James Buchanan," *Slavic Review,* Volume 51, Number 4 (Winter 1992), 758. Herzen, *My Past and Thoughts,* 1164–9. William J. Linton, *Threescore and Ten Years, 1820 to 1890: Recollections,* New York: Scribner's, 1894, 111.

63. Hawthorne to Sanders, May 11, 1854, in Sanders, *Political Correspondence,* 73. Buchanan to Secretary of State Marcy, April 21, 1854, in Buchanan, *Works,* Volume 9, 186–7. Buchanan wrote Pierce on April 7, 1854, that Sanders was a "good and useful officer" who had influence with the "leaders of the revolutionary party from the different Nations of Europe now assembled in London." Buchanan, *Works,* Volume 9, 178.

64. Ettinger, *Soule,* 166, 178, 250–313.

65. Adam Gurowski, *The Turkish Question,* New York: Taylor, 1854, 3, 15. Greeley to Weed, May 28, 1854, Weed Papers, URL. Gurowski to Pike, June 8 and 14, July 30, and August 12, 1854, in Pike, *First Blows,* 253–4, 255–8.

66. *Tribune,* March 6, May 12, 18, and 24, 1854.

67. *Tribune,* May 18 and 24, 1854. E. B. Washburne to James S. Pike, May 24, 1854, in Pike, *First Blows,* 233.

68. Theodore Parker, "The Rights of Man in America," July 2, 1854, in Parker, *Collected Works,* Volume 12, 333–96.

69. Foner, *Free Soil,* 310.

70. *Tribune,* March 28, 1868.

71. Michael Holt, *The Political Crisis of the 1850s,* New York: Wiley, 1987, 258–9. Peterson, *Jeffersonian Image,* 198–201. James McPherson, *Battle Cry of*

Freedom, New York: Oxford University Press, 2003, 40, 240–3. Foner, *Free Soil,* 38, 46.

72. Tyler Anbinder, *Nativism and Slavery: The Northern Know Nothings and the Politics of the 1850s,* New York: Oxford University Press, 1992, 3, 104–6. Holt, *Political Crisis,* 177–9.

73. Greeley to Colfax, September 16, 1849, HGP-NYPL, roll 3, 804. Holt, *Rise and Fall,* 771. Greeley to Weed, August 8, 1853, in Weed, *Autobiography,* Volume 2, 220–1. Hans Trefousse, *The Radical Republicans: Lincoln's Vanguard for Racial Justice,* New York: Knopf, 1969, 85.

74. Hale, *Greeley,* 165. William E. Gienapp, *The Origins of the Republican Party, 1852–1856,* New York: Oxford University Press, 88.

75. D. Homer Batchelder to the *Exeter News-Letter,* August 19, 1857, in Hugh Gregg and Georgi Hippauf, *Birth of the Republican Party: A Summary of Historical Research on Amos Tuck and the Birthplace of the Republican Party at Exeter, New Hampshire,* Nashua: Resources of New Hampshire, 1995, 40–2. On the meeting of future Republicans, see Stackpole, *New Hampshire,* Volume 3, 155.

76. Greeley to Pike, February 24, 1854, Pike Papers, UMO. Gregg and Hippauf, *Birth,* 56–9. Bovay to Greeley, February 26, 1854, in Francis Curtis, *The Republican Party, a History, 1854–1904,* New York: G. P. Putnam's Sons, 1904, Volume 1, 177. Greeley to Bovay, March 7, 1854, in Seitz, *Greeley,* 156–7.

77. Emerson to Carlyle, March 11, 1854, in *Correspondence of Thomas Carlyle and Ralph Waldo Emerson,* Volume 2, 266.

78. Suzanne Schulze, *Horace Greeley: A Bio-Bibliography,* New York: Greenwood Press, 1992, 27.

79. *Tribune,* June 16 and 24, 1854.

80. George W. Patterson to Thurlow Weed, early summer 1854, in Weed, *Autobiography,* Volume 2, 225.

81. Zucker, *Forty-Eighters,* 125. Gienapp, *Republican Party,* 105–6. Greeley to Weed, August 10, 1854, Weed Papers, URL. Hale, *Greeley,* 165–6. Curtis, *Republican Party,* Volume 1, 205.

82. *Tribune,* August 2 and 9, 1854.

83. Parton, *Greeley,* 389–90.

84. Greeley to Seward, November 11, 1854, in Greeley, *Recollections,* 315–20, and Weed, *Autobiography,* Volume 2, 227–81.

85. Stoddard, *Greeley,* 174–5.

86. Van Deusen, *Greeley,* 203, 220.

NOTES TO CHAPTER 7

1. Greeley to George Peabody, October 14, 1854, George Peabody Papers, PEM, MSS 181, Box 193, F7. Claeys, "Mazzini, Kossuth," 254–5.

2. Greeley, *Recollections*, 341. Greeley described the whole episode in pages 332–44.

3. Greeley to Dana, July 12, 1855, HGP-DUL.

4. *Tribune*, April 12, 1855.

5. *Tribune*, September 28, 1855.

6. Greeley to Don Pratt, October 18, 1855, Weed Papers, URL. Greeley to Weed, October 23 and 24, 1855, Weed Papers, URL. Greeley to Marcus Spring, November 4, 1855, SUL. Greeley to Daniel Coit Gilman, November 1, 1855, Gilman Papers, Johns Hopkins University Library, Ms. 1, Box 1, 18, Box 4, 7.

7. Greeley to Dana, December 1, 1855, and January 8, 1856, in Joel Benton, ed., *Greeley on Lincoln, with Mr. Greeley's Letters to Charles A. Dana and a Lady Friend; to Which Are Added Reminiscences of Horace Greeley*, New York: Baker and Taylor, 1893, 87–9, 93–5. Greeley to Dana, January 8, 1856, HGP-NYPL. Greeley to Dana, January 10, 1856, in Benton, *Greeley on Lincoln*, 95–7.

8. Benton, *Greeley on Lincoln*, 100–1. Moncure Conway, *Autobiography, Memories and Experiences*, New York: Houghton Mifflin, 1904, Volume 1, 234–5. Hale, *Greeley*, 172.

9. Greeley to Dana, February 1, 1856, HGP-LC, Box 1. Greeley to Dana, February 3 and 6, 1856. Wilson, *Dana*, 145.

10. Greeley to Pike, February 15, 1856, Pike Papers, UMO. Greeley to Dana, February 27, 1856, Pike Papers, UMO.

11. Greeley to Dana, March 8, 1856, HGP-DUL, also in Benton, *Greeley on Lincoln*, 126–8. Greeley to Dana, April 7, 1856, in Benton, *Greeley on Lincoln*, 142.

12. Patrick W. Riddleberger, *George Washington Julian, Radical Republican: A Study in Nineteenth-Century Politics and Reform*, Indianapolis: Indiana Historical Bureau, 1966, 110–1.

13. Greeley to M. W. Tappan, April 18, 1856, NYHS. On April 27, Greeley again wrote Tappan that "I trust we shall not be divided in the coming struggle. If we do, defeat is inevitable." Greeley to Tappan, April 27, 1856, HGP-DUL.

14. Greeley to E. Winchester, May 1, 1856, HGP-NCHS.

15. Greeley to William M. Chace, S. W. Peckham, and W. Hayes, May 9, 1856, HGP-LC, Box 1.

16. Weed to Seward, May 11, 1856, Seward Papers, URL. Hamilton Fish to Weed, March 22, 1856, Weed Papers, URL.

17. Greeley to Colfax, May 21, 1856, HGP-NYPL, reel 3, 861. *Tribune*, June 6, 7, 11, and 12, 1856.

18. Greeley to Colfax, June 20, 1856, HGP-NYPL, reel 3, 870. Gienapp, *Republican Party*, 358–9, 365–7, and 372–3. Freidel, *Francis Lieber*, 289. Allen Nevins, *Fremont: Pathfinder of the West*, New York: Ungar, 1939, Volume 2, 437. Whittier, *Letters*, Volume 2, 301. Clifford E. Clark, Jr., *Henry Ward Beecher: Spokesman for a Middle-Class America*, Urbana: University of Illinois Press, 1978, 125.

19. Russell B. Nye, *Fettered Freedom*, East Lansing: Michigan State University Press, 1949, 20. Horace Greeley, *A History of the Struggle for Slavery Extension or Restriction in the United States, from the Declaration of Independence to the Present Day*, New York: Dix, Edwards, & Co., 1856. Jeter A. Isely, *Horace Greeley and the Republican Party, 1853–1861: A Study of the New York Tribune*, Princeton: Princeton University Press, 1947, 172. Andrew Rolle, *John Charles Fremont: Character as Destiny*, Norman: University of Oklahoma Press, 1991, 170–1. Greeley to Joshua Giddings, August 27, 1856, Joshua Giddings Papers, LC, Volume 3.

20. Holt, *Rise and Fall*, 976–8. Anon., *The Great Fraud upon the Public Credulity in the Organization of the Republican Party upon the Ruins of the "Whig Party," an Address to the Old-Line Whigs of the Union*, Washington, DC: Union Office, 1856, 9.

21. Greeley to Pike, September 21 and October 6, 1856, Pike Papers, UMO. *Tribune*, October 15, 1856. Rolle, *Fremont*, 174.

22. Greeley to Colfax, November 11, 1856, in O. J. Hollister, *Life of Schuyler Colfax*, New York: Funk and Wagnalls, 1886, 105.

23. Victor von Hagen, *The Germanic People in America*, Norman: University of Oklahoma Press, 1976, 300–2, 309. Zucker, *Forty-Eighters*, 100–1, 301–2. Carl Schurz, *The Reminiscences of Carl Schurz*, New York: Doubleday, 1908, Volume 2, 67, 72.

24. Carl Wittke, *Refugees of Revolution: The German Forty-Eighters in America*, Philadelphia: University of Pennsylvania Press, 1952, 246. Parker, "The Present Crisis in American Affairs," in *Collected Works*, Volume 12, 487.

25. Gunja Sen Gupta, *For God and Mammon: Evangelicals and Entrepreneurs, Masters and Slaves in Territorial Kansas, 1854–1860*, Athens: University of Georgia Press, 1996, 80. Mitford M. Matthews, *A Dictionary of Americanisms on Historical Principles*, Chicago: University of Chicago Press, 1951, Volume 1, 164.

26. Philip S. Foner, *Business and Slavery: The New York Merchants and the Irrepressible Conflict*, Chapel Hill: University of North Carolina Press, 1941, 97. Sen Gupta, *God and Mammon*, 155. *Tribune*, December 7, 1854.

27. Wilson, *Dana*, 148. Charles Robinson, *The Kansas Conflict*, Lawrence, KA: Journal Publishing Company, 1898, 124–6. See also the letter from Olmsted to Edward Everett Hale of October 23, 1855, in *The Papers of Frederick Law Olmsted, Volume 2: Slavery and the South, 1852–1857*, Baltimore: Johns Hopkins University Press, 1981, 368–72. Olmsted wrote Hale that Greeley had not yet done anything "in consequence of my request."

28. Wilson, *Dana*, 133, 137. Pike, *First Blows*, 301–2. Greeley to Dana, February 6 and 16, 1856, in Benton, *Greeley on Lincoln*, 111–7, 120–2.

29. James Redpath, *The Roving Editor*, New York: A. B. Burdick, 1859, 119. Weisberger, *Reporters for the Union*, 25–7.

30. Charles F. Horner, *The Life of James Redpath and the Development of the Modern Lyceum,* New York: Barse and Hopkins, 1926, 42.

31. Greeley to Dana, March 24, 1856, HGP-NYPL. Greeley to Dana, April 2, 1856, in Benton, *Greeley on Lincoln,* 138–42.

32. Barnet Baskerville, *The People's Voice: The Orator in American Society,* Lexington: University Press of Kentucky, 1979, 53–4, on Sumner's speech.

33. Greeley to Rebecca Whipple, June 8, 1856, HGP-LC, Box 1. Greeley, *History of the Struggle,* 2, 164. Alma Lutz, *Crusader for Freedom: Women of the Antislavery Movement,* Boston: Beacon Press, 1968, 261. Greeley to E. H. Hale, July 14 and 30, 1856, New England Emigrant Aid Company Papers, Kansas State Historical Society, MS 619. Sumner, *Letters,* Volume 4, 356.

34. *Tribune,* November 25, 1856.

35. *Dred Scott v. Sanford,* 60 U.S. (19 How.) 393, 400–54 (1857).

36. *Tribune,* March 5, 7, 10, 11, and 16, 1857.

37. Stoddard, *Greeley,* 154–5. Hale, *Greeley,* 157–8. Greeley to Augustus Allen, July 13, 1857, BL.

38. Comparato, *Chronicles of Genius and Folly,* 283. Greeley to Peter Cooper, September 1, 1857, Cooper-Hewitt Business Papers, LC, Box 15.

39. Greeley to E. E. Hale, March 11, July 14, July 30, and November 11, 1857, Emigrant Aid Company Papers, Kansas State Historical Society, Ms 619. Horner, *Redpath,* 91, 95–6.

40. David Shi and George B. Tindall, *America,* New York: Norton, 1989, 390–3.

41. *Tribune,* March 1, 1858.

42. Horace Greeley, "The Christian Spirit of Reform," a lecture given May 13–14, 1858, printed in Martin Thatcher and Orren Hutchinson, eds., *The Religious Aspects of the Age,* New York: Thatcher and Hutchinson, 1858, 54–67.

43. Chapin, in Thatcher and Hutchinson, *Religious Aspects,* 155.

44. *Christian Messenger,* July 6, 1850, 553–4.

45. Horace Greeley, "Life as It Shall Be," *Rose of Sharon,* Volume 12, 1851, 126–37. *Christian Messenger,* Volume 4, Number 1 (December 21, 1850), 110–1. Greeley to John Seville, of Morristown, NJ, April 25, 1853, HGP-NYPL.

46. Horace Greeley, "Growing Old," *Rose of Sharon,* Volume 14 (1853), 9–14. "Letter from Horace Greeley," in *Christian Messenger,* Volume 5 (February 17, 1855). Horace Greeley, "The Death of Children," *Rose of Sharon,* Volume 16 (1855), 65–70. Greeley to W. M. Smith, of Manlius, NY, January 20, 1856, in HGP-NCHS.

47. Horace Greeley, "The Basis of Character," *Rose of Sharon,* Volume 18 (1857), 65–73. Greeley to William H. Fish, December 8, 1857, "A.L.S. Horace Greeley," St. Lawrence University Archives. Eddy, *Sawyer,* 252.

48. Greeley to Colfax, December 21, 1850, HGP-NYPL, reel 3, 832. Greeley to Rebecca Whipple, July 21, 1853, HGP-LC, Box 1. Greeley to John P. Wood-

bury, February 3, 1858, HGP-LC, Box 1. Greeley to Emma W. Newhall, March 9, 1858, HGP-LC, Box 1. Greeley to Theodore Parker, November 5, 1855, Parker Papers, MHS. Greeley to Emma Newhall, April 12, 1856, HGP-LC, Box 1.

49. Schneider and Lawton, *Prophet.* Anne Taylor, *Laurence Oliphant, 1829–1888,* Oxford: Oxford University Press, 1982, 120–1.

50. Schneider and Lawton, *Prophet,* 152–3.

51. Bronson Alcott to his wife in Walpole, NH, October 25, 1856, in Richard R. Herrnstadt, ed., *The Letters of A. Bronson Alcott,* Ames: Iowa State University Press, 1969 (hereafter cited as Alcott, *Letters*), 207–8, 210, 220.

52. Horace Greeley to a lady friend, October 24, 1871, in Benton, *Greeley on Lincoln,* 194–6.

53. Donald, *Lincoln,* 211, 242.

54. *Tribune,* April 18, 1856. Douglas to Colfax, December 1857, in Robert W. Johannsen, ed., *The Letters of Stephen A. Douglas,* Urbana: University of Illinois Press, 1961 (hereafter cited as Douglas, *Letters*), 405–6.

55. Hale, *Greeley,* 203. Lincoln to Lyman Trumbull, December 28, 1857, in Roy P. Basler, ed., *Abraham Lincoln: Collected Works,* New Brunswick, NJ: Rutgers University Press, 1953–5 (hereafter cited as Lincoln, *Collected Works*), Volume 2, 430.

56. Lincoln, "Address before the Young Men's Lyceum of Springfield, Illinois," January 27, 1838, in Lincoln, *Collected Works,* Volume 1, 108–15. Mario Cuomo and H. Holzer, eds., *Lincoln on Democracy,* New York: HarperCollins, 1990, 51.

57. Donald, *Lincoln,* 177. Lincoln, *Collected Works,* Volume 2, 222, 255, 276. Lincoln to Joshua Speed, August 24, 1855, in Lincoln, *Collected Works,* Volume 2, 323.

58. John Ford Newton, *Lincoln and Herndon,* Cedar Rapids, IA: Torch Press, 1910, 72–3, 82–4. Theodore Parker, "The American Idea," May 29, 1850, in William Herndon and Jesse W. Weik, *The Life of Lincoln,* Chicago: Belford Clarke and Co., Volume 2, 32, 65.

59. Greeley to Parker, March 12, 1853, and May 23, 1854, Parker Papers, MHS.

60. Herndon to Parker, March 10 and September 8, 1857, in Newton, *Lincoln and Herndon,* 109–11, 126.

61. Lincoln to Herndon, February 1858, in Emmanuel Hertz, ed., *The Hidden Lincoln: From the Letters and Papers of William H. Herndon,* New York: Viking, 1938, 113–5.

62. Newton, *Lincoln and Herndon,* 140–3. Herndon and Weik, *Lincoln,* 394–5. Herndon to Parker, April 7, 1858, in Newton, *Lincoln and Herndon,* 156–8. Herndon to Weik, April 14, 1858, in Hertz, ed., *Hidden Lincoln,* 14.

63. Herndon to Greeley, April 8, 1858, HGP-NYPL, reel 2, 070. Herndon to

Parker, April 27, 1858, Parker Papers, MHS. *Tribune,* May 17, 1858. Greeley to Herndon, May 29, 1858, in Newton, *Lincoln and Herndon,* 164. Herndon to Parker, June 1, 1858, Parker Papers, MHS. Lincoln to Charles L. Wilson, June 1, 1858, in Nicolay and Hay, *Abraham Lincoln: A History,* New York: Century, 1890, Volume 2, 362–3.

64. Lincoln, *Collected Works,* Volume 2, 461. *Tribune,* June 24 and July 13, 1858. Herndon to Greeley, July 20, 1858, HGP-NYPL, reel 2.

65. Dana to Pike, September 6, 1858, in Pike, *First Blows,* 425. Lincoln's speech at Edwardsville, IL, September 11, 1858, in Lincoln, *Collected Works,* Volume 3, 95.

66. Herndon to Parker, September 20, 23, and October 4, 1858, Parker Papers, MHS.

67. *Tribune,* November 6, 1858. Lincoln to Greeley, November 8, 1858, in Lincoln, *Collected Works,* Volume 3, 336. Herndon to Parker, November 8, 1858, and Greeley to Herndon, November 14, 1858, in Newton, *Lincoln and Herndon,* 234–5, 240.

68. Herndon to Parker, December 15, 1858, in Newton, *Lincoln and Herndon,* 265.

69. Lincoln to Anson G. Henry, December 1858, in Lincoln, *Collected Works,* Volume 3, 339. Parker, *Collected Works,* Volume 7, 211, n.1, and 430. Hertz, ed., *Hidden Lincoln,* 239: "I loaned Lincoln the Parker sermon unmarked and, when it was returned to me, it was marked, and that is all I can truthfully state" (1889).

70. Greeley to Franklin Newhall, January 8, 1859, HGP-LC, Box 1. Stephen A. Douglas to John A. McClernand, December 7, 1859, in Douglas, *Letters,* 478–80. Lincoln to William Kellogg, December 11, 1859, in Lincoln, *Collected Works,* Volume 3, 506–7. *Tribune,* January 25, 1860.

71. Greeley to Amos Tuck, November 17, 1858, Baker Library, DCL. Alcott, *Letters,* 295. Rossi, *Mazzini,* 112–3. Elizabeth A. Daniels, *Jesse White Mario: Risorgimento Revolutionary,* Athens: Ohio University Press, 1972, 74–83, on Mario's trip to the United States.

72. Greeley, *Recollections,* 360.

73. *Tribune,* March 8, 1844, September 11, 1846, May 11, 1849, January 22, 1853, June 15, 1854, November 28, 1856, January 13, 1857, and July 5, 1857. See also Horace Greeley, *An Overland Journey: From New York to San Francisco in the Summer of 1859,* New York: Knopf, 1964.

74. Ray Allen Billington, *The Far Western Frontier,* New York: Harper and Brothers, 1956, 264–5. Jonas Winchester to Horace Greeley, August 20, 1849, Bancroft Library, UCB, Banc MSSC-B547/49, Box 2, California Gold Rush.

75. Greeley to Emma Newhall, February 12, 1859, HGP-LC, Box 1. Greeley to Margaret Allen, February 26, 1857, HGP-FHS. Greeley to Margaret Allen, April 17, 1859, HGP-LC, Box 1.

76. Greeley to Charles Dana, May 20, 1859, in Benton, *Greeley on Lincoln,* 154. Glenn Chesney Quiett, *Pay Dirt: A Panorama of America's Gold Rushes,* New York: D. Appleton–Century, 1936, 162–3.

77. Weisberger, *Reporters for the Union,* 44–5. On Villard, see Henry Villard, *Memoirs of Henry Villard, Journalist and Financier, 1835–1900,* Boston: Houghton Mifflin, 1904, Volume 1, 28–59, 122–6, Volume 2, 267–9.

78. On Greeley among the Mormons, see Greeley, *Overland Journey,* 209–29.

79. On this famous episode, see Richard G. Lillard and Mary V. Hood, *Hank Monk and Horace Greeley: An Enduring Episode in Western History,* George-town, CA: Wilmac Press, 1973; also the *Golden Era,* San Francisco, April 15, 1860. Greeley to A. Hutchinson, August 3, 1859, HGP, Bancroft Library, UCB.

80. James C. Williams, "Horace Greeley in California, 1859," *Journal of the West,* Volume 8, Number 4 (1969), 592–605. Quoted in the *San Francisco Bee,* August 11, 1859.

81. Greeley to George W. Wright, October 8, 1859, Wright Papers, LC.

82. Greeley to George W. Wright, October 18, 1859, Wright Papers, LC.

83. *Tribune,* October 20, 1859.

84. Mark Twain, *The Works of Mark Twain, Volume 2, Roughing It,* Berkeley: University of California Press, 1993, 130–6, and 610–1, n. 135, 26–28. On Artemus Ward and Congress, see Lillard and Hood, *Hank Monk,* 17.

85. *Tribune,* October 19 and December 3, 1859. Seitz, *Greeley,* 150–1.

86. *Tribune,* April 8, 1859. Greeley to G. E. Baker, April 28, 1859, in Weed, *Autobiography,* Volume 2, 255. Seitz, *Greeley,* 150–1.

87. Harry Rudman, *Italian Nationalism and English Letters,* London: Allen and Unwin, 1940, 99. Rossi, *Mazzini,* 44–5. Anna J. Sanders, diary entry for September 12, 1855, George Sanders Papers, LC, Box 1.

88. Hill P. Wilson, *John Brown: Soldier of Fortune,* Cedar Rapids, IA: Torch Press, 1913. Edward Renehan, *The Secret Six: The True Tale of the Men Who Conspired with John Brown,* New York: Crown Publishers, 1995, 123–7, 140. Frederick Douglass, *Autobiographies,* New York: Library of America, 1994, 757.

89. Renehan, *Secret Six,* 151, 165. Theodore Parker to Senator Hale of New Hampshire, May 11, 1858 in Parker, *Collected Works,* Volume 14, 414–5. Thomas W. Higginson, *Cheerful Yesterdays,* Boston: Houghton Mifflin, 1898, 220–1. Wilson, *John Brown,* 400–1.

90. Greeley to William M. Jones, October 23, 1859, HGP-URL. *Albany Evening Journal,* October 27, 1859. Oswald Garrison Villard, *John Brown, 1800–1859: A Biography Fifty Years After,* New York: Houghton Mifflin, 1910, 476. Theodore Parker to Francis Jackson, November 14, 1859, in Parker, *Collected Works,* Volume 14, 426. Seitz, *Greeley,* 151. Seymour Drescher, "John Brown's Body in Europe," in Paul Finkelman, ed., *His Soul Goes Marching On: Responses to John Brown and the Harper's Ferry Raid,* Charlottesville: University Press of Virginia, 1995, 253–95.

91. Greeley to Colfax, November 1859, in Hollister, *Colfax*, 150, n. 1. Greeley to Emma Newhall, December 16, 1859, HGP-LC, Box 1.

92. James Redpath, *The Public Life of Captain John Brown*, Boston: Thayer and Eldridge, 1860, 8, 406. Renehan, *Secret Six*, 257.

93. Renehan, *Secret Six*, 40–1.

94. Weisberger, *Reporters for the Union*, 71–2.

NOTES TO CHAPTER 8

1. Cited in H. W. Burton, *History of Norfolk*, Norfolk, VA: Norfolk Virginian Job Print, 1877, 43–4. Young, *Men and Memories*, Volume 1, 51–2.

2. Greeley to George E. Baker, April 28, 1859, in Weed, *Autobiography*, Volume 2, 255.

3. Letter from three Republicans to Greeley, May 3, 1859, HGP-NYPL, reel 2. Lincoln, *Collected Works*, Volume 3, 375–6.

4. *Tribune*, February 20, 25, 27, and 28, 1860. Lucy Lowden, "The Granite State of Lincoln: New Hampshire's Role in the Nomination of Abraham Lincoln at the Republican National Convention, 1860," *Historical New Hampshire*, Volume 25, Number 1 (1970), 2–26.

5. On the platform, see John F. Cleveland and Horace Greeley, *A Political Textbook for 1860*, New York: Tribune Association, 1860, 26–7; Zucker, *Forty-Eighters*, 134; Horner, *Lincoln and Greeley*, 176; Greeley, *Recollections*, 389–93.

6. Stoddard, *Greeley*, 194–6. Summers, *Plundering Generation*, 268–70.

7. Lowden, "Lincoln," 14–5. *Tribune*, May 15, 17, and 18, 1860. Weed, *Autobiography*, Volume 2, 269. Lincoln, *Collected Works*, Volume 4, 50.

8. *Tribune*, May 19, 22, 23, and June 14, 1860. Joshua Giddings to George Julian, May 25, 1860, Joshua Giddings Papers, LC, Volume 3. Lowden, "Lincoln," 18, on New Hampshire Republicans.

9. Hollister, *Colfax*, 148. Bates to Greeley, May 26, 1860, HGP-NYPL, reel 2.

10. Greeley to Moses Cartland, May 25, 1860, HL, bMS Am 1752 (161). Greeley to Augustus Allen, August 14, 1860, FHS. Greeley and Cleveland, *Political Textbook*.

11. Joshua Leavitt to Salmon P. Chase, November 7, 1860, in American Historical Association, *Diary and Correspondence of Salmon P. Chase*, Washington, DC: Government Printing Office, 1903, 484. Greeley to Beman Brockway, November 11 and 19, 1860, HGP-LC, Box 1. Seitz, *Greeley*, 226–7.

12. *Tribune*, February 6, 1861.

13. On secession, see Edmund S. Morgan, *Inventing the People: The Rise of Popular Sovereignty in England and America*, New York: Norton, 1988; also Greeley, *Recollections*, 397, and *American Conflict*, Volume 1, 380; and Albert Kirwan, *John J. Crittenden: The Struggle for Union*, Lexington: University Press of Kentucky, 1962, 403–4.

14. James B. Stewart, *Wendell Phillips, Liberty's Hero,* Baton Rouge: Louisiana State University Press, 1986, 136–7. Lewis Perry, *Radical Abolitionism: Anarchy and the Government of God in Anti-slavery Thought,* Ithaca, NY: Cornell University Press, 1973, 161. Mayer, *All on Fire,* 327. Foner, *Free Men,* 139–40.

15. *Tribune,* February 20, 23, and April 22, 1850, and May 2, 1854.

16. Pike, *First Blows,* 343–4, 501. Greeley to Pike, June 5, 1856, Pike Papers, UMO.

17. James M. McPherson, *Drawn by the Sword: Reflections on the American Civil War,* Oxford: Oxford University Press, 1996, 50, 60.

18. Dana to Pike, September 1, 1859, and Gurowski to Pike, April 16, May 12, and July 13, 1860, in Pike, *First Blows,* 443–4, 513, 524. Van Deusen, *Seward,* 274. Adam Gurowski, *Slavery in History,* New York: A. B. Burdick, 1860, viii, 248–9, 256, 259.

19. *Tribune,* November 9, 16, 17, 21, 24, 30, and December 6, 1860.

20. *Tribune,* December 17, 1860.

21. Greeley to Lincoln, December 22 and 26, 1860, Lincoln Papers, LC, Volume 23 (5258) and Volume 24 (5334). *Tribune,* December 28, 1860, and January 10, 1861.

22. David Potter in 1941 used the word "duplicity" to describe Greeley's position in "Horace Greeley and Peaceable Secession," *Journal of Southern History,* Volume 7 (1941), 148, 150, 154. Bernard Weisberger argues for Greeley as a principled and consistent pacifist. See Weisberger, "Horace Greeley: The Reformer as Republican," *Civil War History,* Volume 23, Number 1 (1977), 5–25.

23. *Tribune,* January 12, 1861. Lincoln to Weed, February 4, 1861, in Lincoln, *Collected Works,* Volume 4, 185, and in Weed, *Autobiography,* Volume 2, 324.

24. Weed, *Autobiography,* Volume 2, 324.

25. *Tribune,* February 13 and 16, 1861. The train incident is lovingly described in detail by John Hay in Michael Burlingame, ed., *Lincoln's Journalist: John Hay's Anonymous Writings for the Press, 1860–1864,* Carbondale: Southern Illinois University Press, 1998, 32.

26. *Tribune,* February 23 and 27, 1861. Greeley to Brockway, February 28, 1861, HGP-LC, Box 1.

27. Greeley, *Recollections,* 404. *Tribune,* March 4 and 13, 1861.

28. James M. Perry, *A Bohemian Brigade: The Civil War Correspondents—Mostly Rough, Sometimes Ready,* New York: John Wiley, 2000, 6.

29. *Tribune,* July 29, 1861, and June 3, 1862.

30. On soldiers' letters during the Civil War, see James McPherson, *For Cause and Comrades: Why Men Fought in the Civil War,* New York: Oxford University Press, 1997, 20–3, 104–7, 170.

31. Van Deusen, *Weed,* 272. Charlotte Brancaforte, *The German Forty-Eighters in the United States,* New York: Peter Lang, 1989, 34. Ella Lonn, *Foreigners in*

the Union Army and Navy, Baton Rouge: Louisiana State University Press, 1951, 55, 71–2. Lillibridge, *Beacon of Freedom,* 114, 116.

32. *Tribune,* April 15, 17, May 12, 1861.

33. *Tribune,* May 27, 1861. Greeley to Lincoln, Lincoln Papers, LC, Volume 46, 9967. Starr, *Bohemian Brigade,* 33–4.

34. *Tribune,* February 2, 1863. Greeley, *Recollections,* 402–3. Simon Cameron to Greeley, June 10, 1861, HGP-LC, Box 7. On the Sumner visit to New York, see Conway, *Autobiography,* Volume 1, 329.

35. *Tribune,* July 21, 22, and 23, 1861. Starr, *Bohemian Brigade,* 35. Perry, *Bohemian Brigade,* 31–45. See also William Pitt Fessenden to James S. Pike, September 8, 1861, blaming the defeat on the press and "self-appointed generals," James S. Pike Papers, LC.

36. *Tribune,* July 25, 1861. Seitz, *Greeley,* 232.

37. Greeley to Lincoln, July 29, 1861, in Nicolay and Hay, *Abraham Lincoln,* Volume 4, 365–6.

38. Greeley to Beman Brockway, August 8 and 14, 1861, HGP-LC, Box 1. Greeley to Moncure Conway, August 17, 1861, in Conway, *Autobiography,* Volume 1, 336. Greeley to Sam Wilkerson, August 24, 1861, HGP-NYPL.

39. Gurowski to Wendell Phillips, August 16, 1861, HL. Gurowski to James S. Pike, August 19, 1861, in Pike, *First Blows,* 423–4. Gurowski to Pike, August 30, 1861, Pike Papers, UMO. Greeley to Gurowski, September 25, 1861, Gurowski Papers, LC, Box 1. Gurowski to Greeley, October 1, 1861, HGP-NYPL, reel 2. Donald, *Charles Sumner,* 19–20, claims that Sumner got Gurowski his job as translator.

40. Lonn, *Foreigners,* 53, 79. Carl Frederick Wittke, *We Who Built America,* New York: Prentice-Hall, 1939, 250–2. Adam Gurowski, *Diary,* Boston: Lee and Shepard, 1862, Volume 1, 262.

41. Thaddeus Stevens to Simon Stevens, November 5, 1861, Stevens Papers, Volume 1, 226. Gurowski, *Diary,* Volume 1, 131.

42. Greeley to Colfax, January 1862, in Hollister, *Colfax,* 186. George W. Matthews to Colfax, January 3, 1862, in Hollister, *Colfax,* 184.

43. Harper, *Lincoln and the Press,* 119–40.

44. William A. Croffut, *An American Procession 1855–1941: A Personal Chronicle of Famous Men,* Boston: Little, Brown, 1931, 265.

45. Frank L. Mott, *American Journalism,* New York: Macmillan, 1950, 339. Harper, *Lincoln and the Press,* 76. Hollister, *Colfax,* 186.

46. Villard, *Memoirs,* Volume 1, 339. Weisberger, *Reporters for the Union,* 175–6. Starr, *Bohemian Brigade,* 69–70. Harry J. Maihafer, *The General and the Journalists: Ulysses S. Grant, Horace Greeley, and Charles Dana,* Washington, DC: Brassey's, 1998, 74.

47. Greeley to Samuel Strong, March 14, 1861, HGP-NYPL. *Tribune,* July 26, 1861.

48. *Tribune*, August 28, November 7 and 20, 1861.

49. Gilmore, *Personal Recollections*, 39–48. James P. Shenton, *Robert John Walker: A Politician from Jackson to Lincoln*, New York: Columbia University Press, 1961, 186–91.

50. Lincoln, *Collected Works*, Volume 11, 120–2. Horner, *Lincoln and Greeley*, 246–7. Ralph Ray Fahrney, *Horace Greeley and the Tribune in the Civil War*, New York: Da Capo Press, 1970 (originally 1936), 92–5. Gilmore, *Personal Recollections*, 53, 63.

51. Greeley to James R. Gilmore, December 29, 1861, Gilmore Papers, Eisenhower Library, Johns Hopkins University, Ms 37, Scrapbook 1. Seitz, *Greeley*, 238. Burlingame, *Lincoln's Journalist*, 188–9. James H. Trietsch, *The Printer and the Prince: A Study of the Influence of Horace Greeley upon Abraham Lincoln*, New York: Exposition Press, 1955, 201–2.

52. Charles A. Dana, *Recollections of the Civil War*, New York: D. Appleton, 1898, 7–8. Stanton to Greeley, February 19, 1862, Papers of Edwin M. Stanton, LC, Volume 4, 50809–11.

53. Greeley to Samuel Strong, March 14, 1862, HGP-NYPL. Greeley to Colfax, March 20, 1862, in Hollister, *Colfax*, 186. Horace Greeley, "Andrew Johnson," HGP-LC, Scrapbook ac 4322.

54. Wilson, *Dana*, 172, 175–6. Hale, *Greeley*, 253. Marx and Engels, *Collected Works*, Volume 41, 359, 362.

55. Greeley to Hector Orr, April 11, 1862, Horace Greeley Miscellany, WSHS, SC 2019. Maihafer, *General and Journalists*, 134–5.

56. Lloyd Dunlap, "President Lincoln and Editor Greeley," *Abraham Lincoln Quarterly*, Volume 5 (June 1948), 108. Michael Burlingame, ed., *At Lincoln's Side: John Hay's Civil War Correspondence and Selected Writings*, Carbondale: Southern Illinois University Press, 2000, 20. Greeley to Lincoln, January 6, 1863, Robert Todd Lincoln Collection, LC, cited in Harper, *Lincoln and the Press*, 105–6.

57. *Tribune*, May 6, 20, 21, and June 6, 1862. Paul Gates, *The Farmer's Age*, New York: Simon and Schuster, 1960, 75–6.

58. *Tribune*, April 14, 16, 18, 21, 1862. Maihafer, *General and Journalists*, 120–1.

59. Edwin C. Fishel, *The Secret War for the Union: The Untold Story of Military Intelligence in the Civil War*, Boston: Houghton Mifflin, 1996, 87–8. Bayard Taylor to Greeley, July 5, 1862, HGP-NYPL, reel 2, 0373–5.

60. Mark E. Neely, *The Union Divided: Party Conflict in the Civil War North*, Cambridge, MA: Harvard University Press, 2002, 100–1. Harper, *Lincoln and the Press*, 135.

61. Stanton to Greeley, February 10, 1864, HGP-NYPL, reel 2, 0501–2. Crozier, *Yankee Reporters*, 367–9. Nicolay to Greeley, April 24, 1864, HGP-LC, Box 7. Greeley to Nicolay, April 26, 1864, Nicolay Papers, LC, Box 2.

62. Lloyd Chiasson, ed., *The Press in Times of Crisis,* Westport, CT: Praeger, 1995, 88–9. James S. Pike to Pitt, November 30, 1864, James S. Pike Papers, LC.

63. William F. Thompson, *The Image of War: The Pictorial Reporting of the American Civil War,* Baton Rouge: Louisiana State University Press, 1959, 87, 101–2, 166.

64. *Tribune,* May 30, 1861, and January 31, 1862.

65. H. R. Helper, *The Impeding Crisis of the South: How to Meet It,* New York: G. W. Carleton, 1867, 31, 67, 141, 300. Pike, *First Blows,* 469–70.

66. *Tribune,* August 21, October 19, December 4, 1861, and March 6, 7, 8, and 11, April 12, and May 12, 1862. Lincoln to Greeley, March 24, 1862, and Greeley to Lincoln, after March 24, in Lincoln, *Collected Works,* Volume 5, 169. Howard Jones, *Abraham Lincoln and a New Birth of Freedom,* Lincoln: University of Nebraska Press, 1999, 63–5. John Hope Franklin, *The Emancipation Proclamation,* Garden City, NY: Doubleday, 1963, 106.

67. Gilmore, *Personal Recollections,* 76, 81–2. *Tribune,* July 5 and 10, 1862.

68. Horner, *Lincoln and Greeley,* 263. Franklin, *Emancipation Proclamation,* 39.

69. Greeley to R. M. Whipple, August 6, 1862, HGP-LC, Box 1. Greeley to Augustus Allen, August 14, 1862, FHS.

70. *Tribune,* August 20, 1862.

71. Lincoln to Greeley, August 22, 1862, in Lincoln, *Collected Works,* Volume 5, 388–9. Greeley, *American Conflict,* Volume 2, 250–1. Gilmore, *Personal Recollections,* 83–4.

72. Harper, *Lincoln and the Press,* 172–5. *New York Times,* August 25, 1862.

73. *Tribune,* August 22 and 25, 1862. Greeley to George W. Wright, August 27, 1862, HGP-LC.

74. *Tribune,* September 10, 1862. Greeley's remarks in Vermont are in HGP-LC.

75. Gilmore, *Personal Recollections,* 85. *Tribune,* September 23, 1862.

76. Horace Greeley, "Aurora," "Southern Hatred of the North," and "National Unity," *Continental Monthly,* Volume 2 (July–December 1862), 622–5, 448–51, and 357–60.

77. Edwin Stanton to Greeley, October 4, 1862, in Benjamin P. Thomas and Harold M. Hyman, *Stanton: The Life and Times of Lincoln's Secretary of War,* New York: Knopf, 1962, 247. Greeley to James Eveborn, October 11, 1862, HGP-NYPL. Greeley to Ralph Waldo Emerson, November 9, 1862, HL, bMS AM 1280.1263. Franklin, *Emancipation Proclamation,* 89. Lincoln, *Collected Works,* Volume 5, 537. Greeley to Lincoln, December 12, 1862, Robert Todd Lincoln Collection (20115), cited in Horner, *Lincoln and Greeley,* 290–1.

78. Hans Trefousse, *Lincoln's Decision for Emancipation,* New York: Lippincott, 1975, 99. Lincoln, *Collected Works,* Volume 6, 28–30. Horace Greeley, "Abolition," *Johnson's Universal Cyclopedia,* New York: A. J. Johnson, 1887, 13. *Tribune,* January 2 and 3, 1863.

79. *Tribune,* January 5, 7, 1863. Franklin, *Emancipation Proclamation,* 109–10. Greeley to John Nicolay, January 10, 1863, Nicolay Papers, LC, Box 2.

80. Weed to Lincoln, February 1, 1863, in Lincoln, *Collected Works,* Volume 5, 83–4. Gurowski, *Diary,* Volume 2, 173. On Gurowski's street-corner comments on Greeley, see the *Atlantic Monthly,* Volume 18 (November 1866), 633, in Gurowski's obituary.

81. William Lloyd Garrison to Helen Garrison, May 14, 1863, in Walter M. Merrill and Louis Ruchames, eds., *The Letters of William Lloyd Garrison,* Cambridge, MA: Harvard University Press, 1971–81, Volume 5, 153. Greeley to Nicolay, May 24, 1863, Nicolay Papers, LC, Box 2. *Tribune,* June 1, 1863, and March 16, 1864. Greeley to Charles Sumner, June 26, 1863, in Charles Sumner, *The Works of Charles Sumner,* Boston: Lee Shepard, 1870–, Volume 15, 250.

82. Mark Neely, *The Fate of Liberty: Abraham Lincoln and Civil Liberties,* New York: Oxford University Press, 1991, 52–3, 70, 191

83. Vallandigham to Greeley, January 10, 1863, HGP-NYPL.

84. Greeley to I. T. Williams, February 9, 1863, HGP-NCHS. Laura White (Whipple?) to Greeley, February 9, 1863, HGP-NYPL, roll 2, 0402–6.

85. Neely, *Fate of Liberty,* 66. *Tribune,* May 15, 1863.

86. Neely, *Fate of Liberty,* 72.

87. *Tribune,* September 16 and 17, 1863.

88. *Tribune,* December 11, 1863.

89. John Nicolay to Greeley, May 26, 1864, HGP-NYPL, reel 2. *Tribune,* June 17, 1864. Vallandigham to Greeley, April 11, 1865, HGP-NYPL, reel 2.

90. Justin Smith Morrill Papers, LC, Box 53. Greeley was a member of the board and visited Havana on June 22, 1863.

91. *Tribune,* July 4 and 6, 1863.

92. Greeley to Stanton, June 12, 1863, Papers of Edwin M. Stanton, LC, Volume 12, 52634.

93. Gilmore, *Personal Recollections,* 167–205. Bernstein, *New York City Draft Riots,* 19.

94. Harper, *Lincoln and the Press,* 274–6. Starr, *Bohemian Brigade,* 221–4. Gilmore, *Personal Recollections,* 178–9.

95. Gilmore, *Personal Recollections,* 190–5.

96. Gilmore, *Personal Recollections,* 192–4. Seitz, *Greeley,* 212–3.

97. *Tribune,* July 15, 16, 17, and 18, 1863.

98. Greeley to Laura Rowe, August 24, 1863, HGP-NYPL.

99. Mayer, *All on Fire,* 452, 457. *Tribune,* July 4, 1862.

100. Henry S. Commager, *Theodore Parker,* Boston: Beacon Press, 1947, 266. David Donald, *Lincoln's Herndon,* New York: Knopf, 1948, 128. See also Theodore Parker's sermon "The Mercantile Classes" of November 22, 1846, where he wrote that "the government of all, by all, and for all, is a democracy," Parker, *Collected Works,* Volume 10, 26.

101. On the Gettysburg Address, see especially Wills, *Lincoln at Gettysburg*.

102. On the Gilbert text, see Wills, *Lincoln at Gettysburg*, 191. *Tribune*, November 20, 21, and 26, 1863. Gurowski, *Diary*, Volume 3, 33.

103. Lincoln to Michael Hahn, March 13, 1864, in Lincoln, *Collected Works*, Volume 7, 243. Lincoln's "Address to the Sanitary Fair" of April 18, 1864, is in the same collection, Volume 7, 301–2.

104. *Tribune*, July 4, 1864.

105. Alice Fahs, *The Imagined Civil War: Popular Literature of the North and South, 1861–1865*, Chapel Hill: University of North Carolina Press, 2001, 297–8. See also Alice Fahs, "The Market Value of Memory: Popular War Histories and the Northern Literary Marketplace, 1861–1868," *Book History*, Volume 1 (1998), 107–39. Greeley, *Recollections*, 420–1.

106. Greeley, *American Conflict*, Volume 1, 554.

107. Gurowski, *Diary*, Volume 2, 243–5 (June 1, 1864). James Buchanan to Mr. Marble, January 30, 1867, in Buchanan, *Works*, Volume 11, 431–2. *Atlantic Monthly*, Volume 14, Issue 81 (July 1864), 133–5. John Bright to Greeley, August 8, 1864, HGP-NYPL, reel 2, 0562.

108. Fahs, *Imagined Civil War*, 298, 301–2. Greeley, *American Conflict*, Volume 2, 7. Greeley to O. D. Case, July 10 and September 19, 1864; January 10, 1866; February 2, 1867; July 12, 1868; January 25, 1869, HL.

109. Fahs, *Imagined Civil War*, 301–2. Greeley to O. D. Case, February 11, 1870, HGP-NYPL.

NOTES TO CHAPTER 9

1. Starr, *Bohemian Brigade*, 289.

2. On Mercier, see Daniel B. Carroll, *Henri Mercier and the American Civil War*, Princeton: Princeton University Press, 1971, 5–10, 367. On peace settlement ideas, see Jones, *Lincoln*, 159–61.

3. Edward C. Kirkland, *The Peacemakers of 1864*, New York: Macmillan, 1927, 69–71. Reavis, *Greeley*, 156–7. Jones, *Lincoln*, 160. Warren F. Spencer, "The Jewett-Greeley Affair: A Private Scheme for French Mediation in the American Civil War," *New York History*, Volume 51 (1970), 252–3.

4. Greeley to Jewett, January 2, 1863, in *Tribune*, May 5, 1863. Spencer, "Jewett-Greeley Affair," 253–5. *Tribune*, January 9, 1863.

5. Charles Sumner to Francis Lieber, January 23, 1863, in Sumner, *Letters*, Volume 2, 141–2. Sumner to Greeley, March 15, 1863, in Sumner, *Letters*, Volume 2, 147. *Tribune*, May 11, 1863.

6. Horner, *Lincoln and Greeley*, 324–5. Lincoln, *Collected Works*, Volume 6, 225, 330–1.

7. Charles Sumner to Greeley, September 21, 1863, in Sumner, *Letters*, Volume 2, 194–5. *Tribune*, November 23, 1863.

8. John W. Headley, *Confederate Operations in Canada and New York*, Alexandria, VA: Time-Life Books, 1984 (originally New York: Neale Publishing Co., 1906), 218–21. Kirkland, *Peacemakers*, 72–3.

9. On Sanders, see James D. Horan, *Confederate Agent: A Discovery in History*, New York: Crown, 1954, a biography of Thomas Hines, 86–7. Anna J. Sanders in her August 29, 1855, diary entry refers to a meeting between Sanders and Greeley in New York, George N. Sanders Papers, LC, Box 1. On Sanders's naval purchasing work, see U.S. Congress, House Select Committee on Naval Contracts and Expenditures, *Naval Contracts and Expenditures*, Washington, DC: Government Printing Office, 1859, 74–5, 220–31. William A. Tidwell, *Come Retribution: The Confederate Secret Service and the Assassination of Lincoln*, Jackson: University Press of Mississippi, 1988, 124, 332,

10. *Tribune*, April 15, 1864. Greeley to K. E. Horton, May 27, 1864, Young Men's Union Records, PEM, MSS 245, Box 3, folder 1. Sanders to Samuel J. Tilden, July 5, 1864, Tilden Papers, as cited in Alexander C. Flick, *Samuel James Tilden: A Study in Political Sagacity*, New York: Dodd, Mead and Co., 1939, 146. No Tilden letters have been found concerning this episode. Jewett to Greeley, July 5, 1864, in Henry J. Raymond, *The Life and Public Services of Abraham Lincoln*, New York: Derby and Miller, 1865, 571.

11. Lincoln to U. S. Grant, July 6, 1864, in Lincoln, *Collected Works*, Volume 7, 429. Horner, *Lincoln and Greeley*, 300, 325. Greeley to Lincoln, July 7, 1864, in Lincoln, *Collected Works*, Volume 7, 435.

12. William C. Jewett to Greeley, July 7, 1864, in Lincoln, *Collected Works*, Volume 7, 436.

13. Lincoln to Greeley, July 9, 1864, in Lincoln, *Collected Works*, Volume 7, 435. Greeley to Lincoln, July 10 and 13, 1864, in Lincoln, *Collected Works*, Volume 7, 440–1.

14. Lincoln to Greeley, July 15, 1864, in Lincoln, *Collected Works*, Volume 7, 440–2. Hay to Lincoln, July 16, 1864, in Lincoln, *Collected Works*, Volume 7, 443.

15. Michael Burlingame and John Ettlinger, eds., *Inside Lincoln's White House: The Complete Civil War Diary of John Hay*, Carbondale: Southern Illinois University Press, 1997 (hereafter cited as Hay, *Diary*), 224.

16. Gilmore, *Personal Recollections*, 243–5, 258–9. Horner, *Lincoln and Greeley*, 326–7.

17. Greeley telegram to Lincoln, July 18, 1864, in Lincoln, *Collected Works*, 451. Hay, *Diary*, 225.

18. Hay, *Diary*, 224–9.

19. Howard K. Beale, *The Diary of Edward Bates 1859–1866*, Washington, DC: Government Printing Office, 1933, 388–9, Volume 4 of the Annual Report of the American Historical Association for the Year 1930. *Tribune*, July 22, 1864.

20. *Tribune*, July 25, 26, 28, 29, 30, 1864. Correspondence between Greeley

and Lincoln on publishing the letters is in Lincoln, *Collected Works,* Volume 7, 482, 489–90, 494.

21. Lincoln to Abraham Wakeman, July 25, 1864, and Lincoln memorandum on Clement C. Clay, of about the same date, in Lincoln, *Collected Works,* Volume 7, 459–61. The cabinet discussion of August 19 about Greeley is recounted in Howard K. Beale, ed., *The Diary of Gideon Welles,* Boston: Houghton Mifflin, 1911. Greeley to John Nicolay, August 24 and September 4, 1864, in John Nicolay Papers, LC, Box 2. Nicolay to Greeley, October 4, 1864, HGP-LC, Box 7.

22. Dennis K. Wilson, *Justice under Pressure: The St. Albans Raid and Its Aftermath,* Lanham, MD: University Press of America, 1992, 42–3, 103, 136–8. D. P. Crook, *The North, the South, and the Powers, 1861–1865,* New York: John Wiley, 1974, 350. Tidwell, *Come Retribution,* 201–2. See also Oscar A. Kinchen, *Daredevils of the Confederate Army: The Story of the St. Albans Raiders,* Boston: Christopher, 1959, 48.

23. Greeley to Francis P. Blair, December 1, 1864, Abraham Lincoln Papers, LC. Greeley to Isaiah T. Williams, December 16, 1864, HGP-NYHS.

24. Horan, *Confederate Agent,* 289.

25. *Tribune,* January 12, 1863. Greeley to Salmon P. Chase, Chase Papers, LC, Volume 3, 377–8.

26. Gilmore, *Personal Recollections,* 134–47. William M. Lamers, *The Edge of Glory: A Biography of William S. Rosecrans, U.S.A.,* New York: Harcourt, Brace and World, 1961, 259–60. Allen Peskin, *Garfield,* Kent, OH: Kent State University Press, 1978, 178.

27. Salmon P. Chase Papers, Historical Society of Pennsylvania, Volume 1. *Tribune,* December 14, 16, 23, and 24, 1863, February 2, 1864. Hay, *Diary,* 132–3.

28. Greeley to Gideon Welles, January 18, 1864, Welles Papers, LC. Greeley to Frederick Allen, January 24, 1864, HGP-LC, Box 1. Greeley to R. M. Whipple, March 8, 1864, HGP-LC, Box 1.

29. Hay, *Diary,* 193.

30. David E. Long, *The Jewel of Liberty: Abraham Lincoln's Re-election and the End of Slavery,* New York: Da Capo, 1997, 180. *Tribune,* May 13, 1864. Zucker, *Forty-Eighters,* 145. Rolle, *Fremont,* 230. F. B. Carpenter (Francis Bicknell), *Six Months at the White House with Abraham Lincoln,* New York: Hurd and Houghton, 1866, 153, on Lincoln's refusal to see Greeley.

31. *Tribune,* June 14, 1864. Greeley to George Opdyke, August 1864, in Trietsch, *Printer and the Prince,* 276. Brisbane to Greeley, August 20, 1864, HGP-NYPL, reel 2, 0554–6. The August 30 meeting was at David Dudley Field's home. See Sumner, *Letters,* Volume 2, 251–2. Greeley to W. O. Bartlett, August 30, 1864, HGP-NYPL.

32. Ruth J. Bartlett, *John C. Fremont and the Republican Party,* Columbus:

Ohio State University Press, 1930, 94–103, 111–3. Greeley to John Nicolay, September 19, 1864, Nicolay Papers, LC, Box 2. Eduard Laboulaye, *The Election of the President of the United States,* Washington, DC: Union Congressional Committee, 1864, 9, first published in the *Tribune,* October 25, 1864.

33. *Tribune,* November 10, 1864. Long, *Jewel of Liberty,* 233, 258.

34. Greeley to Margaret Allen, December 5, 1864, HGP-LC, Box 1. Ellis P. Oberholtzer, *Jay Cooke: Financier of the Civil War,* Philadelphia: George W. Jacobs & Co., 1907, Volume 1, 488. Greeley to William Pitt Fessenden, February 17, 1865, George Wright Papers, LC. *Tribune,* April 14, 1865.

35. Greeley, *American Conflict,* Volume 2, 748–9.

36. Tidwell, *Come Retribution,* 332. Lincoln, *Collected Works,* Volume 3, 541, from Lincoln's February 27, 1860, speech at Cooper Union.

37. *Tribune,* January 13, 25, March 19, April 23, December 16, 1864, January 7 and 11, 1865. Joseph George, Jr., "Black Flag Warfare," *Pennsylvania Magazine of History and Biography,* Volume 115, Number 3 (July 1991), 291–318. Edward Steers, Jr., *Blood on the Moon: The Assassination of Abraham Lincoln,* Lexington: University Press of Kentucky, 2001, 47–53. Tidwell, *Come Retribution,* 240, and facing photograph.

38. *Tribune,* October 17, 1864. Tidwell, *Come Retribution,* 144, 330–3. William Hanchett, *The Lincoln Murder Conspiracies,* Urbana: University of Illinois Press, 1983, 19, 43.

39. Greeley to Rebecca Whipple, April 13, 1865, in Stoddard, *Greeley,* 330–1. *Tribune,* April 14, 1865.

40. *Tribune,* April 17, 18, and 19, 1865.

41. Hanchett, *Conspiracies,* 65. *Tribune,* May 4, 5, and 6, 1865.

42. Roy Z. Chamlee, *Lincoln's Assassins: A Complete Account of Their Capture, Trial, and Punishment,* Jefferson, NC: McFarland, 1990, 235. *Tribune,* May 11, 1865, article on Sanders reprinted from the *Cincinnati Times,* and May 12 article by Greeley on "Liberty." Hanchett, *Conspiracies,* 74.

43. Hanchett, *Conspiracies,* 75.

44. Bingham Duncan, *Whitelaw Reid: Journalist, Politician, Diplomat,* Athens: University of Georgia Press, 1975, 37–49. Greeley had approached Reid about editing the *Tribune* as early as January 1866, Greeley to Reid, January 19, 1866, HGP-NYPL. Thayer, *John Hay,* Volume 1, 334. Most of the younger men joining the newspaper were born between 1833 and 1838, and were in their thirties after the Civil War. In 1865, George Ripley was sixty-three, Charles T. Congdon was forty-four, and Bayard Taylor was forty.

45. Summers, *Plundering Generation,* 10–4. Bayard Taylor to John Russell Young, September 19, 1866, Papers of John Russell Young, LC, Volume 3. Greeley to Isaiah T. Williams, April 2, 1868, HGP-NCHS.

46. Victor Fischer and Michael B. Frank, eds., *Mark Twain's Letters, Volume*

2, 1867–1868, Berkeley: University of California Press, 1990, 117–8, 166; also in that volume, Twain to Frank Fuller, November 24, 1867 (pp. 111–2), and to Jervis Langdon, December 2, 1868 (p. 298).

47. Reid, *Horace Greeley,* 11. Greeley to Isaiah T. Williams, February 14, 1868, HGP-NCHS.

48. George P. Fletcher, *Our Secret Constitution: How Lincoln Redefined American Democracy,* Oxford: Oxford University Press, 2001, 26–7. Mark Van Doren, ed., *The Portable Walt Whitman,* New York: Penguin, 1974, 245–6, from "Years of the Modern" (1865).

49. *Tribune,* December 10, 1863, and April 14, 1865. Greeley to Margaret Allen, April 12, 1865, in the *Patent Trader* of February 2, 1961, Mt. Kisco, New York. Greeley to George Wright, April 19, 1865, George Wright Papers, LC. Greeley to Thomas Dixon, June 2, 1865, HGP-NYPL.

50. Greeley to Benjamin Butler, August 24, 1865, Papers of Benjamin F. Butler, LC, Box 46. Greeley's comment on Chinese immigration (September 3, 1865) is cited in Stuart C. Miller, *The Unwelcome Immigrant: The American Image of the Chinese, 1785–1882,* Berkeley: University of California Press, 1969, 170.

51. Linn, *Greeley,* 219.

52. Bernstein, *New York City Draft Riots,* 239–41. Lewis Tappan to Greeley, April 10, 1866, HGP-LC, Box 7. Greeley to a friend, May 12, 1866, HGP-NYPL. Greeley to Margaret Allen, September 14, 1866, HGP-LC, Box 1. Anna Sanders's diary for June 25 and 27, 1866, and February 7, 1867, in George N. Sanders Papers, LC, Box 1. *Tribune,* November 24, 1866.

53. *Tribune,* November 27, 1866. Sam Wilkeson to John Young, December 1, 1866, Papers of John Russell Young, LC, Volume 3. Greeley to James Lawrence, December 16, 1866, HGP-NYPL. Greeley to H. Sedley, January 5, 1867, HGP-NYPL.

54. Greeley to Lavinia Phelps, October 27, 1867, HGP-LC, Box 1. Greeley to Zachariah Chandler, August 25, 1867, Papers of Zachariah Chandler, LC, Volume 4, 772. Samuel May, Jr., to Greeley, October 25, 1867, HGP-NYPL, reel 2, 0907–8. Horace Greeley, *An Address on Success in Business Delivered Before the Students of Packard's Bryant and Stratton New York Business College,* New York: S. S. Packard, 1867, 29, 37, 38. Greeley to Samuel Sinclair, November 21, 1867, HGP-NYPL. Greeley to Joseph R. Hawley, November 27, 1867, Joseph R. Hawley Papers, LC. On the Dickens banquet at Delmonico's, see Young, *Men and Memories,* Volume 1, 134, 139. Seward to Greeley, December 3, 1867, HGP-LC, Box 1 (the diplomatic position was Minister Plenipotentiary to Austria).

55. *Tribune,* June 10, 1865. Foner, *Freedom,* 103, citing Howard in the *New Orleans Tribune,* November 6, 1865. McFeeley, *Howard,* 231. *Tribune,* December 18 and 20, 1865.

56. Horace Greeley to Josephine Griffey, September 7, 1870, and Griffey to

Greeley, September 12, 1870, in Elizabeth Cady Stanton et al., eds., *History of Woman's Suffrage, Volume 1,* New York: Source Book Press, 1970 (originally 1881), 36–7. *Tribune,* April 8, 1870.

57. On William Wirt and the original company, see Charles Royster, *The Fabulous History of the Dismal Swamp Company,* New York: Knopf, 1999, 7–9, 401–5, 430–4. The story of Greeley and Bean's swamp project is contained in the papers of Isaiah T. Williams, NYPL, Boxes 27 and 28.

58. Jonathan T. Dorris, *Pardon and Amnesty under Lincoln and Johnson: The Restoration of the Confederates to Their Rights and Privileges, 1861–1898,* Chapel Hill: University of North Carolina Press, 1953, 218, 263–71, 300. *Tribune,* June 19, 1854, June 22, 1866. Greeley to Salmon P. Chase, May 30, 1866, in Salmon P. Chase Papers, LC, Volume 97, 14536–7.

59. *Tribune,* August 24, 1866. Varina Davis to Greeley, September 2 and October 16, 1866, HGP-NYPL, reel 2, 0757–8 and 0773–5.

60. Greeley, *Recollections,* 410–6.

61. Greeley to Charlotte Allen, May 20, 1866, FHS. Lately Thomas, *The First President Johnson,* New York: William Morrow, 1968, 526–7. Linn, *Greeley,* 220–1. The Union League Club, founded in February 1863, was an offshoot of the U.S. Sanitary Commission and emphasized loyalty to the Union. See Henry Bellows, *Historical Sketch of the Union League Club of New York,* New York: G. P. Putnam, 1879.

62. John Jay, president of the Union Club, to Horace Greeley, May 16, 1867, HGP-NYPL. *Tribune,* May 23, 1867 (Greeley's open letter to the Club). Bellows, *Union Club,* 102–3. Reavis, *Greeley,* 298–9. The Tribune Association also published as a pamphlet the *Letter of Hon. Horace Greeley to the Union Club of New York Who Threatened Him with Expulsion for Signing Jefferson Davis's Bail Bond* (n.d.).

63. Horace Greeley, "The Fruits of the War," *The Galaxy,* Volume 4 (July 1867), 364–6. *Tribune,* September 5, 1867. Greeley to Rebecca Whipple, December 7, 1867, HGP-LC, Box 1. Seitz, *Greeley,* 286.

64. Linda Kerber, *Women of the Republic: Intellect and Ideology in Revolutionary America,* Chapel Hill: University of North Carolina Press, 1980, 278. Bonnie S. Anderson, *Joyous Greetings: The First International Women's Movement, 1830–1860,* Oxford: Oxford University Press, 2000, 108–10, 114–5. Miriam Gurko, *The Ladies of Seneca Falls: The Birth of the Women's Rights Movement,* New York: Schocken, 1976, 307–11.

65. Seitz, *Greeley,* 61–2. Greeley to Rufus Griswold, January 21, 1849, thanking him for an anthology of female poets, Griswold Collection, BPL. Brian Roberts, *American Alchemy: The California Gold Rush and Middle-Class Culture,* Chapel Hill: University of North Carolina Press, 2000, 233. Horace Greeley, "Felicia Hemans," *Rose of Sharon,* Volume 2 (1841), 83–93.

66. Gurko, *Seneca Falls,* 104. *Tribune,* May 1, 1850, in Linn, *Greeley,* 89, n. 1. Elizabeth C. Stanton, *Eighty Years and More, Reminiscences 1815–1897,* New York: Schocken, 1971, 152.

67. Tyler, *Freedom's Ferment,* 450. Greeley to Mrs. C. M. Severance, October 2, 1853, in the *Proceedings of the Women's Rights Convention, Cleveland, Ohio, 1853,* Cleveland: Gray, Beardsley, Spear, 1854, 10.

68. Stanton et al., eds., *History of Woman's Suffrage,* 424, 509.

69. Susan B. Anthony to John Russell Young, November 16, 1866, Papers of John Russell Young, LC, Volume 3. Greeley to L. U. Reavis, March 4, 1867, Special Collections, UNHL.

70. Goldsmith, *Other Powers,* 132–3. New York State Constitutional Convention, *New York Convention Manual,* Albany: Weed, Parsons & Co., 1867, vii. Flick, *Tilden,* 160–1.

71. Ellen Carol Du Bois, *Feminism and Suffrage: The Emergence of an Independent Women's Movement in America 1848–1869,* Ithaca, NY: Cornell University Press, 1978, 87–8. Greeley to Isaiah Williams, August 7, 1867, Isaiah T. Williams Papers, NYPL, Box 27, folder 5. Kathleen Barry, *Susan B. Anthony: A Biography of a Singular Feminist,* New York: Ballantine, 1988, 176. T. Stanton and H. S. Blatch, eds., *Elizabeth Cady Stanton: Diaries and Letters,* New York: Harpers, 1922, Volume 2, 116–8.

72. Susan B. Anthony to Horace Greeley, July 8, 1868, HGP-NYPL, reel 2, 1024–5. *Tribune,* October 1, 1867. James Garfield to Whitelaw Reid, December 9, 1868, in Margaret Leech and Harry J. Brown, *The Garfield Orbit,* New York: Harper and Row, 1978, 265–6. On Woodhull, see the *Tribune,* May 12, 1871.

NOTES TO CHAPTER 10

1. John Bright to Greeley, November 28, 1866, HGP-NYPL, reel 2, 0780–3. Greeley to Senator E. D. Morgan, February 5, 1867, in Stoddard, *Greeley,* 258–9.

2. *Tribune,* February 22, 24, 25, and 26, 1868.

3. *Tribune,* March 16, 1868. Greeley to Thaddeus Stevens, April 20, 1868, Papers of Thaddeus Stevens, LC, 06/1136. Greeley to Rebecca Whipple, May 4, 1868, HGP-NCHS. Greeley to Charlotte Block, May 1, 1868, FHS.

4. *Tribune,* May 27 and 28, 1868.

5. *Tribune,* April 1, 6, 8, 9, and 10, 1867, and July 16, 1868.

6. *Tribune,* January 19, 23, and 30, and February 8 and 10, 1869.

7. *Tribune,* April 28, 1851. Benjamin Quarles, *Lincoln and the Negro,* New York: Oxford University Press, 1962, 99–100, 119–21.

8. Smiley, *Lion of White Hall,* 217–9. Greeley to U. S. Grant, January 31, 1870, HGP-LC, Box 1. Allan Nevins, *Hamilton Fish: The Inner History of the Grant Administration,* New York: Dodd, Mead and Co., 1936, 179–80, 184, 348.

9. *Tribune,* June 14 and 15, 1870.

10. W. S. Neidhardt, *Fenianism in North America*, University Park: Pennsylvania State University Press, 1975, 4–7, 15, 119–20.

11. Neidhardt, *Fenianism*, 44–50, 59–75. *Tribune*, June 7, 1866. Keneally, *Great Shame*, 443.

12. *Tribune*, August 25, October 24, 29, and 31, 1866. John C. O'Brien to Greeley, December 13, 1867, HGP-NYPL, reel 2, 0912.

13. Robert Fishman, *Bourgeois Utopias: The Rise and Fall of Suburbia*, New York: Basic Books, 1987. Kenneth Jackson, *Crabgrass Frontier: The Suburbanization of the United States*, New York: Oxford University Press, 1985, 85.

14. On Meeker, see Robert Emmitt, *The Last War Trail: The Utes and the Settlement of Colorado*, Norman: University of Oklahoma Press, 1954, 45–7.

15. Hayden, *Seven American Utopias*, 261–87. Donald Worster, *Rivers of Empire: Water, Aridity and the Growth of the American West*, New York: Oxford University Press, 1985, 83–96. William Wyckoff, *Creating Colorado: The Making of an American Landscape*, New Haven: Yale University Press, 126–9.

16. Nathan Meeker, "A Western Colony," *Tribune*, December 14, 1869. Barbara Smith, *The First Hundred Years of Greeley, Colorado, 1870–1970*, Greeley, CO: Journal Publishing Company, 1970. David Boyd, *A History: Greeley and the Union Colony of Colorado*, Dubuque, IA: Kendall Printing, 1987, 36–7.

17. Greeley to Meeker, January 31, 1870, HGP-DPL. *Daily Colorado Tribune*, April 9, 1870, 1.

18. Record of Greeley's payments and deeds in Greeley Papers, City of Greeley Archives, Greeley, Colorado. Greeley to Nathan Meeker, July 10, 1870, HGP-DPL. Accounts of Greeley's visit are in the *Greeley Tribune*, November 16, 1870; the *Daily Rocky Mountain News*, October 13, 1870; and the *Colorado Tribune*, October 15, 1870.

19. Horace Greeley, "The Plains—As I Crossed Them Ten Years Ago," *Harper's New Monthly Magazine*, Volume 38, Number 228 (May 1869), 789–95. Boyd, *Union Colony*, 53, 79, 87. The Illinoisan was George Augustus Hobbs, editor of the Genesseo, Illinois, *Republic*.

20. *Greeley Tribune*, November 16 and 25, 1870.

21. On Barnum, see the *Denver Tribune*, April 25, 1871, and the *Greeley Tribune*, March 15, 1871. Also see Walter Stewart, *P. T. Barnum's Colorado Connection*, Greeley, CO: Elmarry Publications, 2001; and Ida Libert Uchill, *What P. T. Barnum Did in Colorado*, Denver: Pioneer Peddler Press, 2001.

22. Greeley to Meeker, September 1, 1871, and February 28 and March 23, 1872, HGP-DPL. Greeley to R. L. Sanderson, November 15, 1871, GLC.

23. Greeley, *What I Know about Farming*, 34, 188, 310. Greeley, *Recollections*, 295–310.

24. Twain, *Roughing It*, 728, n. 483.7.8. Twain to Greeley, May 7, 1871, Mark Twain Papers, UCB.

25. *Buffalo Express*, May 10, 1871, 2, as described in Twain, *Roughing It*, 728.

26. Worster, *Rivers of Empire*, 92–6. Wyckoff, *Creating Colorado*, 126–9.

27. On Carl Schurz, see especially Hans Trefousse, *Carl Schurz: A Biography*, Knoxville: University of Tennessee Press, 1982; and Carl Schurz, *The Reminiscences of Carl Schurz*, New York: Doubleday, 1908, three volumes.

28. Schurz, *Reminiscences*, Volume 1, 4–6, 17, 28, Volume 2, 39–43, 52–4.

29. Carl Schurz, "True Americanism," April 18, 1859, in his *Reminiscences*, Volume 1, 48–72. See also his "The Doom of Slavery," August 1, 1860, in *Reminiscences*, Volume 1, 122–60.

30. Trefousse, *Schurz*, 119. Schurz, "The Treason of Slavery," October 7, 1864, in *Reminiscences*, Volume 1, 225–48.

31. Greeley to Carl Schurz, March 4 and November 27, 1867, Papers of Carl Schurz, LC, Volume 7, 1310–1. Schurz to his wife, October 19, 1867, in Joseph Schafer, ed., *Intimate Letters of Carl Schurz, 1841–1869*, Madison: State Historical Society of Wisconsin, 1928, 408–9. Schurz to Greeley, July 9, 1868, HGP-NYPL, reel 2, 1026–7.

32. Greeley to Rebecca Whipple, November 8, 1868, HGP-LC, Box 1.

33. Matthew Hale Smith, *Sunshine and Shadow in New York*, Hartford, CT: J. B. Burr, 1869, 654, 657. Review of Greeley's *Recollections* in the *Atlantic Monthly*, Volume 23, Number 136 (February 1869), 260–2. Greeley to Rebecca Whipple, May 16, 1869, HGP-LC, Box 1. R. W. McAlpine, *The Life and Times of Col. James Fisk, Jr.*, New York: New York Book Company, 1872, 448–9.

34. Horace Greeley, *Essays Designed to Elucidate the Science of Political Economy*, Philadelphia: Porter and Coates, 1869, 13, 40, 135, 169, 286, 337, 341. Vermont's Justin Morrill, father of the land-grant colleges, thanked Greeley for "exposing many of the sophisms of the Free Traders" in his letter to Greeley of January 15, 1870, HGP-LC, Box 7.

35. Earle Dudley Ross, *The Liberal Republican Movement*, New York: H. Holt and Co., 1919, 18–9. Reavis, *Greeley*, 179–80. Whitelaw Reid to Hamilton Fish, July 3, 1870, Papers of Hamilton Fish, LC, Volume 70, 10232. Hollister, *Colfax*, 359. Grant to Schuyler Colfax, August 21, 1870, in John Y. Simon, ed., *Papers of Ulysses S. Grant*, Carbondale: Southern Illinois University Press, 1967– (hereafter cited as Grant, *Papers*), Volume 20, 229–33.

36. U. S. Grant to J. R. Young, November 15, 1870, in Young, *Men and Memories*, Volume 1, 164–5. Grant to Greeley, December 10, 1870, in Grant, *Papers*, Volume 21, 84.

37. Beman Brockway to Greeley, December 12, 1870, HGP-LC, Box 1.

38. Greeley to George Wright, January 9, 1871, George Wright Papers, LC. Horace Greeley, "Counsel to Young Men," *Wood's Household Magazine*, January 1871. Ross, *Liberal Republican Movement*, 36–8. Charles Sumner to Whitelaw Reid, February 25, 1871, in Sumner, *Letters*, Volume 2, 545.

39. Ross, *Liberal Republican Movement*, 38–9, 47–8. Horace Greeley, *Mr.*

Greeley's Letters from Texas and the Lower Mississippi, New York: Tribune Office, 1871, 35, 55.

40. *New York Herald,* September 13, 1871, cited in Ross, *Liberal Republican Movement,* 39. Hollister, *Colfax,* 355. Grant to Henry Wilson, November 15, 1871, in Grant, *Papers,* Volume 22, 231–3.

41. Greeley to a lady friend, December 25, 1871, in Benton, *Greeley on Lincoln,* 202.

42. Ross, *Liberal Republican Movement,* 79.

43. Norma L. Peterson, *Freedom and Franchise: The Political Career of Benjamin Gratz Brown,* Columbia: University of Missouri Press, 1965, 162, 164, 205.

44. *Tribune,* January 29, 1872. Seitz, *Greeley,* 369. William Lloyd Garrison to Mary Grew, January 24, 1872, in Garrison, *Letters,* Volume 6, 219.

45. Reavis, *Greeley,* 169–70. *Tribune,* February 5, 1872.

46. Justin S. Morrill to Greeley, March 11, 1872, HGP-LC, Box 7. Greeley to Morrill, March 12, 1872, Papers of Justin S. Morrill, LC, Box 57. Greeley to Josiah Grinnell, March 13, 1872, Grinnell College Archives.

47. Ross, *Liberal Republican Movement,* 57–60.

48. Ross, *Liberal Republican Movement,* 86–105. Linn, *Greeley,* 242–4. Patrick W. Riddleberger, *George Washington Julian, Radical Republican: A Study in Nineteenth-Century Politics and Reform,* Indianapolis: Indiana Historical Bureau, 1966, 270–1. The quotation (of Henry D. Lloyd) is from the *Tribune,* May 31, 1872.

49. John Greenleaf Whittier to Edwin Morton, May 10, 1872, published in the *Springfield Republican* of May 17, in Whittier, *Letters,* Volume 3, 267–8. Schurz to Greeley, May 6, 1872, and Greeley to Schurz, May 8 and 10, 1872, in Papers of Carl Schurz, LC, Volume 16, 3243–8, Volume 17, 3276–7. Peterson, *Freedom and Franchise,* 219–9.

50. James G. Smart, "Whitelaw Reid and the Nomination of Horace Greeley," *Mid-America,* Volume 49, Number 4 (1967), 227–43.

51. Ross, *Liberal Republican Movement,* 129–49.

52. Edward A. Pollard, *A Southern Historian's Appeal for Horace Greeley,* Lynchburg, VA: Daily Republican Book and Job Printing Establishment, 1872, 10, 15, 17, 19, 27–8.

53. Greeley lectured in Poughkeepsie, New York, on May 16, 1872. See HGP-LC, Box 5. Greeley to James Dunn, May 22, 1872, Hargrett Library, University of Georgia, MS 1007. Charles Sumner to Whitelaw Reid, May 15, 1872, in Sumner, *Letters,* Volume 2, 592. Horace Greeley, *The Great Industries of the United States,* Hartford, CT: J. B. Burr and Hyde, 1872, 868–73. Greeley wrote Samuel Sinclair on June 5 that he was not well and that his doctor urged him to "go away for a few days," HGP-NYPL.

54. Montezuma, Iowa, *Weekly Republican,* June 5, 1872, quoted in Payne,

Grinnell, 266–7. Gerrit Smith, June 22, 1872, speech in Peterboro, New York, in African-American Pamphlet Collection, LC. Ross, *Liberal Republican Movement,* 176. Greeley to Charles Lanman, June 27, 1872, Papers of Charles Lanman, LC, Volume 2, 2269.

55. George T. McJimsey, *Genteel Partisan: Manton Marble, 1834–1917,* Ames: Iowa State University Press, 1971, 159–61. Henry Watterson to Samuel Bowles, May 19, 1872, BPL, Ms 307. Lydia M. Child to Sara Blake Shaw, May 20, June 23, July 7 and 13, and September 26, 1872, in Lydia M. Child Papers, Anti-Slavery Collection, Cornell University Libraries, Microform 78, number 2053. George Bancroft to Hamilton Fish, June 1872, and Fish to John Jay, June 2, 1872, in Nevins, *Hamilton Fish,* 598. On Schurz's attempt to form a new faction, see Linn, *Greeley,* 247 n.1.

56. Peterson, *Freedom and Franchise,* 222–3.

57. Garrison to Samuel May, Jr., July 13, 1872, in Garrison, *Letters,* Volume 6, 235. Brockway, *Fifty Years,* 328. W. O. Duvall to Gerrit Smith, July 19, 1872, HGP-NYPL. Ross, *Liberal Republican Movement,* 162.

58. Stackpole, *New Hampshire,* Volume 4, 200. *Horace Greeley's Jokes! Written by Old-Time Editors and Reporters of the Tribune.* New York: George Gilluly & Co., 1872. Amos J. Cummings, *The Greeley Campaign Songster,* Chicago: Halpin & McClure, 1872. Hale, *Greeley,* 342–3.

59. Cummings, *Campaign Songster,* 14, 20, 23, 27–9, 53–4, 58, 64, 66.

60. Greeley to John T. West, July 15, 1872, HGP-NYPL. Ross, *Liberal Republican Movement,* 177. Charles Sumner to Heman Chase, July 20, 1872, in Sumner, *Letters,* Volume 2, 602, 604–5. Greeley to Sumner, July 31, 1872, Papers of Charles Sumner, LC. Greeley to Gabrielle Greeley, July 28, 1872, HGP-LC.

61. Ross, *Liberal Republican Movement,* 156, 178–9. Freidel, *Francis Lieber,* 411. LeRoy P. Graf and Ralph W. Haskins, eds., *The Papers of Andrew Johnson,* Knoxville: University of Tennessee Press, 1967–2000, Volume 16, 337–8, 347. Stevens, *Typographical Union,* 623–4.

62. Albert B. Paine, *Thomas Nast: His Period and His Pictures,* New York: Pearson, 1904, 45–68, 129, 234.

63. Charles Sumner, "Greeley or Grant?" September 3, 1872, an address not given at Faneuil Hall in Boston because the Senator was ill. Sumner, *Collected Works,* Volume 15, 209–54. John Greenleaf Whittier to Miles Newton, Joseph Disbrow, and Robert Hubbard, September 3, 1872, in Whittier, *Letters,* Volume 3, 274–7. Ross, *Liberal Republican Movement,* 158.

64. Oberholtzer, *Jay Cooke,* Volume 2, 165. David Howard Bain, *Empire Express: Building the First Transcontinental Railroad,* New York: Penguin, 2000, 171–2. Clifford Browder, *The Money Game in Old New York: Daniel Drew and His Times.* Lexington: University Press of Kentucky, 1986, 182–3.

65. Gerrit Smith to Horace Greeley [printed], October 1, 1872, Baker Library, DCL. See Andrew Johnson's speech at Brownsville, TN, of October 17,

1872, in Graf and Haskins, eds., *Papers of Andrew Johnson*, Volume 16, 396. Gabrielle Greeley Clendenin Notebooks, NCHS. Greeley to Mr. and Mrs. R. M. Whipple, October 18, 1872, HGP-LC, Box 1. Greeley to his nephew, Horace Greeley II, October 29, 1872, HGP-LC, Box 1.

66. Elizabeth Cady Stanton to Susan B. Anthony, November 5, 1872, in Ann D. Gordon, ed., *The Selected Papers of Elizabeth Cady Stanton and Susan B. Anthony*, New Brunswick, NJ: Rutgers University Press, 1997, Volume 2, 140–1. Elmer R. Hays, *Morning Star. A Biography of Lucy Stone, 1818–1893*, New York: Harcourt, Brace, and World, 1961, 237. Linn, *Greeley*, 254–5. James McPherson, "Grant or Greeley? The Abolitionist Dilemma in the Election of 1872," *American Historical Review*, Volume 71 (1965), 43–61.

67. Greeley to Col. Tappan, November 1872, in Hollister, *Colfax*, 387. Greeley to a lady friend, November 8, 1872, in Benton, *Greeley on Lincoln*, 235. Grinnell, *Men and Events*, 226–7.

68. Greeley's note "Out of the Depths," November 13, 1872, HGP-NYPL, reel 3, 0710.

69. Charles Sumner to Whitelaw Reid, November 29, 1872, in Sumner, *Letters*, Volume 2, 614. Greeley to William M. Smith, January 20, 1856, HGP-NCHS. *Tribune*, November 29, 1872.

NOTES TO CHAPTER 11

1. Schuyler Colfax to Samuel Sinclair, December 1, 1872, in Hollister, *Colfax*, 386. John Greenleaf Whittier to Edwin H. Chapin, December 2, 1872, in Whittier, *Letters*, Volume 3, 282. Bayard Taylor to Whitelaw Reid, December 2, 1872, in Taylor, *Life and Letters*, 607–8. Theodore C. Smith, *The Life and Letters of James Abram Garfield*, New Haven: Yale University Press, 1925, Volume 1, 497.

2. *Atlantic Monthly*, Volume 30 (December 1872), 762–3. Lydia M. Child to Sarah Shaw, December 18, 1872, Anti-Slavery Collection, Lydia M. Child Collection, Cornell University, Ithaca, NY.

3. Wills of September 21, 1857, and January 9, 1871, Isaiah T. Williams Papers, NYHS (hereafter cited as ITW), Box 28, folder 6. On probating Greeley's will, see also the Surrogate's Court Records in the Westchester County Archives (hereafter cited as WCA).

4. See Thomas Rooker's December 18 testimony in ITW, Box 28, folder 6. Greeley's list of his lands is dated November 13, 1872, and is in HGP-NYPL.

5. ITW, Box 28, folders 5 and 6. Oberholtzer, *Jay Cooke*, 413–4.

6. WCA, December 14, 1877. According to Schedule E, Ida Greeley received $725.67, Gabrielle $1,840.19, Margaret Bush $2,259.40, Arminda Greeley $1,075.20, and Esther Cleveland $1,250.55.

7. Wheaton J. Lane, *Commodore Vanderbilt: An Epic of the Steam Age*, New York: Knopf, 1942, 324.

8. Ida and Gabrielle Greeley to Ralph Meeker, January 20, 1879, Hazel E. Johnson Collection, Greeley History Museum.

9. George Ripley, quoted in Octavius B. Frothingham, *George Ripley*, Boston: Houghton Mifflin, 1883, 275. On the Greenwood Cemetery statue, see Stevens, *Typographical Union*, 626–8; and *The Greeley Monument Unveiled at Greenwood, December 4, 1876*, New York: Francis Hart & Co., 1877, 20.

10. Stevens, *Typographical Union*, 635.

11. For a list of towns, see the Greeley, Colorado, *Tribune*, March 3, 1997.

12. *Tribune*, September 17, 1867.

13. Horace Greeley, "The Disciplines and Duties of the Scholar," *The Nineteenth Century*, Volume 4 (1849), 25–44, from a speech given at Hamilton College in New York. Gamaliel Bradford, *As God Made Them: Portraits of Some Nineteenth-Century Americans*, Boston: Houghton Mifflin, 1929, 131–66.

14. Reavis, *Greeley*, 186.

15. Greeley to Margaret Allen, 1864, in Stoddard, *Greeley*, 159. Greeley to a lady friend, April 20, 1871, in Benton, *Greeley on Lincoln*, 180–1. Greeley to Isaiah Williams, December 16, 1864, HGP-NCHS.

16. Peyton McCrory, "The Party of Revolution: Republican Ideas about Politics and Social Change, 1862–1867," *Civil War History*, Volume 30 (December 1984), 337.

17. Editorial, *National Quarterly Review*, Volume 26 (December 1872), 154–60.

Selected Bibliography

The following bibliography is brief and selected. It emphasizes the life of Horace Greeley and the theme of American freedom. A full indication of sources consulted is given in the footnotes throughout the book.

ARCHIVES AND MANUSCRIPT COLLECTIONS

Baker Library, Dartmouth College, Hanover, NH: Greeley Miscellany.
Barker Library, Fredonia, NY: Papers of Horace Greeley.
Beinecke Library, Yale University, New Haven, CT: A. J. Macdonald Collection of Utopian Materials.
Boston Public Library, Boston, MA: Correspondence of Rufus Wilmot Griswold.
Brooks Memorial Library, Brattleboro, VT: Papers on Water Cure Establishments.
California State Library, Sacramento, CA: Jonas Winchester Collection.
City of Greeley Museums, Greeley, CO: Papers of Horace Greeley.
Concord Public Library, Concord, MA: Papers of Concord Lyceum.
Denver Public Library, Denver, CO: Letters of Horace Greeley to Nathan Meeker.
Duke University Library, Durham, NC: Papers of Horace Greeley.
Fenton Historical Society, Jamestown, NY: Letters of Horace Greeley.
Gilder Lehrman Collection, New York City, NY: Correspondence of Horace Greeley.
Grinnell College Library, Grinnell, IA: Greeley Letters to Josiah Grinnell.
Houghton Library, Harvard University, Cambridge, MA: Papers of Ralph Waldo Emerson, Margaret Fuller, Adam Gurowski, Francis Lieber, Charles Sumner.
Library of Congress, Washington, DC: Papers of James G. Birney, Salmon P. Chase, Moncure Conway, Adam Gurowski, Horace Greeley, Julia Ward Howe, George Julian, Francis Lieber, Abraham Lincoln, Frederick Law Olmsted, George N. Sanders, Carl Schurz.
Massachusetts Historical Society, Boston, MA: Papers of James T. Fisher, Theodore Parker, George Ripley.
Milton S. Eisenhower Library, Johns Hopkins University, Baltimore, MD: Papers of James Robert Gilmore.

Minnesota Historical Society, St. Paul, MN: Papers of William S. King, Emma Dewey.

New Castle Historical Society, Chappaqua, NY: Horace Greeley Collection.

New Hampshire State Library, Concord, NH: Publications of Horace Greeley, *Jeffersonian.*

New-York Historical Society, New York City, NY: Papers of Horace Greeley, Thurlow Weed, Isaiah T. Williams.

New York Public Library: Papers of Horace Greeley, Isaiah T. Williams.

New York State Library, Albany, NY: Horace Greeley Collection.

North Carolina State Archives, Raleigh, NC: Marriage Bond of Horace Greeley and Mary Cheney.

Peabody Essex Museum, Salem, MA: George Peabody Papers, Gilbert L. Streeter Papers, Young Men's Union Records, Autograph Collection.

Poultney Historical Society, Poultney, VT: Greeley Miscellany.

Rochester Public Library, Rochester, NY: Papers of Horace Greeley and Thurlow Weed.

St. Lawrence University, Canton, NY: Greeley Letters.

Stanford University Libraries, Stanford, CA: Papers of Rebecca Spring.

State University of New York at Stony Brook: Papers of Hamilton Fish.

University of California, Berkeley, CA: Papers of Horace Greeley.

University of Georgia Libraries, Athens, GA: Letter of Horace Greeley to James Dunn, May 22, 1872.

University of Iowa Libraries, Iowa City, IA: Papers of Josiah Grinnell.

University of Maine Libraries, Orono, ME: Papers of James S. Pike.

University of New Hampshire Libraries, Dover, NH: Letter to L. U. Reavis.

University of Rochester, Rush Rhees Library, Rochester, NY: Papers of Horace Greeley, Thurlow Weed.

University of South Carolina, Columbia, SC: Papers of Francis Lieber, Campanella Collection on Giuseppe Garibaldi.

University of Virginia, Charlottesville, VA: Letters of Horace Greeley to Henry Thoreau.

Westchester County Archives, Westchester, NY: Wills and Probate Records of Horace Greeley.

Wisconsin Historical Society, Madison, WI: Papers of Horace Greeley, Marvin Bovee.

PRIMARY SOURCES

Ames, Mary Clemmer. *A Memorial of Alice and Phoebe Cary, with Some of Their Poems.* New York: Hurd and Houghton, 1875.

Bancroft, F., ed. *Speeches, Correspondence, and Political Papers of Carl Schurz.* New York: G. P. Putnam's Sons, 1913.

Basler, Roy P., ed. *Abraham Lincoln, 1809–1865: Collected Works.* New Brunswick, NJ: Rutgers University Press, 1953–5, nine volumes.

Bates, Edward. *Diary of Edward Bates, 1859–1866.* Washington, DC: Government Printing Office, 1933.

Beale, Howard K., ed. *Diary of Gideon Welles.* New York: Norton, 1960, three volumes.

Beard, James F., ed. *The Letters and Journals of James Fenimore Cooper.* Cambridge, MA: Harvard University Press, 1968, six volumes.

Benton, Joel. *Greeley on Lincoln, with Mr. Greeley's Letters to Charles A. Dana and a Lady Friend; to Which Are Added Reminiscences of Horace Greeley.* New York: Baker & Taylor, 1893.

———. *Persons and Places.* New York: Broadway, 1905.

Bingham, Caleb. *The Columbian Orator.* Boston: Manning and Loring, 1800, third edition.

Bishop, Joseph Bucklin. *Notes and Anecdotes of Many Years.* New York: Scribner's, 1925.

Borden, Morton. "Five Letters of Charles A. Dana to Karl Marx." *Journalism Quarterly,* Volume 36 (Summer 1959).

———. "Some Notes on Horace Greeley, Charles Dana, and Karl Marx." *Journalism Quarterly,* Volume 34, Number 4 (Fall 1957), 457–65.

Brisbane, Albert. *Albert Brisbane: A Mental Biography with Character Study.* New York: Burt Franklin, 1969 (originally Boston, 1893).

Brockway, Beman. *Fifty Years in Journalism.* Watertown, NY: Daily Times Printing and Publishing House, 1891.

Burlingame, Michael, ed. *Lincoln's Journalist: John Hay's Anonymous Writings for the Press, 1860–1864.* Carbondale: Southern Illinois University Press, 1998.

———. *At Lincoln's Side: John Hay's Civil War Correspondence and Selected Writings.* Carbondale: Southern Illinois University Press, 2000.

Burlingame, Michael, and John Ettlinger, eds. *Inside Lincoln's White House: The Complete Civil War Diary of John Hay.* Carbondale: Southern Illinois University Press, 1997.

Chappaqua Historical Society. *The Centenary of Horace Greeley.* Chappaqua, NY: Chappaqua Historical Society, 1911.

Chase, Salmon P. *The Salmon P. Chase Papers, Volume 1: Journals, 1829–1872.* Kent, OH: Kent State University Press, 1993, five volumes.

Christman, Henry M., ed. *The American Journalism of Marx and Engels: A Selection from the New York Daily Tribune.* New York: New American Library, 1966.

Congdon, Charles T. *Recollections of a Journalist.* Boston: James R. Osgood and Co., 1880.

Cummings, Amos J. *The Greeley Campaign Songster.* Chicago: Halpin and Mc-Clure, 1872.

Dana, Charles A. *Recollections of the Civil War.* New York: D. Appleton, 1898.

Dean, Bradley P. "Henry D. Thoreau and Horace Greeley Exchange Letters on the 'Spontaneous Generation of Plants.'" *New England Quarterly,* Volume 66, Number 4 (1993), 630–8.

Edgerton, Sarah C., ed. *The Rose of Sharon: A Religious Souvenir.* Boston: A. Tomkins and B. B. Mussey, 1842–9.

Forbes, Hugh. *Manual for the Patriotic Volunteer on Active Service in Regular and Irregular War.* New York: De Witt and Davenport, 1855, two volumes.

Gilmore, James R. *Personal Recollections of Abraham Lincoln and the Civil War.* Boston: L. C. Page and Co., 1898.

Golovin, Ivan. *Stars and Stripes, or American Impressions.* New York: D. Appleton, 1856.

———. *Zapiski Ivana Golovina.* Leipzig: Wolfgang Gerhard, 1859.

Greeley, Horace. *The American Conflict: A History of the Great Rebellion in the U.S.A., 1860–1864.* Hartford, CT: O. D. Case and Co., 1864–6, two volumes.

———. *The Crystal Palace and Its Lessons: A Lecture.* New York: Dewitt and Davenport, 1852.

———. *Essays Designed to Elucidate the Science of Political Economy While Serving to Explain and Defend the Policy of Protection to Home Industry.* Boston: Fields, Osgood, & Co., 1870.

———. *Glances at Europe.* New York: Dewitt and Davenport, 1851.

———. *The Great Industries of the United States.* Hartford, CT: J. B. Burr and Hyde, 1872.

———. *Hints toward Reforms.* New York: Harper & Brothers, 1850.

———. *A History of the Struggle for Slavery Extension and Restriction in the United States.* New York: Dix, Edwards & Co., 1856.

———. *Life of Colonel Fremont.* New York: Greeley and McElrath, 1856.

———. *Mr. Greeley's Letters from Texas and the Lower Mississippi.* New York: Tribune Office, 1871.

———. *An Overland Journey: From New York to San Francisco in the Summer of 1859.* New York: Knopf, 1964, ed. Charles T. Duncan, from the *Tribune.*

———. *Political Textbook for 1860.* New York: Tribune Association, 1860.

———. *Recollections of a Busy Life.* New York: J. B. Ford and Co., 1868.

———. "A Sabbath with the Shakers." *Knickerbocker, or New-York Monthly Magazine,* Volume 11, Number 6 (June 1838), 532–7.

———. *What I Know about Farming.* New York: G. W. Carleton, 1871.

———. *The Writings of Cassius Marcellus Clay.* New York: Harper, 1848.

Grinnell, Josiah B. *Men and Events of Forty Years.* Boston: D. Lothrop, 1891.

Gurowski, Adam. *America and Europe.* New York: D. Appleton, 1857.

———. *Diary.* Three volumes: Boston: Lee and Shepard, 1862; New York: Carleton, 1864; Washington, DC: Morrison, 1866.

———. *Le Panslawisme, son histoire, ses veritables elements: religieux, sociaux, philosophiques, et politiques.* Florence, Italy, 1848.

———. *Russia as It Is.* New York: Appleton, 1854.

———. *Slavery in History.* New York: A. B. Burdick, 1860.

———. *The Turkish Question.* New York: Taylor, 1854.

———. *La verite sur la Russie et sur la revolte des provinces polonaise.* Paris: Delaunay, 1834.

———. *A Year of the War.* New York: Appleton, 1855.

Hansen-Taylor, Marie, ed. *Life and Letters of Bayard Taylor.* Boston: Houghton Mifflin, 1884, two volumes.

Harding, Walter, and Carl Bode, eds. *The Correspondence of Henry David Thoreau.* New York: New York University Press, 1958.

Hopkins, James F., ed. *The Papers of Henry Clay.* Lexington: University Press of Kentucky, 1959–, ten volumes.

Hudspeth, Robert N., ed. *The Letters of Margaret Fuller.* Ithaca, NY: Cornell University Press, 1983, six volumes.

Lieber, Francis. *Miscellaneous Writings.* Philadelphia: Lippincott, 1880, two volumes.

———. *On Civil Liberty and Self-Government.* Philadelphia: Lippincott, 1853.

Marx, Karl, and Friedrich Engels. *Collected Works.* New York: International Publishers, 1982.

Merrill, Walter M., and Louis Ruchames, eds. *The Letters of William Lloyd Garrison.* Cambridge, MA: Harvard University Press, 1971–81, six volumes.

Moore, John B., ed. *The Works of James Buchanan.* Philadelphia: J. B. Lippincott, 1909.

Packard, John B., ed. *The Letters of John Greenleaf Whittier.* Cambridge, MA: Harvard University Press, 1975, three volumes.

Parker, Theodore. *The Collected Works.* Boston: American Unitarian Association, 1907–13, fifteen volumes.

Pierce, Edward L., ed. *Memoirs and Letters of Charles Sumner.* Boston: Roberts Bros., 1877, four volumes.

Proceedings at the Unveiling of a Memorial to Horace Greeley at Chappaqua, N.Y., February 3, 1914. Albany: University of the State of New York, 1915.

Rusk, Ralph L., ed. *The Letters of Ralph Waldo Emerson.* New York: Columbia University Press, 1939, six volumes.

Sanders, George N. *The Political Correspondence of the Late Hon. George N. Sanders.* New York: American Art Galleries, 1914.

Saxon, A. H., ed. *The Selected Letters of P. T. Barnum.* New York: Columbia University Press, 1995 (1983).

Schurz, Carl. *The Reminiscences of Carl Schurz*. New York: Doubleday, Page & Co., 1908, three volumes.

Snow, Frederick E. "Unpublished Letters of Horace Greeley." *The Independent*, Volume 59, Number 2968 (October 19, 1905), 912–5.

Stanton, Elizabeth Cady, and Susan B. Anthony. *The Selected Papers of Elizabeth Cady Stanton and Susan B. Anthony, Volume 1: In the School of Anti-Slavery 1840 to 1866*. New Brunswick, NJ: Rutgers University Press, 1997.

Swisshelm, Jane. *Half a Century*. Chicago: Jansen, McClung & Co., 1880.

Twain, Mark. *The Works of Mark Twain, Volume 2: Roughing It*. Berkeley: University of California Press, 1993.

Villard, Henry. *Memoirs of Henry Villard: Journalist and Financier, 1835–1900*. Boston: Houghton Mifflin, 1904, two volumes.

Webster, Noah. *American Dictionary of the English Language*. New York: 1830, 1847, 1857, and 1870 editions.

Weed, Thurlow. *Autobiography*. Boston: Houghton Mifflin, 1884, two volumes.

Whittier, John Greenleaf. *The Complete Poetical Works of John Greenleaf Whittier*. Boston: Houghton Mifflin, 1892.

Young, John Russell. *Men and Memories: Personal Reminiscences by John Russell Young*. New York: F. Tennyson Neely, 1901, two volumes.

SECONDARY SOURCES

Alentieva, T. V. "Kh. Grili I Amerikanskii Fur'erizm v seredine XIX veka." *Amerikanskii ezhegodnik*, 1989, 190–209.

Anderson, David D. "Horace Greeley on Michigan's Upper Peninsula." *Inland Seas*, Volume 17, Number 4 (1962), 301–6.

Bartlett, Ruth J. *John C. Fremont and the Republican Party*. Columbus: Ohio State University Press, 1930.

Baxter, Maurice G. *Henry Clay and the American System*. Lexington: University Press of Kentucky, 1995.

Beecher, Jonathan. *Charles Fourier: The Visionary and His World*. Berkeley: University of California Press, 1986.

Bellows, Henry W. *Historical Sketch of the Union League Club of New York*. New York: G. P. Putnam, 1879.

Bernstein, Iver. *The New York City Draft Riots: Their Significance for American Society and Politics in the Age of the Civil War*. New York: Oxford University Press, 1990.

Bestor, Arthur. "Albert Brisbane—Propagandist for Socialism in the 1840s." *New York History*, Volume 28 (1947), 128–58.

Bilotta, James D. *Race and the Rise of the Republican Party, 1848–1865*. New York: Peter Lang, 1992.

Bjork, Ulf Jonas. "Sketches of Life and Society: Horace Greeley's Vision for

Foreign Correspondence." *American Journalism*, Volume 14, Numbers 3–4 (1997), 359–75.

Blue, Frederick J. *The Free Soilers: Third Party Politics 1848–1854*. Urbana: University of Illinois Press, 1973.

Blumin, Stuart M. *Rude Republic: Americans and Their Politics in the Nineteenth Century*. Princeton: Princeton University Press, 2000.

Bovee, Warren G. "Horace Greeley and Social Responsibility." *Journalism Quarterly*, Volume 63, Number 2 (1986), 251–9.

Boyd, David. *A History: Greeley and the Union Colony of Colorado*. Dubuque, IA: Kendall Printing, 1987.

Bressler, Ann Lee. *The Universalist Movement in America, 1770–1880*. New York: Oxford University Press, 2001.

Burrows, Edwin G., and Mike Wallace. *Gotham: A History of New York City to 1898*. New York: Oxford University Press, 1999.

Capper, Charles. *Margaret Fuller: An American Romantic Life*. New York: Oxford University Press, 1992.

Carner, Vern. "Horace Greeley and the Millerites." *Adventist Heritage*, Volume 2, Number 1 (1975), 33–4.

Clark, J. C. D. *The Language of Liberty, 1660–1832*. Cambridge: Cambridge University Press, 1994.

Cmiel, Kenneth. *Democratic Eloquence: The Fight over Popular Speech in Nineteenth-Century America*. Berkeley: University of California Press, 1990.

Commons, John R. "Horace Greeley and the Working Class Origins of the Republican Party." *Political Science Quarterly*, Volume 24 (1913), 468–88.

Cornell, William M. *The Life and Public Career of Hon. Horace Greeley*. Boston: D. Lothrop & Co., 1872.

Cross, Coy F. *"Go West, Young Man!" Horace Greeley's Vision for America*. Albuquerque: University of New Mexico Press, 1995.

Cushman, Ralph S. "Horace Greeley's Early New England Home." *New England Magazine*, Volume 21 (1900), 556–65.

Downey, Matthew T. "Horace Greeley and the Politicians: The Liberal Republican Convention in 1872." *Journal of American History*, Volume 53, Number 4 (1967), 727–50.

Eddy, Richard. *The Life of Thomas J. Sawyer, and of Caroline M. Sawyer*. Boston: Universalist Publishing House, 1900.

Ellis, Sumner. *Life of Edwin H. Chapin*. Boston: Universalist Publishing House, 1883.

Erlich, Jacob. *Sketch of the Life of Horace Greeley, with Brief Extracts from His Writings and Biographical Notes*. Chappaqua, NY: Chappaqua Historical Society, 1911.

Fahrney, Ralph Ray. *Horace Greeley and the Tribune during the Civil War*. Cedar Rapids, IA: Torch Press, 1936.

Fischer, David H. *Albion's Seed: Four British Folkways in America.* New York: Oxford University Press, 1989.

Fischer, L. H. *Lincoln's Gadfly, Adam Gurowski.* Norman: University of Oklahoma Press, 1964.

Foner, Eric. *Free Soil, Free Labor, Free Men: The Ideology of the Republican Party before the Civil War.* New York: Oxford University Press, 1970.

———. *The Story of American Freedom.* New York: Norton, 1998.

Freidel, Frank. *Francis Lieber: Nineteenth-Century Liberal.* Baton Rouge: Louisiana State University Press, 1947.

Gienapp, William E. *The Origins of the Republican Party, 1852–1856.* New York: Oxford University Press, 1987.

Golemba, Henry L. *George Ripley.* Boston: Twayne, 1977.

Greeley, George Hiram. *Genealogy of the Greely-Greeley Family.* Boston: Frank Wood, 1905.

Gunderson, Robert Bray. *The Log-Cabin Campaign.* Lexington: University Press of Kentucky, 1957.

Gurko, Miriam. *The Ladies of Seneca Falls: The Birth of the Women's Rights Movement,* New York: Schocken, 1976.

Gustafson, Thomas. *Representative Words: Politics, Literature and the American Language, 1776–1865.* Cambridge: Cambridge University Press, 1992.

Haffner, Gerald O. "Horace Greeley's Impressions of Indiana, 1853." *Indiana Historical Bulletin,* Volume 52, Number 6 (1975), 65–7.

Hale, William Harlan. *Horace Greeley: Voice of the People.* New York: Harper & Brothers, 1950.

———. "When Karl Marx Worked for Horace Greeley." *American Heritage,* Volume 8, Number 3 (1957), 20–5, 110–1.

Handlin, Oscar. *Liberty in America, 1600 to the Present.* New York: Harper and Row, 1986, three volumes.

Harding, Walter. *The Days of Henry Thoreau: A Biography.* New York: Knopf, 1965.

Harper, Robert. *Lincoln and the Press.* New York: McGraw-Hill, 1951.

Hess, Earl J. *Liberty, Virtue, and Progress: Northerners and Their War for the Union.* New York: New York University Press, 1988.

Hollister, O. J. *Life of Schuyler Colfax.* New York: Funk and Wagnalls, 1886.

Holt, Michael F. *The Rise and Fall of the American Whig Party: Jacksonian Politics and the Onset of the Civil War.* New York: Oxford University Press, 1999.

Horner, Harlan Hoyt. *Lincoln and Greeley.* Urbana: University of Illinois Press, 1953.

Howe, Daniel. *The Political Culture of the American Whigs.* Chicago: University of Chicago Press, 1979.

Ingersoll, L. D. *The Life of Horace Greeley.* Philadelphia: John E. Potter & Co., 1874.

Isely, Jeter A. *Horace Greeley and the Republican Party, 1853–1861: A Study of the New York Tribune.* Princeton: Princeton University Press, 1947.

James, Howard. *Abraham Lincoln and a New Birth of Freedom.* Lincoln: University of Nebraska Press, 1999.

Kammen, Michael. *Spheres of Liberty: Changing Perceptions of Liberty in American Culture.* Madison: University of Wisconsin Press, 1986.

Kirkland, Edward Chase. *The Peacemakers of 1864.* New York: Macmillan, 1927.

Kirkwood, Robert. "Horace Greeley and Reconstruction." *New York History,* Volume 40, Number 3 (1959), 270–80.

Kluger, Richard. *The Paper: The Life and Death of the New York Herald Tribune.* New York: Knopf, 1985.

Komlos, John H. *Louis Kossuth in America, 1851–1852.* Buffalo, NY: East European Institute, 1973.

Krieger, Leonard. *The German Idea of Freedom: History of a Political Tradition.* Boston: Beacon Press, 1957.

Lillard, Richard G., and Mary V. Hood. *Hank Monk and Horace Greeley: An Enduring Episode in Western History.* Georgetown, CA: Wilmac Press, 1973.

Linn, William A. *Horace Greeley, Founder and Editor of the New York Tribune.* New York: D. Appleton, 1903.

Lunde, Erik S. *Horace Greeley.* Boston: Twayne, 1981.

Maihafer, Harry. *The General and the Journalists: Ulysses S. Grant, Horace Greeley, and Charles Dana.* Washington, DC: Brassey's, 1998.

Mayer, Henry. *All on Fire: William Lloyd Garrison and the Abolition of Slavery.* New York: St. Martin's, 1998.

McPherson, James M. "Grant or Greeley? The Abolitionist Dilemma in the Election of 1872." *American Historical Review,* Volume 71 (1965), 43–61.

Metz, Timothy R. "Horace Greeley's Rhetoric as Seen in the Light of Cicero's." Master's thesis, Marquette University, Milwaukee, WI, 1965.

Neale, Richard L. *The 1872 Nomination and Presidential Campaign of Horace Greeley.* Chappaqua, NY: New Castle Historical Society, 1980.

Neeley, Mark. *The Fate of Liberty: Abraham Lincoln and Civil Liberties.* New York: Oxford University Press, 1991.

Nevins, Allen. "Greeley, Horace." *Dictionary of American Biography.* New York: Scribner's, 1931, Volume 7, 528–34.

Oakes, James. *Slavery and Freedom: An Interpretation of the Old South.* New York: Vintage, 1991.

Pangle, Thomas. *The Spirit of Modern Republicanism: The Moral Vision of the American Founders and the Philosophy of Locke.* Chicago: University of Chicago Press, 1988.

Parton, James. *The Life of Horace Greeley, Editor of the New York Tribune.* New York: Mason Brothers, 1855.

Patterson, Orlando. *Freedom, Volume 1: Freedom in the Making of Western Culture.* New York: Basic Books, 1991.

Perry, James M. *A Bohemian Brigade: The Civil War Correspondents—Mostly Rough, Sometimes Ready.* New York: John Wiley, 2000.

Peterson, Norma L. *Freedom and Franchise: The Political Career of B. Gratz Brown.* Columbia: University of Missouri Press, 1965.

Pike, James S. *First Blows of the Civil War: The Ten Years of Preliminary Conflict in the United States from 1850 to 1860.* New York: American News Co., 1879.

Pitkin, Hannah. "Are Freedom and Liberty Twins?" *Political Theory,* Volume 16 (November 1988), 523–52.

Potter, David M. "Horace Greeley and Peaceable Secession." *Journal of Southern History,* Volume 7 (1941), 145–59.

Radomsky, Susan M. "The Idolized Pursuit: Horace Greeley and the Farm." Master's thesis, University of Texas, Austin, 1990.

Reavis, Logan Uriah. *A Representative Life of Horace Greeley.* New York: G. W. Carleton, 1872.

Reid, Whitelaw. *Horace Greeley.* New York: Charles Scribner's, 1879.

Reynolds, Larry J. *European Revolutions and the American Literary Renaissance.* New Haven: Yale University Press, 1988.

Rickert, William E. "Horace Greeley on the Stump: The Presidential Campaign of 1872." *Western Speech,* Volume 39, Number 3 (1975), 175–83.

Robbins, Peggy. "Where Do You Stand, Horace Greeley?" *Civil War Times Illustrated,* Volume 29, Number 5 (1990), 50–5, 83–4.

Robbins, Roy M. "Horace Greeley: Land Reform and Unemployment, 1837–1862." *Agricultural History,* Volume 8 (1933), 18–41.

———. "Horace Greeley and the Quest for Social Justice, 1837–1862." *Indiana History Bulletin,* Volume 16 (1939), 68–84.

Roeber, A. G. *Palatines, Liberty, and Property: German Lutherans in Colonial British America.* Baltimore: Johns Hopkins University Press, 1999.

Ross, Earle Dudley. "Horace Greeley and the South: 1865–1872." *South Atlantic Quarterly,* Volume 16 (1917), 324–38.

———. *The Liberal Republican Movement.* New York: H. Holt and Co., 1919.

Rossi, Joseph. *The Image of America in Mazzini's Writings.* Madison: University of Wisconsin Press, 1954.

Rumiantseva, Nelly. "Karl Marx, Correspondent for the *New York Tribune.*" *Soviet Life,* Number 318 (March 1983), 8–9, 30.

Saalberg, Harvey. "Bennett and Greeley, Professional Rivals, Had Much in Common." *Journalism Quarterly,* Volume 49, Number 3 (1972), 538–46, 550.

Schanck, Peter C. "Of Gregory, Gold and Greeley." *Quarterly Journal of the Library of Congress,* Volume 26, Number 4 (1969), 226–33.

Schulze, Suzanne. *Horace Greeley: A Bio-Bibliography.* New York: Greenwood, 1992.

Seitz, Don. *Horace Greeley, Founder of the Tribune.* Indianapolis: Bobbs-Merrill, 1926.

Sen, Amartya. *Development of Freedom.* New York: Knopf, 1999.

Skinner, Quentin. *Liberty before Liberalism.* Cambridge: Cambridge University Press, 1998.

Smart, James G. "Whitelaw Reid and the Nomination of Horace Greeley." *Mid-America,* Volume 49, Number 4 (1967), 227–43.

Smith, Barbara. *The First Hundred Years of Greeley, Colorado, 1870–1970.* Greeley, CO: Greater Greeley Centennial Commission, 1970.

Somkin, Fred. *Unquiet Eagle: Memory and Desire in the Idea of American Freedom, 1815–1860.* Ithaca, NY: Cornell University Press, 1967.

Sotheran, Charles. *Horace Greeley and Other Pioneers of American Socialism.* New York: Humboldt Publishing Co., 1892.

Spencer, Warren F. "The Jewett-Greeley Affair: A Private Scheme for French Mediation in the American Civil War." *New York History,* Volume 51 (1970), 238–68.

Stackpole, Everett S. *History of New Hampshire.* New York: American Historical Society, 1916, four volumes.

Stasik, Florian. *Adam Gurowski: 1805–1866.* Warsaw, Poland: Panst. Wydaw. Naukowe, 1977.

———. "Adam Gurowski's Road to Abolitionism." *Acta Poloniae Historica,* Volume 35 (1977), 87–112.

Steele, Janet. *The Sun Shines for All: Journalism and Ideology in the Life of Charles A. Dana.* Syracuse, NY: Syracuse University Press, 1993.

Steer, Edward, Jr. *Blood on the Moon: The Assassination of Abraham Lincoln.* Lexington: University Press of Kentucky, 2001.

Stoddard, Henry Lothrop. *Horace Greeley: Printer, Editor, Crusader.* New York: G. P. Putnam's, 1946.

Taylor, John M. *William Henry Seward: Lincoln's Right Hand.* New York: HarperCollins, 1991.

Taylor, Sally. "Marx and Greeley on Slavery and Labor." *Journalism and History,* Volume 6, Number 4 (1979–80), 103–6, 122.

Trefousse, Hans. *Carl Schurz: A Biography.* Knoxville: University of Tennessee Press, 1982.

Trietsch, James H. *The Printer and the Prince: A Study of the Influence of Horace Greeley upon Abraham Lincoln.* New York: Exposition Press, 1955.

Tyler, Alice Felt. *Freedom's Ferment: Phases of American Social History to 1860.* Minneapolis: University of Minnesota Press, 1944.

Van Deusen, Glyndon G. *Horace Greeley, Nineteenth-Century Crusader.* Philadelphia: University of Pennsylvania Press, 1953.

Van Deusen, Glyndon G. "The Nationalism of Horace Greeley." In E. M. Earle, ed., *Nationalism and Internationalism: Essays Inscribed to C. J. H. Hayes.* New York: Columbia University Press, 1950, 431–54.

———. *Thurlow Weed: Wizard of the Lobby.* Boston: Little, Brown, 1947.

———. *William Henry Seward.* New York: Oxford University Press, 1967.

Wallace, Irving. *The Fabulous Showman: The Life and Times of P. T. Barnum.* New York: Knopf, 1959.

Weisberger, Bernard A. "Horace Greeley: Reformer as Republican." *Civil War History,* Volume 23, Number 1 (1977), 5–25.

Widmer, Edward L. *Young America: The Flowering of Democracy.* New York: Oxford University Press, 1999.

Wierzbicka, Anna. *Understanding Cultures through Their Keywords.* New York: Oxford University Press, 1997.

Wilentz, Sean. *Chants Democratic: New York City and the Rise of the American Working Class, 1788–1850.* New York: Oxford University Press, 1984.

Williams, James C. "Horace Greeley in California." *Journal of the West,* Volume 8, Number 4 (1969), 592–605.

Williams, Mentor. "Horace Greeley at Niagara Falls." *Inland Seas,* Volume 4, Number 2 (1948), 96–100.

———. "Horace Greeley at the Northwest River and Harbor Convention, 1847." *Inland Seas,* Volume 3, Number 4 (1947), 218–23.

Wills, Gary. *Lincoln at Gettysburg: The Words That Remade America.* New York: Simon and Schuster, 1992.

Wilson, James H. *The Life of Charles A. Dana.* New York: Harper, 1907.

Wittke, Carl. *Refugees of Revolution: The German Forty-Eighters in America.* Philadelphia: University of Pennsylvania Press, 1952.

Wolloch, Isser. *Revolution and the Meanings of Freedom in the Nineteenth Century.* Stanford, CA: Stanford University Press, 1996.

Zabriskie, Francis. *Horace Greeley, the Editor.* New York: Funk and Wagnalls, 1890.

Zahler, Helene Sara. *Eastern Workingmen and National Land Policy, 1829–1862.* New York: Columbia University Press, 1941.

Zubkov, A. Iu. "Kh. Grili I N'iu Iork Tribun vo vremia grazhdanskoi voiny I rekonstrukstii." *Amerikanskii ezhegodnik,* 1985, 124–42.

Zucker, A. E. *The Forty-Eighters: Political Refugees of the German Revolution of 1848.* New York: Russell and Russell, 1950.

Index

"HG" signifies "Horace Greeley."

164; presidential election (1856), 184–187; presidential election (1860), 196, 199, 201, 205, 210–214; presidential election (1864), 196, 256–259; presidential election (1868), 293; Reconstruction, 266–269; Republican Party politics, 178, 181–182, 184–185, 210–214, 256–259; Whig Party politics, 31, 44, 51–55, 57, 60, 102, 109–111, 113–114, 161–162, 171, 181–182

• **political positions/stances:** abolitionism, 35–37, 99, 100, 101, 172, 297; "bleeding Kansas," 187–193; class harmony, 65, 69, 71, 97, 136; distrust of masses, 32; disunionism, 37, 153, 216–217, 254; opposition to annexation of Texas, 43, 104; opposition to capital punishment, 103; opposition to Chinese immigration, 267; opposition to Compromise of 1850, 153; opposition to Democratic Party, 16, 20; opposition to expansionism, 281–283; opposition to Freemasonry, 17, 18, 19–20, 25–26, 29; opposition to Fugitive Slave Act, 161; opposition to Jackson (Andrew), 16, 20, 27, 32, 46; opposition to "Know-Nothings," 103, 174, 184; opposition to Ku Klux Klan, 295; opposition to Lecompton Constitution, 201; opposition to Lincoln in Illinois race (1858), 195–197; opposition to Lincoln in presidential race (1864), 257–258; opposition to McClellan, 103, 227, 228–229; opposition to Mexican War, 108; opposition to single-issue parties, 99, 109, 113; opposition to strikes, 35, 133, 342n21; opposition to voting rights for women, 275–278; private property, 67, 76; support for American System, 32; support for amnesty toward the South, 266, 272, 274; support for anti-slavery movement,

1–2, 29, 35, 98, 99, 100–102, 103–108, 111, 116, 133, 172, 178–179, 180–209, 207, 230–236; support for Choctaw Indians, 294–295; support for Congressional reform, 115–116; support for Cuban independence, 67; support for development of wilderness areas, 87; support for distributing income from sale of public lands, 33, 58, 89; support for Douglas in Illinois race (1858), 195–196, 199–200, 210; support for eighthour day for workers, 267; support for elimination unemployment, 67; support for emancipation, 214, 227, 240; support for emigration of New Englanders to Kansas, 188–189, 192; support for farmers, 67, 89; support for free homesteads in the West, 43; support for free labor, 96–98; support for free land to actual settlers in the West, 91, 92–94; support for Free Soil ideology, 109, 112–113; support for freedom of the press, 62, 223–230; support for Hungarian independence, 142; support for Irish famine relief, 140; support for Irish independence, 114, 140, 141–142, 282–283; support for Jefferson Davis, 245–246, 271–274, 279–280; support for land reform, 115, 116, 186; support for mediated peace settlement, 247–256; support for moving unemployed from cities to the West, 42; support for one-term presidency, 256, 295; support for organized labor, 97–98, 132–133; support for personal liberty, 236–239; support for protectionism, 31, 58, 96–97, 103, 281, 293–294, 301; support for sale of public lands in the West, 30, 42; support for technical education for young men, 67; support for Texas independence, 34, 103–104;

About the Author

Robert C. Williams has taught modern history at Williams College, Washington University in St. Louis, and Davidson College. A co-founder of History Associates Incorporated, he lives in Center Lovell, Maine, with his wife, Ann, and teaches part-time at Bates College.